To Die Gallantly

HISTORY AND WARFARE
Arther Ferrill, *Series Editor*

To Die Gallantly

The Battle of the Atlantic

EDITED BY

Timothy J. Runyan
and Jan M. Copes

Westview Press

BOULDER • SAN FRANCISCO • OXFORD

History and Warfare

Published in 1994 in the United States of America by Westview Press, Inc., 5500 Central Avenue, Boulder, Colorado 80301-2877, and in the United Kingdom by Westview Press, 36 Lonsdale Road, Summertown, Oxford OX2 7EW

Library of Congress Cataloging-in-Publication Data
To die gallantly : the battle of the Atlantic / edited by Timothy J.
  Runyan and Jan M. Copes.
    p.   cm.
  Includes bibliographical references (p.) and index.
  ISBN 0-8133-8815-5 — ISBN 0-8133-2332-0 (pbk.)
    1. World War, 1939–1945—Campaigns—Atlantic Ocean.   2. World War,
1939–1945—Naval operations.   I. Runyan, Timothy J.   II. Copes,
Jan M.
D770.T6   1994
940.54'5—dc20   94-10715
                                                                          CIP

Printed and bound in the United States of America

⟨∞⟩ The paper used in this publication meets the requirements
     of the American National Standard for Permanence of Paper
     for Printed Library Materials Z39.48-1984.

10   9   8   7   6   5   4   3   2

Contents

Photographs and Maps

Preface

When Admiral Erich Raeder heard Adolf Hitler's demand in 1939 that the German Navy prepare for war against the Allies, Raeder responded that the *Kriegsmarine* could do little more than show the world "how to die gallantly." He knew that the German surface navy was not prepared for war, a fact that Hitler refused to recognize. However, the U-boat war in the Atlantic began with disastrous consequences for Allied shipping. This was the "Happy Time" Germany enjoyed before the United States, Britain, Canada, and their allies united to reverse the toll of ships and men while confirming Raeder's prophecy.

Recognizing the pivotal importance of the Atlantic campaign in World War II, the North American Society for Oceanic History (NASOH) devoted its 1992 annual meeting to a commemoration of the fiftieth anniversary of the Battle of the Atlantic. NASOH, which has served as a forum for students of naval and maritime history for over twenty years, was ably assisted in this effort by the Naval Historical Center (NHC) of Washington, D.C.; the Center's facilities at the Washington Navy Yard provided a most appropriate setting for a conference focused on the war at sea. The opportunity brought together scholars from Europe and the Americas to exchange views on various aspects of the conflict, and most of the chapters printed here were first presented as papers at NASOH's Battle of the Atlantic conference. Both NASOH and the NHC are pleased to be able to bring such recent research to a wider audience through the publication of this volume.

The early stages of the war in the Atlantic were a disaster for the Allies, especially for convoys from North America headed to Europe. German U-boats ruled the sea, flaunting American coastal defenses by cruising the waters from the Caribbean to New England. Only the Allies' incredible will to fight and to send newly built ships out into the Atlantic made possible the continuation of war against Germany. The losses were greater than ever experienced by American merchant mariners in any previous conflict. Allied, and especially United States, naval forces were uncertain and ineffective during the early stages of conflict in 1941-1942, unable to respond to the underwater terror that took away the logistical support necessary to supply Britain and Russia in their struggle against the *Wehrmacht*.

A solution emerged, although painfully slowly, in the form of intelligence technology coupled with the recognition of the benefits of escorted convoys and the work of hunter-killer groups. The secret code of the German high command was broken by the hard work and good fortune of Polish, British, and other counter-intelligence specialists. This most dramatic breakthrough provided an advantage to the Allies that the Germans refused to acknowledge. Furthermore, the development of HF/DF (high frequency/direction finding) technology enabled escorts and hunter-killer groups to seek out the wolfpacks with terrible effect. The employment of long-range air-surveillance planes stationed on aircraft carriers completed the assortment of weapons needed to turn the hunters into the hunted. At the end of the war nearly all German submarines, out of the hundreds sent into combat, had been destroyed.

A study of the Battle of the Atlantic is rightly focused on submarines and intelligence warfare, but there is much more to the conflict, as demonstrated by the essays in this volume. Readers may find it discomforting to learn of conflict between commanders and of arguments among the Allies over issues of control or policy. The Canadians found the Americans short in recognition of their convoy work, and the Americans faulted the British deployment of resources. The U.S. Navy complained that the army failed to provide air support it vitally needed so it decided to create its own air force. Admirals quarreled with politicians, generals, and other admirals. They postured, protested, resigned, or were removed from office. But the war continued, exacting a terrible emotional and physical toll.

The concerns of the Americans, Canadians, and others on the western coast of the Atlantic in the early stages of the war were genuine. American vulnerability to coastal submarine attack is readily apparent in the tales of those North Carolinians who stood shocked while watching torpedoed freighters burn only a few miles off the Atlantic coast. One response was the rapid employment of new and expanded security forces to protect ports such as New York and to guard the coasts. Fear and panic at home had to be controlled. But merchant marine casualties of both ships and men reached unacceptable levels. New approaches had to be found to prevent a German victory in the Atlantic that would direct the course of the war. This book addresses the Battle of the Atlantic from the multiple perspectives of the strategists and political leaders, of those serving on ships at sea, and of the codebreakers. As the numerous films produced about the war make clear and the bibliography at the end of this work demonstrates, the passage of fifty years has not dulled public interest. A half-century of scholarship has provided insight but not the last word on this terrible yet decisive struggle. Sir Winston Churchill claimed that during World War II only the U-boat war truly frightened him. He felt that the Battle of the Atlantic was the dominating factor in the war. It is certainly appropriate to reconsider this important conflict as so much new information has come to light.

As is true of any publishing venture, this volume owes its life to many contributors. The first to be thanked are those representatives of the North American Society for Oceanic History and the Naval Historical Center, who organized the conference at which this research was first presented. This includes Center Director Dean C. Allard, Senior Historian William S. Dudley (who also served as conference coordinator for NASOH), Head of the Contemporary History Branch Edward Marolda and Publications Editor Sandra Doyle. Thanks are also due to NASOH officers Barry Gough (Wilfred Laurier University), Briton C. Busch (Colgate University), and William N. Still (East Carolina University) for their support of the conference and this publication. Both NASOH and the Naval Historical Center deserve thanks for their financial support of the project. Our personal thanks must also go to Mary Szymczyk for the many hours in front of the word processor required to prepare the text for press. She was supported at times by Darlene Sanders and Tami Ward. Chris Dawson deserves a special thanks for his help in compiling the bibliography. All are associated with Cleveland State University, which has been supportive throughout this project. Of course, credit must also be given to the diligent work of all the authors whose contributions appear here. Peter Kracht and Cindy Hirschfeld of Westview Press deserve special thanks for their prompt and professional assistance. And finally, we must acknowledge with respect the role of all those from both sides of the Atlantic who faced its challenge fifty years ago.

Timothy J. Runyan
Jan M. Copes
Cleveland, Ohio

Introduction:
An American Assessment

From the perspective of fifty years, several major issues arise in an American assessment of the Battle of the Atlantic. First, what was our essential strategic objective? Second, what was the role played by international and inter-service politics? Third, what basic factors explain American operational effectiveness? Finally, what was the relationship between the threat of advanced German undersea technology at the end of World War II and the menace posed by Soviet submarines in the Cold War era?[1]

Various definitions of the strategic objective in the Battle of the Atlantic can be offered. For the United States Navy, however, the overwhelming purpose was to enable Allied land power to operate ashore in Northern Europe to defeat Nazi Germany.[2] As Russell Weigley has noted, it is typical of the American way of war to seek out and confront an enemy at the principal source of his strength. That is exactly what the United States did in the World War II European campaign.[3]

It is important to note that the ultimate purpose was *not* to destroy U-boats. In fact, the major American naval leaders, including Admirals King, Stark, and Low, stated that they would be satisfied if not a single U-boat was sunk, providing U.S. convoys safely crossed the North Atlantic.[4] Nevertheless, we must remember that in 1943 the United States did seize the opportunity presented by Ultra intelligence and the

---

[1] The views expressed here were first presented at the International Historical Conference on the Battle of the Atlantic held at Liverpool, England, in May 1993. They are solely those of the author. They do not represent the views of the Department of the Navy or Defense.

[2] This analysis is based especially upon the following accounts: Robert W. Love, Jr., *History of the United States Navy*, 2 vols (Harrisburg, PA: Stackpole Books, 1992) 2: 64-119; and his "The Battle of the Atlantic," in *The Second World War: Europe and the Mediterranean*, ed. Thomas B. Buell et al. (Wayne, NJ: Avery Publishing, 1984), 205-26; and Ernest J. King and Walter Muir Whitehill, *Fleet Admiral King: A Naval Record* (New York: W. W. Norton, 1952).

[3] See Russell F. Weigley, *The American Way of War* (Bloomington, Indiana: Indiana University Press, 1973), 312-59.

[4] See Francis S. Low's report forwarded by his memorandum of 28 Oct 1944 in the Papers of Ernest J. King, series XI, Box 13, Operational Archives, Naval Historical Center, Washington, D.C. (hereafter Low Report of 28 Oct 1944); B. Mitchell Simpson, III, *Admiral Harold R. Stark* (Columbia, SC: University of South Carolina Press, 1989), 194; and Love, *History* 2: 66-68.

availability of new hunter-killer task forces built around escort carriers to launch an effective assault on German submarines in the Central Atlantic. Pragmatic American naval leaders set aside their longstanding belief that it was inefficient to use naval forces to seek out and destroy U-boats operating on the high seas. The success of the hunter-killer groups in 1943-1944 was one of the major contributions made by the United States to victory in the Battle of the Atlantic.[5]

Did American leaders also recognize the defense and sustenance of Great Britain as a key objective? Obviously that was the case. But that was not the first priority. To draw a somewhat fine distinction based on the hard-headed logic of the leading admirals, they did so because Britain was a vital military ally and because the British Isles represented an essential base for the invasion of Northern Europe, which was the prime objective. This position is reminiscent of the U.S. Navy's appreciation of the situation in World War I. At that time, Captain William Veazie Pratt, then the principal assistant to Admiral William S. Benson, the American chief of naval operations, observed that the U.S. Navy's key contribution in the Great War was to "mobilize and transport America's great reserve power to the European war front." Observing that our "major part" was in "getting our troops and munitions and supplies over there," Pratt contrasted this with "the impelling reason of the British," which "was protection to food and war supplies in transit."[6] This position is illustrated very clearly in World War II by the insistence of Admiral Ernest J. King that priority must be given to the protection of U.S. troop convoys. Another indication of the tendency in strategic thinking to value military need over civil necessity was the willingness of American leaders in the spring of 1944 to gamble on the well-being of the British civilian population, which faced a critically short food supply, in order to give maximum shipping support to the military requirements of the Normandy operation.[7]

If the grand strategy of the navy's World War II leaders was the same as in World War I, there also was continuity in the strategic means they

---

[5] Love, *History* 2: 111-15; Samuel Eliot Morison, *History of United States Naval Operations in World War II*, vol. 10, *The Atlantic Battle Won, May 1943-May 1945* (Boston: Little, Brown, 1956), 363.

[6] Quoted in Dean C. Allard, "Anglo-American Naval Differences in World War I," in *In Defense of the Republic*, eds. David C. Skaggs and Robert S. Browning, III (Belmont, CA: Wadsworth Publishing Co., 1991), 245.

[7] Love, *History* 2: 66-70.

adopted. True to the concept of going to the source of the enemy's strength, an objective shared by America's political and military leaders during the First World War, Admiral King consistently stressed that U-boats must be attacked *before* reaching the high seas.[8] One of the major reasons King joined General George C. Marshall, chief of staff of the U.S. Army, in championing an immediate cross-channel operation in 1942 was to seize the U-boat bases in Western France, which were vital for the success of Germany's underseas campaign. For the same purpose, King urged leaders of the Allied air forces to target U-boat bases and factories in their strategic bombing campaign. If U-boats could not be destroyed at their source, then the next best tactic was to attack them while transiting to their operating areas. The Bay of Biscay antisubmarine air offensive that was endorsed in 1943 with enthusiasm by Admiral King and Admiral Harold R. Stark (overall commander of U.S. Naval Forces in Europe) can be seen as the equivalent of the antisubmarine mine and ship barriers in the North Sea and English Channel that the United States championed in the First World War.[9]

It is an irony of the classic maritime struggle known as the Battle of the Atlantic that for the United States its ultimate effect must be measured by the success of the Western Allies in bringing their strength to bear ashore. "Maritime strategy," a phrase that became famous in the United States during the 1980s, describes this way of thinking. That term is traditionally associated with the Reagan administration's defense posture. But as Michael Palmer tells us, the tendency of American strategists to emphasize the use of naval forces to support land campaigns long antedates the decade of the 1980s.[10]

The role of international and inter-service politics in the Battle of the Atlantic is a second subject that deserves attention. Despite the pious American saying that politics stops at the water's edge, individual nations involved in coalition campaigns obviously have distinctive and sometimes conflicting national interests. Further, each military service has its own perspective and goals. Neither international nor bureaucratic politics could be adjourned entirely, even as the various nations and services involved in the Battle of the Atlantic were fighting shoulder to shoulder in their prolonged and bitter conflict with Nazi Germany.

The political story continues to be a subject of controversy. Robert

---

[8] For World War I, see Allard, "Anglo-American Naval Differences," 248-50. King's stress on going to the source of the enemy's strength is indicated, for example, in King and Whitehill, *King*, 457.

[9] King and Whitehill, *King*, 457 ; Simpson, *Stark*, 187-92; Love, *History* 2: 118.

[10] Michael A. Palmer, *Origins of the Maritime Strategy* (Washington D.C.: Naval Historical Center, 1988).

Love, for example, recently claimed that the British sought to use charges of American ineptitude during the initial German U-boat blitz off the United States as a pretext for establishing British strategic control of the entire Atlantic in 1942.[11] Whether or not that charge is valid, it is possible that jockeying for international position was involved in the rather vivid British reactions, that persist to the present time, to German success in Operation *Paukenschlag* (*Roll of Drums* or *Drumbeat*). One can second-guess Admiral King for his refusal to immediately initiate coastal convoys, even if initially these could only be provided with under-strength escort forces or with no escorts at all. It is puzzling, however, that his British critics did not take into account another fact that was well known to them. That was King's decision to give priority to the military mission of assuring the safety of American troop convoys to the United Kingdom and elsewhere, as compared to the protection of mercantile convoys off the East Coast. Obviously, this allocation of naval forces stripped key defenses from the Eastern Seaboard. Here again we see a distinction between military and civil requirements.[12]

A full discussion of Operation *Paukenschlag* cannot be undertaken at this point. But since it is a subject that deserves considerable attention, let me enumerate a few questions that deserve consideration by future researchers.

To what extent were the reactions of Admiral King and his senior colleagues, all of whom had served as middle-grade officers in World War I, influenced by recollections of the German submarine offensive off the U.S. East Coast in 1918? The contemporary view on that earlier operation was that it was a German attempt to mount a minor operation aimed at diverting U.S. attention from the major theater of war, which was in Europe. Despite German success during 1918 in sinking about one hundred ships and smaller craft, accompanied by great public alarm, U.S. naval leaders of the Great War refused to make basic changes to the

---

[11] Love, *History* 1: 79. Other works on the dual themes of cooperation and competition in Anglo-American military relations during World War II include James R. Leutze, *Bargaining for Supremacy: Anglo-American Naval Collaboration, 1937-1941* (Chapel Hill: University of North Carolina Press, 1977); Christopher G. Thorne, *Allies of a Kind: The Allies, Britain and the War Against Japan, 1941-1945* (New York: Oxford University Press, 1978); and Alex Danchev, *Very Special Relationship: Field-Marshal Sir John Dill and the Anglo-American Alliance, 1941-1945* (London: Brassey's Defence Publishers, 1986).

[12] For balanced accounts of Operation *Paukenschlag*, see Love, *History* 2: 66-70; and Dan van der Vat, *The Atlantic Campaign* (New York: Harper and Row, 1988), 237-48. In my opinion, Michael Gannon's *Operation Drumbeat* (New York: Harper and Row, 1990) is unreliable.

deployment of their forces. Was this precedent not to alter policy a basic factor in the outlook of Admiral King in 1942?[13]

U.S. and Allied losses off the American coast during the first six months of 1942 were considerable. In the Eastern Sea Frontier alone, they amounted to about 100 merchantmen.[14] But, even if the American slaughter had continued, one can ask whether the U-boat campaign promised any decisive strategic result, especially against a continental power such as the United States that was well endowed with natural resources and a well-developed internal transportation network. In any case, to put the magnitude of those losses in perspective, one should remember that more than 2,500 Allied merchantmen were lost to enemy action throughout the war. A related and more cosmic question, of course, is whether Admiral Dönitz's tonnage warfare concept in general was strategically sound. Was there really any prospect that the simple sinking of merchant ships, without regard to the geographic importance of the areas in which these losses occurred, could win the war for Germany?

Lastly, to what extent was the United States Navy inhibited in its response to *Paukenschlag* by the demands of the Pacific War? One must remember that the navy needed to organize and protect major troop movements into the Pacific early in 1942.[15] Further, Japanese submarines were operating off the West Coast at this time.[16] There also were distinct fears that the Japanese would invade Hawaii or even the West Coast of the United States.[17] In other words, one should bear in mind that U.S. naval leaders were fighting a two-ocean war. They were not able to concentrate exclusive attention on the Atlantic coast.

But, setting aside the controversial issue of *Paukenschlag*, the influence of the Anglo-American dispute on the opening of a second front in Northern Europe must be addressed. Following the British refusal to launch a cross-channel operation in 1942, King and Marshall proposed that the United States should shift its attention almost exclusively to the Pacific. That position probably was little more than a bluff. In any case,

---

[13] Samuel Eliot Morison, *History of United States Naval Operations in World War II*, vol. 1, *The Battle of the Atlantic, 1939-1943* (Boston: Little, Brown and Company, 1956), 125-26.

[14] Ibid., 413.

[15] Samuel Eliot Morison, *History of United States Naval Operations in World War II*, vol. 3, *The Rising Sun in the Pacific, 1931-April 1942* (Boston: Little, Brown and Company, 1956), 265.

[16] Clark G. Reynolds, "Submarine Attacks on the Pacific Coast, 1942," *Pacific Historical Review*, (May 1964), 183-93.

[17] See Stetson Conn et al., *Guarding the United States and Its Outposts* (Washington: GPO, 1964); and John J. Stephan, *Hawaii Under the Rising Sun: Japan's Plan for Conquest After Pearl Harbor* (Honolulu: University of Hawaii Press, 1984).

it was specifically overridden when Franklin Roosevelt directed the mounting of Operation *Torch* in North Africa later that year. These high-level decisions had tangible impacts on the antisubmarine campaign. For example, the deferral of a major amphibious operation in Northern Europe allowed King to persuade President Roosevelt to downgrade the construction priority for landing craft and to expedite the building of destroyer escorts, a class of warships essential for the anti-U-boat campaign.[18] On the other hand, the diversion of naval assets to the *Torch* landings in November 1942 was one factor contributing to the growing success of German submarines in the North Atlantic during the bloody winter of 1942-1943.[19]

Two other instances of the major influence of international politics in the Battle of the Atlantic can be noted. One was the decision taken at the Atlantic Convoy Conference that convened in Washington during March 1943 to shift strategic control of Canadian ASW forces in the Northwest Atlantic from the United States to Canada herself. This was, in part, a military decision. But it also had a significant political dimension. In fact, as Marc Milner has pointed out, this adjustment was a "watershed in Canadian" history as a "recognition of Canada's special interest in the North Atlantic."[20]

The second example is provided by the North Russian convoys. These were viewed by Western naval officers as highly risky operations that diverted essential ships from more important tasks, notably the Battle of the Atlantic. For Winston Churchill and Franklin Roosevelt, however, the convoys to Murmansk and Archangel were essential symbols of Western support for a hard-pressed Soviet ally. Hence, political require-ments overrode strategic considerations.[21]

Inter-service or bureaucratic politics also are evident in the Battle of the Atlantic, as they are endemic in so much of military history. From the U.S. Navy's point of view, the major story was its conflict with the Army Air Forces with regard to the role played by land-based, long-range air-craft in the antisubmarine campaign. A major lesson learned early in the Battle of the Atlantic was the enormous value of these planes in detecting and deterring the U-boat. The U.S. Navy, which entered the war without its own land-based aircraft, initially depended on the cooperation of the Army Air Forces, using a system that roughly paralleled the maritime air support provided by the RAF's Coastal Command to the Royal Navy. But

---

[18] Love, *History* 2: 100.
[19] Ibid., 97.
[20] Marc Milner, *North Atlantic Run* (Annapolis: Naval Institute Press, 1985), 234.
[21] van der Vat, *The Atlantic Campaign*, 203-04, 278-80.

by the summer of 1943, it became clear that there were irreconcilable differences between the two U.S. services with regard to the command and tactical employment of land-based aircraft. Understandably, ASW operations, especially convoy protection duty, were not of primary importance to the Army Air Forces, which viewed strategic bombing as its primary mission. Insofar as the navy was concerned, ASW was crucial. Instead of continuing to dispute these issues, the two services agreed to shift the army's long-range ASW aircraft to the navy, where they were manned by naval personnel. In return, the navy provided the army with replacement aircraft. With this step, an important bureaucratic conflict ended. Thereafter the U.S. Navy had direct control of all of the critical assets for waging modern antisubmarine warfare.[22]

What can one say about the tactical, organizational, and technical factors that allowed the U.S. Navy to make significant contributions to the campaign against enemy U-boats? Under the U.S. Navy's strategic concept, the victory achieved by Allied armies in Western Europe was the ultimate measure of success in the Battle of the Atlantic. As previously noted, U.S. naval leaders saw the destruction of enemy U-boats as secondary in importance. But out of a total of 606 German submarines sunk in action on the high seas, 132 kills were scored by forces under the operational control of the United States, which did not fully enter the war until December 1941.[23] The massive production by U.S. shipyards and factories of the merchantmen, naval ships, aircraft, and many other weapons and systems employed in the Battle of the Atlantic must also be acknowledged in evaluating the overall American contribution to that campaign.

During and after the war, Francis S. Low, Admiral King's principal assistant for ASW, made several analyses of the requirements for operational success in this field of naval warfare. Admiral Low concluded that operational training, adequate ASW force levels, and intelligence on the location of enemy submarines were three key factors.[24] Somewhat

---

[22] Morison, *History* 10: 26-31. A recent history by a serving U.S. Army officer, Montgomery C. Meigs, *Slide Rules and Submarines* (Washington D.C.: National Defense University Press, 1990) is of interest in giving a contemporary restatement of the U.S. Army's partisan views regarding the alleged shortcomings of the U.S. Navy in the Battle of the Atlantic.

[23] This statistic is derived from a table appearing in Admiralty Historical Section, *The Defeat of the Enemy Attack on Shipping 1939-1945* (London, 1957), 245. U-boats lost through bombing raids, by mines, other causes, or unknown causes are not included.

[24] In addition to ibid. and Low's studies that appear as annexes to that report, see Low, "Study of Undersea Warfare," 22 April 1950, and Low, "Presentation to the Fifth Undersea Symposium," 15-16 May 1950, both of which are in the Command File, Operational Archives, Naval Historical Center, Washington D.C. The Top Secret annex (now declassified) to the 22 April 1950 study stresses the vital importance of Ultra intelligence.

surprisingly, considering the U.S. Navy's traditional aversion to centralization and to organizational solutions to problems, the 1943 establishment of the central ASW command known as the Tenth Fleet (in which Admiral Low served as chief of staff to Admiral King) was viewed by Low and his colleagues as a crucial step. Further, Low's assessments acknowledged the important role of scientific analysis or operational research in developing effective doctrine and tactics.[25] Of course, he also enumerated the role played by a myriad of new weapons and detection systems, such as hedgehogs, magnetic detection devices, anti-homing torpedo gear, direction-finding equipment, the Leigh light, and improved radar and sonar. As was true for operational research, many of these devices were British innovations.[26] But Low and his fellow officers in the navy did not subscribe to a simple materialistic explanation of the Allied success. Instead the dominant theme in their analysis was the overarching need to coordinate all elements of the ASW problem, including capable and sufficient quantities of ships, aircraft, weapons, and other systems; the proper allocation of these forces and their effective operational training; and the availability of good intelligence and scientific analysis by an organization such as the U.S. Navy's Tenth Fleet. In effect, the manifold facets of the ASW problem were recognized as being part of a seamless web. Writing for the benefit of future naval commanders, Admiral Low stressed that success in subsequent campaigns depended above all else on the integration of these manifold elements under central control.

The United States Navy could congratulate itself at the end of World War II for its role in the maritime alliance that mastered the U-boat. But at the same time there was a sobering recognition that the new underseas technology developed by Germany late in the war represented a radically different problem. If Germany's advanced weapons had been deployed in a major way, the United States would have faced an entirely new Battle of the Atlantic. To be sure, the ASW barriers established by U.S. naval forces engaged in Operation *Teardrop* during April-May 1945 were highly successful in countering the final U-boat threat in the Western Atlantic. During *Teardrop* surface ships operating at the peak of their efficiency destroyed five of the six snorkel U-boats deployed by Admiral Dönitz. Nevertheless, the employment of the snorkel undercut the effectiveness of American ASW aircraft. Further, there was deep

---

[25] A comprehensive account of U. S. operations research appears in Keith R. Tidman, *The Operations Evaluation Group* (Annapolis: Naval Institute Press, 1984).

[26] For an excellent account of British-American technical cooperation in the Battle of the Atlantic, see William Hackman, *Seek and Strike* (London: Her Majesty's Stationery Office, 1984), especially 250-65.

anxiety on the American side because of intelligence assessments, now known to be false, that the Germans planned to use submarine-launched rockets against East Coast cities. There was no effective defense against those weapons in 1945.[27]

In November 1949, a little more than four years after the end of World War II, the chief of naval operations appointed Admiral Low to conduct another comprehensive study of undersea warfare. By that time, the Cold War was fully underway and the Western democracies recognized the Soviet Union as a hostile power intent on establishing hegemony in Europe. This was precisely the threat posed by Germany in 1939 that led to World War II. For naval officers, there was yet another arresting transference from Hitler's Germany to the Soviet Union. Bearing in mind the success of the Soviets in exploiting the human and industrial resources of the German undersea warfare organization at the end of the war, Low made this sobering observation in his final report of April 1950:

> All the improvements made by the Germans in submarines, weapons and mines are available to the Russians. These include snorkel, closed cycle propulsion, Types XXI and XXIII submarines, pattern running and acoustic torpedoes, guided missiles and influence mines. . . . They have the industrial capacity and technical knowledge [to put these developments into production] if they decide to give the effort high priority. German submarine production during World War II approached 30 boats per month and Russian shipbuilding capacity approximates that of pre-war Germany.[28]

Admiral Low then made an even more alarming statement:

> The Anti-Submarine Warfare techniques and equipment in use by the U.S. Navy at the present time, while adequate to defeat the conventional World War II type submarine, are inadequate to deal with an advanced-type of submarine and improved weapons that the Russians can build now. Echo ranging by sonar is still the only effective method of locating a fully submerged submarine which is running quietly. The nature of the ocean and the physics of underwater sound propagation make it appear that there is no early prospect of increasing sonar echo range in practicable equipment for surface craft sufficiently to deal with the submarine of the future.[29]

---

[27] Morison, *History* 10: 344-56.
[28] Low, "Study of Undersea Warfare," 22 April 1950, 2.
[29] Ibid.

Clearly, there are many similarities between the Battle of the Atlantic and the American naval experience in the World War I campaign of 1917–1918. The Cold War flowed directly out of World War II. That development plus the decisive Allied victory in Europe must be viewed as the major outcomes of the Battle of the Atlantic.

Despite the fact that outright hostilities were avoided, the new ASW campaign between NATO and the Soviet Union in the Atlantic absorbed enormous attention for more than forty years after World War II. Many of the points made previously with regard to the strategic objective, politics, and the war-fighting principles involved in the Battle of the Atlantic could also apply to the Cold War era. It would not be the first time that one can discover more continuities than discontinuities within the history of the North Atlantic community.

Dean C. Allard
Naval Historical Center
Washington, D.C.

PART ONE

The Early Years

1

The Atlantic in the Strategic Perspective of Hitler and Roosevelt, 1940-1941[1]

Werner Rahn

In his "Directive No. 9" of 29 November 1939, entitled "Principles of Warfare Against the Economy of the Enemy," Adolf Hitler considered interference with the British economy as the "most effective means" to defeat Great Britain.[2] Hitler was prepared to adopt this strategic concept for the navy, hitting Great Britain in her most vulnerable spot by disturbing her sea lines of communication. However, Hitler and his Naval Staff[3] moved on different planes of strategic thinking: Hitler expected a short war limited to Europe, and he did not want to jeopardize the hope of better relations with Great Britain by launching a radical war on its economy. The Naval Staff, on the other hand, was convinced from a very early date that the conflict with the Anglo-Saxon opponent would be very long. It would have to be won in the Atlantic, even if that would mean the entry of the United States into the war.

[1] This paper is based on my "Der Seekrieg im Atlantik und Nordmeer" ("Naval Warfare in the Atlantic and Arctic"), published in the German World War II Series *Das Deutsche Reich und der Zweite Weltkrieg*, vol. 6, Horst Boog, Werner Rahn, Reinhard Stumpf, and Bernd Wegner, *Der globale Krieg. Die Ausweitung zum Weltkrieg und der Wechsel der Initiative 1941-1943* (Stuttgart, 1990), 275-297. The author thanks John B. Hattendorf and Martin Alexander for their assistance, especially for reading and correcting the first draft of the translation.
[2] Walther Hubatsch, ed., *Hitlers Weisungen für die Kriegführung*, 2d rev. ed. (Koblenz, 1983), 40-42.
[3] The Naval Staff (*Seekriegsleitung or Skl*) was the key element in the German Naval Command (*Oberkommando der Kriegsmarine*), responsible for strategic and operational planning. From the beginning of World War II, Grand Admiral Erich Raeder held two positions: commander in chief of the navy and chief of Naval Staff. See Michael Salewski, *Die deutsche Seekriegsleitung 1935-1945*, vol. 1 (Frankfurt/M. 1970), 102.

From the experience of the First World War, the German Naval Staff knew that the economic link between Great Britain and the North American continent was the lifeblood of the island kingdom. It also knew that, in a war against the economy of a country so dependent on its sea lanes, Germany would have to reckon with the opposition of the United States as soon as the existence of Great Britain became seriously threatened.

After France had been defeated in the summer of 1940, Great Britain was the only nation able to fight Germany and was not prepared to deny Germany's dominant position on the continent. American policy soon began to develop in directions that became more and more dangerous for German strategy and warfare. President Franklin D. Roosevelt clearly favored this pro-British policy. Beginning his career in national politics as Assistant Secretary of the Navy from 1913 to 1920, Roosevelt had felt strong ties with the U.S. Navy, and this experience during World War I had an influence on his later strategic thinking. To him, safe sea lines of communication and a strong navy were indispensable prerequisites for a power wishing to promote liberal world trade and to protect its overseas interests.[4]

As president, Roosevelt did all that was in his power to have the navy's armament program ratified in Congress. The defeat of France in June 1940 changed the attitude in Congress towards the authorization of military expenses and led to the adoption of the "Two-Ocean Expansion Act" of 19 July 1940. This started a large-scale expansion of the U.S. Navy and gave proof of the United States' intention to become a dominant naval power in both the Atlantic and the Pacific. In view of this imminent armament program, time was becoming the most important factor for German war strategy: Great Britain had to be hit decisively in the Atlantic theater before the U.S. had the chance to engage its potential military power. The German Naval Staff foresaw that there were limits to the Reich's own production capacities and its material resources. As early as December 1940, it viewed America's growing support of Britain as a dangerous development "towards a marked *prolongation of the war.*" This, the Naval Staff considered, would have a "very negative effect on

---

[4] American policy and strategy from the beginning of World War II to the deepening participation in the war against Germany 1941 is fully discussed by Waldo Heinrichs, *Threshold of War. Franklin D. Roosevelt and American Entry into World War II* (New York: Oxford, 1988). See also William L. Langer and S. Everett Gleason, *The Undeclared War, 1940-1941* (New York, 1953); William Carr, *Poland to Pearl Harbor. The Making of the Second World War* (London, 1985), 134-144; David Reynolds, *The Creation of the Anglo-American Alliance 1937-41. A Study in Competitive Cooperation* (London, 1981); and Andreas Hillgruber, *Hitlers Strategie. Politik und Kriegführung 1940-41* (Frankfurt/M., 1965), 90-102, 192-206, 310-316 and 398-408.

the overall German war strategy."[5] This cautiously worded statement obviously expressed the fact that Germany would not be able to win a prolonged war of attrition against the two Anglo-Saxon naval powers.

For this reason, in December 1940, at a time when the Führer was still firmly determined to attack the Soviet Union, Grand Admiral Erich Raeder, the commander in chief of the navy, asked Hitler "to recognize that the greatest task of the hour is concentration of all our power against Britain." To Raeder, this meant the concentration of air force and navy ordnance items against the British supplies. The admiral was "firmly convinced that German submarines, as in the World War, are the decisive weapons against Britain." Yet Raeder also thought that Germany needed to promote submarine construction within the overall armament program more than had been the case so far. Although Hitler did not explicitly reject Raeder's view, he did refer to the allegedly new political situation — "i.e., Russia's inclination to interfere in Balkan affairs" — requiring Germany "to eliminate at all cost the last enemy remaining on the continent, before he can collaborate with Britain . . . . After that everything can be concentrated on the needs of the Air Force and the Navy."[6] In saying this in a very skilled and obvious way, Hitler used a strategic argument which has a long tradition in navies — the argument that a naval power can only be defeated after the last continental bulwark of that power has fallen.

It seemed, however, that the intensive efforts of the Naval Staff to win Hitler over to its strategic program were beginning to bear fruit. This much can be seen by statements in the Führer's speech to the *Wehrmacht* command in January 1941. In it he said that in combatting Great Britain, Germany ought to put its main emphasis on naval and air attacks on Britain's supplies and on its armament industry, a tactic which might be crowned by success in the following summer. It was not clear what Hitler meant by "success" in this context. However, he continued to say that he was "in principle" prepared to "conclude a mutual peace with England."[7]

---

[5] Werner Rahn and Gerhard Schreiber, eds., *Kriegstagebuch der Seekriegsleitung 1939-1945, Teil A*, vol. 16 (December 1940) (Herford, Bonn: Mittler, 1990), 233 and 238 (20 December 1940), emphasis added by author.

[6] Gerhard Wagner, ed., *Lagevorträge des Oberbefehlshabers der Kriegsmarine vor Hitler 1939-1945* (Munich, 1972), 171-173 (27 December 1940). For a translation in a different order and selection of documents, see *Fuehrer Conferences on Naval Affairs* (Annapolis: Naval Institute Press, 1990, reprint of *Brassey's Naval Annual 1948*), 29-496. For the above cited document, see ibid., 160-163. Compare also the typewritten edition of the U.S. Navy: *Fuehrer Conferences in Matters Dealing with the German Navy* , 7 vols. (Washington D.C.: Secretary of the Navy 1947), in this context for 1940, vol. 2, 68-71 (Library of Naval War College, Newport, RI).

[7] Memo of Rear Admiral K. Fricke, 21 January 1941, in Wagner, *Lagevorträge*, 183-184.

Adolf Hitler and Admiral Erich Raeder, shown here in 1933. Photo courtesy of the Naval Academy Historical Collection, Flensburg, Germany.

This again made clear that Hitler and the Naval Staff were pursuing different stratego-political aims in the war against the British. When, a few weeks later, Hitler consented to Raeder's request for concerted air and navy attacks against the British maritime transport capacity, this appeared to be a short-term success for the navy. In reality, however, it was a formal recognition that a basic change in the overall strategy of the Reich, for Operation *Barbarossa* was already in place. The massive employment of the *Luftwaffe* against British shipyards and harbor facilities could not be sustained for long. The use of the *Luftwaffe* in other theaters of war clearly indicated the "limited role"[8] Hitler was assigning to the Atlantic naval war in the framework of his overall strategy. In his eyes, Great Britain was not *the* enemy on whom all weapons had to be concentrated in order to defeat him, but a potential partner who had to be made to "see reason" by applying an appropriate amount of military pressure. Hitler also knew, having been reassured by the navy's arguments, that a forced economic war, even with the utmost effort, could not lead to any marked success in one year. Furthermore, an effort of this kind would risk provoking U.S. entry into the war, which he was seeking to avoid at this point. His principal aim was to defeat the Soviet Union in order to create a large continental European area that could not be blockaded and which could form the economic basis for a future conflict with the U.S.[9]

Roosevelt's reelection as president on 5 November 1940 secured domestic support for America's policy of supporting Great Britain against Germany. Most importantly, America could now take additional supporting measures and, at the same time, speed up her arms production. In December 1940, Churchill realized that soon Britain would no longer be able to pay for the arms supplied by the American government according to the principle of "cash and carry." Soon afterwards, however, the United States established the Lend-Lease system, enabling Roosevelt to give material support to any state "whose defense in the opinion of the President is vital for the defense of the United States."[10] Sustaining British defense had, in this way, become a component of American security policy, and the basic structure of the Atlantic Alliance was set. By suggesting that his country would not be able to win the war against Germany with its own resources, Churchill practically offered Britain to the United States as a "junior partner" in a future alliance.[11]

---

[8] Hillgruber, *Hitlers Strategie*, 165. See Salewski, *Die Deutsche Seekriegsleitung* 1: 430-431.

[9] See Hillgruber, *Hitlers Strategie*, passim.

[10] Ibid., 398. See also Reynolds, *Creation of the Anglo-American Alliance*, 145-150.

[11] Andreas Hillgruber, *Der Zweite Weltkrieg 1939-1945. Kriegsziele und Strategie der großen Mächte* (Stuttgart, Berlin, 1982), 55.

In view of the danger from a constant reduction in the available maritime transport capacity, the British command saw as its primary task the reduction or the limitation of the tonnage loss in the Atlantic. This could either be done by reinforcing the naval forces or by constructing more merchant ships. However, in both sectors, British shipyards were operating at full capacity. A further increase could only be achieved by harvesting American capacities.

At the end of the year 1940, Washington came to the conclusion that, compared to Japan, Germany was not only the stronger enemy but, due to its position of power in Europe and its offensive conduct of war in the Atlantic, a much more dangerous enemy — one which directly threatened not only Britain, but also the United States. With this attitude, Washington was agreeing to the fundamental basis of British strategy, concentrating on the security of the Atlantic sea lanes as fundamental to all further offensive operations in Europe.[12]

The ABC-1 Agreement, concluded at the end of March 1941, determined the joint strategy for coalition warfare by giving top priority to the European-Atlantic theater of war and the defeat of Germany. Only when this goal had been reached would all efforts be concentrated on the war against Japan. Although in this agreement the United States did not commit itself to entering the war and did not even give a statement on when and under what circumstances it might do this at all, the basic strategic decision soon brought about consequences for the distribution of British and American forces. This was a logical consequence of the establishment of the Lend-Lease system — the need to find ways and means to make sure that the material supplies which were considered vital for the defense of the U.S. reached their destination. This meant that the protection of the Atlantic convoy routes had already become part of the U.S. security policy, although Roosevelt denied this fact in public in January.[13]

The political intention and strategic importance of the Lend-Lease system were recognized at once in Berlin. As early as 18 March 1941, Raeder took various measures to obtain unrestricted rules of engagement for the German Navy in order to make it more effective. But Hitler was not willing to grant more than an extension of the area of operations to the Northwest, as far as the territorial waters of Greenland. The American reaction to this measure was not long in coming and made it clear that

---

[12] Maurice Matloff and Edwin M. Snell, *Stratiegic Planning for Coalition Warfare, 1941-1942* (Washington D.C.: Office of the Chief of Military History, Department of the Army, 1953).

[13] Thomas A. Bailey and Paul B. Ryan, *Hitler vs. Roosevelt. The Undeclared War* (New York, London, 1979), 109-112.

Roosevelt was prepared to escalate the conflict. In April, the United States took over the protection of Greenland by establishing military bases there. On 18 April, the Pan-American safety zone was shifted to the East as far as 30° W longitude. With the resulting obligation to safeguard its own security interests and to provide indirect support for the Royal Navy, the U.S. Navy relocated three battleships, one carrier, four cruisers, and eighteen destroyers from the Pacific into the Atlantic in intervals between March and June 1941.

This redeployment of naval forces brought a few problems with it, since the conclusion of the neutrality agreement between the Soviet Union and Japan on 13 April had changed the situation in the Pacific to the benefit of Japan. The American naval command had to realize that, by creating what was potentially a one-ocean navy, it was running the risk of a global war being fought in two oceans too early.[14] For despite the reinforcement from the Pacific, the U.S. Atlantic Fleet was unprepared — both in terms of materiél and personnel — for permanent convoy operations in the western part of the Atlantic. In view of this situation, and due to a lack of support in Congress, operations of this kind were delayed for the time being. As an alternative measure, patrol cruises in the Pan-American safety zone were extended and intensified. This led to an impairment of German naval warfare, since the safety zone between Iceland and Greenland jutted far out into the declared German area of operations in which U-boats were allowed to deliver their weapons unimpeded. Hostile incidents were inevitable, or maybe they were meant to be provoked to hasten the United States' entry into war as the situation in Europe dramatically worsened, with the number of monthly ship losses increasing from 320,000 gross registered tons to 688,000 tons. If the rate of sinkings had continued on this scale, the supplies sent to the Allies through the Lend-Lease system would have drained American resources without any strategic effect. Other factors, now causing great worries in Washington, were the catastrophic developments in the Mediterranean and in the Balkan states.[15]

On 10 April, Roosevelt decided to lend additional support to Great Britain. Since British forces in East Africa dominated the unsupplied Italian troops, there was no longer any reason for regarding the Red Sea as a war zone. This made it possible for American merchant ships to

---

[14] Douglas M. Norton, "The Open Secret. The U.S. Navy in the Battle of the Atlantic, April-December 1941," *Naval War College Review* 26, no. 4, (1974): 65; and Heinrichs, *Threshold of War*, 39-50.

[15] Reynolds, *Creation of the Anglo-American Alliance*, 196-197; Robert Dallek, *Franklin D. Roosevelt and American Foreign Policy 1932-1945* (New York, 1979), 260-261.

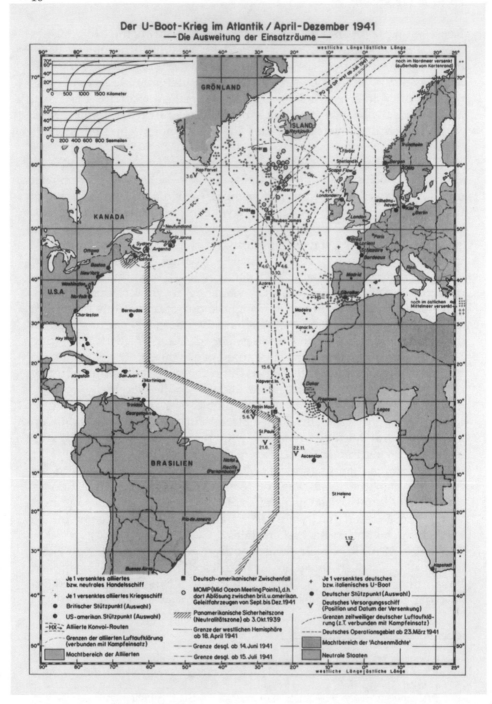

Der U-Boot-Krieg im Atlantik / April-Dezember 1941
—— Die Ausweitung der Einsatzräume ——

transport war material via the Cape route directly to the Middle East theater of war, helping to relieve the critical supply situation for the British.[16] In Berlin, Raeder had to accept the fact that Hitler had rejected his plans aimed at disrespecting American neutrality. It was plain that Hitler wanted to avoid a conflict with the United States in view of his imminent military campaign against Russia. However, within the German Naval Staff there were those who realized that Roosevelt's pro-British foreign policy created domestic political problems for him. Not only was the military strength of the United States insufficient, but American public opinion was "the strongest bulwark against the entry into war by the USA." This led the Naval Staff to conclude that "*an entry into war by the USA must not be considered inevitable*"[17] and that the Reich should assume a cautious attitude towards the United States.

Germany's policy of avoiding provocations which could negatively influence American public opinion was justified in view of the dilemma which Hitler faced since his decision to undertake Operation *Barbarossa*. In Hitler's view the Atlantic could not become the strategic center of German warfare before the last potential ally of the naval powers on the continent had been defeated.

In May 1941, the Naval Staff considered the extensive operations of the U.S. Atlantic Fleet as a particular danger to German surface units operating as merchant raiders. The latter, when encountering American units, were running the risk of their position being reported. Hence, for Raeder the moment had come "when it is necessary to point out to the President and the people of the USA the limits, in an appropriate manner avoiding any kind of provocation, at which point the measures for the support of Great Britain must come to an end." If Germany was putting up with everything, he continued, there was the danger of further American measures "leading either to a serious impairment of the German naval warfare against British supply lines or to an armed conflict."

Hitler's reaction was not to be mistaken. In view of what he saw as Roosevelt's insecure attitude, he wanted to avoid incidents, "under no circumstances" running the risk of the U.S. entering the war. This was especially the case given the probability that Japan would only intervene "if the U.S. is the aggressor."[18]

---

[16] Bailey and Ryan, *Hitler vs. Roosevelt*, 125-126.

[17] Naval Staff, War Diary, Part C VIII, 10 May 1941, Bundesarchiv-Militärarchiv (hereafter BA-MA), RM 7/206, 191-193, emphasis added by author.

[18] Conference, Raeder and Hitler, 22 May 1941, Annex 1, in Wagner, *Lagevorträge*, 231-234. Annex 1 entitled "The Present Problem of Naval Warfare in the Atlantic in view of the Attitude of the U.S.A. May 1941" is *not* included in the 1990 edition of *Fuehrer Conferences*, but compare the edition of the U.S. Navy: *Fuehrer Conferences* for 1941, vol. 1, 68-73.

Although Roosevelt knew very well that his policy was aimed at the massive material support of Great Britain, Hitler's impression of him as being insecure was not entirely wrong. In Roosevelt's speeches, which had rather a pretentious character, the president would not make a statement as to whether, or under what circumstances, he would enter into an armed conflict with the Reich. On 27 May 1941 he graphically depicted the dangers lying ahead if Germany were to continue its extension of power. His only action, however, was to proclaim a state of unlimited national emergency in order to accelerate the extension of arms and ship construction at a time when British shipping losses had taken on alarming dimensions and considerably exceeded the construction rate in both Great Britain and the United States.[19]

In July 1941, American troops replaced British units stationed in Iceland and gave proof of Roosevelt's determination to extend the American position in the Atlantic farther out to the east. The American occupation of Iceland must also be seen in connection with the German attack on the Soviet Union. In Washington, it was generally expected that the Red Army would collapse within the next two or three months and that, as a consequence, the main emphasis of German warfare would then be shifted to the west. In view of Great Britain's critical situation, it was quite natural for Washington to use this unique opportunity to contain the German military potential in the east by intensified support for the British war effort. Politically influential circles pressed Roosevelt to act more determinedly in the Atlantic,[20] but he preferred to remain cautious, choosing an indirect and more secure approach. The first logical consequence of the occupation of Iceland was to extend the corresponding safety zone, giving British ships the opportunity to join U.S. convoys which were being assembled to supply the troops stationed in Iceland.

The American assessment of the chances of the German *Wehrmacht*'s ability to defeat the Soviet Union, as well as the assessment of the future German strategy against the Anglo-Saxon naval powers, corresponded closely with Hitler's own expectations and goals. In July 1941, shortly after the United States had occupied Iceland, Raeder requested him to issue a political directive as to whether this should be viewed as "an entry into the war, or as an act of provocation which should be ignored." Hitler pointed out that he was "most anxious to postpone the United States' entry into war for another one or two months." For this reason,

---

[19] Dallek, *Franklin D. Roosevelt*, 265-267; Reynolds, *Creation of the Anglo-American Alliance*, 202-203; Carr, *Poland to Pearl Harbor*, 139-140.
[20] See Langer and Gleason, *Undeclared War*, 537-538.

attacks on American merchant ships and warships should be avoided.[21] Apart from this measure, Hitler even seemed to have taken into consideration the possibility of temporarily suspending the submarine war altogether in order to avoid incidents of this kind. Obviously, he was counting on the military campaign in the East to bring success within only a few months. Such an outcome, from his point of view, would have extremely positive effects on the Reich's overall strategic situation. In this case, Germany's position on the European continent for quite a long time would be so firm and secure that a conflict with the United States need not be feared any more. The global dimensions of such a *Weltkriegstrategie* (world war strategy), as Hillgruber calls it,[22] are also obvious in the offer to ally with Japan. Hitler told the Japanese ambassador Oshima on 14 July that when Russia was destroyed, which would soon be the case, a common enemy would be exterminated "once and for all." He continued to say that since the United States and Britain would always be the enemies of Germany, an alliance with Japan had to become the "basis of our state policy." Hitler had not failed to perceive the strategic pressure being exerted by the United States, to the west into the Pacific as well as to the east into the Atlantic: "Germany is threatened by Russia in the East and by America in the West. Japan is threatened by Russia in the West and America in the East," Hitler said. "This is why I think that we must destroy them together."[23]

It was not only the geographical distance between the two potential allies that made this worldwide war plan remain both illusion and utopia. It was also the fact that, apart from a lack of resources, a wide gap separated the strategic goals of the two countries. Within the Japanese command there were only a few who would have been willing to follow Germany unreservedly on this dangerous line of confrontation.

Against a background of considerable initial successes in the military campaign against Russia and threatening developments in the Atlantic, the Naval Staff tried at various levels in July 1941 to convince both the *Wehrmacht* command and Hitler of the immediate strategic necessity to concentrate German warfare on fighting the Anglo-Saxon naval powers. Matter-of-factly analyzing the threats to which the Reich was exposed, as well as its possibilities, the Naval Staff pictured the dilemma of a

---

[21] Conference, Raeder and Hitler, 9 July 1941, in Wagner, *Lagevorträge*, 264-265. Compare *Fuehrer Conferences* (1990), 221. See also Janet M. Manson, *Diplomatic Ramifications of Unrestricted SubmarineWarfare, 1939-1941* (New York: Greenwood Press, 1990), 129.

[22] Hillgruber, *Der Zweite Weltkrieg*, 72.

[23] Memo of Ambassador Hewel of a conference between Hitler and the Japanese Ambassador Oshima, 15 July 1941, *Akten zur deutschen auswärtigen Politik 1918-1945*, Series D: 1937-1945, vol. 13, 2, 829-834. The quotation is on page 833.

European continental power lacking the vital elements of a naval power
which was forced to fight against the greatest naval powers of the world:
"While in World War I we had the second strongest battle fleet in the
world but no appropriate operational base, we now dispose of a
strategically favorable operational base; however, we do not have the
required battle fleet to operate within the Atlantic."[24] The Naval Staff
predicted that the two allied naval powers would continue to fight even
if the Soviet Union collapsed in order to reach their "final goal" of
destroying Germany on the continent. In view of the American ship
construction program, which would make itself felt from 1942 onward,
the Germans would have to increase the number of enemy ships they
sank ". . . until the British supply situation will have reached a critical
point again." Allowing for this time factor, the Naval Staff came to the
conclusion that "the enemies' prospect for the battle in the Atlantic . . . for
the year 1942 must be assessed as favorable." For this reason, the Naval
Staff advocated that Germany take advantage of the political assets of
cooperation with France and Japan in order to bring about a decision in
the Atlantic through concentrated employment of all available forces, and
in particular with the help of submarines and the air force. At the same
time, Raeder tried to influence Hitler into making a clear decision on the
matter. Some of the dictator's statements had made Raeder doubtful as
to whether Hitler still ranked the naval war in the Atlantic highly. By
contemplating a temporary suspension of the submarine war altogether,
and by criticizing the employment of heavy surface units in the Atlantic,
Hitler suggested that he was going to increase his influence in naval warfare in the future. Raeder, on the other hand, tried to convince Hitler to
authorize more freedom of action for the navy. Hitler was not prepared
to do this in view of the still undecided situation in Russia. However,
when Raeder hinted at the hazards arising from a possible occupation of
Northwest Africa by British and American forces, he revealed the great
strategic weakness of the Axis powers in Europe. Indeed, this weakness
soon developed into a crisis. If the enemy lodged in this area, it would
no longer be possible to defeat the British; on the contrary, the other side
would in this case dispose of a much larger deployment area to be used
for operations directed against the European south flank. So Raeder demanded "a clearing up of the relations between Germany and France" as
a basis for a political and military cooperation. The Admiral wished to be
able to use positions in North Africa, including French colonies, as bases

---

[24] "Denkschrift zum gegenwärtigen Stand der Seekriegführung gegen England Juli 1941"
(21 July 1941), in Salewski, *Die deutsche Seekriegsleitung* 3: 189-221. The quotation is on pages
195-196.

for "the decisive fight in the battle in the Atlantic." Moreover, he advocated an extension of the naval war against U.S. merchant ships by stopping and sinking them in accordance with prize regulations. This would be a further step in cutting the growing American support to the British.

In saying that this political decision probably could not be made unless the military campaign in the east was brought to an end, Raeder expressed the entire dilemma which lay at the heart of the German prosecution of the war in the summer of 1941. Hitler immediately took the cue and assured the commander in chief of the navy that he still had the same concept of the effects of obstructing British supply lines. Hitler continued to say that he was only trying "to avoid having the U.S.A. declare war while the Eastern Campaign is still in progress," and that afterwards he would reserve "the right to take severe action against the U.S.A. as well."[25] As for his policy concerning France, Hitler did not agree with the ideas of the Naval Staff, mainly out of consideration for his Italian ally. The German strategy thus did not and could not change. The Naval Staff's large-scale plans could not be realized, not only because of the lack of forces to carry them out but also because there was no "afterwards" to the military campaign in the east.

Meanwhile, on the other side of the Atlantic, it became clear that the United States was firmly determined to intensify its support for Great Britain short-of-war, and, in doing so, to become more and more the dominant partner, trying to assert American political and economic ideals for a peaceful worldwide postwar order. The critical situation of the British partner, as well as the fact that the decision on American entry into war had not yet not been made, were a favorable basis for the imminent negotiations. In this respect, it can be said that the outcome of the conference between Roosevelt and Churchill from 9 to 12 August 1941, at Placentia Bay in Newfoundland, was really pre-programmed. In these negotiations, Washington could assert most of its political and military ideas, whereas Great Britain was forced to realize that the United States did not plan to intensify its direct or indirect support and seemed to be a long way from entering into war.[26]

The political signal was the so-called Atlantic Charter of 14 August signed by Roosevelt and Churchill, in which both sides not only defined their common war goal as "the final destruction of the Nazi dictatorship" but also defined the fundamental elements of a postwar worldwide peace. The latter involved pledges that there would be no territorial

---

[25] Conference, Raeder and Hitler, 25 July 1941, in Wagner, *Lagevorträge*, 271-273. Compare *Fuehrer Conferences*, 222-223 and Salewski, *Die deutsche Seekriegsleitung* 1: 407-412.
[26] Heinrichs, *Threshold of War*, 146-154.

changes or extensions of areas of influence, the restoration of the national rights of self-determination regarding forms of government, global free trade on the basis of equal access to raw materials and sales markets, freedom of the seas, a repudiation of violence, and the establishment of an international security system. In the wake of these principles, not only did elementary British interests resulting from economic advantages of the Commonwealth fall by the wayside, but those of the new participant in the war, the Soviet Union, did as well. Hence the first material supply deliveries for this "unnatural ally" were correspondingly low. The threatening development in the Asiatic-Pacific area caused by Japan's occupation of Indochina made it absolutely necessary from the British point of view for a concerted action to convey an unmistakable warning signal to Tokyo. Strategic positions like Singapore and the Dominions in Australia and New Zealand were in jeopardy. Their security, in view of the British ties in Europe and the Middle East, could only be maintained with the help of the United States. Roosevelt, however, had already taken measures by blocking Japanese funds and imposing an oil embargo. Evidently, he wanted to avoid further escalations and did not want to risk a premature conflict; he preferred to gain time for his own arms program.

Skillfully taking advantage of his position as commander in chief of all U.S. forces, Roosevelt used the U.S. Navy as a military instrument in the framework of his pro-British foreign policy. It was in the security interests of the United States to transport its own arms material safely to where the partner needed it on the other side of the Atlantic. So when Churchill requested at the Placentia Bay conference that units of the U.S. Navy participate in the securing of the North Atlantic convoys as well as in the surveillance of the Denmark strait, Roosevelt made the appropriate concessions. In doing so, the president also pointed out to Churchill that, in view of his difficult position vis-á-vis the Congress, he meant to avoid submitting a formal request for a declaration of war against Germany and that he would prefer to provoke "incidents" which would justify the commencement of hostilities by taking part in security operations within the German blockade area.[27] Such "incidents" were not long in coming.

Shortly afterwards, on 4 September 1941, approximately two hundred nautical miles southwest of Iceland, the American destroyer *Greer* and the German submarine *U 652* became involved in an inconclusive fight. This was the first fight between German and American forces in the war. Both sides claimed that the enemy had attacked first. The commanding officers

---

[27] Report, Churchill to War Cabinet, 19 August 1941, in Dallek, *Franklin D. Roosevelt*, 285.

U 652 at her commissioning ceremony in Kiel on 3 April 1941, with her commanding officer Lieutenant Fraatz in the tower. Photo courtesy of Commander Lichtenberg, FGN (Ret.), who was a petty officer on *U 652* in 1941.

of *U 652* had not noticed the close cooperation between the destroyer and a British patrol aircraft which had begun the attack by depth-charging the submarine.[28]

Roosevelt at once considered this incident a good opportunity for a further escalation of the American activities in the Atlantic. Although the naval command had informed him about the real course of events, on 11 September he related the incident saying that the *Greer* had done nothing to provoke the enemy but that she had suddenly been attacked by a German submarine. He used this incident to make a sharp comment on Hitler's aggressive war policy aimed at ruling the world and the German naval warfare in the Atlantic connected with it. In the maritime areas that were necessary for America's own defense, he said, American naval and air forces would no longer wait for attacks but would protect all merchant ships within their own waters, regardless of whether they were

---

[28] Manson, *Diplomatic Ramifications*, 138-140; Bailey and Ryan, *Hitler vs. Roosevelt*, 168-171.

flying American or foreign flags. Churchill commented on this development, which was extremely favorable for his aims, saying that now Hitler's only choice was either to lose the battle in the Atlantic or to engage in a permanent conflict with American naval forces.[29]

This assessment of the situation, which was basically correct, was shared by the Naval Staff in Berlin. The German Naval Staff characterized Roosevelt's order to attack as a "locally restricted declaration of war," having as the "only possible consequence" the military necessity to answer each open warlike act by the employment of weapons. On 17 September, Raeder pointed out to Hitler that Roosevelt's measures were designed to "make us restrict our attacks through fear of incidents," and that to yield would not only reduce the number of ships sunk but also encourage Washington to increase its interference constantly. He continued to say that a strong reaction "would probably induce the president to restrict his measures rather than to intensify them, since he evidently still meant to avoid open war, at least as long as it was quite sure that Japan was going to remain neutral."

At the time, Raeder's assessment of the situation was quite correct. Hitler, however, was still hoping for the "great decision" in the east and therefore gave orders for German naval units to avoid further incidents in the war on merchant shipping before about the middle of October.[30]

One important area in which the United States could support Great Britain was that of maritime transport capacity. Since it was within the strategic interests of the United States to defend and to strengthen the British position in Europe, it was only logical for the U.S. to use its merchant fleet to further this aim. However, such action would violate the 1939 laws of neutrality unless, through the operations of the U.S. Atlantic Fleet, Hitler could be provoked to declare war on the United States. In fact, this was what Roosevelt was still hoping for, since the prospects of Congress ratifying an American declaration of war were still poor. For this reason, the torpedoing of the destroyer *Kearny* on 17 October, far within the German extended area of operations and close to the American safety zone, usefully served as a further escalation through a revision in the American policy of neutrality.

The *Kearny* was part of a Task Unit to reinforce British escort security for a convoy exposed to U-boat attacks. Eleven sailors were killed in the

---

[29] Langer and Gleason, *Undeclared War*, 744-747.

[30] Conference, Raeder and Hitler, 17 September 1941, in Wagner, *Lagevorträge*, 286-288. Compare *Fuehrer Conferences* (1990), 231-233. Annex 1 of the conference with the title "The Speech made by the President of the U.S.A. on 11 September 1941" is *not* published in the 1990 edition, but see the 1947 edition of the U.S. Navy for 1941, vol. 2, 37-40.

attack. These were the first casualties of American forces in World War II.[31] In this case, Roosevelt took ten days to react, and on 27 October he used harsh words criticizing the German war policy and Hitler in particular, without elucidating the exact circumstances under which the incident had taken place. He said that shooting had begun, and that history would tell who had fired the first shot. He repeated his order saying that the U.S. Navy would shoot first and announced a revision of the neutrality policy that would include the arming of U.S. merchant ships and the transporting of war material with American merchant ships to ports in friendly countries. In effect this meant opening the existing war zones in Europe, which previously had been closed to American merchant ships.

When Hitler did not react as expected and London, as well as Washington, learned from deciphered radio signals that German submarines were receiving restrictive orders to avoid all incidents with American naval forces, Roosevelt refrained from engaging in any further escalations. Even the 31 October sinking of the destroyer *Reuben James*, with 115 casualties, scarcely had any effect on what remained of relations between Germany and the United States. It did contribute, however, to strengthening the president's position in Congress for the final vote of 13 November on revising American neutrality. The relatively weak majority of eighteen votes in the House of Representatives showed that, with his cautious policy on the verge of war, Roosevelt was running a great risk, although polls conducted in mid-October had revealed that 70 percent of American citizens thought it more important to defeat Hitler than to keep out of the war. The narrow majority in Congress also made it clear that, in order to justify a declaration of war, there had to be more serious incidents in foreign policy or, at least, more important incidents than fighting along the convoy routes in the Atlantic.[32] From the diplomatic cables of the Japanese, Roosevelt knew that the critical situation in the Pacific was more likely to turn into a crisis than the situation in the Atlantic.

In order to maintain the German position in North Africa, in October 1941 Hitler had seen the strategic necessity not only to continue the potentially wearing military campaign in the east but also to solve the crisis in the Mediterranean, which was a vital precondition for the successful ending of the overall war situation for the Naval Staff.[33] Since

---

[31] Bailey and Ryan, *Hitler vs. Roosevelt*, 196-198; Manson, *Diplomatic Ramifications*, 142-146.

[32] Dallek, *Franklin D. Roosevelt*, 292.

[33] Salewski, *Die deutsche Seekriegsleitung* 1: 474.

there were no other forces available, submarines had to be withdrawn from the Atlantic to stabilize the situation. The transfer of U-boats into the Mediterranean and the concentration of additional boats off Gibraltar seriously weakened the concept of sea denial in the Atlantic. It soon became clear at this point that the Axis Powers had overreached their potential and that they were only able to maintain their respective positions by alternating their concentration of forces. However, an analysis of the war situation from Hitler's point of view shows that he still had the illusion that he had achieved his great goal to defeat the Soviet Union.[34]

On 27 October 1941, Hitler informed Vice Admiral Kurt Fricke, the chief of staff of the Naval Staff,[35] that "to win the military campaign in the East" was a necessary "precondition for a successful fight against Great Britain." To "*secure the continental zone*," he said, was now the "*prime necessity of the hour*." This, he added, also meant the securing of the Mediterranean position. Morale in Italy was going from bad to worse, with everyone, except in fascist circles, growing tired of the war and wanting peace and talking about the "war of the Germans." Under the circumstances, Hitler's view was a very shrewd and honest assessment of the situation! This critical development in Italy made Hitler determined to reinforce German air and naval forces in the Mediterranean. Fricke, however, was in line with the Naval Staff's point of view, saying that it was necessary to concentrate all forces available for the disruption of British supply lines in the Atlantic. Hitler was not prepared to change his attitude and said that there had to be "an immediate concentration of forces" in the Mediterranean, since "a German/Italian loss of position in this area represented an intolerable hazard for the European continent."

When Fricke brought up the "question of the final, successful ending of the war," expressing his opinion that "the total defeat of England was necessary to guarantee a new order in Europe," Hitler frankly let him know that he and Naval Staff saw the enemy with quite different eyes. Even then Hitler was still prepared to conclude peace with England, since the geographic area in Europe, which Germany had been able to occupy so far, was sufficient to secure the future of the German people. Fricke got the impression that Hitler was prepared to make concessions on the colonial question but that he did not expect Churchill to give way. "Obviously the Führer would be pleased if, after the military campaign in the East, England would be prepared to conclude peace of her own

---

[34] Hillgruber, *Hitlers Strategie*, 537, n. 3.
[35] The best summary of the conference between Vice Admiral K. Fricke and Hitler is in *Kriegstagebuch der Seekriegsleitung, Teil A*, vol. 26, October, 1941 (Herford, Bonn, 1991), 474-478. Quotations ibid., emphasis added.

accord . . . even if in this case Germany would have no more possibilities to occupy *more* space than had been the case so far." Hitler's directives were unmistakable, and so the German Navy had to send the requested number of submarines into the Mediterranean. Meanwhile, the number of submarines in the Atlantic had diminished to an extent that Admiral Karl Dönitz, Flag Officer U-boat Command, was speaking of a "submarine vacuum" which the enemy could not but welcome.[36]

The inferior status of the Atlantic within the framework of German strategy became very clear when Germany declared war against the United States on 11 December 1941. Of ninety-one operational submarines, only six were immediately assigned for the American East coast.

In April of 1941, Hitler told the Japanese Foreign Minister Matsuoka that the fighting against maritime transport capacities was a "decisive weakening of Britain *and* America" and that he was sure that no American could "set foot on the European continent."[37] At the end of 1941, he was rather inclined to neglect the possible long-term results of effective warfare in the Atlantic. Now he was more concerned about "sinking 4 ships in the Arctic Waters delivering tanks to the Russian front line than to sink 100,000 GRT in the South Atlantic."[38] Apart from the fact that tank deliveries of the Western powers were insignificant compared to the Soviet tank production rate, this brought up again the fundamental question: What was the strategic goal of German naval warfare in the Atlantic? Would the fight be decided by a "race" between the number of ships sunk and ships constructed? Or should the Atlantic be the front court of the "Fortress Europe" that had to be defended against an enemy who was definitely superior in terms of matériel and personnel? So far, the submarines had turned out to be very effective. However, this led Hitler and others to overestimate a weapons system which surely was an effective instrument to solve critical situations in the Mediterranean. But by the end of the following year, it would lose its ability to avoid enemy surveillance and attacks.

In December 1941, Pearl Harbor and the Japanese offensives drew Washington's attention to the events in the Pacific, but the Atlantic continued to be a bridge to the "junior partner," Great Britain. She held the key positions in the eastern Atlantic that were to become the starting bases for successful allied offensives against the Axis Powers in Europe.

---

[36] U-Boat Command to Naval Staff, 3 November 1941, BA-MA RM 7/845, fol. 220-221. See also Rahn, "Der Seekrieg im Atlantik und Nordmeer," *Der globale Krieg*, 296.

[37] Memo of a conference between Hitler and the Japanese Ambassador, 4 April 1941, *Akten zur deutschen auswärtigen Politik*, Series D, vol. 12, 1, document no. 266.

[38] Memo of Captain von Puttkamer of a conference between Raeder and Hitler, 29 December 1941, BA-MA RM 7/133, fol. 331-335.

2

The Views of Stimson and Knox on Atlantic Strategy and Planning

Jeffrey G. Barlow

Some forty-five years have passed since former Secretary of War Henry L. Stimson published his memoirs, entitled *On Active Service In Peace And War*, and staked out the high ground in the debate as to whether the War Department or the Navy Department deserves more of the credit for reacting effectively to the German U-boat threat in U.S. waters in 1942 and 1943.[1] In this debate, Stimson held all the advantages. He based his memoirs on the extensive private diaries which he had dictated during his years of public service. These diaries, together with the rest of his papers, were subsequently donated to Yale University and were made available to interested scholars beginning in the 1960s. On the other hand, his counterpart in the Navy Department during much of the turbulent wartime period, Frank Knox, had died in office in the spring of 1944, and his classified personal-official correspondence remained unavailable to historians until very recently.

In more recent decades, a number of historians have used Stimson's memoirs and, more importantly, his diaries to bolster claims that under his guidance the War Department moved quickly to defeat the German U-boat threat, while the Navy Department, under the dead hand of traditionalist admirals, continued to flounder about in ignorance of the proper way to deal with it. In 1960, the well-known naval historian Elting E. Morison elaborated upon this theme in his biography of Stimson,

---

[1] Henry L. Stimson and McGeorge Bundy, *On Active Service In Peace And War* (New York: Harper & Brothers, 1948).

Turmoil and Tradition: A Study of the Life and Times of Henry L. Stimson.[2] A current example which continues to rely on this basic theme is a 1990 book by Army officer Montgomery Meigs entitled *Slide Rules and Submarines: American Scientists and Subsurface Warfare in World War II.*[3]

It is time to look at the issue anew, using both Stimson's diaries and Frank Knox's letters to his principal correspondent, Admiral Harold R. Stark. Such an analysis provides a sense of how each man viewed the strategy and planning related to the U-boat war in the Atlantic and leads to a few observations on how accurate the accepted Stimson version of the events really is. From the outset, however, several caveats must be made about the nature of the Stimson diaries. First of all, because he dictated the entries a day or more after the events, and because the entries were typed up in finished form by a secretary rather than being hand-written by the man himself, Stimson's diaries rarely show any sense of hesitancy or rethinking with regard to the events described. In addition, during his time as Secretary of War (if not before), Stimson was dictating these diary entries at least in part with an eye toward history, and this historical "self consciousness" should be taken into account. As General George C. Marshall's biographer, Forrest C. Pogue, remarked some years ago, "Stimson's diary says constantly, 'Marshall came in; he was much worried.' After a time you wonder whether the entry reflects Marshall's state of mind or Stimson's."[4]

Stimson's Views

To understand Henry Stimson's approach to Atlantic strategy and planning, one must also understand two important things about him. First, as a former National Guard officer with a much earlier tour as Secretary of War under his belt, Stimson thought himself a military strategist. In this he was much like Winston Churchill, who, as Britain's wartime Prime Minister, liked to sign himself "Former Naval Person" in his communications with President Franklin Roosevelt. It would have been difficult to convince Colonel Stimson (had anyone tried) that his

---

[2] Elting E. Morison, *Turmoil and Tradition: A Study of the Life and Times of Henry L. Stimson* (Boston: Houghton Mifflin Company, 1960).

[3] Montgomery C. Meigs, *Slide Rules and Submarines: American Scientists and Subsurface Warfare in World War II* (Washington, D.C.: National Defense University Press, 1990).

[4] Forrest C. Pogue, "Commentary," in *Air Power And Warfare: The Proceedings of the 8th Military History Symposium, United States Air Force Academy, 18-20 October 1978,* ed. Alfred F. Hurley and Robert C. Ehrhart (Washington, D.C.: Office of Air Force History and United States Air Force Academy, 1979), 206.

Colonel Henry L. Stimson, Secretary of War during World War II. Photo courtesy of the National Archives, Washington, D.C.

earlier, rather brief associations with the army had not endowed him with a general officer's grasp of the finer points of military strategy. In addition, his years of Cabinet-level public service and a certain patrician background encouraged him in the general correctness of his own viewpoint on matters that arose.

The second important point is that Henry Stimson possessed an almost visceral dislike of the navy and its senior officers, which appeared to stem in large part from that service's entirely different approach to looking at the world. That it differed in organizational structure, concepts of command, and prerogatives from his beloved army, which at the turn of the century had been restructured around the concept of the General Staff by Elihu Root, was, to Stimson, indicative of its underlying flaws. As an oft-quoted sentence from his memoirs (although undoubtedly coined by his co-author McGeorge Bundy, rather than by Stimson himself) intoned, ". . . some of the army-navy troubles . . . grew mainly from the peculiar psychology of the Navy Department, which frequently seemed to retire from the realm of logic into a dim religious world in which Neptune was God, Mahan his prophet, and the United States Navy the only true Church."[5] It didn't seem to bother him that he really had no knowledge of the navy; nor did it stop him from assuming that strategy, tactics, and logistics were handled pretty much alike whether they were employed on land or at sea.

During 1941, Stimson was strongly in favor of the United States rendering whatever help it could to the United Kingdom's beleaguered war effort. He saw U.S. convoying of merchant ships carrying British war supplies as a vital part of this effort. For example, following an evening meeting with Navy Secretary Frank Knox in late March 1941, he noted in his diary, "We both agreed that the crisis is coming very soon and that *convoying is the only solution* and that it must come practically at once."[6] A month later, when President Franklin Roosevelt was giving serious consideration to how the United States could carry out its projected patrolling in the Atlantic with inadequate forces then in the Atlantic Fleet, Stimson recommended withdrawing the major portion of the Pacific Fleet from Hawaii and sending it into the Atlantic Ocean to beef up Admiral King's forces.[7] Stimson noted:

> [W]hen I got back to the office in the afternoon I had a long conference with Marshall and Stark. Marshall was particularly strong in thinking I had done a great thing in getting the chance of having the main fleet sent over to the Atlantic. He was strongly of the opinion that the psychological benefit of moving the fleet to the Atlantic would far outweigh any encouragement that it would give to Japan. Japan would recognize that we meant business and would be just as cautious about going down to Singapore as if we stayed there. Stark, when he came in

---

[5] Stimson and Bundy, *On Active Service*, 506.

[6] Emphasis in original. Entry for 24 March 1941, Henry Lewis Stimson Diaries (hereafter Stimson Diaries), vol. 33, 112, Manuscripts and Archives, Yale University Library, New Haven Connecticut, microfilm edition, reel 6. The author used the copy of the microfilm edition in the Manuscript Division, Library of Congress.

[7] Entry for 24 April 1941, Stimson Diaries, vol. 33, reel 6, 182-183.

and was told about the discussion in the morning, felt about the same
way too.[8]

Less than two weeks later, however, in a meeting with the president,
Admiral Stark stepped back from full support for Stimson's position. This
change of heart quickly brought on the Secretary's scorn. As Stimson
dictated to his diary, "to my utter surprise, *Stark switched around* and
trimmed on the subject and was only for moving three ships — three
capital ships. . . . I came out of the meeting with a renewal of my original
impression of *Stark — that he is a timid and ineffective man* to be in the post
he holds."[9]

America's entry into the war in December 1941 did little to dampen
Stimson's harsh criticisms of the navy. Just days after the Japanese attack
on Pearl Harbor, following General Douglas MacArthur's urgent pleas for
help in the Philippines, the secretary was castigating Admiral Thomas C.
Hart, commander in chief of the Asiatic Fleet, for taking "*the usual Navy
defeatist position*" in daring to tell MacArthur that the islands could not
long be held with the forces available.[10] Convinced that he had a better
understanding of naval strategy than the admirals in the Navy
Department, Stimson continued to lobby the president for his pet schemes
during December 1941 and January 1942. One of these was a push for
small aircraft carriers (ACVs, later redesignated CVEs) which could be
produced quickly and used to take the fight to the Japanese while their
offensives were still in progress.[11] Convinced that the navy was not
moving fast enough, on 13 January 1942 Stimson approached the
president with the proposal that the War Department be allowed to build
the ships. As he noted, "I had called up the President and told him that
I wanted him to authorize me to build a navy. He was rather startled by
the proposition but I got his attention thereby to the pressing carrier
situation and I told him that the Netherlands [Netherlands East Indies]
campaign depended upon our getting at once some small carriers and
that I had been hammering at the navy for a month without any
success."[12] The president suggested that Stimson talk over the small
carrier issue with Rear Admiral John H. Towers, the Chief of the Bureau
of Aeronautics. This the Secretary of War did, but he found out that none
of these ships would be ready until June. As he gloomily recorded in his

---

[8] Ibid., 185.

[9] Emphasis in original. Entry for 6 May 1941, Stimson Diaries, vol, 34, reel 6, 13.

[10] Emphasis in original. Entry for 14 December 1941, Stimson Diaries, vol. 36, reel 7,
105.

[11] See entry for 28 December 1941, Stimson Diaries, vol. 36, reel 7, 152.

[12] Entry for 14 January 1942, Stimson Diaries, vol. 37, reel 7, 32.

diary, "at present it looks as if we should not be able to get any carriers to help in the fight against the Japanese advance in the New Netherlands unless we can get one of the Navy's real carriers which they are fighting strongly against giving to us."[13]

With such an active interest in the naval aspects of the war, it is little wonder that Henry Stimson soon began occupying himself with the progress of the war against the U-boats in the Atlantic. In mid-March 1942 he sent President Roosevelt an outline report on his recent visit to Panama. The report proposed a number of suggestions for providing a defense of the Panama Canal against attack by an enemy aircraft carrier. For protection of the canal's Pacific side, Stimson reported the Bomber Command's idea of an outer patrol by Army Air Force (AAF) long-range bombers out to 1,000 miles from the canal. All of these patrolling bombers were to be equipped with ASVs (radar) to enable them to locate the enemy carrier at some distance.[14] Two days later Stimson took up the issue of providing additional long-range bombers for protection of the canal with Army Air Forces Commanding General Henry H. Arnold.[15]

The next day an issue arose which was to plague army-navy relations for the next sixteen months. During a visit to Stimson's office by Frank Knox, Admiral Ernest J. King (commander in chief and newly appointed CNO), and Admiral Towers, King raised the question of the navy obtaining from the AAF's aircraft production allocation some six hundred B-24 and B-25 bombers by mid-1943 (and an additional seven hundred by mid-1944) for use in the Atlantic and Pacific for convoy escort, patrolling, and shipping protection in coastal waters.[16] Stimson, Marshall, and Arnold did not greet the idea positively. Stimson commented:

> The issue is whether, now that the Navy has discovered that their air development has been ineffective and disappointing, we shall give them outright large numbers of our big bombers for their pilots to fly, or whether we shall turn over to them to serve under their command the

[13] Ibid.

[14] Memorandum from Stimson to President Franklin D. Roosevelt, 14 March 1942, filed with entry for 14 March 1942, Stimson Diaries, vol. 38, reel 7, 29-30.

[15] Entry for 16 March 1942, Stimson Diaries, vol. 38, reel 7, 37.

[16] King had first raised the issue in a letter to AAF Commanding General Hap Arnold several weeks before but had gotten a highly negative response. See copies of the five letters on this subject exchanged between King and Arnold from 20 February through 18 March 1942, all enclosures to the memorandum from Captain L. A. Thackrey to the Secretary of the Navy, 4 February 1948; "Review of the Marshall-Arnold-King Correspondence on ASW—1942-1943" Folder, Box 13, Ernest J. King Papers, Operational Archives, Naval Historical Center (hereafter OA, NHC).

A U.S. Army Air Forces B-25 bomber on antisubmarine patrol off the east coast of Florida, 12 May 1942. Photo courtesy of the Naval Historical Center, Washington, D.C.

bombers and our Army pilots who know them. . . . This last is the method we wish. The bombers and the pilots represent a unit which is the fruit of a great organization on the part of the Army. It could not be extemporized early in the Navy, and simply to turn over the bombers for them to learn to use without the schools and the vast system of ground troops in other respects which support the men in the air, would involve the delay in their use until the Navy built up virtually another army to support them.[17]

Having rejected the navy's initial attempt to obtain its own long-range aircraft for convoy escort and antisubmarine patrols, Stimson began thinking about setting up an Army Air Forces antisubmarine warfare (ASW) capability. A significant impetus to his thinking was a meeting he had with the heads of the major U.S. oil companies on 26 March 1942. At this meeting, the executives told Stimson that tanker sinkings by U-boats were so serious in scope that if they continued at the present rate, "the

---

[17] Entry for 17 March 1942, Stimson Diaries, vol. 38, reel 7, 42.

whole fleet would be destroyed in a very few months."[18] This was an extremely sobering conclusion. The following day, Stimson recorded in his diary: "The sinkings of tankers on the eastern coast lie heavy on my feelings and I had a talk with [Assistant Secretary of War for Air Robert A.] Lovett about them in an effort to do everything I can to press forward the equipment of our planes with the radio eye [radar]."[19]

During the next several days, the secretary continued to mull over the question of how to introduce radar-equipped bomber aircraft into the antisubmarine campaign. This culminated in a decision on 1 April 1942 to bring in Dr. Edward L. Bowles of the Massachusetts Institute of Technology as Stimson's special consultant to administer the Army's airborne radar program.[20] Within days, Bowles was expanding his area of interest into the larger question of overall antisubmarine warfare.[21] Yet, even as Bowles was getting down to work, Stimson was lamenting the state of the U.S. Navy. As he dictated in his diary on 14 April, "I have been more discouraged today over the situation of our own navy than I think I have ever been before. Here it is nearly two years since we came in here and the Navy is still badly organized and I do not feel any confidence in the men at the head of it."[22]

On 20 May 1942, Edward Bowles came to the secretary of war with a proposal for establishing a special antisubmarine bombardment group for developing the equipment, tactics, and techniques necessary for effective ASW. As Bowles explained, airborne radar was not at a stage where it could be treated as "a magic gadget which, when installed in a depth-charge-carrying aircraft . . . creates an effective anti-submarine weapon." To be effective the aircraft also needed special ordnance, the proper navigational equipment, and possible other means to detect submerged submarines, and all of this required a center organized expressly for exploiting airborne antisubmarine warfare.[23] Stimson approved the proposal in principle.[24] Ten days later, General Arnold directed the establishment of the Sea-Search Attack Development Unit (SADU) at Langley Field, Virginia. Its primary mission was to "Develop

---

[18] Entry for 26 March 1942, Stimson Diaries, vol. 38, reel 7, 62.

[19] Entry for 27 March 1942, Stimson Diaries, vol. 38, reel 7, 64.

[20] Entry for 1 April 1942, Stimson Diaries, vol. 38, reel 7, 79.

[21] See, for example, the entry for 14 April 1942, Stimson Diaries, vol. 38, reel 7, 113.

[22] Ibid.

[23] Memorandum from Bowles to the Secretary of War, 20 May 1942, 1-2; "X" Folder, Box 3, Correspondence & Reports Re: Edward L. Bowles's Anti-sub Warfare Office, Expert Consultant To The Secretary Of War, Record Group 107, National Archives, Washington D.C. (hereafter Bowles Correspondence, RG 107, NA.)

[24] Entry for 20 May 1942, Stimson Diaries, vol. 39, reel 7, 31.

tactics and technique in order that the submarine destructive devices known, and those which may be developed, be used to the greatest advantage."[25]

As the weeks passed, Henry Stimson continued to worry over the dangerous situation in the Atlantic, where U-boats continued to sink U.S. and British merchant ships at an alarming rate. On 7 June 1942, he talked over the situation with John J. McCloy, one of his chief advisers, and Lewis Douglas. He commented, "We are disgusted at the handling of the matter by the Navy. They have not risen to it as a great occasion. They are too slow."[26] Several weeks later, in a conversation with Dr. Vannevar Bush, Director of the Office of Scientific Research and Development, the subject arose of the need for reorganization of the Navy Department in order to effectively prosecute the antisubmarine war. Stimson noted, "This leaves me with a rather stiff problem of how to get another Department pushed along into the right channels on what is probably the most critical problem that now threatens our war effort."[27]

In early August 1942, Edward Bowles recommended to Secretary Stimson that the time was ripe for the formation of an Air Antisubmarine Force which would incorporate all army and navy land-based aircraft of the antisubmarine forces. While it would confine its operations to U.S. coastal waters, it would be free to send detachments to other parts of the world.[28] Five weeks later, Army Chief of Staff George Marshall sent a memorandum to Admiral King informing him that he was directing the organization of the First Antisubmarine Army Air Command, whose primary mission would be submarine destruction. Marshall informed King that he proposed to centralize the control of this command in the War Department, so that it could be promptly dispatched to the scene of current enemy submarine activities. He noted, however, that the unit's operations would be under the control of the Sea Frontiers Command.[29] A few days later, Admiral King responded by commenting that this organization would add "materially" to the effectiveness of available ASW aircraft. However, he made it clear that, as commander in chief, he would continue to exercise operational control of these aircraft through the Sea Frontier Commanders.[30] As subsequently formed, the First Antisubmarine

---

[25] Directive by the Commanding General, AAF for the Director of Technical Services, AAF, 30 May 1942; "XI-A" Folder, Box 3, Bowles Correspondence, RG 107, NA.

[26] Entry for 7 June 1942, Stimson Diaries, vol. 39, reel 7, 76.

[27] Entry for 23 July 1942, Stimson Diaries, vol. 39, reel 7, 195.

[28] Memorandum from Bowles to the Secretary of War, 7 August 1942; "XIII" Folder, Box 3, Bowles Correspondence, RG 107, NA.

[29] Memorandum from Marshall to King, 14 September 1942; "XIV-A" Folder, ibid.

[30] Memorandum from King to Marshall, 17 September 1942; "XIV-B" Folder, ibid.

Army Air Command conducted its ASW operations under the operational control of the navy.[31]

Secretary Stimson was not content to let the matter remain here, however. Some three months later, on 27 December 1942, he talked with the president about allowing the Army to pursue an offensive posture against the U-boats. As he remarked:

> I took up the question of a submarine offensive as distinguished from the defensive work the Navy was doing by building more and more ships to be sunk and escort vessels. . . . I . . . said that I thought the matter was being held back by the conservatism and lack of imagination of the higher Navy command; that there were plenty of brains lower down in the Navy; and that in my opinion the thing to do was similar to what I had done in regard to microwaves in the Army—to pick out the best man in the Navy for the purpose and give him charge; . . . .[32]

In January 1943, Stimson urged on Navy Undersecretary James V. Forrestal the idea that the navy create a small "killer" group of surface vessels which could be placed in areas where German U-boat "wolf packs" were operating and could keep the submarines submerged; smashing those that surfaced.[33] Even though this seemed not to garner much navy attention, Stimson continued pressing his case for taking the offensive against the U-boats.

In early March 1943, Dr. Bowles presented the secretary with his report, which called for carrying out aggressive air warfare against the U-boats. A memorandum was subsequently drawn up to show the changes which would be necessary to effect such a campaign. The memo stated that the mission of navy-operated aircraft would be to provide convoy cover for the protection of convoys. On the other hand, the mission of army-operated aircraft would be hunting and destroying submarines in those localities where intelligence information indicated they were operating. The paper stressed that this hunting would be done "by a command which is not guarding slow-moving convoys nor shackled by traditions of surface vessel maneuvers."[34] During the rest of March,

---

[31] See memorandum from Major General Joseph T. McNarney, Deputy Chief of Staff, to Commanding General, AAF, 22 September 1942; "XIV-C" Folder, ibid.

[32] Entry for 27 December 1942, Stimson Diaries, vol. 41, reel 8, 120-121.

[33] See entry for 25 January 1943, Stimson Diaries, vol. 41, reel 8, 180-181, and letter from Stimson to Forrestal, 28 January 1943, attached after entry for 28 January 1943, ibid., 188-189.

[34] "Memorandum of operational changes which are necessary to put into effect Dr. Bowles' study of antisubmarine warfare," 10 March 1943, attached after entry for 10 March 1943, Stimson Diaries, vol. 42, reel 8, 100-101.

Secretary of the Navy Frank Knox and Admiral Harold Stark on the River Clyde
in Scotland during a 1944 inspection tour of U.S. naval facilities in the United
Kingdom. Pictured left to right are Secretary Knox, Captain Lyman S. Perry, and
Admiral Stark. Photo courtesy of the Naval Historical Center, Washington, D.C.

Stimson worked to figure out how he could force this new organizational scheme on the navy.[35] On 26 March 1943, he made his pitch to
President Roosevelt, arguing on the basis of charts that in May 1942 the
attacks on the U-boats by the AAF's little group of B-18 bombers "were
effective" in driving them away from the U.S. coast.[36]

In the end, though, it was all for nought. Admiral King and the navy
were not about to surrender any significant portion of the service's
responsibility for antisubmarine warfare. Several months later, following
a series of memoranda between Admiral King and General Marshall, the
army agreed to turn over the land-based air ASW mission entirely to the

[35] See entry for 25 March 1943, Stimson Diaries, vol. 42, reel 8, 116-117.
[36] Entry for 26 March 1943, Stimson Diaries, vol. 42, reel 8, 119.

navy.[37] By the beginning of 1944 all of the antisubmarine warfare duties being performed by AAF squadrons had been assumed by navy outfits.

Knox's Views

Unlike Henry Stimson, Frank Knox came to his job as Secretary of the Navy unable to claim any share of military or naval expertise. Up to the time he was appointed by President Roosevelt, he had been a newspaper publisher. Nonetheless, he grew in his new job, and as he became more accustomed to navy ways he began according his senior officers his trust.

From the outset of his correspondence with Admiral Harold Stark, the former CNO who was now Commander, United States Naval Forces in Europe, Frank Knox, like his senior uniformed counterparts in the Navy Department, believed that convoying was vital to the protection of merchant shipping and that the navy's lack of suitable escort vessels and well-trained crews was the principal handicap in the initial months of the U-boat campaign in U.S. coastal waters. As he wrote to Stark in early June 1942:

> I have been considerably appalled by a study of the submarine menace made by Admiral Reeves and Admiral Dorling. . . . Their remedy is a faster proportion in the construction of escort vessels and the use of escorts for convoys wherever they are needed. I think their reasoning is logical and sound. We have finally brought about a fairly good situation along the Atlantic Coast by the use of convoys. We do not yet have convoys in the Caribbean and there the sinkings continue. This gives us a new and more recent illustration that the submarine can be beaten when you have escort vessels.[38]

In this same letter, Knox went on to add:

> I have given more time and thought to this submarine thing than I have to any other responsibility I have had during the last three or four months, and I still feel serious doubts as to when we can turn the tide in our favor. We are getting quite a respectable number of sub-chasers in actual service, but the necessity for well-trained crews and the lack of them is slowing down the effect their use ought to have on sinkings.[39]

---

[37] Copies of this exchange of memos between King and Marshall can be found as attachments to the memo from Thackrey to the Secretary of the Navy, 4 February 1948, Box 13, King Papers, OA, NHC.

[38] Letter from Knox to Stark, 5 June 1942; "June 1942" Folder, Box A1, Harold R. Stark [Personal-Official] Papers, OA, NHC.

[39] Ibid.

Three weeks later, Knox was again stressing to Stark the navy's need for crews well trained in ASW techniques. He commented:

> You are right about the submarine menace but I think we are gradually making progress. The more I get into it, the more I am convinced that its ultimate solution is to be found in the right kind of sub-chasers equipped with adequate devices and weapons plus properly trained crews. The public is hepped up over the idea of sending two or three thousand 40 or 50-foot launches out to sea and wiping the submarines out overnight. There seems to be little or no appreciation of the difficulty of submarine hunting and the skill required to make a kill.[40]

In July 1942, Secretary Knox went on an inspection tour of the Eastern Sea Frontier, accompanied by Rear Admiral Richard S. Edwards, King's Chief of Staff. A major purpose of the trip for the secretary was to inculcate in the forces patrolling for submarines a greater spirit of endeavor by letting the personnel know that the department's senior people were "deeply interested" in what they were doing.[41]

In early August 1942, Frank Knox was writing in a hopeful manner about the positive effect that the establishment of the coastal convoy system had had on the U-boats sinkings. He told "Betty" Stark: "At long last, we seem to have made considerable progress in the anti-submarine fight. The figures for the month of July for United Nations losses are the lowest they have been since last January and, in our waters, alone, showed a very sharp drop of about 40 percent." In a more somber vein, however, he went on to note the great difficulty they were having in establishing a convoy system in the Gulf of Mexico the "lack of escort vessels and properly equipped aircraft for patrol purposes."[42] Late that same month, he returned to the issue of the need for more escorts, telling Stark, "We are by no means producing enough escorts to provide sufficient convoys and it seems to me blind folly to ignore the implications of this policy. It does us little good to produce one hundred cargo ships a month if we do not produce enough escort vessels during that month to enable us to protect them when they go to sea."[43]

It was in large part because he knew just how fluid the U-boat situation was that Frank Knox remained so focused on the escort ship

---

[40] Letter from Knox to Stark, 27 June 1942, ibid.

[41] Letter from Knox to Stark, 13 July 1942; "July 1942" Folder, Box A1, Stark Papers, OA, NHC.

[42] Letter from Knox to Stark, 5 August 1942; "August 1942" Folder, Box A1, Stark Papers, OA, NHC.

[43] Letter from Knox to Stark, 29 August 1942, ibid.

issue. In September 1942, when U-boat sinkings of merchant ships in the U.S. coastal waters from Maine to Florida had dropped almost to zero, he was well aware that other areas were receiving their full share of the German skippers' attentions.[44] In mid-October 1942, the navy secretary made a major pitch to President Roosevelt for doubling the construction of escorts during 1943 at the expense of cargo ship building and other production programs.[45]

Frank Knox's inherent caution held steady into the new year as shipping losses continued to mount. He wrote Admiral Stark in March, just after the conclusion of the Convoy Conference. He commented, "We are going to go into the spring in pitifully weak condition both as regards surface anti-submarine craft for mid-Atlantic work, and air. Whether we shall get the reinforcements in aircraft soon enough to be effective this spring, I do not know and I doubt it." He wrote further: "Already the total for this month foreshadows as heavy, if not heavier, losses than those of last fall and summer. I am doing everything I can to prepare the public for this but, despite it, the Navy is sure to take it on the chin until we have the submarine finally licked."[46] The secretary returned to that same note of caution a week later, when he wrote to Stark:

> One of the discouraging phases of the situation is the length of time it takes to get any kind of equipment ready for actual service at sea. We need about 130 big, long-range, four-engine planes to cover the area thoroughly between Newfoundland and Iceland. We only have about forty or fifty assigned but it is going to be thirty to sixty days before they are properly prepared for that kind of duty and, in the meantime, the slaughter of ships goes on.[47]

In late May 1943, Knox began sounding a bit more optimistic about the U-boat war situation, telling "Betty" Stark: "The news about the submarine warfare continues to be exceptionally good, almost too good to last."[48] A few days later, though, he expressed his concern that British

---

[44] See letter from Knox to Stark, 17 September 1942; "September 1942" Folder, Box A1, Stark Papers, OA, NHC.

[45] See letter from Knox to President Roosevelt, 19 October 1942, enclosed with letter from Knox to Stark, 20 October 1942; "October 1942" Folder, Box A1, Stark Papers, OA, NHC.

[46] Letter from Knox to Stark, 24 March 1943; "March 1943" Folder, Box A1, Stark Papers, OA, NHC.

[47] Letter from Knox to Stark, 29 March 1943, ibid.

[48] Letter from Knox to Stark, 28 May 1943; "May 1943" Folder, Box A1, Stark Papers, OA, NHC.

leaders, including Churchill, were talking too much about submarine activities. He remarked, "Already the more optimistic in this country are assuming that the battle with the submarines is won. Although we know it is not won, things are looking better." He cautioned that when in a few weeks the antisubmarine forces began to lose a lot of the destroyers then engaged in escort duties because large-scale troop convoying began to take place, the losses could well go up again.[49]

Frank Knox did not know then that the tide indeed had turned in the Allies' favor. Following unsupportable losses to his U-boats (running at fifteen to seventeen boats a month), German Navy Commander in Chief Karl Dönitz had decided in May 1943 to withdraw his U-boats from the North Atlantic until such time as they could be equipped with new weapons which would allow them to reassert their primacy against the Allied forces. From that point on, however, they were forced into a losing battle with new Allied ASW assets that were becoming operational on a steadily-increasing scale.

A Few Comparisons

Much of the credit that Secretary of War Henry Stimson took (or was given) for his role in pushing the American development of airborne search radar for the antisubmarine mission was deserved. His appointment of scientist Edward Bowles as his expert consultant for radar matters provided impetus to a program that otherwise might not have advanced as rapidly as it did.

Nonetheless, it was only a partial success. Despite the grandiose dreams of Bowles and Stimson, the Army Air Forces Antisubmarine Command did not become the major offensive U-boat killer that both men had envisioned. In mid-February 1943, out of a total complement of 235 aircraft (scattered over twenty-one different bases), the Antisubmarine Command had only seventy-one aircraft which were equipped with radar of any kind, and thirty-four of these (48 percent of the number so equipped) were obsolete B-18B twin-engine bombers.[50] Six weeks later the Antisubmarine Command was down to 231 aircraft, of which thirty-five were undergoing depot- or sub-depot-level maintenance; while only four

---

    [49] Letter from Knox to Stark, 5 June 1943; "June 1943" Folder, Box A1, Stark Papers, OA, NHC.

    [50] "Airplanes and Equipment of the Antisubmarine Command," 17 February 1943; "ASC" Folder, Box 2, Bowles Correspondence, RG 107, NA.

of the Command's twenty-three squadrons were fully operational and another four were rated capable of limited operations.[51]

Moreover, Stimson's dismissive appraisal of the navy's convoying and air escort operations as merely defensive in nature and his happy-go-lucky concept of surface ship killer operations were indicative of an intelligence that reflected no serious understanding of naval matters. On balance, then, one can conclude that however great he may have deemed his gifts as a strategist of the Atlantic campaign, Henry Stimson clearly was not on a par with the admirals he loved to deride and was less realistic than Navy Secretary Frank Knox, who claimed to possess no special strategic insights.

All in all, Knox's innate caution (one could even term it mild pessimism) about the course of the Battle of the Convoys served him rather better than one would have expected, given the unheralded position in history his wartime service has so far accorded him. He was loath to see an early decision in the U-boat/merchant ship war arising from miracle weapons or offensive shortcuts. The acquisition of sufficient numbers of adequate escorts and antisubmarine aircraft, and practical ASW training for their crews, were the factors he saw as pulling the Allies through in the long run. Knox may have lacked Stimson's ability to use the "bully pulpit" to invigorate the search for new solutions to the problems at hand, but he made up for this lack with his stolid talent for allowing his people to "stay the course" during the rough months of heavy shipping losses, when radical solutions to the problem were all-too-evident in other quarters of the government.

---

[51] See the Command status memorandum prepared for the Commanding General, Army Air Forces Antisubmarine Command, 31 March 1943; "3A Submarines-Antisubmarine Command" Folder, Box 5, Bowles Correspondence, RG 107, NA.

3

Codes and Ciphers:
Radio Communication
and Intelligence

Jürgen Rohwer

From the outset of World War II, radio communications were crucial
to both sides in the conflict. The Allies used radio signals to direct the
operations of their convoys, and the Axis to direct surface raiders and
U-boat groups. Both sides used codes and ciphers to protect these
communications, and both were successful in their efforts to gain
intelligence out of the enemy's communications by some form of radio or
signal intelligence.[1]

When Hitler decided in May 1938 that he had to reckon with the
opposition of Great Britain against his policy of territorial expansion by
military force, he confronted the navy with a drastic change in its
strategic and operational planning. Such planning had been focused up
to that time on France and Poland as opponents. A war game in the
autumn of 1938 came to the conclusion that in a campaign against the
Anglo-French sea lines of communication (SLOCs), the use of heavy
surface ships might be more successful than the use of U-boats. The
report concluded: "As long as a German merchant warfare is mainly

---

[1] This analysis is based on Jürgen Rohwer, "Radio Intelligence and its Role in the Battle
of the Atlantic," in *The Missing Dimension. Governments and Intelligence Communities in the
Twentieth Century*, ed. E. Christopher Andrews and David Dilks (London: Macmillan, 1984),
159-168 and notes on sources, 280-281; and "Allied and Axis Radio Intelligence in the Battle
of the Atlantic. A Comparative Analysis," in *The Intelligence Revolution. A Historical
Perspective*, ed. Walter T. Hitchcock (Washington: U.S. Air Force Academy, Office of Air
Force History, 1991), 77-109, with extensive documentation of the sources.

based only on U-boats, the core of the British Fleet cannot be broken."[2]

On 17 August 1938, the navy's commander in chief Generaladmiral Erich Raeder formed a planning committee to develop the recommendations for a building program. The committee offered two options, which Raeder presented to Hitler. If a new fleet was needed quickly, the committee recommended building pocket battleships and U-boats. If there was more time, the preferred option was to build a balanced fleet, including heavy battleships, cruisers, and U-boats, to force the British fleet to disperse its ships. Then task forces of heavy battleships could destroy them piecemeal while cruisers and U-boats attacked merchant ships.

Hitler, assuring Raeder that he needed the fleet not earlier than 1944 or 1946 (and probably already looking into the future when he might need a large high-seas fleet for the confrontation with the Anglo-American sea powers), chose the second option. Thus, on 27 January 1939, he announced the "Z-Plan" aimed at a big balanced fleet including heavy super battleships.

Besides the ships commissioned or already building (four battleships, three pocket-battleships, two carriers, five heavy cruisers, six light cruisers, twenty-three destroyers, thirty torpedoboats, and sixty-three U-boats), the plan called for completing by 1945 no less than six battleships of 56,200 tons, eight pocket battleships of 22,145 tons (later changed to three battlecruisers of 32,300 tons), two additional carriers, five light cruisers, twelve recce cruisers, twenty-two destroyers, forty-six torpedoboats, and 186 U-boats (later augmented up to 1947 by an additional four pocket battleships, four carriers, eighteen light cruisers, twenty-four recce cruisers, twenty-five destroyers, fourteen torpedoboats and twenty U-boats).[3] However, Commander U-Boats Karl Dönitz, then only a Commodore and not directly participating in the high-level deliberations, was of the opinion that Great Britain would not wait for the completion of this fleet without countermeasures. In his view, only a large fleet of U-boats might be able to cut the Allied SLOCs by concentrating in groups to attack merchant ships in convoys.[4]

Contrary to many erroneous statements in Anglo-American publications, Dönitz had developed his operational and tactical concepts

---

[2] Michael Salewski, *Die deutsche Seekriegsleitung 1935-1945*, vol. 2: 1935-1941 (Frankfurt/Main: Bernard & Graefe, 1980), 44ff; Jost Dülffer, *Weimar, Hitler und die Marine. Reichspolitik und Flottenbau 1920-1939* (Düsseldorf: Droste, 1973), 477ff.

[3] Dülffer, *Weimar, Hitler und die Marine*, 500, 569. From Bundesarchiv/Militärarchiv (BA/MA): Case 1504. Anl. 1/Skl.IIIa 5/39 gKdos.

[4] Karl Dönitz, *Memoirs. Ten Years and Twenty Days*, trans. R.H. Stevens (London: Greenhill, 1990), 37-50.

From left, Admiral Erich Raeder, Commander U-boats Karl Dönitz, and Adolf
Hitler with the crew of *U 29*. Photo courtesy of the Bibliothek für Zeitgeschichte,
Stuttgart.

before the war. His idea was not based, as one might expect, on the
critical historical analysis of the U-boat war of 1917-18. At the time, only
the first three volumes of the official analysis of that conflict, *Der
Handelskrieg mit U-Booten* by Rear Admiral Arno Spindler, were available
and only covered the period up to January 1917, before the Allies
introduced the convoys. Because of internal opposition to Spindler's
analysis of the reasons for U.S. entry into the war, the last two volumes
were not finished then and were published only after World War II from
the materials given back to the Germans by the British in the 1960s.[5]
Dönitz used only his personal recollection of an attack against a convoy
as captain of *UB 68* in October 1918 and his experiences with night

---

[5] Arno Spindler, *Der Handelskrieg mit U-Booten*, vol. 1, *Vorgeschichte* (Berlin: Mittler,
1922); vol. 2, *Februar bis September 1915* (Berlin: Mittler, 1933); vol. 3, *Oktober 1915 bis Januar
1917* (Berlin: Mittler, 1934); vol. 4, *Februar bis Dezember 1917* (Berlin: Mittler, 1941, not
distributed, republished privately, Hamburg, 1964); vol. 5, *Januar bis November 1918*
(Frankfurt/Main: Mittler, 1966.)

attacks of torpedoboats when he was commander of a *Halbflottille* in the *Reichsmarine*. Knowing of the danger from the British ASDIC (echo-ranging sonar) to submerged U-boats, he thought that it might be possible to concentrate a group of U-boats, tactically led by a flotilla commander as "pack-leader" and directed by radio from the shore command, to attack a convoy simultaneously at night, when the low silhouettes of the surfaced U-boats were difficult to detect against the black sea from the higher standing lookouts on the surface ships.[6]

From war games in the winter of 1938-39, Dönitz concluded that about three hundred U-boats would be needed to fight a successful war against the the Allied SLOCs. In May 1939 he sent his U-boats into the Atlantic for an exercise to check his idea of radio-controlled group operations,[7] and the plan proved feasible. To lead the groups or "packs," he ordered a series of new type IX-B U-boats with extra communications equipment to act as command boats.[8]

When the war started, however, Dönitz had only twenty-two U-boats capable of operating in the Atlantic. He wanted to hold back half of the boats to have some available to send against the first convoys expected at the end of September, but the *Seekriegsleitung* (Naval Staff) ordered all usable U-boats into the Atlantic on 19 August to intercept many of the then still independently running ships and to search or sink them according to prize regulations. So when the first convoys were reported in mid-September, Dönitz had to call back the newest U-boats to have them resupplied for a first attempt at a controlled group operation in mid-October.[9] He planned to concentrate nine U-boats south of Ireland, and even though only three were able to operate together against a convoy, the operation proved that it was possible to hold contact for several days and to home in other U-boats for their attacks by radio signals. Of the nine U-boats, *U 38* and *U 41* were not ready in time to depart, *U 47* had to be detailed for the attack against Scapa Flow, and *U 40*, sent out late through the Channel to save time, was lost on a mine there. Of the five boats which arrived, *U 42* and *U 45* were sunk after successful attacks against convoys before they could call up other boats. The other three sank four independent ships and one more in an individual attack against a convoy before *U 46* was able to locate convoy

---

[6] Dönitz, *Memoirs*, 18-24.

[7] Ibid., 18-50.

[8] Erich Groener, *Die deutschen Kriegsschiffe 1815-1945*, ed. Dieter Jung and Martin Maass, vol. 3, *U-Boote* . . . (Koblenz: Bernard & Graefe, 1985), 66-149.

[9] Jürgen Rohwer, "The U-Boat War Against the Allied Supply Lines," in *Decisive Battles of World War II: The German View*, ed. Hans-Adolf Jacobsen and Jürgen Rohwer, trans. Edward Fitzgerald (London: André Deutsch, 1965), 259-312.

HG 3 and to lead *U 48* and *U 37* to the convoy. Dönitz ordered a patrol line, which found the convoy again. All three boats attacked and sank one ship each before they had to go off after the arrival of the air escort. Only after the return of the boats did it become clear that misfiring torpedoes had prevented additional successes.[10]

Dönitz planned another attempt in November with five U-boats, but again only three came to the assembly point in time to operate against another HG convoy reported by *U 53* off Lisbon. This time the operation failed because of the aggressive escort, and again, torpedo failures. After *U 53* had lost contact, *U 49* found the French convoy KS 27, but she had to break off because of damage to her torpedo tubes from depth charges. Attempts by *U 41* and *U 43* to attack failed, but *U 41* sank five independents and *U 43* sank two ships out of convoys and two more sailing independently.[11]

In February 1940 *B-Dienst*, the German decryption service, located the British carrier *Ark Royal*, the battlecruiser *Renown*, and the heavy cruiser *Exeter* coming up from Freetown. Three U-boats in the area west of the Channel were ordered to intercepting positions, but when *U 48* reported a westbound convoy and followed, its signal seemed to be intercepted by the French and British D/F stations and the naval ships were rerouted.[12] That incident illustrates a problem inherent in radio-communications and signal intelligence, or SigInt. Dönitz feared the Allied ability to pinpoint the positions of U-boats when they used their radios. So the standing order to the U-boats was to keep strict radio silence and to send signals only when in contact with the enemy. To make it more difficult for the enemy to take bearings, the Germans introduced a *Kurzsignalheft*, a code which allowed a convoy to send a contact signal with all necessary dates in only about ten seconds. To make it impossible for the enemy to read the messages, they were enciphered before being sent with the daily setting of the Enigma cipher machine "Schlüssel M-3."[13] German experts were of the opinion that this machine, with its system of independent

---

[10] Günter Hessler, *The U-Boat War in the Atlantic 1939-1945* (London: HMSO, 1989), 7-13; Jürgen Rohwer, "Die erste Geleitzugschlacht des Zweiten Weltkrieges (1939)," in *Köhlers Flottenkalender 1970* (Herford: Koehler, 1969), 172-176.

[11] Jürgen Rohwer, "Die zweite Geleitzugschlacht im November 1939," in *Köhlers Flottenkalender 1971* (Herford: Koehler, 1970), 128-131, and *Axis Submarine Successes 1939-1945* (Annapolis: Naval Institute Press, 1983), 6-7.

[12] Hessler, *U-Boat War*, 14.

[13] Jürgen Rohwer, *The Critical Convoy Battles of March 1943* (Annapolis: Naval Institute Press, 1977), 11-17, 221-234; Władysław Kozaczuk, *Geheimoperation WICHER. Polnische Mathematiker knacken den deutschen Funkschlüssel 'Enigma'*, trans. Theodor Fuchs, ed. Jürgen Rohwer (Koblenz: Bernard & Graefe, 1989), 34-41.

An Enigma machine. Photo courtesy of the Bibliothek für Zeitgeschichte, Stuttgart.

settings for the rotor sequence, the ring position, and the plugboard and its individual indicator system, offered the greatest number of possible cipher alphabets. Even if a machine were captured, without all the settings it would be impossible to break the cipher by analytical means in time for some operational use. Cipher materials were printed with water-soluble ink to prevent their capture from sunken vessels or U-boats. In addition, there was a separate secret list of cue words, known only to the commanding officers, which allowed them to change compromised settings with a short signal.[14]

When the war started, almost 90 percent of the messages sent with the "Schlüssel M-3" were enciphered with the circuit "Heimische Gewässer" (Home Waters), including the messages of the Atlantic U-boats. Only the armed merchant Raiders used the circuit "Außerheimische Gewässer" in which only very few messages in the same daily setting were ever sent.[15] To reduce the number of signals sent in the same setting on any day, additional special circuits were introduced from time to time. For example, in September 1939 a special circuit was introduced for U-boat training, in 1940 for the connection to the Naval Attaché Tokyo, and 1941 for the Mediterranean, for the Main Fleet, and for the Baltic. Later, many new circuits were established for other areas.[16]

It is well known that the Allied efforts to break into the Enigma ciphers were successful at first only against some Air Force systems and that the "Schlüssel M-3" resisted all attempts. The main challenge facing the Allies was to find out the inner wirings of the additional three cipher rotors (VI, VII, and VIII) that the German Navy used in addition to the five rotors already known from the efforts of Polish cryptanalysts. However, even with the capture of three rotors (including VI and VII) from survivors of *U 33*, sunk in February 1940, the cipher documents taken from the trawler *Schiff 26* on 26 April 1940 by the destroyer *Griffin* (which allowed the Allies in May to read messages of six days of April), and the capture of rotor VIII in August 1940, the British at Bletchley Park could not decipher messages in the short time necessary for operational use.[17] During that time, *B-Dienst* was clearly more successful.[18]

The Royal Navy used two main cipher systems. The first was a "Naval Cipher," operated by officers only, for operational signals mainly

---

[14] Alberto Santoni, "Die Entstehung der 'Enigma'," in Alberto Santoni, *Ultra siegt im Mittelmeer* (Koblenz: Bernard & Graefe, 19859), 26-35; David Kahn, *Seizing the Enigma. The Race to Break the German U-Boat Codes, 1939-1943* (Boston: Houghton Mifflin, 1991).

[15] F.H. Hinsley, E.E. Thomas, C.F.G. Ransom, and R.C. Knight, *British Intelligence in the Second World War. Its Influence on Strategy and Operations*, 3 vols. (London: HMSO, 1979-1988), 1: 163, 336-348.

[16] Hinsley, *British Intelligence* 2: 663-664, 667.

[17] Patrick Beesly, *Very Special Intelligence* (London: Hamish Hamilton, 1977), 24-41; Kahn, *Seizing the Enigma*, 112-126; Jürgen Rohwer, "Die Funkaufklärung im Seekrieg," in Kozaczuk, *Geheimoperation WICHER*, 182-202.

[18] Heinz Bonatz, *Seekrieg im Äther. Die Leistungen der Marine-Funkaufklärung 1939-1945* (Herford: Mittler, 1981).

concerning ships down to destroyers. The second was the "Administrative or Naval Code" operated by ratings, used first for administrative signals and messages covering small ships and later also for signals about ship movements. The first was based on a four-figure codebook and the second on a five-figure codebook, and both were super-enciphered by long-subtractor tables of 5,000 groups each, changing every month or two months.[19]

The *B-Dienst* achieved the first breaks into the Naval Code in peacetime, when it was often used without super-enciphering. By the end of 1939 a great part of the codebook had been reconstructed, as had been parts of the long-subtractor tables. Against the "Naval Cipher," the *B-Dienst* was also more and more successful. In April 1940, during the Norwegian operation, the *B-Dienst* was able to decrypt some 30 to 50 percent of the signals in the "Naval Cipher" and could deliver to the operational commands good estimates about the location and the movements of the main units of the Home Fleet. But because of the small number of intercepts, it was never possible to break into the subtractor tables of the Flag Officers.[20]

In January 1940 one more code appeared which had great importance during the Battle of the Atlantic. It was the "Merchant Navy Code" for radio signals to and between merchant ships. The *B-Dienst* achieved the first breaks in this code in March 1940 and could decrypt most of the signals using code materials captured at Bergen in May 1940 and later from captures during the operations of the armed merchant raiders.[21]

The French Navy used as its main cipher, in addition to some other not so important systems, the "TBM/Touts Bâtiments Militaires," a five-digit code which was super-enciphered up to the beginning of the war with numeral exchange tables. By the time the war started, *B-Dienst* had completely broken this code. When the French then introduced a super-encipherment with a long-subtractor system, they made a big cryptological mistake by taking the subtractor numerals from the code, so that the *B-Dienst* could achieve a new break in a short time.[22]

As far as U-boat operations were concerned, up to the summer of 1940 the main problem was that there were seldom enough U-boats in the area where the *B-Dienst* had decrypted positions of convoys to

---

[19] Hinsley, *British Intelligence* 2: 631-642.
[20] Bonatz, *Seekrieg im Äther*, 24-45.
[21] Ibid., 65-86.
[22] Ibid., 45-47.

achieve successful intercepts. When there were more U-boats available, as was first the case in mid-June 1940, sometimes their attacks against the many independents still in the area were followed by SOS-signals of the attacked vessels or success reports of the U-boats. Such signals in turn gave the British D/F stations the positions of the U-boats, and the Submarine Tracking Room could reroute the convoy around the dangerous area.[23]

So, when on 12 June 1940 the *B-Dienst* decrypted the position where convoy HX 48 was to be taken over by the A/S escort and the route order for the troop convoy US 3 coming from Freetown, Dönitz ordered the group "Prien" with seven U-boats against HX 48 and group "Rösing" with five U-boats against US 3. The latter convoy was routed clear, however, because group "Rösing" had marked the area as dangerous by sinking eleven independents, including the armed merchant cruiser *Carinthia*." Prien" with U 47 came into contact with only a straggler of HX 48 and sank it, then the *B-Dienst* reported the ordered route change to the south and the operation was broken off. Only by chance U 38 met the convoy and sank two ships. The twelve U-boats of both groups found so many targets, and made some individual attacks on convoys HGF 34 and HX 49, that after four weeks they had fifty-nine ships to their account, even without a coordinated group operation against a convoy.[24]

Operations against British armed merchant cruisers of the Northern Patrol were very successful at this time. When the *B-Dienst* decrypted their patrol orders in late May and early June, two outgoing U-boats, U 25 and U A, were sent to their area, and they found and sank the *Scotstoun* and the *Andania*.[25]

At the end of June 1940 most of the U-boats had used up their torpedoes and had to return, so in July there were very few U-boats at sea. By mid-August a greater number of U-boats, some of them already replenished at the newly won bases in Western France, arrived in their operational areas. The first attempt to bring three U-boats into contact with convoy HX 63 at the pick-up point of the A/S escort, decrypted by the *B-Dienst*, failed because the U-boats sank three independents in the area and the convoy was rerouted to the south. This signal was decrypted too late to send the U-boats to the new position in time. But during the last six days of August, ten U-boats in individual attacks against convoys

---

[23] Hessler, *U-Boat War*, 27-29; Bonatz, *Seekrieg im Äther*, 204-212; Beesly, *Very Special Intelligence*, 42-60.

[24] Hessler, *U-Boat War*, 48, diagram 3, point 5, 6; Rohwer, *Axis Submarine Successes*, 18-22.

[25] Hessler, *U-Boat War*, 28.

sank sixteen ships and one escort, torpedoed five ships, and sank four stragglers from convoys.[26]

In September the first real convoy battle took place when the *B-Dienst* decrypted the route order for the convoy SC 2 four days in advance. One of the three assigned boats intercepted the convoy and was able, notwithstanding the severe weather with wind up to force 8, to hold the contact for three days and to lead three other boats in. Five ships were sunk.[27]

Now the German *B-Dienst* experienced its first setback. On 20 August the Admiralty had replaced the "Naval Cipher No. 1" with a new "Naval Cipher No. 2," and the "Administrative Code" was replaced by a new "Naval Code No. 1." Both now had four-figure code books to make the distinction between them more difficult. The *B-Dienst* needed some time to decipher the new code books and the new tables. By 9 October, 5 percent of the" Naval Cipher" and 19 percent of the "Naval Code" were reconstructed, and by 1 January 1941 the percentage was up to 19 percent and 26 percent.[28]

While the *B-Dienst* could not help much, the next three big convoy battles against HX 72 in September and SC 7 and HX 79 in October brought important experiences in other fields of communications. During these months the German preparations for Operation *Sealion*, the landing in England, made it necessary to get weather reports from the Atlantic. Besides the disposition of some disguised trawlers as weather reporting ships in Arctic waters, the only way to get data from the Central North Atlantic was from U-boat reports.[29]

The U-boats far out to the west had to send their reports two times daily. Dönitz had to accept the dangerous possibility that the signals might be intercepted by the D/F stations. To his great surprise, however, these weather-reporting U-boats intercepted these three convoys far out in the west, allowing the concentration of the other available boats for massed night attacks. HX 72 lost twelve ships, SC 7 twenty-one ships, and HX 79 twelve ships. Dönitz saw this as evidence that his fears about the Allied D/F system were unwarranted.[30] Such fears had already been weakened by decrypts of French signals in the spring of 1940, which showed the problems of pinpointing the positions of radio signals of

[26] Ibid., 47-49; Rohwer, *Axis Submarine Successes*, 22-27.

[27] Bonatz, *Seekrieg im Äther*, 208-213, 218; Hessler, *U-Boat War*, 49-50.

[28] Hinsley, *British Intelligence 2*: 635; Bonatz, *Seekrieg im Äther*, 29-36.

[29] Rohwer, *Critical Convoy Battles*, 16-21; Hinsley, *British Intelligence 1*: 565-569.

[30] Dönitz, *Memoirs*, 100-112; Hessler, *U-Boat War*, 50-53; Rohwer, *Axis Submarine Successes*, 29-34.

U-boats at some distance from the coast. At a distance of more than three hundred miles from the shore stations, the fixes seemed to be so far off the mark that convoys which were probably rerouted ran exactly over the positions where U-boats had sent weather reports for many days. This would have grave consequences later on.[31]

On the British side, the first surprise was the inefficiency of the highly regarded Asdic against the night surface attacks of the U-boats. The need to hold back the destroyers for the anti-invasion operations had led to very weak escort groups which were assembled as vessels were available. During night battles, the escort commander had no way to advise his vessels because of the lack of an ultra short-wave communication system. The Admiralty took several steps to remedy the situation. First, it sent radio-observation vessels into the Atlantic to analyze the German methods of radio-directed convoy operations by the wolf packs. The results of this traffic analysis led to improvements in the shore-based direction finding system that gave the Submarine Tracking Room and the Trade Plot of the Admiralty better options for rerouting the convoys around the dispositions of the still relatively few German U-boats.[32]

The Admiralty also realized the great importance of the contact signals, and on the recommendation of Sir Robert Watson-Watt it developed an automatic HF/DF set for small escorts. Watson-Watt thought it might be possible to take bearings on the first contact signal on the ground wave and to send out a fast escort to force the contact-holding U-boat to dive while the convoy made a detour away from the U-boat position. A similar development based on the research and tests of two French experts, Deloraine and Busignies, was continued in the United States after the French collapse. In mid-1941 the first British destroyers got the FH3 set which was successfully used for the chase of the German weather-reporting ships in May and June. Tests with the improved automatic set FH4 were interrupted, however, when *U 105* sank the test sloop *Culver* on 31 January 1942. After some delays in early and mid-1942, the equipment of convoy escorts finally began. In Britain the first to be so equipped were the rescue vessels assigned to convoys and then the destroyers of the Senior Officer Escort of the now consistent escort groups; in the U.S., the big Coast Guard cutters were equipped first, then the destroyers.[33]

German *B-Dienst* reports from the spring of 1943 contain entries about HF/DF-equipped Allied escort vessels, so one must question why this

---

[31] Rohwer, *Critical Convoy Battles*, 17.

[32] Beesly, *Very Special Intelligence*, 42-60; Rohwer, *Critical Convoy Battles*, 17-19.

[33] Rohwer, *Critical Convoy Battles*, 19-21.

was not taken into account. It must have been due partly to negligence resulting from the experience with the D/F system in 1940, and partly because attention was by then so fixed on the fear of Allied radar that indications of other methods were overlooked.[34]

Allied escorts were equipped with the 1.5 meter ASV-II radar in 1940 and 1941 to improve their ability to locate surfaced U-boats at night, but the Germans greatly overestimated its effectiveness against the U-boats. Under normal conditions, U-boats could detect the ships of a convoy by optical means earlier than the ASV-II radar could locate a low-lying U-boat in the sea clutter. Furthermore, when the 10cm ASV-III radar was introduced in late 1942 and early 1943, it achieved real success only in fog and bad sighting conditions. The British type 271 lanternas were installed on the bridge, too low for enough range. The mast-top installation of the U.S. destroyers was much more efficient, as was proved in the convoy battles of March 1943.[35]

In late 1940 the Admiralty had requested the assignment of more long-range planes with ASV-II radar to cover the convoys at least by day against the contact-holding U-boats. When the RAF Coastal Command got such planes in the spring of 1941 with the Catalinas and the first few Liberators, the German U-boats were forced more and more away from the area close off the Northern Channel, making it more and more difficult for the Germans to intercept convoys. Still, many more U-boats were sighted by optical means than located by radar. Even in the big convoy battles against HX 229 and SC 122 in March 1943, of twenty-nine U-boats detected by planes only one was located by radar! There is no question that the German's great overestimation of the effectiveness of air- or shipborne radar up to mid-1943 blocked their realization of the much greater danger from the HF/DF in the convoy battles, to say nothing of the well-kept secret of Ultra, the decryption of the German radio messages.[36]

On 1 February 1941, however, the German Navy reached its lowest figure of only twenty-one U-boats, of which only nine were in the operational area. At this time the Italians had twenty-three submarines operating out of Bordeaux, and six were in the North Atlantic. Trained for stationary operations in the Mediterranean, they could not help much to bring their German comrades to the convoys they reported because

---

[34] Ibid., see the texts to pictures between pp. 192-193.

[35] Ibid., 186-200.

[36] Alfred Price, *Aircraft versus Submarine* (London: Kimber, 1973). See also Price, "Development of Equipment and Techniques," and Rohwer, "A German Perspective," both in *Search and Sink*, Bracknell Paper No. 2, A Symposium on the Battle of the Atlantic, 21 October 1991 (Bracknell: Royal Air Force Staff College, 1992), 48-67.

they were not accustomed to holding the contact in the rough conditions of the North Atlantic.[37]

The small number of operational German U-boats forced Dönitz to look for improved reconnaissance to find the convoys. One possibility was the use of long-range aircraft, but it took several months before the 1st Group/Kampfgeschwader 40 got its twelve long-range Focke-Wulf 200 Condor planes and was, by order of Hitler on 7 January, put under operational control of the Commander U-boats. The planes had to fly from Merignac, near Bordeaux, west around Ireland to Stavanger in Norway and back on the next day. Seldom were more than one or two planes operational daily, and their reconnaissance signals were difficult to use because they often fixed positions badly in the adverse weather conditions of the North Atlantic. This was finally improved in the summer of 1941 when the Condors sent homing signals which were evaluated by D/F onshore stations and U-boats at sea to give the other U-boats a more exact position of the reported convoy.[38]

In February 1941 neither the aircraft nor the B-Dienst could help much to find the convoys. More often, the U-boats got the first contact themselves and led the others to their targets. For example, on the evening of 8 February U 37 sighted convoy HG 53 of sixteen ships southwest of Cape St. Vincent. After sinking two ships on the 9th, the U-boat was ordered to maintain contact and send homing signals for five Condors, which arrived at midday and sank five more ships. Maintaining its contact, U 37 sank one more ship on 10 February and tried to lead the heavy cruiser Admiral Hipper to the scene. But this ship found only one straggler, which was sunk, and then made contact with the convoy SLS 64 coming up from Freetown, sinking seven of its nineteen unescorted ships on the morning of 12 February. Then, on the night of 26 February, U 47 sank three vessels of convoy OB 290 and damaged one more tanker before homing in six Condors, which sank seven more ships and damaged four others.[39]

During the operations of the German pocket battleship Admiral Scheer, the heavy cruiser Admiral Hipper, and the battleships Gneisenau and Scharnhorst from November 1940 to March 1941, the German B-Dienst could provide the ships with good background information about the

---

[37] Hessler, U-Boat War, 57-62; Ubaldino Mori-Ubaldini, I Sommergibili negli Oceani. La Marina Italiana nella Seconda Guerra Mondiale, vol. 12 (Roma: Ufficio Storico della Marina Militare, 1963), 23-178.

[38] Hessler, U-Boat War, 62-64; Rohwer, "A German Perspective," 55-67.

[39] Hessler, U-Boat War, 67-68; Jürgen Rohwer and Gerhard Hümmelchen, Chronology of the War at Sea 1939-1945. The Naval History of World War Two (London: Greenhill Books, and Annapolis: Naval Institute Press, 1992), 50-53.

general dislocation of British ships and could follow the operations of the German ships from their observation of the QQQ- or RRR- signals of attacked ships or convoys and from the results of traffic analysis of British fleet radio traffic. This information was seldom of tactical use for the German ships, however, because there were no signals such as route orders intercepted which could be used.[40]

More important was the possibility of decrypting many signals in the Merchant Navy Code for the operations of the German armed merchant raiders in all three oceans. Such decrypts were partly done at home but also on board the ships at sea by special *B-Dienst* groups. One such case was the raid of the *Pinguin* into the Antarctic. On 18 December 1940 *B-Dienst* information about Norwegian whale factory ships was radioed by the *Seekriegsleitung* to the *Pinguin*, which approached the area where the "Bord-B-Dienst-Gruppe" observed from 27 December to 12 January the radio traffic of the whale factories to lay down the best tactical plan for the attack. All three, including eleven whale-catchers, were captured and sent successfully with prize crews to France.[41]

One other important case was the interception of the British freighter *Automedon* on 11 November 1940 by the *Atlantis*. The capture yielded important courier post, including new code tables for the Eastern Fleet and other operational materials of great use to the Japanese, which were sent with the prize ship, *Ole Jacob*, to Japan.[42]

In April 1941 the British convoy routing in the North Atlantic became more successful for two reasons. First, the still relatively few U-boats were now forced more to the west by the long-range planes of the RAF Coastal Command and the strengthened escort groups which had in March succeeded in sinking four U-boats, including the three most successful commanders — Prien, Schepke, and Kretschmer. A second factor was the improved net of D/F stations around the North Atlantic, as the *B-Dienst* recognized when signals of a new station in Iceland were intercepted on 21 April.[43]

By this time, Bletchley Park had begun the decryption of the cipher "Home Waters" following the capture of important cipher materials from the German patrol vessel *Krebs* during the Lofoten raid of 3-4 March 1941. At the time the Germans did not realize the consequences of this and

[40] Bonatz, *Seekrieg im Äther*, 170-175.

[41] Ibid., 39-40; Gerhard Hümmelchen, *Handelsstörer. Handelskrieg deutscher Überwasser-streitkräfte im Zweiten Weltkrieg* 2. Aufl (München: Lehmanns, 1967), 201-312.

[42] Hümmelchen, *Handelsstörer*, 204-205.

[43] D.M. Watson and H.E. Wright, *Radio Direction Finding* (London, 1971); Ralph Erskine, "From the Archives: U-Boat HF WT Signalling," *Cryptologia* 12, no. 2, 98-106

other captures from *U 110* and the weather- reporting ships *München* and *Lauenburg* in May and June.[44] But was this pure negligence and blind trust in the Enigma machine?

As early as 1940, suspicions arose about the security of the communications and the cipher system. The then chief of staff to the Naval Communications Department, Captain Stummel, had investigated the cases of suspicious losses, especially of U-boats in shallow enemy-held areas, but he remained convinced that even if a machine might have been recovered the necessary papers with the settings must have been soaked and were of no use anymore.[45]

But on 18 April 1941 the Commander U-boats noted in his war diary suspicions that the enemy might have further unknown sources of information on U-boat dispositions when some planned operations against convoys reported by the *B-Dienst* or air reconnaissance failed. Dönitz thought a security leak might be the reason, and he tried to restrict at all costs the dissemination of details about U-boat operations beyond the staffs in real need of such information.[46]

The *B-Dienst* and the staff of the Commander U-boats started to compare their findings about the possible reasons for the Allied evasion of the U-boat dispositions. All details of naval and merchant traffic collected from U-boat reports, air reconnaissance, the reports of agents, meteorological trawlers, and other German or Italian units were entered onto a map, as was all information the *B-Dienst* had collected from SOS-reports, signals of torpedoed ships, decrypted U-boat warning reports, sighting reports by aircraft, and decrypted British reports about D/F bearings of U-boat signals. This comparison seemed to show that the enemy measures were not the result of the U-boat's use of the radio but were mainly due to U-boat sightings, sinkings, and other indications, while the D/F bearings seemed still not exact enough for tactical use.[47]

For a short time the fears were lessened when on 7 May *U 110* sighted convoy OB 318 and was able to bring in three other boats. Only a week later these boats, which were formed up with other boats to a "Western Group," intercepted the convoy HX 126 south of Greenland, notwithstanding its attempted detour to the north, and sank nine ships.[48]

---

[44] Stephen W. Roskill, *The Secret Capture* (London: Cassell, 1959); Hinsley, *British Intelligence*, 333-339; Kahn, *Seizing the Enigma*, 1-14, 112-160.

[45] Timothy Mulligan, "The German Navy Examines its Cryptographic Security, October 1941," *Military Affairs* 49, no. 2 (April 1985): 75ff.

[46] Kriegstagebuch (KTB) des Befehlshabers der U-Boots (BdU), 18 April 1941, Bundesarchiv-Militärarchiv, Freiburg; Mulligan, "Cryptographic Security."

[47] Hessler, *U-Boat War*, 77-79; Mulligan, "Cryptographic Security."

[48] Hessler, *U-Boat War*, 73.

The well-known *Bismarck* operation was tactically influenced by radio intelligence almost exclusively by traffic analysis and direction finding. The many reports in recent publications about the decryption of a signal by a high-ranking Air Force general questioning the whereabouts of the *Bismarck* had only minimal influence on the interception of the vessel.[49]

After the break of the *Bismarck* operation, the U-boat patrol lines searched for convoys in vain for weeks. When the Commander U-boats changed his tactics into a wide dispersion of his now more than twenty boats on 23 June, the convoy HX 133 was sighted at the corner of this disposition, while a few days later an operation against a southbound convoy sighted by a Condor completely failed.[50]

At the same time, the destruction of the German surface supply system organized in the Atlantic for the *Bismarck* operation led to a new investigation, because it seemed impossible that the dispersed supply tankers were intercepted by chance at their replenishment points.[51] There must have been a break into the German signal traffic. But when the Germans learned that the tanker *Gedania* was abandoned in panic when intercepted by a British warship and taken to Gibraltar, the experts saw there the source of a non-cryptanalytical compromise which led to the capture or sinking of most of the supply ships. On 22 June the cue-word "Perseus" was sent to change the cipher settings, but this could not offset the unknown captures from *U 110* and the *München* and *Lauenburg*.[52]

Admiral Dönitz still had doubts. He pressed now for a separation of the U-boat radio traffic from the surface traffic and tried to introduce other security measures, including ordering by a code word the change of the cipher settings. On 16 June he introduced a reference-point system to designate positions instead of the two-letter-four-numbers code from the grid maps. When this system proved too cumbersome, Dönitz reintroduced the grid-square system on 11 September but with randomly chosen two-letter digraphs.[53]

New fears about cipher security came up when on 28 September the British submarine *Clyde* surprised two German U-boats during a replenishment operation in the Tarafal Bay on the Cape Verde Islands.

---

[49] Elmer B. Potter, Chester W. Nimitz, and Jürgen Rohwer, *Seemacht. Eine Seekriegsgeschichte von der Antike bis zur Gegenwart* 3.Aufl. (Herrsching: Pawlak, 1982), 508-518, with maps; Beesly, *Very Special Intelligence*, 73-87; Hinsley, *British Intelligence* 1: 339-346.

[50] Hessler, *U-Boat War*, 75-76.

[51] Hinsley, *British Intelligence* 1: 344-346; Rohwer and Hümmelchen, *Chronology of the War at Sea*, 63-66.

[52] Kahn, *Seizing the Enigma*, 195-205.

[53] Mulligan, "Cryptographic Security"; Hinsley, *British Intelligence* 2: Appendix 9, Devices for Disguising U-Boat Positions in Enigma Signals, 681-682.

On 5 October, the U-boat signal traffic was finally separated from the circuit "Heimische Gewässer" and placed into the new special U-boat cipher "Triton." But it took up to 1 February 1942 before the new cipher machine "M-4" with one additional "Greek" rotor was ready and distributed for operational use, so the new circuit had to be used first with the old "M-3" machine.[54]

The problem remained, however, only partly covered up by the change of the main operational area to the east against the U.K.-Gibraltar convoys where the agents at Algeciras or the five Condors could help with the now-proven homing system. When more U-boats came into the Atlantic in September and new operations to the west were started, some chance interceptions of SC convoys led to successful attacks and caused some unwarranted relaxation.[55] In the second part of 1941, however, U-boats could not find the convoys and experienced their first decisive setback.

---

[54] Ralph Erskine, "Naval Enigma: The Breaking of Heimisch and Triton," *Intelligence and National Security* 3, no. 1, 162-183; Kahn, *Seizing the Enigma*, 204-208.

[55] Hessler, *U-Boat War*, 79-87.

4

Planning the Defense of the South Atlantic, 1939-1941: Securing Brazil

Theresa L. Kraus

For the most part, World War II historiography has neglected the importance of the South Atlantic, and particularly Brazil, in the prewar preparations of the United States. By concentrating on developments in Europe instead of in the Western Hemisphere, many studies seem to lose sight of issues instrumental in moving the Roosevelt administration away from isolationism and toward greater military preparedness.

In the early 1930s, American defense prospects were good because of the geographic position of the Western Hemisphere. Separated from potential European and Asian aggressors by thousands of miles of ocean, the United States would have ample warning of any attack. Military planners also knew that, despite recent advances in military technology, any foreign nation would find it extremely difficult to make anything other than a nuisance raid on the U.S. Bombing aircraft did not have the necessary range to attack across the ocean, and Japan lacked the bases in the eastern Pacific to support a naval attack on the American west coast.

War plans written after World War I focused exclusively on repelling foreign invasion. The immediate defense of the U.S. lay in the hands of the navy, positioned to control the seaward approaches to the American shores. The much smaller army focused its attention on coastal defenses to deny any potential enemy the use of ports.

American strategists had traditionally assumed that any military threat to the hemisphere would take the form of a naval attack followed by the landing of ground forces. The late 1930s, however, witnessed the advent of significant increases in the range and striking power of land- and carrier-based aircraft. These new developments in air power coincided with Hitler's rise to power and created a new and viable threat to hemispheric security. In particular, the Munich crisis of September 1938 marked a turning point in American defense policy. By that time, both military and naval staffs in the U.S. had noted rapid improvements in military technology and the greatly increased range and striking power of armed forces. Military analysts concluded that, while no foreign nation had gained the capacity to launch an attack on the United States directly across oceans, an attack from land bases within the hemisphere was possible. Therefore, the basic U.S. defense policy quickly became one of preventing the establishment of any hostile air base in the Western Hemisphere from which the United States might be bombed or from which a seaborne invasion could be supported.

Army planners believed that any air attack on the hemisphere would probably follow the air route which stretched from Africa to the Brazilian bulge. The region was 1,800 nautical miles and six hours by air from Dakar, West Africa. The area was underdeveloped, underpopulated, undefended, inaccessible to Brazilian military forces, and beyond the protection of U.S. forces stationed in the Caribbean. In the event of an attack, the closest U.S. forces were 2,600 miles away in Puerto Rico, and those troops could do little to divert an Axis invasion. Any nation controlling the region would command the shortest sea and air routes from Europe and Africa to the Atlantic coast of South America, the water routes into the rubber producing areas of the Amazon Basin, and more importantly, the South Atlantic routes northward toward the Atlantic coast of North America, the Gulf of Mexico, the Caribbean, and the Panama Canal.

A surface attack on Brazil was unlikely to succeed as long as friendly naval powers patrolled the South Atlantic, but an African-based air attack was feasible. According to American intelligence sources, an air attack combined with fifth column revolutionary activity in southern Brazil could easily bring about the downfall of the Brazilian government. Military planners feared that the resultant chaos would lead to the establishment of a pro-Axis government in Brazil from which anti-U.S. activities could be carried out. Although not a very realistic possibility, some believed that from a foothold in Brazil the Axis powers would move to positions from which they could attack the Panama Canal.

U.S. military observers realized that Brazilian military forces were incapable of stopping any type of invasion. The Brazilian army, with an active strength of approximately sixty-six thousand men, was little more than a militarized police force. It lacked the organization, training, and equipment to meet first-class troops in battle. In addition, Brazil's defense policy called for the concentration of its forces in the more populated southern regions, rather than in the northeast, the one region the U.S. military believed vulnerable to attack.

Furthermore, the political orientation and motives of the Brazilian government also concerned the Roosevelt administration. On 10 November 1937, in ·an attempt to centralize rule and bring industrial development to the country, Brazilian President Getulio Vargas had, with the help of his military force, announced the creation of his *Estado Novo* (New State). The new Brazilian constitution, with its cooperative governmental system and its fascist provisions, led many in the United States to speculate that the Brazilian president's sympathies lay with Hitler and Mussolini. In addition, Vargas's desire to industrialize and to enhance Brazil's position within Latin America led him to look to Europe for developmental aid and new markets. Although Vargas continually reasserted Brazil's friendship with the United States, he invited German and Italian military missions to Brazil, strengthened economic ties to Germany, and purchased increasing amounts of armament from Germany's Krupp munitions factory.

Adding to U.S. fears of Brazilian sympathy to the Fascists were the large numbers of German, Italian, and Japanese nationals residing in Brazil.[1] These groups, according to U.S. consular and FBI reports, seemed extremely vulnerable to increasing Axis propaganda efforts. U.S. observers worried that, in case of a German invasion into the northeast, Axis sympathizers in the south would rise and overthrow the government.[2]

Throughout the 1930s, Germany's primary interest in Brazil, like that

---

[1] In 1940, the total Brazilian population numbered 41,236,314 persons, according to that year's census. This number included 122,735 naturalized citizens and 1,283,833 foreigners. German nationals represented the largest percentage of the foreign and naturalized population. See Brasil, Commissao Censitaria Nacional Recenseamento Geral do Brasil, *Censo Demografico Populacao e Habiracao*, vol. 2 (Rio de Janeiro: Servico Grafico do Instituto Brasileiro de Geografia e Estatistica, 1950), 12, 14, 20.

[2] See for example, Memorandum, Nazi-Fascist Propaganda in Brazil, 17 December 1937, File 800.20210/13; Memorandum, Welles to Caffery, 31 January 1938, File 800.20210/24C; Memorandum, Scotton to Hull, 25 February 1938, File 800.20210/41; and Memorandum, Italian Fascist and German Nazi Activity in the American Republics, February 1938, File 810.00 F/32, all in Record Group 59, Department of State Decimal Files, National Archives, Washington, D.C. (hereafter RG 59, NA). See also FBI Report on Totalitarian Activities in Brazil, December 1942, Harry L. Hopkins Papers, Franklin Delano Roosevelt Library, Hyde Park, NY (hereafter FDRL); Memorandum, The Brazilian Situation, 29 May 1941, Modern Millitary Branch, Record Group 165, National Archives (hereafter RG 165, NA); Hugo Fernandez Artucia, *La Organizacion Secreta Nazi en Sudamerica* (Mexico: A. Artis, Impresor, S. de R.L., n.d.), 62; Alton Frye, *Nazi Germany and the American Hemisphere, 1933-1941* (New Haven: Yale University Press, 1967), 75; and Stanley E. Hilton, *Hitler's Secret War in South America, 1939-1945* (New York: Ballantine Books, 1981), 23.

of the United States, had been commercial in nature.[3] When the war began in Europe, however, the economic interests of both countries gave way to political and military concerns. Brazil's strategic position in the hemisphere, its production of strategic materials such as rubber, iron ore, manganese, and quartz, and its large unassimilated German population made it a prime target for Axis espionage activities.[4] Both the German and Italian governments actively encouraged the sale of civil and military equipment to the South American republics by offering extremely liberal credit terms based on trade or barter agreements. German and Italian training missions often accompanied the equipment deliveries. The German- and Italian-controlled commercial airlines also worked to expand their routes throughout Brazil in the immediate prewar period. To American observers, the German airline Condor in particular appeared to be interested in obtaining routes located in strategic areas regardless of their commercial potential. The expansion of commercial routes into northeast provincial towns seemed peculiar to U.S. officials, especially when they noted that Condor made little attempt to expand operation into heavily populated areas such as Saõ Paulo.[5]

As the Axis countries increased their political, economic, and cultural propaganda efforts, foreign policy experts in Washington became increasingly preoccupied with the thought that Vargas might ally his country to, or at least cooperate with, Nazi Germany if war came to the hemisphere. This fear led the State Department to pursue the Good Neighbor Policy actively in the hope of gaining Brazilian support for U.S. foreign policy goals.[6] At one point, the influx of Americans into Brazil promoting hemispheric cooperation led Brazilian Foreign Minister (and

---

[3] President Vargas hoped to give Brazil economic independence; therefore, his economic policies were aimed at expanding foreign sales. Although the United States was Brazil's primary trade partner, Germany's trade barter agreements offered Vargas a chance to expand markets and purchase finished goods without the expenditure of hard currency. See Frank McCann Jr., *The Brazilian-American Alliance, 1937-1945* (Princeton, NJ: Princeton University Press, 1973), 148-175.

[4] For more on German espionage efforts, see Leslie B. Rout, Jr. and John F. Bratzel, *The Shadow War: German Espionage and United States Counterespionage in Latin America During World War II* (Frederick, MD: University Press of America, Inc., 1986).

[5] William A.M. Burden, *The Struggle for Airways in Latin America* (New York: Council on Foreign Relations, 1943), 42. For the United States' struggle to eliminate Axis-controlled commercial airlines in Brazil, see Theresa L. Kraus, "Clipping Axis Wings," *Air Power History* (Spring 1990): 19-26.

[6] For more on the Good Neighbor Policy, see Irwin F. Gellman, *Good Neighbor Diplomacy: United States Policies in Latin America, 1933-1945* (Baltimore: Johns Hopkins University Press, 1979) and Bryce Wood, *The Making of the Good Neighbor Policy* (New York: W.W. Norton, 1967).

former ambassador to the United States) Oswaldo Aranha to joke: "One more goodwill mission and Brazil will declare war on the U.S.A."[7]

While Secretary of State Cordell Hull encouraged hemispheric solidarity through reciprocal trade agreements, Pan-American meetings, cultural exchanges, and goodwill tours, Secretary of War Harry Woodring began promoting a reorientation in military strategy from a passive continental defense to a more active hemispheric defense policy. Woodring argued that planning for the defense of U.S. national boundaries was not sufficient. The army and navy had to be ready to take the initiative and to prepare to protect the entire hemisphere.[8] War Department planners believed that, while strengthening economic and cultural ties would yield long-term dividends in Latin America, the Axis threat was immediate, and only military aid would provide the necessary short-term means of establishing goodwill and cooperation.

Hence, U.S. Army planners began urging the administration to combine its goodwill efforts with military objectives. In particular, the War Department wanted to use commercial aviation assets in Brazil for military purposes. Army planners believed that the successful protection of the South Atlantic necessitated the acquisition of a string of air bases first throughout Brazil and then in the rest of the hemisphere. Testifying before the Senate Military Affairs Committee in February 1938, General "Hap" Arnold of the Army Air Corps stated that the Germans alone had 1,700 planes capable of crossing the Atlantic from Africa to South America.[9] Arnold and other military leaders argued that the U.S. would not be safe if the hemisphere was lost, and they encouraged Roosevelt to aid American aviation interests in Latin America by building airfields, establishing meteorological stations, and training Latin American nationals in American civil aviation schools. In the absence of bilateral defense agreements, such action, they felt, would not only promote U.S. goodwill but also give the United States bases from which to operate in case of war.[10]

---

[7] For example, during the war Nelson Rockefeller's Office of the Coordinator of Inter-American Affairs spent approximately $13,500,000 on public works programs in Brazil; OCIAA's next highest expenditure was in Mexico, where it spent $7,500,000. See "The Wooing of Brazil," *Fortune* 25 (October 1941): 97, and Records of the OCIAA, Record Group 229, Federal Records Center, Suitland, MD.

[8] Mark S. Watson, *Chief of Staff: Prewar Plans and Preparations* (Washington, D.C.: Office of the Chief of Military History, Department of the Army, 1974), 88.

[9] William Langer and S. Everett Gleason, *The Challenge to Isolation, 1937-1940* (New York: Harper Brothers, 1952), 623.

[10] In January 1937, President Vargas offered the use of naval base facilities to the United States and suggested to Assistant Secretary of State Sumner Welles that bilateral conversations be undertaken to determine where the U.S. would like to construct such a base. Vargas also suggested that the United States might want to utilize a portion of

Under the leadership of Cordell Hull, however, State Department officials lobbied against greater military cooperation with Latin America. Anything which could be interpreted as military interest in Latin America, they argued, would adversely affect U.S. goodwill projects. The State Department succeeded in convincing Roosevelt of its views, and as a result, until the State Department provided the impetus for change, army and navy planners could gain White House approval to plan only for specific and short-term contingency measures.

Despite State Department attitudes, military planners continued pushing for a greater hemispheric role. The Joint Army and Navy Board, which began functioning with renewed vigor as the situation in Europe deteriorated throughout 1939,[11] undertook an investigation of the Axis threat to Latin America. In April 1939, the Joint Planning Committee, a subcommittee of the Joint Board, completed an exploratory study which outlined three ways the Axis powers might intervene in Latin America. The study suggested that they might openly and actively support revolutionary movements designed to set up a government sympathetic to fascist powers, establish Axis-controlled submarine and air bases, or move actual armed forces into Latin America. The Planning Committee warned that "he who controls the coast of South America may control the hinterlands." Planners recommended that, in view of the strategic importance of the northeastern tip of Brazil near Natal, measures should be taken to deny an air base in this area to the Axis.[12]

The U.S. occupation of air bases in Brazil, however, had to be undertaken with the permission of the Vargas government. Joint military planning with Brazil began with the visit of Chief of Staff designate George C. Marshall to Brazil in May 1939. In mid-June, Brazilian Chief of Staff Pedro Aurelio de Goes Monteiro returned to the U.S. with Marshall on the USS *Nashville*, and the two military leaders began two months of defense talks.[13]

During the Marshall - Goes Monteiro talks in June and July, the

---

Brazilian territory as a means of safeguarding the eastern approach to the Panama Canal. The Roosevelt administration, not yet ready to undertake a program of bilateral defense preparations, declined the proposal. See Welles to Roosevelt, 26 January 1937, President's Personal Files, #4473 Vargas, FDRL.

[11] In July 1939, Roosevelt instructed the Joint Board to report directly to him rather than to the Secretaries of War and Navy.

[12] "Joint Planning Committee Exploratory Studies in Accordance with J.B. 325 (Serial 634)," Joint Board Color Plans, Secretary of State-JCS, World War II Plans, Department of the Navy Operational Archives, Naval Historical Center, Washington, D.C. (hereafter OA, NHC).

[13] Forrest Pogue, *George C. Marshall: Education of a General* (New York: The Viking Press, 1963), 338-342.

Brazilian Chief of Staff offered the use of air and naval facilities in the northeast. He proposed that the two countries jointly construct bases which would be available to U.S. naval and air forces in case of war. Under this proposal Brazilian forces, supplied with American arms, would provide the ground defense. President Vargas approved Goes Monteiro's offer in August, and joint staff conversations began immediately in an effort to work out the details. The plan provided for the construction of airfields by the Brazilian government with Brazilian labor. Brazil would furnish materials such as sand, gravel, and lumber, with the balance of the material to be provided by the United States. The U.S. would also supply the necessary technical help to design the plans and specifications for the bases.[14] Brazilian and U.S. officials met throughout 1939 and into early 1940 in an futile attempt to reach some kind of agreement on the proposal.

The attempt proved futile because the question of arms supplies slowed and then halted negotiations on joint defense measures. Since the British blockade had cut off deliveries of German arms, the Brazilian government wanted guarantees for deliveries of new arms, not surplus. The United States, however, gearing up for possible war, did not have excess arms. As discussions lagged, Brazilian Foreign Minister Aranha informed U.S. Ambassador Jefferson Caffery that "if the United States authorities were interested in keeping his country from going Nazi, good will and speeches would no longer satisfy the Brazilian people. They needed to see a few results."[15] Likewise, Chief of Staff Goes Monteiro claimed that he had personally received enough Lucky Strike cigarettes and scotch whiskey to last him for two years, but that that was the only tangible result he could see of Brazil's requests for military equipment.[16] As one historian has noted, from these talks "Marshall received fairly accurate data on Brazil's military capabilities . . . while Goes Monteiro received little more than smiles and handshakes."[17] No agreements resulted from the staff conversations.[18]

---

[14] Report of Meeting of the War Plans Division, 13 October 1940, Foreign Files, Record Group 18, National Archives (hereafter RG 18, NA).

[15] Memo, Caffery to Hull, 14 June 1940, 810.20 DEF/163 2/3, Department of State Decimal Files, RG 59, NA.

[16] Charles D. Fellows, "Vargas to Ingram: The Big Play in the South Atlantic, World War II," Spring 1984, World War II Command File, OA, NHC.

[17] Frank McCann, Jr., "Brazil, the United States, and WW II: A Commentary," *Diplomatic History* (Winter 1979): 66.

[18] Ironically, the United States had more success in delivering German arms to the Brazilians than it had in delivering U.S. arms. In November 1940 the British had seized a Brazilian vessel, *Siquiera Campos*, carrying European arms to Brazil. Brazilian authorities appealed to the United States for help in getting the ship released. Not until the summer

Although the danger to South America seemed a possibility to U.S. observers in 1939 and early 1940, most Latin American leaders felt no imminent threat to the sovereignty of their countries. Further, despite promises of cooperation in U.S. defense measures, many Latin American leaders feared Axis reprisals and a further disruption of trade, and they hesitated to take more than rhetorical actions.[19] Brazilian President Vargas was particularly cautious and, realizing that he had more to gain by remaining neutral as long as possible, was unwilling to commit Brazil openly to one side or the other. In addition, Vargas's cabinet and advisors were divided on which side to support in the European war. By vacillating, Vargas kept Brazilian politicians guessing as to his next move and therefore unable to threaten his rule.[20] Furthermore, until the spring of 1940, Brazil, like most of its Latin American counterparts, saw no difference in the war aims of the Axis and the Allies.[21] A fundamental change did not occur until the *blitzkrieg* of April and May and the subsequent fall of France and the Low Countries. Latin America suddenly came to the realization that neutrality alone could not insure safety.

---

of 1941 did the British permit a U.S. ship to pick up a load of arms and ship them to Brazil on a U.S. vessel. Stetson Conn and Byron Fairchild, *The Framework of Hemisphere Defense* (Washington, D.C.: Office of the Chief of Military History, Department of the Army, 1978), 271.

[19] For example, at the Eighth Pan-American Conference in Lima, Peru in December 1938, the conferees met to discuss the Axis threat to the hemisphere and again in September 1939 and the July 1940 Act of Havana.

[20] Throughout the immediate prewar period, Vargas received pro-Axis information and advice from his diplomats abroad. Luiz Sparano, the Brazilian Ambassador in Italy, sent continuous reports that the Axis looked to Brazil as a future ally. Cyro de Freital Valle, the Brazilian ambassador in Berlin, reported that the Germans considered themselves invincible and later wrote that the continued inactivity of the Allies seemed to give the Axis increased hope for victory. Compared to the quiescence of the Allies, the Germans seemed to be making great achievements. On the other hand, Oswaldo Aranha continually reassured his American friends that Brazil would side with the U.S. if war came to the hemisphere. For example, in January 1940 Aranha wrote American columnist Drew Pearson that "90 % of the public opinion [in Brazil] is not only favourable to France and England but unmistakably and ostensibly contrary to Germany and Russia." Despite Vargas's maneuvering, Aranha reassured his friend that "more than any other Brazilian President, [Vargas] is 100% in favour of a Pan American policy and cooperation with the United States in all international questions." Letter, Sparano to Vargas, 26 September 1940, 40.09.26/2, Archivo Getulio Vargas; Freitas Valle to Aranha, 27 September 1939, 39.09.27, Archivo Oswaldo Aranha; and Freitas Valle to Vargas, 16 February 1940, 40.03.05, Archivo Getulio Vargas; Letter, Aranha to Pearson, 2 January 1940, 40.01.02/3, Archivo Oswaldo Aranha, Centro de Pesquisa e Documentacao de Historia Contemporanea do Brasil, Instituto de Direito Publico e Ciencia Politica Fundacao Getulio Vargas, Rio de Janeiro, Brazil.

[21] John Lloyd Mecham, *The United States and Inter-American Security* (Austin, TX: University of Texas Press, 1961), 185.

As events in Europe became more critical, U.S. strategists began to pressure the administration for action. War Department planners still believed that northeast Brazil had to be defended by U.S. troops if German forces moved into West Africa. A successful defense of this region would ensure the whole South Atlantic front against external attack. To make this position defensible, strategists considered it crucial to establish U.S. bases in northeast Brazil to prevent Axis machinations there.[22] Roosevelt, sympathetic to the military planners but also looking for a means to increase U.S. military readiness without alienating the isolationists, believed that the isolationist Congress would approve funds for the defense of Latin America since even the staunchest isolationists felt that the United States should build up the defenses of the Western Hemisphere. Hence, the president began a campaign to convince Congress of the need for additional military expenditures. On 16 May 1940, six days after Hitler's forces invaded Belgium and the Netherlands, President Roosevelt pointed to Brazil as a prime example of hemisphere vulnerability when he asked Congress for $896,000,000 to modernize the U.S. military. Stressing the vulnerability of the hemisphere, the president pointed out:

> The islands off the west coast of Africa are only 1,500 miles from Brazil. Modern planes starting from the Cape Verde Islands can be over Brazil in seven hours. . . . And, Para, Brazil, near the mouth of the Amazon River, is but four hours to Caracas, Venezuela; and Venezuela is but two and one-half flying hours to Cuba and the Canal Zone. . . .

Roosevelt claimed that enemy forces could easily move from Brazil to Mexico's Yucatan Peninsula and Tampico. Aiming his next remarks at the midwestern isolationists, he stated that he would be "safer on the HudsonRiver than if [he were] in Kansas" because of the proximity of Kansas to Mexico by air.[23]

Eight days after the president's speech, the War Department's fears of an Axis invasion of Brazil seemed to have been fulfilled. On 24 May British intelligence in London warned that 6,000 *Wehrmacht* soldiers loaded aboard merchant ships were possibly headed for Brazil, to be joined there by additional troops on other German merchantmen already in harbor and by Nazi elements already in Brazil. To cope with the possibility of such an invasion, on 25 May President Roosevelt directed his

---

[22] Conn and Fairchild, *The Framework of Hemisphere Defense*, 33.

[23] Quoted in R.W. Hodge, "Lining Up Latin America: The United States Attempts to Bring About Hemisphere Solidarity, 1939-1941" (Ph.D. diss., Michigan State University, 1968), 57.

military chiefs to devise plans for moving 10,000 troops to Brazil by air to be followed by 100,000 by sea to coastal points from Belém to Rio de Janeiro as soon as an Axis move occurred.[24] In two days, navy and army planners had drafted a plan codenamed "Pot of Gold." Military planners did express concern that the dispatch of military forces to Brazil without an invitation from the Brazilian government might lead to cries of American imperialism and result in Latin American charges of a renewed U.S. policy of interventionism.[25] Although the scare proved without merit, it increased the demands of military planners for acquiring air bases in Brazil.

A breakthrough in achieving War Department goals came when the State Department called an interdepartmental meeting to discuss the army's requirements for airdromes beyond the continental limits of the United States. This meeting led to the formation of a subcommittee to prepare specific recommendations as to the best ways to obtain air base facilities throughout Latin America. On 22 May the subcommittee had responded that there were only three viable options for obtaining bases. The government could create a new agency under the supervision of the Civil Aeronautics Administration to look into the matter; it could contract with the various Latin American nations to carry out the project; or it could contract with a civilian agency to build the facilities on a nonprofit basis. Since the War Department considered the acquisition of the bases an absolute necessity and did not trust Latin American zeal or competence, the subcommittee recommended that the work be undertaken by a civilian company. The committee members suggested using Pan American Airways, since it already operated an extensive service throughout Latin America.[26]

Pan American seemed the logical choice for several reasons. The airline had just inaugurated routes across the interior of Brazil, so it could justifiably argue that it needed to construct better land bases as the company made the switch from sea to land planes. The airline could also obtain permission from the countries involved without diplomatic negotiations, simply as a matter of routine. And, perhaps most important, Pan American employees could go where soldiers could not.[27]

---

[24] Conn and Fairchild, *The Framework of Hemisphere Defense*, 33.

[25] Joint Army and Navy Plan for the Support of the Brazilian Government, 27 May 1940, CominCh-CNO Files, World War II Plans, OA, NHC.

[26] Report of the Subcommittee on Caribbean Airways, 22 May 1940, 4815, G-2 Decimal Files, RG 165, NA.

[27] Bynum E. Weathers, Jr., *Acquisition of Air Bases in Latin America, June 1939-June 1943*, USAF Historical Study no. 63 (Alabama: USAF Historical Division, Research Studies Institute, Maxwell, AFB, 1960), 133; Report by Robert L. Cummings, Jr. regarding the

Representatives of the U.S. government negotiated with Pan American Airways President Juan Trippe throughout the summer in an effort to convince the airline to undertake a massive construction project. On 19 July Trippe formally agreed to undertake the project, but it took four months of negotiations before he actually signed a contract with the government. In November 1940 officials of Pan American Airports Corporation, a subsidiary of the airline, signed a secret contract with the U.S. government for the construction of a number of airfields in the South Atlantic and Caribbean. (By the end of the war, Pan Am had built and maintained fifty-nine air bases in fifteen countries, opening 9,500 miles of strategic air lanes for the high-speed transports and bombers of the U.S. Army and Navy).

With the U.S. government contract in hand, Pan American Airways then negotiated with the Brazilian government for approval of its Airport Development Program (ADP) to develop airfields in northeast Brazil. Because Brazil maintained its neutrality until August 1942, any base agreement had to be disguised as commercial in nature; the airline's involvement with the U.S. government remained secret to many Brazilians. By the end of the war, the United States military, through the ADP, obtained both airfields and a military transport system along the Brazilian bulge. The United States Army Forces South Atlantic, headquartered in Recife, Brazil, operated from these bases to transport supplies and equipment to Allied forces in North Africa, the Middle East, and the Far East.

While negotiations with Pan American were still underway, the War Department had continued its hemisphere planning. A plan, based on the newly approved Joint Board Rainbow 4, projected a theater of operations in northeastern Brazil if Great Britain was defeated. Army and navy planners believed that if Germany defeated Great Britain it would then drive through Africa into Brazil. When it appeared in the fall of 1940 that Great Britain would hold on, the urgency for contingency planning for Brazilian operations subsided. Even though the hemisphere was safe from immediate invasion, U.S. military planners continued to call for action. Although the possibility of an Axis invasion into Brazil was minimal, army planners still wanted a string of air bases in northeast Brazil to use for ferrying aircraft and supplies to the various theaters of war.

Although Pan American had already agreed to undertake construction, military planners hoped for an overt military agreement with Brazil which would serve to hasten completion of the bases. Not until the

Construction of Airports in Latin America, 24 August 1942 and Working Note on ADP, n.d., Pan American Airlines Archives, Pan Am Building, New York, New York.

United States agreed to help finance and provide technicians for the construction of the Volta Redonda steel mill, however, did the Brazilian president's attitude toward U.S. pressure for defense arrangements change. Vargas believed the mill was crucial to the industrial development of his country, and for months he had been negotiating with both the Germans and Americans for financing. The mill agreement signaled the end of the period in which Brazil could gain advantages by maneuvering between the United States and Germany. Brazil was now firmly tied to the U.S. and its foreign policy and military objectives.[28]

Soon after the steel mill agreement was signed, Lt. Colonel Lehman W. Miller, Corps of Engineers, chief of the U.S. military mission in Brazil, began formal staff conversations with Brazilian Chief of Staff Goes Monteiro. In October 1940, Goes Monteiro travelled to the United States to discuss the tentative military cooperation agreement worked out with Miller. By 29 October, U.S. Chief of Staff George Marshall and Goes Monteiro had worked out a draft agreement in which Brazil promised the United States use of air and naval bases if the Axis invaded any American nation. In return, the United States agreed to supply Brazil with arms and with material to develop its war industries and railway system.[29] Although the final agreement was not signed until April 1941, the draft agreement provided the base for subsequent cooperation. Brazil was now firmly in the U.S. camp.

By the end of 1940, then, United States military planners had succeeded in convincing the Roosevelt and Vargas administrations to accept their proposals for defense of the Western Hemisphere, although it would take one more year to finalize and execute these plans. As fear of seeming Nazi infallibility approached paranoid levels, calls for greater military preparedness drowned out individuals and organizations voicing isolationist sentiment. One immediate result of the fall of France was that the military received increasingly larger budgets — and supplementary appropriations — that allowed it to finance the projected Brazilian defense policy. In the same respect, while the consummate politician Vargas frustrated military planners, once he gained economic and military concessions from the United States he became a willing supporter of U.S. political and military wartime objectives in his country. Hence, although the War Department had been unable to achieve its objectives in Brazil quickly, complete Brazilian cooperation was ultimately secured.

---

[28] McCann, *The Brazilian-American Alliance*, 193-200.
[29] Conn and Fairchild, *The Framework of Hemisphere Defense*, 277-278.

5

Brazil, Espionage, and Dönitz's Dream

John F. Bratzel

In his dreams, Karl Dönitz pictured a fellow German, sitting quietly in the cellar of an out-of-the-way house, tapping out code to a waiting U-boat. The message would give the name, type, tonnage, and cargo of the next sailing from Rio de Janeiro. The U-boat commander would leisurely position his craft and at the appointed time, assuming the allies were punctual, fire a torpedo and destroy the ship. Despite this information, some ships still might escape the submarines. It would make no difference, however, because in Dönitz's dream, other German agents had secreted bombs on board Allied ships. Three or four days out of port, an internal explosion would do the job the submarines had failed to do.

Luckily, Karl Dönitz's dreams weren't realized, but it was not for lack of effort. The Germans did attempt to use Brazil as a base to broadcast shipping information and did attempt to sabotage Allied shipping. Indeed, the Germans sent more agents, recruited more local agents, and spent more money on intelligence gathering in Brazil than in any other place in Latin America. At times Germany was successful, but a variety of factors combined to make Germany's overall effort a failure.

Brazil and the United States generally maintained good relations from the turn of the century to the beginning of World War II. The basic reason was relatively simple; the two countries had complementary rather than competing products. The U.S. bought Brazilian coffee and minerals, while Brazil purchased U.S. manufactured items. This situation changed after Adolf Hitler came to power. He had no cash to buy Brazilian products, but he did work out a barter arrangement. When the war started, Germany was Brazil's best customer.

The British blockade immediately slowed German traffic, but for a brief period Brazil enjoyed an enviable position, with powerful countries outbidding each other to gain Brazilian friendship. This situation, however, did not last. Germany could not ship goods; promises of German weapons seemed to assume that tanks and planes could be transported by submarines. Only the U.S. was in a position to supply the necessary goods, so Brazil moved closer to the U.S. Each step of closeness, however, cost Uncle Sam money because the Brazilians drove a hard bargain.

The story of German espionage attempts in Brazil is a story of too little, too late. Many historians have suggested that German U-boats would have done better had the war been delayed. Similarly, German espionage would have been better if the war had been delayed.

In May 1940, the Germans planned to smash across France, but they seem to have been surprised when they were successful. Quickly, the requirements for war and the requirements for a Brazilian espionage structure changed. The initial networks that had been established consisted primarily of individual German businessmen sending material to letter drops in Spain or other non-belligerent nations. Indeed, some of the material was sent to Germany by way of LATI, the Italian airline. It consisted mostly of information gleaned from the press and trade publications. The magazine of the steel industry, for example, would be the source for indicating tonnage produced.[1] If this were World War I again, such information would have been sufficient.

World War II, however, was very different, and slow communications, often taking four to six weeks, were no longer of any particular value. What was needed was instant information. The Germans asked their spymasters to establish radio-based networks, each of which would have a number of agents collecting information for dispatch to Germany. The information desired principally concerned shipping, although knowledge of air activities and air ferrying from Natal (in the bulge of Brazil) to Africa was also of great interest to the Germans.

The problem was that it was not easy to establish the kind of networks the Germans desired. German businessmen, turned spy, were not inconspicuous. Moreover, the various networks got into enormously self-destructive battles with each other over who would be in charge of Brazilian spying. One agent, for example, had money and he was supposed to give it to other agents but refused unless they swore allegiance to him. Another invented material he knew Germany wanted to hear in order to curry favor with Berlin. Unfortunately for the Germans, this gambit was successful and Berlin sent adulatory messages to an agent

---

[1] See Leslie B. Rout Jr. and John F. Bratzel, *The Shadow War: German Espionage and United States Counterespionage in Latin America during World War II* (Frederick, MD: University Publications of America, 1986), 112-113, 334.

who made it up as he went along. One other spy only went to Brazil to escape military service. Another became a playboy, bought fancy cars, acquired a mistress, and kept a secret file on all of the other German agents. The Brazilian authorities were delighted when this cache of information was discovered upon his capture.[2]

In spite of the problems with the German networks and the truly amazing characters who ended up working for the Germans, Nazi agents did manage to produce a considerable amount of intelligence information and broadcast it to Germany using clandestine radios.[3] In February 1942, the current routing of ships heading north to the U.S. from Brazil was dispatched to Germany. In June 1942, navigation charts for the east coast of the United States were sent. But most messages were similar to these:

> December 25, 1941 — arrived from England: English refrigerator ship *Viking Star* — 6,445 tons.

> December 26, 1941 Leaving for New York: American liner, *Brazil* — 20,614 tons.[4]

While this information was undoubtedly useful to the Germans, there is no conclusive proof that in even one instance it led directly to the sinking of an Allied ship. What this information did suggest was the general pattern of Allied activity. Had things been different, had the Germans had more and better U-boats, had the German's had time to set up a better, more complete spy apparatus, Karl Dönitz's dream of U-boats idling off the coast of South America, not bothering to stir until their compatriots on shore identified a target for them, may have come true.

But if submarines could not do the job, there were still German agents in Brazil who could take direct, covert action to aid their cause. Almost immediately after the declaration of war in Europe, Germany sent two ships, the *Dresden* and *Babitonga*, to Brazil. Each ship was well stocked with the accoutrements of war necessary to sustain a German commerce raider. The ships docked in the port of Santos and remained there until March of 1941 when orders were received for the *Dresden* to rendezvous with the commerce raider *Atlantis*. The Germans feared, however, that the British would attack the *Dresden*, or worse, follow it to its destination. To counter this possibility, Albrecht Engels, a leader of

---

[2] Superintêndencia de Sequrança, Politica de Saõ Paulo, *A Rede de Espionagem Nazista chefiada por Niels Christian Christiansen* (Saõ Paulo, 1943), 9, 11-12.

[3] *Files of the German Naval Staff, German Naval Attache in Brazil*, T-65, PG-32004, 198. U.S. Department of the Navy, Naval Historical Center, Washington Navy Yard, Washington DC.

[4] See ML-170, roll 22, Record Group 242, National Archives, Washington D.C.

one of the German spy rings, arranged to fly out to sea, scout the escape route for the *Dresden*, and report back. This was done successfully, the *Dresden* sailed, met and replenished the *Atlantis*, took off prisoners, and successfully reached Bordeaux.[5]

The *Babitonga* was supposed to leave a week later, but this time the air search by Engels turned up two British warships waiting outside Santos harbor. Sailing was delayed. A few days later, when the coast was clear, *Babitonga* left Santos and also met the *Atlantis*. As that ship needed relatively few supplies, *Babitonga* was sent to another rendezvous point only to be subsequently spotted by the British. Her crew scuttled her,[6] but this development does not diminish the initial contribution of Brazilian-based German agents in getting both ships out of Brazilian waters.

Not only supply ships for commerce raiders benefited from clandestine sea searches. Three German freighters that were trapped by the British in either Santos or Rio de Janeiro wanted to break through the British blockade. Another reconnaissance flight was needed. This time, Nazi agent Josef Starziczny arranged for Fritz Weissflog, another German agent and pilot, to fly both of them along the coast of Brazil. They spotted no British ships, and all three vessels sailed. Two made it to Germany with their cargoes of war materials; only the *Hermes* was eventually caught and sunk.[7]

Not every ship, however, got away, and it was one that didn't, the *Windhuk*, which created a success for the counterespionage forces of Brazil and the United States. In 1942, the Germans recruited Captain Tulio Regis do Nascimiento as an agent. The captain was a fascist sympathizer whose recruitment promised to pay high dividends. The Americans uncovered do Nascimiento, however, when in an effort to aid the Germans, he asked to go to the United States and examine the newest equipment the Sperry Corporation was producing. Whether he would have been invited is impossible to determine, but U.S. cryptographers intercepted the message to Germany indicating that one of its agents had asked to visit the Sperry plant. Do Nascimiento may have the record for remaining secret the shortest time following recruitment. The Brazilians did not arrest him immediately. He was an army officer, and absolute proof did not yet exist, but he was being watched.

---

[5] Reiner Pommerien, *Das Dritte Reich and Lateinamerika: Die deutsche politik gegenüber Süd und Mittelamerika, 1939-1942* (Düsseldorf, 1977), 215.

[6] See August K. Muggenthaler, *German Raiders in World War II* (Englewood Cliffs, NJ, 1977), 103-105; Pommerein, *Das Dritte Reich*, 215.

[7] See Decimal File 862.20210/1930 1/2, pp. 10-11 Record Group 59, National Archives, Washington, D.C. (hereafter RG 59, NA).

In 1941, the German ship *Windhuk* lay at Guanabara Bay, Rio de Janeiro's harbor. She was loaded, and the Germans planned to slip through the British blockade and make for Europe. The request for departure papers, however, was still pending when the Japanese attacked Pearl Harbor. The Brazilians refused to issue a certificate to allow the *Windhuk* to depart; moreover, there was a strong rumor that the ship would be seized by the Brazilians.

In July the Germans finally concluded that their ship would never be allowed to leave Rio de Janeiro. They decided to blow it up, an action which would demonstrate power and ability. Do Nascimiento and his recruit, Gerardo Melo Mourão, built a crude bomb using an alarm clock and flares. All that was necessary was to place the bomb in *Windhuk's* hold. The person chosen, another *integralista* named Alvaro da Costa e Souza, agreed to place to bomb in the hold for $6,000. He lost his courage when he realized that Brazil would soon be at war with the Axis and that activity such as this would likely be defined as treason with its concomitant penalties. However, he still wanted the money. To cover himself, he told the Brazilian secret service that the Germans were planning to blow up the *Windhuk* but failed to mention he was supposed to be the agent of *Windhuk's* demise. After implicating his Nazi friends, he told them that since Brazil was now at war, payment would have to come in advance. But Costa e Souza was too clever. Following his meeting with the Germans, the Brazilians arrested all of them. Costa e Souza later received twenty-five years in prison, but he, at least, was scheduled to be out five years before Melo Mourão and do Nascimiento who each received thirty years. The others were out by 1950, but do Nascimiento was not released until 1954.[8]

While the Germans exerted considerable energy to blow up the *Windhuk*, they couldn't win the war by blowing up their own ships. The trick is to blow up the enemy's ships. This is exactly what a super-secret organization established by the Germans in Rio de Janeiro was supposed to do. It was to remain unknown to all other German networks and only go into action when it received a coded message from Germany. Agents were trained, and by November 1940, sabotage chief Georg Konrad Friedrich Blass sent a telegram to Germany indicating that Operation *South Pole* (the placing of bombs on Allied ships) could begin at any time. All that was needed was a coded message containing the word "cyclops," and ships in Brazil, Argentina, and Chile would be attacked.

The war went on, but the agents received no word from Germany. The reason was that regular Nazi agents supplying shipping data and the

---

[8] Decimal File 862.202109/2076, pp. 1-2, RG 59, NA.

German Foreign Office opposed sabotage. They concluded that the resultant clamor would mean a break in diplomatic relations as well as an end to shipping information while sinking very few British ships. Proof of this assertion came when agents in Argentina could contain themselves no longer and put two bombs on the British freighter *Gascony*. One bomb exploded, killed the Argentine sailor hired to place it, damaged the engine, and put a hole in the side of the ship, but it did not sink the vessel. The result was a special espionage and sabotage investigation that forced German agents to go underground.[9]

The Allies first learned of this unit through intercepted radio communications. This sabotage group was supposed to be separate, but to communicate with Germany it had to use other German agents' radios. The United States picked up these transmissions, broke the low level code that enciphered them, and learned of the network. Still, it wasn't enough for arrest. Indeed, it was only after agents in Chile started to set fires in British ships that counterespionage agents realized the scope of the *South Pole* organization. The arrest of the Chilean perpetrators, their identities learned through intercepted radio messages, their subsequent questioning by the Chileans, and their "decision" to talk led to the unmasking of *South Pole*. The fear by elements in Germany that this sabotage effort would hinder the intelligence effort and have negative political effects were borne out. Indeed, it is difficult to believe that such a unit was even seriously considered.

The German efforts in Brazil had their genesis in an old-fashioned view of espionage. Agents gleaned material from a variety of sources and sent it to neutral nations to be forwarded to Germany. If it took two months, it mattered little because the material was strategic rather than tactical. The U-boat changed that. For information to be useful immediately, radios and complicated information-gathering mechanisms were required. As spy organizations grew and began to broadcast, their increased activity increased the ability of counterespionage to stop them. Had the war gone differently, however, these radio stations might have proven very effective; as it was, they gave Berlin the broad outlines of shipping in the South Atlantic, but the information never sank ships. U-boats were the key. Attempts at do-it-yourself sabotage were a total failure, and the go-it-alone attempts produced only negative results. The real success for the Germans came early in the war, when through air surveillance they were able to help supply commerce raiders in the South Atlantic. Karl Dönitz "dream," therefore, was never realized.

---

[9] Decimal File 862.20210/4-545, p. 1, RG 59, NA and *Axis Espionage and Propaganda in Latin America*, p. 41, Box 966, Record Group 165, NA.

PART TWO

The "Happy Time"

6

The Character of the German Naval Offensive: October 1940-June 1941

Donald P. Steury

In the spring and summer of 1940, the German naval high command saw vast new opportunities for the use of its surface fleet in offensive action. The conquests of France and Norway brought the Germans a network of naval bases that extended from the North Cape to the Spanish border, outflanking the blocking position held by Great Britain across the Atlantic passages. The elimination of the French fleet substantially reduced the margin of superiority enjoyed by the Western allies, while Italy's entry into the war gave Germany a new ally, powerful at sea, to balance British naval superiority. With the German fleet freed from the "wet triangle" of the North Sea, operational planning, hitherto focused on northern waters, now shifted to the broad reaches of the Atlantic.[1]

The small size of the German surface fleet — never more than about eleven large warships, of which no more than four were ever available for Atlantic operations — belied the importance attached to it in German strategy. Germany's naval planners, in attempting to learn from their defeat in the First World War, viewed the failure of the 1917-18 U-boat offensive as an indication of the limitations of the submarine as a principal weapon of war and the danger of relying too much on a "single dimension" of naval power.[2] At the same time, they rejected the

---

[1] Klaus A. Maier, et al., *Germany and the Second World War, vol. 2, Germany's Initial Conquests in Europe*, trans. Dean S. McMurry and Ewald Osers (Oxford: Oxford University Press, 1991), 352.

[2] Philip K. Lundeberg, "The German Critique of the U-Boat Campaign, 1915-1918," *Military Affairs* (1963); Bundesarchiv-Militärarchiv (hereafter BAMA), Freiburg im Breisgau, RM 6/57 OKM *Kriegsspiel Feb-März 1939*.

Tirpitzian strategy of a decisive naval battle in the North Sea. In its stead, the Naval War Staff (*Die deutsche Seekriegsleitung,* or Skl,) argued for the more fluid concept of an ocean war on communications. In war, the focus of surface naval operations would be the North Atlantic convoy routes; fleet actions would not occur as stand-up gun duels between opposing battle lines but would evolve out of running convoy actions between heterogeneous groups of surface ships, with submarines and aircraft playing subordinate roles.

In consequence, prewar Germany built heavy ships — battleships, pocket battleships, heavy cruisers, and aircraft carriers — designed for independent operations in distant waters. All were fast, had respectable cruising ranges for their type, and were given better than average firepower and superior protection. The war had begun with only a part of the first generation of planned warships in service, but the ships that had been completed were regarded as individually superior to their opposite numbers in the Royal Navy, which was to make up somewhat for their numerical inferiority.[3] Moreover, Skl planned to supplement the regular warships with a fleet of auxiliary cruisers similar to those that had proved so successful in World War I. Disguised, heavily-armed converted merchant ships, these twentieth-century privateers could remain at sea to prey upon enemy shipping for a year or more. Although not approaching the combat potential of a regular warship, in the second war they proved to be raiders as effective as in the first, and they remained in operation long after the battle fleet had abandoned the Atlantic.[4]

Faced with the still substantial numerical superiority of the Royal Navy, Skl could not contemplate a direct challenge to British command of the North Atlantic but planned to wear down British naval supremacy through a strategy of attrition. It would be an unequal battle: with almost no reserves, Skl could not afford to allow the few German warships and

---

[3] German warship designs did not live up to expectations, proving to be too short-legged for Atlantic operations. Moreover, postwar analyses show that German efforts to achieve a qualitative advantage did not result in warships measurably superior to their contemporaries in other navies. However, in 1940-41 the navies of Germany's principal antagonists were still made up largely of older warships, inferior to the more modern German designs. Furthermore, German ships in this period had the advantage of radar (not yet fitted to most Allied warships) and a significant intelligence superiority. See William H. Garzke Jr. and Robert O. Dulin Jr., *Battleships: Axis and Neutral Battleships of World War II* (Annapolis, MD: Naval Institute Press, 1985), 195-96, 296-303; M. J. Whitley, *German Cruisers of World War II* (Annapolis MD: Naval Institute Press, 1985), 72-75.

[4] Having neglected the concept in peacetime, Skl revived it on the outbreak of war, so that by the summer of 1940 some half-dozen merchant ships had been converted and were ready for operations. Maier, *Germany and the Second World War* 2: 349.

raiders to seek combat at even equal odds, but it reasoned that German warships operating as a "fleet in being" on the convoy routes would have an effect all out of proportion to their strength. For example, the identified presence of a single U-boat or auxiliary cruiser in an area would force merchant shipping into escorted convoys, with the strength of the escort increasing relative to the weight of the opposition. Destroyers would be adequate to deal with U-boats, but a German cruiser would compel the British to escort their convoys with like force, while a pocket battleship would tie up several cruisers or a battleship with each convoy.[5] With eleven convoys present in the North Atlantic on any given day and more scattered across the South Atlantic, Pacific, and Indian Oceans, the British Admiralty would soon find its resources stretched thin. Continuous pressure would be necessary: although German forces were too small to bring about a decisive result, Skl believed that much could be achieved through "psychological effect," arguing that repeated appearances by German warships on the high seas "in widely varied areas" would "force enemy import traffic to make detours, . . . necessitate the stoppage of merchant traffic on the sea route concerned, and . . . discourage the readiness of neutrals to export to the enemy . . . ."[6]

German surface force strategy thus aimed at nothing less than a breakdown of the whole mechanism of British overseas supply. This was to be achieved not so much by the destruction of enemy shipping as by incessant attacks that overstressed the system as a whole, ultimately inducing a general state of paralysis. In Skl's view, the "preponderant responsibilities and interests" of the British empire left Great Britain particularly vulnerable to a campaign of this kind, one to which Germany — with no overseas interests to protect — was virtually immune.[7] The Admiralty itself they viewed as "orthodox and conservative," not unlike an aging boxer who was ponderous and past his prime but still packed a powerful punch.[8]

As such, Skl's strategy contrasts starkly with that of the other side to German sea power, the U-boat arm. Although it made the most of German strengths and exploited British weaknesses, at no time did German surface force strategy contemplate a direct attack on the edifice of British maritime supremacy. This was precisely what was attempted

---

[5] BAMA RM 6/57 PG341348-1/111 Skl 1a *Kriegsspiel 1938-39*, *"Einfluß der Wahl des Handelskriegstyps auf den Geleitdienst."*

[6] *Battle Instructions for the (German) Navy* (Issue of May 1939), 3-4, ADM 223/25, Public Record Office (hereafter PRO), London.

[7] BAMA RM 6/57 OKM *Kriegsspiel Feb-März 1939*, 13.

[8] Hansjürgen Reinicke, "German Surface Force Strategy in World War II," United States Naval Institute *Proceedings* (1957): 185.

by the Flag-officer U-boats, Vice Admiral Karl Dönitz, in what he called the "tonnage war" — the effort to cripple the British war effort by sinking merchant ships faster than they could be built.[9] Whereas Skl sought to disperse British naval power, Dönitz, by concentrating his U-boats on the North Atlantic convoy routes, was pursuing a course calculated to concentrate it. While Skl avoided direct confrontation with British naval forces, Dönitz sought them out in massed attacks on British convoys.

Clearly, the whole of these two strategies pursued in combination would be greater than the sum of its parts, particularly if combined with an air campaign on the part of the *Luftwaffe* and the available naval aircraft. Indeed, a combined arms effort of this nature *(Gesamtkrieg-führung)* was at the heart of German prewar planning and formed part of Skl's rationale for committing German surface forces to the Atlantic campaign.[10] In practice, however, the *Kriegsmarine's*[11] divided command structure, failure to complete the two aircraft carriers that had been laid down, and interservice rivalry made this difficult to achieve.[12] Coordinated efforts involving surface ships and U-boats foundered on an excessively complex communications system, and, without aircraft carriers, German surface forces never had direct access to the air support they needed. The *Luftwaffe* waged its own, independent war on merchant shipping with little more than a nod toward cooperation with the *Kriegsmarine*, apart from a few, specialized reconnaissance units. In effect, Germany waged naval war in three independent, unrelated campaigns: above, below, and on the surface of the ocean.

Atlantic operations with surface ships had begun with the outbreak of war, two pocket battleships having been deployed to the open ocean in August 1939, before the opening of hostilities. The initial campaign was comparatively brief, however, and did not live up to expectations. It ended with the destruction of the *Admiral Graf Spee* and the return of *Lützow* (ex-*Deutschland*) to home waters. There then followed a hiatus of nearly eight months which were occupied, first, with the Norwegian campaign and then with the repair and refit of the ships involved.

---

[9] Maier, *Germany and the Second World War* 2: 349.

[10] BAMA RM 6/53 PG32625 *Generaladmiral* Erich Raeder: *Grundsätzliche Gedanken der Seekriegführung*, 3 February 1937. See also the summary discussion in Donald P. Steury, *Germany's Naval Renaissance: Ideology and Sea Power in the Nazi Era* (University Microfilms, 1991), 206-12, 295-97. For evidence of the concept of *Gesamtkriegführung* in Skl's summer 1940 planning, see Maier, *Germany and the Second World War* 2: 352.

[11] The German navy, 1935-45.

[12] U-boats were not directly subordinated to the Naval War Staff, which retained direct control only of surface combatants. All aircraft in Germany were subject to the authority of the commander of the *Luftwaffe* (and the navy's arch-rival)Reichsmarschall Hermann Göring.

The German heavy cruiser *Admiral Hipper* at the ancient French naval port of Brest. In 1940 and 1941, the cruiser used Brest as a base for attacks on the North Atlantic convoy routes. Photo courtesy of the Imperial War Museum, London.

German heavy ships did not return to the Atlantic until late October 1940, when the pocket battleship *Admiral Scheer* sortied on what was to be a successful five-month cruise in the Atlantic and Indian oceans. The next German warship to take to the high seas was a heavy cruiser, *Admiral Hipper*, which passed into the North Atlantic on 7 December, there to engage in a none-too-successful three-week search for unescorted convoys along the Halifax route. On 27 December she put into Brest, the first major German warship to reach a French port. After a four-week refit in Brest she sortied again into the Atlantic, sighting and sinking seven ships of a northbound convoy. After another refit in Brest, *Admiral Hipper* returned to home waters via the Denmark Straits, north of Iceland.

The high point in German Atlantic surface force operations occurred between January and June 1941, beginning with the cruise of the battleships *Gneisenau* (wearing the flag of the fleet commander, Admiral Günther Lütjens) and *Scharnhorst* (Operation *Berlin*). These powerful warships were loose in the North Atlantic for about six weeks, sinking a total of twenty-two merchant ships of 115,622 tons. Contacted on three separate occasions by British battleships and once by aircraft from a carrier, *Ark Royal*, they were never successfully engaged and on 21 March put into Brest.

The next operation, codenamed *Rheinübung*, was planned to be the most ambitious to date, employing *Scharnhorst* and *Gneisenau* from France and two newly completed ships from home waters, the heavy cruiser

Prinz Eugen and the battleship *Bismarck*. The scale of the operation was reduced, however, when repairs and subsequent torpedo damage removed the two Brest-based battleships from the board. It then was delayed when one of the remaining participants, *Prinz Eugen*, ran onto a mine in the Baltic. *Bismarck*, with Lütjens on board, and *Prinz Eugen* finally departed the German base at Gotenhafen (Gdynia, Poland) on 19 May.

Ill fortune dogged this, the last German heavy ship operation in the Atlantic, from the start. Sighted in the Skagerrak and reported to the British Admiralty, the two German ships were spotted again by aerial reconnaissance in Grimstadfjord, off the Norwegian port of Bergen. Later, in attempting to pass the Denmark Straits, they were caught and shadowed by two patrolling British heavy cruisers — the first time this had happened in the whole campaign. Undeterred, Lütjens nevertheless pressed forward, to be engaged by the battle cruiser *Hood* and battleship *Prince of Wales*. Although this action ended with *Hood* sunk and *Prince of Wales* damaged and beaten off, *Bismarck* herself was damaged and Lütjens could not shake off his pursuers. He decided to make for France. Harassed and finally crippled by carrier aircraft, on 27 May *Bismarck* was caught by two British battleships within six hundred miles of Brest and finally sank after being bombarded by over seven hundred heavy shells for a period of nearly two hours.[13] *Prinz Eugen*, having been dispatched on independent operations earlier, cruised fruitlessly for seven days in the Atlantic before mechanical difficulties forced her into Brest.

Long after the event, the commander in chief of the German Navy, Grand Admiral Erich Raeder, wrote of the "lasting effects" the loss of the *Bismarck* had on the war at sea.[14] The sinking of the *Bismarck* was indeed an event of profound importance: for the British it was a badly needed victory, a reminder that command of the sea was still in the hands of the Royal Navy and that, despite the terrible toll in lives and ships, the *Kriegsmarine* had yet to win the Battle of the North Atlantic. To pro-British neutrals — particularly those in the United States — it was evidence that Great Britain was still an important factor in the war. Along with the check to the *Luftwaffe* in the Battle of Britain and the recent decisive defeat of the Italian navy off Cape Matapan, the chase and sinking of the battleship *Bismarck* went a long way to offset the disasters in Norway, France, North Africa, Yugoslavia, and Greece, to say nothing of the then ongoing debacle off Crete. To Adolf Hitler, the sinking of the *Bismarck* was confirmation — if ever he needed it — that his intuition

---

[13] Garzke and Dulin, *Battleships*, 238-41.
[14] Erich Raeder, *My Life* (Annapolis MD: Naval Institute Press, 1960), 358.

that his commanders could not be trusted was correct, and it marked the beginning of a resolve to exercise much tighter control over naval operations.

To the German Naval War Staff the failure of *Rheinübung* was a bitter blow, but in the summer of 1941 it was not seen as the decisive turning point in the fortunes of the German surface fleet. *Bismarck* was a powerful unit, but in the eyes of the naval high command her loss did not substantially alter the strategic balance. Most of the German surface fleet was either refitting or in training, but substantial forces would be available for a fall offensive. Plans for an immediate breakout with *Lützow* (Operation *Sommerreise*) went ahead, to be followed in August by a sortie with the other remaining pocket battleship, *Admiral Scheer*. *Bismarck's* sister ship *Tirpitz* was nearly operational, the heavy cruiser *Admiral Hipper* would be ready in September, and *Scharnhorst* and *Gneisenau* would be repaired and ready for operations "early in the Fall," as would *Prinz Eugen*.[15]

If anything, Skl's plans for the second half of 1941 were more ambitious than those that had been laid for the first half of the year. Operations were planned for three areas: *Tirpitz* and *Admiral Hipper* would deploy to Trondheim, where they would act as a "fleet in being," tying down elements of the British Home Fleet based in Scapa Flow. Meanwhile, the Brest squadron would raid the convoy routes in the middle and southern Atlantic, while *Lützow* and *Admiral Scheer* would operate in the lucrative Indian Ocean area. Skl also planned continuing operations with armed merchant raiders, four of which were at sea during this period.

The principles governing German strategy remained the same: dispersal of Britain's naval forces and disruption of her sea lines of communication. The Germans recognized that the outcome of the *Bismarck* operation signaled the existence of a distinctively more hostile operational environment than hitherto had been the case — British cruisers were now equipped with radar, the fast, new *King George V* class battleships were appearing, and the Royal Navy was making effective use of land-based patrol planes and aircraft carriers. But Skl believed the importance of these developments could be minimized by avoiding the long cruises that had characterized past German heavy ship operations in the Atlantic. When British naval forces made a clean sweep of the overseas network of German tankers and supply ships that supported Atlantic operations in June, it only confirmed Skl in that opinion while

---

[15] Michael Salewski, *Die deutsche Seekriegsleitung, 1935-1945*, 3 vols. (Frankfurt am Main: Bernard und Graife, 1970), 1: 454.

British Halifax heavy bombers over Brest, sometime late in 1941. The German battleships *Scharnhorst* and *Gneisenau* are in dry dock, at right, partially covered by camouflage netting. The heavy cruiser *Prinz Eugen* is moored at the lower left. RAF bombers raided Brest incessantly while it was under German occupation, frustrating *Kriegsmarine* plans to use the French Atlantic ports as bases for anything larger than U-boats or destroyers and putting an end to Atlantic surface ship operations. Photo courtesy of the Imperial War Museum, London.

failing to alert Germany's naval planners to another development, more ominous for German naval operations as a whole: the growing ability of British intelligence to predict German deployments, largely through penetration of the Enigma machine cipher.[16]

In fact, the RAF struck the most immediately decisive blows to Skl's strategic ambitions. On 13 June the pocket battleship *Lützow*, bound for the North Atlantic via Norway, was attacked and badly damaged by Beaufort torpedo bombers. *Lützow* returned safely home but was out of action until March 1942. On 2 July the heavy cruiser *Prinz Eugen*, dry-docked in Brest, was hit by two bombs and taken out of action until February 1942. Three weeks later the battleship *Scharnhorst*, working up at La Pallice following completion of her engine repairs, was hit by five bombs. On 27 July she was back in the dock at Brest, having taken on some 3,000 tons of water. Her repairs would not be completed until December. All this additional repair work overburdened the Brest dockyard, so *Gneisenau's* repairs were extended, with completion also delayed until the end of the year. Finally, in August the pocket battleship *Scheer* was badly damaged when she ran aground in the Baltic, sustaining damage that prohibited an Atlantic deployment before December.[17] Although no ships were actually lost, by the end of July the RAF had effectively neutralized the entire German surface fleet until the end of the year. With *Hipper* still in the dockyard, only *Tirpitz* remained operational of the ships that had been available for Atlantic operations.

In September, Hitler finally put an end to Skl's plans by banning Atlantic surface operations until the successful conclusion of the Russian campaign (anticipated by the end of the year).[18] Fearing another *Rheinübung* disaster, the Führer also was increasingly preoccupied with the war in Russia as well as with the possibility of a British landing in Norway. The convergence of these three ideas in Hitler's mind — all eventually were to become obsessions — transformed Norway into a "Zone of Destiny" for the German surface fleet. In December he ordered a reconcentration of the German fleet along the Norwegian coast, including the Brest squadron, which returned home via the English Channel in February 1942 (Operation *Cerberus*). "Every ship that is not in

---

[16] F.H. Hinsley, *British Intelligence in the Second World War*, 3 vols. (London: HMSO, 1979), 1: 345-46.

[17] Salewski, *Die deutsche Seekriegsleitung* 1: 456.

[18] In September, *Tirpitz* and *Scheer* were somewhat fatuously employed containing the ineffective Soviet Baltic Fleet. M.J. Whitley, *German Capital Ships of World War II* (London: Arms and Armour Press, 1989), 176-77.

Norway is in the wrong place," he told Raeder.[19] No German heavy ship ever again entered the Atlantic.

Operations with armed merchant raiders were much longer-lived. Auxiliary cruisers were sent out in two "waves": the first wave beginning in March 1940 with the sortie of Ship 16 *Atlantis*.[20] Six ships put to sea in this period, the last departing on 3 July. A second wave of four ships deployed beginning on 3 December 1940, but difficulties in fitting out the raiders meant that only two ships departed in 1940 (one of which, Ship 10 *Thor*, was on a second cruise), followed by two more in 1942. A fifth auxiliary cruiser, Ship 14 *Coronel*, attempted to break out as late as February 1943 but was heavily damaged and never left home waters. Another two ships were fitted out as raiders but never attempted a sortie. Although made increasingly difficult by the growing strength of Allied naval forces, the disguised raider campaign continued to meet with success on the open ocean and was halted only when the Allied stranglehold on the exits to the Atlantic grew tight enough to block completely the egress of German ships.

A total of six regular German warships and seven auxiliary cruisers were present in the Atlantic between the end of October 1940 and the beginning of June 1941. The greatest period of concentration was in February 1941, when four heavy ships were at large — *Scharnhorst*, *Gneisenau*, *Admiral Hipper*, and *Admiral Scheer* — along with seven auxiliary cruisers. All told, regular warships sank or captured fifty-one merchant ships and tankers of 257,381 tons over the fall and winter of 1940-41, while the disguised raiders accounted for another fifty-six ships of 321,989 tons. By comparison, in the same period U-boats sank a total of 395 ships of 2,163,205 tons (see Table 1).[21]

More significant was the actual impact of the surface campaign in terms of delays and diverted shipping. In November 1940, for example, *Admiral Scheer* succeeded in suspending North Atlantic convoy traffic for twelve days following her attack on a single convoy, HX 84.[22] The following February, the period of greatest activity, the North Atlantic convoy cycle was "completely disrupted."[23] The real, total effect of the German surface campaign, measured in terms of its effect on the all-important British import economy, is more difficult to determine,

---

[19] Heinrich Bredemeier, *Schlachtschiff Scharnhorst* (Herford: Koehlers Verlagsgesellschaft, 1962), 206.

[20] Maier, *Germany and the Second World War* 2: 349-51.

[21] S.W. Roskill, *The War at Sea, vol. I, The Defensive* (London: HMSO, 1954), 615-18.

[22] Whitley, *German Capital Ships*, 130-31.

[23] Roskill, *War at Sea* 1: 379.

Table 1
Allied Shipping Losses and Source, Sept. 1939-Dec. 1941

Month/Year	U-boat	Aircraft	Warship	Armed Merchant Raider
September 1939	153,879		5,051	
October 1939	134,807		32,058	
November 1939	51,589		1,722	
December 1939	80,881	2,949	22,506	
January 1940	111,263	23,693		
February 1940	169,566	853	1,761	
March 1940	62,781	8,694		
April 1940	32,467	13,409		5,207
May 1940	55,580	158,348		6,199
January 1941	126,782	78,597	18,738	78,484
February 1941	196,783	89,305	79,086	7,031
March 1941	243,020	113,314	89,838	28,707
April 1941	249,375	323,454		43,640
May 1941	325,492	146,302		15,002
June 1941	310,143	61,414		17,759
July 1941	94,209	9,275		5,792
August 1941	80,310	23,862		21,378
September 1941	202,820	40,812	7,500	8,734
October 1941	156,554	35,222		
November 1941	62,196	23,015		
December 1941	124,070	72,850	6,661	

Source: S.W. Roskill, *The War at Sea*, *vol.1*, *The Defensive* (London: HMSO, 1954), 615-18.

Table 2
Relationship of Import Tonnage to the UK and Shipping Losses
September 1939-December 1941

Month/Year	Imports to UK (tonnage)	Losses to Enemy Action (tonnage)
September 1939	3,297,070	158,930
October 1939	3,576,135	166,865
November 1939	4,408,689	53,311
December 1939	4,466,664	106,336
January 1940	4,847,044	134,956
February 1940	4,348,820	172,180
March 1940	4,970,525	71,475
April 1940	5,336,917	51,083
May 1940	5,362,873	220,127
January 1941	2,651,399	302,601
February 1941	2,621,795	372,205
March 1941	2,864,121	474,879
April 1941	2,620,531	616,469
May 1941	3,466,204	486,796
June 1941	3,594,684	389,316
July 1941	3,765,724	109,276
August 1941	4,002,450	125,550
September 1941	4,267,134	259,866
October 1941	4,203,224	191,776
November 1941	3,336,789	85,211
December 1941	3,735,419	203,581

Source: W.K. Hancock, ed., *Statistical Digest of the War* (London: HMSO, 1951), 184-85.

bound up as it is with seasonal factors, the direct and indirect influences of the air and submarine campaigns, and — not least important — the general impact of the war upon British trade. Nevertheless, the steady drop in the volume of British imports throughout the summer, fall, and winter of 1940-41, reaching a nadir between January and March, gives some indication of the results achieved by Germany's deployed surface ships and disguised raiders (see Table 2).[24]

The opening of the 1940-41 German surface campaign coincided with the end of the first U-boat "Happy Time," (June-October 1940) in which Germany's most successful commanders — Kretschmer, Prien, and Schepke — made their reputations. During this period a small number of U-boats (never more than eighteen, but generally eleven to thirteen)[25] operating from the newly acquired French Atlantic bases sank a total of 1,395,298 tons of merchant shipping, an average of 279,060 tons per month. Thereafter sinkings fell off somewhat, due to the conditions of the North Atlantic winter, the presence of larger numbers of British convoy escorts, and the development of improved ASW tactics. The delays, diversions, and forced convoy dispersals caused by the appearance of German heavy ships on the North Atlantic sea lanes alongside the U-boats doubled the effectiveness of the war on enemy trade, even though the average level of sinkings due to U-boats dropped slightly to 264,723 tons per month and the average total British losses to enemy action only rose by some 66,401 tons monthly (from 452,249 to 518,650 tons per month). In June, following the sinking of the *Bismarck* and the end of the German surface campaign, the volume of British imports began to rise again, despite a dramatic rise in sinkings by U-boats now reinforced by increased *Luftwaffe* participation. Not until the second "Happy Time" (January-June 1942)[26] were British imports reduced to that of the winter of 1940-41, and not until the grim, dark winter of 1942-43, when Dönitz was briefly able to deploy more than one hundred U-boats to the North Atlantic convoy routes, did the *U-bootwaffe* exceed the results achieved in that period.[27]

Probably the greatest disappointment to the Naval War Staff was its

---

[24] W.K. Hancock, ed., *Statistical Digest of the War* (London: HMSO, 1951), 184-85.

[25] V.E. Tarrant, *The U-Boat Offensive, 1914-1945* (Annapolis, MD: Naval Institute Press, 1989), 96.

[26] Operation *Paukenschlag*, Dönitz's offensive against the shipping routes along the east coast of the United States, dominated the second "Happy Time" (January-July 1942). Due to the primitive state of American ASW measures, U-boats were able, once again, to operate virtually unmolested during this period, sinking a total of 3,376,966 tons of shipping. See Tarrant, *U-Boat Offensive*, 104-07.

[27] Ibid., 111-16.

inability to make effective use of the Atlantic naval bases available in occupied France. Only one major German warship, *Admiral Hipper*, could really be said to have used one of the French ports as an operating base and that only briefly, early in 1941. Brest, the ancient French naval arsenal and principal Atlantic fleet base, proved to be too near British bomber bases. *Hipper* had eighty-five tons of bombs dropped on her during her brief tenure (albeit without result) while *Scharnhorst*, *Gneisenau*, and *Prinz Eugen* were bombed incessantly, enduring 1,971 tons of bombs dropped by 1,875 aircraft during one three-month period.[28] Initially optimistic — despite early warnings from the responsible flag officer, General Admiral Albert Saalwächter (Group West) — Skl had its hopes dashed within weeks of the battleships' arrival in France.[29] By 11 April, Skl had been forced to conclude that Brest was not a viable operating base in the face of concerted RAF bombing raids and began to consider falling back to Trondheim or (with Spanish cooperation) the use of Ferrol as an Atlantic base.[30] By this time, however, both battleships were in dry dock — *Scharnhorst* due to her engine repairs and *Gneisenau* because of torpedo damage. Extensive raids continued throughout most of 1941, so that these warships were never able to remain operational for any length of time while they were in France. The U-boats based in France during this period, however, were protected by concrete bunkers and thus escaped largely unscathed.[31]

That German surface forces were able to operate in distant waters to the length and breadth of the British convoy system, despite the lack of a secure base on the Atlantic or friendly neutrals in areas close to concentrations of British shipping, was due in part to their superior mobility but mostly to the prewar development of a naval supply service.[32] The *Kriegsmarine* was the only European navy to incorporate at-sea replenishment into its overall strategic conception, and in 1940 it had under construction a fleet of big, fast supply ships *(Troßschiffe)* built specifically to accompany and provide logistical support to regular warships engaged in ocean warfare. Four supply ships were completed in time for the Atlantic surface campaign. To these purpose-built ships were added a number of tankers captured or requisitioned in the course of the war. All proved to be remarkably successful and continued their

---

[28] Maier, *Germany and the Second World War* 2: 355; Roskill, *War at Sea*, 487.

[29] Salewski, *Die deutsche Seekriegsleitung* 1: 387.

[30] Ibid., 388.

[31] Karl Dönitz, *Memoirs: Ten Years and Twenty Days* (London: Weidenfeld and Nicholson, 1959), 409-10.

[32] BAMA RM 6/53 PG 32635, 18.

operations long after the end of the surface campaign, acting as floating supply bases for U-boats, auxiliary cruisers, and blockade runners in distant waters.

Conduct of an ocean campaign of this nature was no mean feat of organization, requiring the coordination of diverse types of ships — warships, auxiliary cruisers, supply ships, and U-boats — on a worldwide basis. No fewer than seven supply ships and tankers were mobilized for the first battleship operation *(Berlin)* and nine for the second *(Rheinübung)*. Some of these ships were already in the Atlantic, some came from France, and others had to break out ahead of the warships from German home waters. No less impressive was the endurance of the crews, many of whom were impressed from the merchant service. For example, the tanker *Friedrich Breme* put to sea in December 1940 in support of the cruiser *Admiral Hipper*. She remained at sea continuously, alone in the North Atlantic, for nearly seven months, including the whole of the winter of 1940-41, until finally captured in June by the British cruiser *Sheffield*.[33]

As remarkable a logistical achievement as the German surface campaign was, its success only underscores the extent to which the German naval offensive was conducted on a shoe string. The lack of overseas bases meant that any damage suffered when actually in the Atlantic could not be repaired, while return to Germany through the Atlantic passages with a warship that was less than fully operational was problematic — a major factor in Lütjens' decision to take *Bismarck* into a French port. The few heavy ships that were available could not be replaced. This meant that the single-ship actions so much in the British naval tradition had to be avoided as much as the Nelsonian decisive battle.

In fact, Skl demanded of its seagoing commanders a mixture of strategic boldness and tactical caution that was difficult for most of them to understand, leading two fleet commanders to resign within the first ten months of the war. Not until Günther Lütjens took the helm did Skl acquire a seagoing commander in chief who seemed to grasp the importance Skl attached to achieving a broader psychological effect through the mere presence of German heavy ships on the open ocean.[34] There is no doubt that the German surface fleet more than fulfilled Skl's expectations in its ability to influence British dispositions: preoccupied

---

[33] Erich Gröner, Dieter Jung, and Martin Maas, *Die deutschen Kriegsschiffe, vol. 4: Hilfsschiffe I: Werkstattschiffe, Tender und Begleitschiffe, Tanker und Versorger* (Koblenz: Bernard und Graefe Verlag, 1985), 169-71.

[34] Salewski, *Die deutsche Seekriegsleitung* 1: 387.

with the threat — real and potential[35] — presented by German heavy ships in home waters, as well as by two to four German warships cruising in the open ocean, the Admiralty kept four to five capital ships in Scapa Flow, along with aircraft carriers, throughout the period of the German naval offensive. Another five to seven battleships were constantly employed on convoy escort — in all, about three-quarters of the British battle fleet and an equal proportion of cruisers, a force many times that which Germany had committed to Atlantic operations.

Not surprisingly, Skl rated the deterrent role of the German surface fleet very highly. Tying up British capital ships and cruisers on convoy duty prevented them from being sent to the Mediterranean, where the Italians were already hard-pressed. More importantly, perhaps, escort duty consumed men and material, putting additional strain on an already fully extended support infrastructure. Moreover, the need to escort the capital ships while they were at sea occupied destroyers that otherwise might have been used as convoy escorts. Finally, the preoccupation of the British battle fleet with the defense of maritime communications prevented the Royal Navy from attacking the German iron ore route along the Norwegian coast or from launching raids against German ports and coastal installations, such as occurred later in the war. (The first British carrier raids on the Norwegian coast did not occur until July 1941, *after* the sinking of the *Bismarck* had brought an end to the surface campaign.)

Thus, if the German surface fleet perhaps was not, as Skl believed, "capable of working the strongest strategic influence upon the course of the war as a whole," the German naval leadership had some justification for their belief that it was the one weapon "whose strength the enemy fears above all else."[36] Such was the impression made by *Bismarck*, Germany's most famous battleship, upon the minds of Churchill and the Admiralty that the continued existence of her sister ship *Tirpitz* worked a powerful influence upon British dispositions, particularly in the crucial winter of 1941-42. The opening of a third front in the Pacific meant that

---

[35] Throughout most of 1940 the Admiralty believed the German naval construction program to be more advanced that it actually was and took precautions against potential deployments by ships that were not yet complete, and in some cases never were. Apart from the extant active German warships, as of 27 March 1940, for example, the Admiralty believed that *Bismarck* was all but ready for sea (in fact, she did not leave the builder's yard until September) and that the (never completed) aircraft carrier *Graf Zeppelin* had already begun her sea trials and could be expected to deploy anytime after 1 April 1940. PRO ADM 1/10617.

[36] *Denkschrift des Chef der Seekriegsleitung vom 10.1.43*, T1022/reel 3467/PG 33959, National Archives, Washington D.C.

there were too few capital ships to go around, largely because a high proportion of them were held in home waters or the North Atlantic in anticipation of a possible German breakout. Indirectly at least, the German surface fleet thus may be said to have contributed to the Singapore disaster and the sinking of the *Prince of Wales* and *Repulse*. Finally, Skl scored at least one significant, if isolated, coup: in late February and March 1941, with the Royal Navy preoccupied with searching for German surface ships in the North Atlantic, the Western Mediterranean was denuded of British naval forces. It was then that Erwin Rommel and the *Afrika Korps* were transported, unmolested, across the Mediterranean to North Africa.[37]

Significantly greater results might have been achieved had Skl been able to coordinate surface ship actions with those of the *Luftwaffe* and the U-boat arm. The lack of an indigenous air arm meant that U-boats and surface ships alike were dependent upon inadequate numbers of shore-based *Luftwaffe* aircraft for air reconnaissance, while the inability to coordinate the actions of the two arms of the *Kriegsmarine* considerably eased the task of British convoy escorts.

Simultaneous attacks by U-boats and surface ships in the Atlantic occurred (almost serendipitously) on two occasions. On 11 February 1941 the heavy cruiser *Admiral Hipper* sank one merchant ship after being directed to the area of a dispersed North Atlantic convoy by signals from Flag Officer U-Boats in Lorient.[38] One month later, on the night of 8-9 March, Lütjens, with *Scharnhorst* and *Gneisenau*, encountered a north-bound convoy, SL 67, in the Cape Verde narrows. Deterred from attacking the convoy by its heavy escort — which included the battleship *Malaya* and a number of destroyers (some of which were incorrectly identified as cruisers) — Lütjens chose to act as contact holder, broadcast-ing position reports to bring U-boats into attack. While *Scharnhorst* and *Gneisenau* drew off the convoy's escort, U-boats sank five steamers and forced the convoy to disperse.[39]

On neither occasion were combined attacks possible, because German surface ships were unable to communicate directly with the U-boats in the vicinity: Lütjens' signals had to be relayed via Berlin! A combined operation with U-boats, surface ships, and aircraft was not attempted until July 1942 in the attack on convoy PQ 17. On that occasion the mere presence of German heavy ships in the general area of a convoy under

---

[37] Reinicke, "German Surface Force Strategy in World War II," 186.

[38] Whitley, *German Cruisers*, 115.

[39] Peter Handel-Mazzetti, "The *Scharnhorst-Gneisenau* Team at Its Peak," United States Naval Institute *Proceedings* (1956): 138.

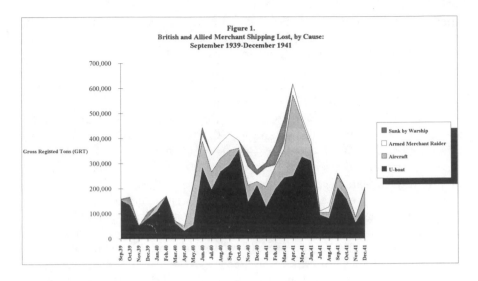

Figure 1.
British and Allied Merchant Shipping Lost, by Cause:
September 1939-December 1941

air and submarine attack was enough to cause the escort to be with-drawn, leaving the hapless merchant ships to be nearly annihilated by U-boats and land-based bombers.

Thus, despite the prewar planning and preparation, the German campaign with surface ships remained an isolated series of events in the war at sea. German conduct of an Atlantic campaign in three dimensions mirrored the polycratic structure of the Third Reich as a whole. In the *Kriegsmarine's* overlapping command structure and the incipient rivalry with the *Luftwaffe* may be found, writ small, the multiple, competing fiefdoms and struggles between petty party bureaucrats that sapped the strength of Germany's war effort and helped to prevent the Nazi leadership from attaining its goal of global conquest.

At bottom, however, the character of the German naval offensive was defined not so much by this fact, or its various components, as by its underlying conception. Skl's "psychological" strategy of dispersion and disruption was — and could be — no more than a holding action fought against the superior maritime power of the Royal Navy. Moreover, members of the German Naval War Staff simply had no understanding of the enormity of the total war in which they were engaged — a failing they most certainly shared with their colleagues in the *Luftwaffe* and the army, not to mention their Führer and supreme commander. Although the resiliency of Britain's 1940-41 maritime infrastructure would be difficult to measure, the judgment of the Chief of the Kaiser's Naval Staff,

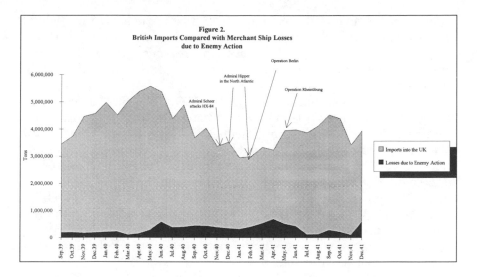

Figure 2.
British Imports Compared with Merchant Ship Losses
due to Enemy Action

Admiral Henning von Holtzendorff, may be taken as a starting point. In 1916 he estimated that the destruction of 600,000 tons of shipping a month for six consecutive months would drive Great Britain out of the war.[40] In the spring and summer of 1917 the Imperial Navy came close to achieving this goal with U-boats alone (3,765,758 tons sunk in six months — an average of 627,626 tons per month), but ultimately failed.[41] In 1940-41 the *Kriegsmarine* and *Luftwaffe* together not only sank fewer ships overall[42] but fell short of the Imperial Navy's success in sustained sinkings, approximating Holtzendorff's criterion for victory on only two widely separated occasions: June 1940 (585,496 tons sunk) and April 1941 (687,901 tons sunk). At the height of the naval offensive, German surface warships were able to harass British convoy traffic for a few months and disrupt it for several weeks, but at no point were Britain's overseas communications in danger of being severed irrevocably, nor did either U-boats or surface ships approach the level of success achieved in World War I, when Great Britain was in real danger of starvation. Moreover, the

---

[40] Tarrant, *U-Boat Offensive*, 44.

[41] Ibid., 58.

[42] Between March and December 1917 (over a period of ten months, the height of the first campaign), German U-boats accounted for 5,303,267 tons of British, Allied, and neutral shipping. Between October 1940 and June 1941 (nine months), German U-boats, aircraft, and surface ships sank a total of 4,062,575 tons. See Tarrant, *U-Boat Offensive*, 58; Roskill *War at Sea* 1: 615-18.

inability of Britain's west coast harbors to handle the import traffic that
was arriving muted the impact of the German naval offensive. In the
winter of 1940-41, the backlog was such that cargoes and merchant ships
equal in tonnage to those being sunk on the high seas were trapped in
British ports, waiting to be unloaded.[43]

Again, the strategic conception of the Naval War Staff may be contrasted with that of the U-boat high command. Dönitz significantly overestimated Germany's industrial potential and capability to win the war
at sea, but he correctly understood it to be a war between economies, one
that could only be won by attacking the industrial strength of the enemy
at its source. Therein lay the reasoning behind the strategy of the tonnage
war.[44] By comparison with this grim vision of destruction, the ambitions
of the Naval War Staff seem hopelessly unrealistic, reflecting attitudes
towards naval warfare passed down from the seventeenth century. Yet
even three hundred years ago, it was not "the taking of individual ships
or convoys" that was decisive, but:

> . . . the possession of that overbearing power upon the sea which drives
> the enemy's flag from it, or allows it to appear only as a fugitive; and
> which, by controlling the great common, closes the highways by which
> commerce moves to and from the enemy's shores.[45]

In first half of the twentieth century, the fully mobilized war economy of
the British Empire was still capable of sustaining the kind of maritime
supremacy of which Mahan wrote. In the winter and spring of 1941 this
truth was evident in the British ability to bear losses, the growing
numbers of convoy escorts, the toughness and endurance of the Royal
Navy in the face of determined attacks on the convoy system, and in the
bombs raining down on German warships in harbor.

---

[43] C.B.A. Behrens, *Merchant Shipping and the Demands of War* (London: HMSO, 1955),
128.

[44] Maier, *Germany and the Second World War 2*: 349.

[45] Alfred Thayer Mahan, *The Influence of Sea Power upon History, 1660-1783* (Boston:
Little, Brown and Company, 1908), 138.

7

The U.S. Navy and Operation
Roll of Drums, 1942

Robert W. Love, Jr.

The reasons for the success of the German Navy's Operation *Roll of Drums (Drumbeat)* in 1942 remain one of the most controversial aspects of the U.S. Navy's conduct of the Second World War.[1] Previous accounts have failed to place *Roll of Drums* within the context of American global strategy, competing theater demands, or institutional history.[2]

The September 1939 German proclamation of a blockade of Allied trade, to be enforced by submarines, neither surprised nor alarmed the British Admiralty or the U.S. Navy Department. The German Navy's employment of U-boats to implement a commerce raiding strategy against Allied merchant shipping in declared war zones off France, around the British Isles, and in the Mediterranean had been a major feature of the naval aspect of the Great War; Kaiser Wilhelm's authorization of "unrestricted submarine warfare" in January 1917 brought the United States into the European conflict, and both London and Washington viewed the successful Anglo-American campaign to thwart the enemy offensive as an important contribution to the November 1918 Allied victory.[3] What impressed both British and American naval

---

[1] Robert W. Love, Jr., "Admiral King, Operation 'Roll of Drums', and the Historians: What Really Happened off the East Coast in Early 1942?," paper presented at the Annual Meeting of the Society for Military History, Fredericksburg, Virginia, 10 April 1992.

[2] Recent examples of this tradition include Homer H. Hickham, Jr., *Torpedo Junction* (Annapolis: Naval Institute Press, 1989); and James T. Cheatham, *The Atlantic Turkey Shoot: U-Boats off the Outer Banks in World War II* (Greenville, North Carolina: Williams and Simpson, 1990).

[3] Robert W. Love, Jr., *History of the United States Navy*, 2 vols., (Harrisburg, PA: Stackpole Books, 1992), vol. 1, chs. 28-30.

men about the German campaign was that, even though Allied naval headquarters appeared to react slowly in instituting a convoy system and undertaking escort-of-convoy operations by ocean escort groups in early 1917, the costly German offensive failed. In 1917-1918, German U-boat operations did not isolate Britain, significantly reduce her imports, exports, or industrial production, drive London to the peace table, or prevent the American Expeditionary Force from safely reaching its French ports of debarkation.[4] From the U.S. Navy's viewpoint, moreover, the German's mid-1918 submarine minelaying campaign off the northeastern Atlantic coast of the U.S. was an embarrassing, desperate, and ultimately futile operation that resulted in the loss of relatively little shipping tonnage.[5]

The Navy Department watched, and the Admiralty watched much more attentively, the German naval renaissance after 1934 with trepidation, but neither London nor Washington focused on the rebirth of the U-boat arm. The Admiralty faced threats from German capital ships in the North Sea, the Italian Navy in the Mediterranean, and the Japanese Navy in the Far East. Reasoning that if the Royal Navy's Home Fleet could not command the North Sea then nothing else mattered, the Admiralty's building policy aimed increasingly at that objective to the exclusion of others. Nonetheless, the Admiralty made plans to implement an escort-of-convoy strategy for some merchant shipping at the onset of hostilities, confident that this approach would succeed, as it had in 1917-1918, owing to the small number of U-boats in the German fleet, the short cruising radius of most of those vessels, and the great distances from the German Navy's submarine bases on the Baltic to the Western Approaches to the British Isles. The Admiralty also placed great faith in its secret ASDIC, or echo-ranging sonar, system, which endowed an escort with a vastly more accurate means of locating an opposing submerged submarine than the primitive World War I-era hydrophones.[6]

For its part, the Navy Department paid little heed to the growth of

---

[4] For various analyses of the U.S. Navy's response to the German offensive of 1917-18, see Kenneth J. Hagan, *This People's Navy* (New York: Free Press, 1991), 296; Tracy B. Kittredge, *Naval Lessons of the Great War* (New York: Doubleday, 1921); Love, *History* 1: 500. Gary E. Weir, *Building American Submarines* (Washington D.C.: Government Printing Office, 1991).

Comparing the strategic dilemmas of 1917-1918 and 1942-43 is a staple of accounts of the 1939-45 Battle of the Atlantic. See, for example John Terraine, *The U-Boat Wars: 1916-1945* (New York: G. P. Putnam's Sons, 1989), 413; Correlli Barnett, *Engage the Enemy More Closely: The Royal Navy in the Second World War* (New York: Norton, 1991), 441-42. Both sources suggest that the U.S. Navy learned nothing from the World War I experience.

[5] Love, *History* 1: 507-10.

[6] Barnett, *Engage the Enemy*, 45.

the U-boat arm for different reasons. The first derived from the repeated declarations of President Franklin D. Roosevelt and Secretary of State Cordell Hull that the United States would not participate in another general European war.[7] The various neutrality measures, proposed by the president and passed by Congress over little opposition, carved this policy into American law. Regardless of their personal political sympathies, navy men accepted these declarations as guideposts for naval policy. The second reason was the Navy Department's overriding concern with the Japanese. Once Tokyo suggested, in 1934, that Japan would not renegotiate the 1922 Five Power Treaty on terms acceptable to the United States, American naval building policy aimed at realizing the goal of a "treaty fleet" so as to restore the 1922 treaty ratios in all types of major combatants. So closely related were these issues to the mission of defending the Philippine Commonwealth — which was, after all, American territory — that Pacific defense overshadowed any serious conside-ration of German naval rearmament until the president signaled a major shift in foreign policy after the Munich Conference in September 1938.[8]

Hard upon the dismemberment of Czechoslovakia, the Joint Army-Navy Board instructed its subordinate War Plans Committee to consider American strategy in the event of a global conflict pitting the Anti-Comintern Powers — Germany, Italy, and Japan — against a coalition composed of Britain, France, Soviet Russia, and the United States.[9] Of the resulting RAINBOW Plans, only RAINBOW FIVE envisioned an American strategy of "Germany-first" in which the navy's primary mission might be in the Atlantic theater of operations.[10]

Even as navy planners looked more frequently at the Atlantic as a likely theater of operations, naval strategy remained rooted in the Pacific conundrum, and that strategy drove doctrine. Because most Japanese submarines had a short cruising radius and exercised with the battleships during prewar fleet exercises, U.S. Navy analysts correctly reasoned that

[7] Robert W. Love, Jr., "From Neutrality to Belligerence: New Evidence on American Military and Naval Preparations for World War II," paper presented at a meeting of the World War II Studies Association, National Archives, Washington, D.C., 28 May 1993.

[8] Lawrence Pratt, "The Anglo-American Naval Conversations on the Far East of January 1938," *International Affairs* (1971): 749-54; Entry, for 13 Dec. 1937, Diary of Admiral William D. Leahy, Leahy Mss, Manuscript Division, Library of Congress (hereafter LC).

[9] "Report of the Planning Committee," 21 April 1939, Joint Board of the Army and the Navy, section 3, serial 634, Record Group 225, National Archives, Washington, D.C. (hereafter RG 225,NA)..

[10] The other RAINBOW Plans envisioned U.S. Navy operations almost entirely in the Pacific or Atlantic home waters. John Major, "The Navy Plans for War," in Kenneth J. Hagan, ed., *In Peace and War*, 2d ed. (Westport, CT: Greenwood Press, 1984), 246.

the Japanese Navy eschewed a commerce-raiding strategy and intended instead to concentrate its attacks on opposing capital ships and cruisers. This led U.S. Navy tacticians to perfect systems and doctrine to screen heavy combatants, while improving escort-of-convoy doctrine was limited to the problem of defending the movements of small formations of rearward Fleet Train auxiliaries and troop transports. Like the Admiralty, the Navy Department assessed the development of its own, highly secret echo-ranging sonar system as endowing the defending escort ship with a critical, perhaps decisive, technological edge over an opposing submarine.[11]

The transformation of the naval war against Germany from a replay of 1917-1918, which the admiralties anticipated, into the struggle Prime Minister Winston Churchill labelled the Battle of the Atlantic, resulted not from any Allied strategic misappreciation, but rather from the entirely unexpected German conquest of Norway, her defeat of the Belgian, French, and British air forces and armies in May 1940, and the surrender of France in June. The establishment of the German Air Force on the Norwegian coast underlined the need for the British to maintain a powerful, well-escorted Home Fleet at Scapa Flow capable of commanding the North Sea, while the new German Air Force bases in Belgium and northern France by themselves endangered British shipping in the Channel and the Western Approaches. But the real enhancement to German naval power resulting from the French surrender derived from the German occupation and development of the naval bases on the Bay of Biscay. The deployment of German Air Force units to the coast not only made credible the invasion threat but also made possible air attacks on British ports and shipping in home waters and, in 1941, ill-coordinated combined air-sea arms attacks on inbound and outbound British merchant convoys.

Roosevelt's response to the outbreak of war in Europe moved the Navy Department to consider measures to wage a two-ocean war. On 6 September 1939, only hours after Britain declared war on Germany, he directed the State Department to proclaim a Neutrality Zone, bounded by a line three hundred miles seaward of coasts of the nations of North and Central America and the Caribbean, in which belligerent naval operations were prohibited, and ordered Admiral Harold R. Stark, the Chief of

---

[11] Barnett, *Engage the Enemy*, 45. Barnett's criticism supposed that British and American naval men expected wartime antisubmarine and submarine technology to remain static. More likely, they expected that the levels of both technologies would rise and that echo-ranging sonar would prove decisive. They were, of course, essentially correct.

Naval Operations, to establish a Neutrality Patrol to enforce this policy.[12] Practice differed from declared policy, however. Roosevelt instructed Stark to order Rear Admiral Alfred Johnson's Atlantic Squadron, reinforced to accomplish its new mission, to locate German merchant ships in the Neutrality Zone, broadcast their positions in plain English, and trail them until they were intercepted, seized, or sunk by Royal Navy patrols. The first Neutrality Patrol operations convinced Stark that the fleet was short of rugged destroyers, so he quickly asked Congress for funds to recommission and modernize over one hundred mothballed, World War I-era four-stack destroyers, ships the navy had regarded in the 1930s as a reserve escort force. This work was scarcely underway when, during the Battle for France, Churchill asked Roosevelt for the "loan" of some destroyers for the hard-pressed Royal Navy, an appeal that led in September 1940 to the controversial Destroyer Deal.[13]

By then, the Navy's War Plans Division was fully committed to a "Germany-first" strategy, even proposing in May to shift most of the U.S. Fleet, then based at Pearl Harbor, to the Atlantic should Britain collapse following the French surrender.[14] Next, in mid-June, Captain Charles M. Cooke of the War Plans Division persuaded Admiral Stark to ask Congress for an emergency authorization measure, known as the Two-Ocean Navy Act, and a supplemental appropriation to pay for the first installment.[15] Stark formally codified this grand strategy in his November 1940 "Plan Dog" Memorandum, and Roosevelt approved of this approach in conversations with Stark.[16]

The adoption of the "Germany-first" strategy led the CNO to re-establish the Atlantic Fleet, disestablished in 1922, and to call for staff talks with representatives of the British Chiefs of Staff Committee with the objective of formulating a wartime grand strategy for the emerging Anglo-American coalition.[17] When Admiral Ernest J. King assumed command of the Atlantic Fleet on 1 February 1941, a delegation from London was already in Washington negotiating with an army-navy team

---

[12] Patrick Abbazia, *Mr. Roosevelt's Navy* (Annapolis, MD: Naval Institute Press, 1975), 61-81; B. Mitchell Simpson, "Harold Raynsford Stark," in Robert W. Love, Jr., ed., *The Chiefs of Naval Operations* (Annapolis MD: Naval Institute Press, 1980), 109-36.

[13] Simpson, "Harold Raynsford Stark," 122-23.

[14] Captain Russell Crenshaw [Director WPD] to CNO, 17 June 1940, Signed Letters, Box 79, Series 4, Strategic Plans Collection, Operational Archives, Naval Historical Center, Washington Navy Yard Washington D.C.(hereafter OA, NHC).

[15] Major, "Navy Plans for War," 250-51.

[16] Stark explained the implications of Plan Dog in Stark to Ghormley, 16 Nov. 1940, Anglo-American Relations 1940-41, Misc. Items, Box 5, Stark Mss, NHC.

[17] Report on British-United States Staff Conferences, 29 Jan-March 1941, US-UK Conversation Reports, January-March 1941, Box 118, Strategic Plans Collection, OA, NHC.

representing the Joint Board.[18] The product of these talks, ABC-1, divided the Atlantic into two "areas of strategic responsibility" and broadly defined the missions of the new Atlantic Fleet.[19] King incorporated these missions into his first Atlantic Fleet Operating Plans.[20] To implement ABC-1 and the various Lant Fleet OpPlans, Admiral Stark proposed increasing the Atlantic Fleet from fewer than 60 ships in February to over 175 units in December by transferring ships from the Pacific Fleet and assigning newly commissioned combatants to King's command.[21]

Neither the British nor the Americans had much experience with the unique challenge of transatlantic escort-of-convoy operations, and both started in effect from scratch in the spring of 1941. The breakout of the battleship *Bismarck*, and the commerce raiding operations of the *Admiral Scheer*, the *Hipper*, and others, led the First Sea Lord, Admiral of the Fleet Sir Dudley Pound, to order that the first transatlantic escort groups include a capital ship or heavy cruiser, and Admiral King's early LantFleet OpPlans[22] This was overly expensive, and British ocean escort groups consisted mostly of destroyers and frigate- and corvette-type vessels. What made possible the inauguration of transatlantic convoys in May 1941 was the deployment of three British escort groups to Hvalfjordur, Iceland and the establishment of the Royal Canadian Navy's Newfoundland Escort Force operating out of St. Johns.[23] As for the U.S. Navy, not only was the Atlantic Fleet unready to participate in escort-of-convoy operations but also Roosevelt was unwilling, probably

---

[18] A.T. Cornwall-Jones, Secretary to the UK Delegation, "Report on British-US Staff Conversations, 21st Meeting," 27 Feb. 1941, US-UK Conversation Reports, Jan-March 1941, Box 118, Strategic Plans Collection, OA, NHC.

[19] In light of subsequent events, it is ironic that the British naval delegation to the ABC staff talks proposed wording that would have, in effect, made the U. S. Navy responsible for the entire Atlantic theater. Annex V of the British-United States Staff Conversations Report, 1941, "Coordination of Command Between the Fighting Services of the Associated Powers," ibid.

[20] "CinCLant Administrative History," no. 138, 1946, *Administrative Histories of World War II*, vol. 1, 141-43, Library, NHC.

[21] DirWPD to CNO, 2 April 1941, Signed Letters April 1941, Box 81, Series 4, Strategic Plans Collection, OA, NHC; CinCLant to OpNav, 25 April 1941, File: CinCLant, Box 61, RG 38, NA.

[22] Captain Francis B. Low, "Report on Ocean Escort in the Western Atlantic," 1 April 1941, Box 1, King Mss, OA, NHC. For all LantFleet OpPlans for 1941-42, see Box 147K, Series 9, Strategic Plans Collection, OA, NHC.

[23] When organized, the Newfoundland Escort Force consisted of thirty-one British destroyers, nine sloops, and twenty-nine Canadian corvettes. "The completion of end-to-end A/S escort in the North Atlantic was only possible with the commissioning of sufficient numbers of Canadian corvettes," according to Marc Milner, *North Atlantic Run* (Annapolis, MD: Naval Institute Press, 1985).

for reasons of domestic politics, to take that step; as an alternative, he ordered the Coast Guard to transfer ten modern cutters to the Royal Navy under the Lend-Lease Act, an arrangement completed on 30 April 1941. Anxious to suspend the futile Neutrality Patrols, Roosevelt instead approved a proposal by Stark and King to inaugurate mid-Atlantic "sweeps" by task forces built around battleships and heavy cruisers.[24] Clearly an interim measure offering no clear military benefit, these sweeps bridged the gap in Atlantic Fleet activity between the conclusion of the Neutrality Patrols and the inauguration of U.S. Navy participation in escort-of-convoy operations.

Roosevelt's decision to extend Lend-Lease military assistance to Soviet Russia hard upon the German invasion in June 1941 led directly to the order to undertake Atlantic escort-of-convoy operations under the terms of ABC-1. Despite significant losses in the Mediterranean that spring, by June the Royal Navy and the rapidly enlarged Royal Canadian Navy had organized an efficient escort-of-convoy system for merchant shipping. This, and the adoption of an evasive routing strategy resting on Ultra radio intelligence, dramatically increased the safety of the Atlantic convoys.[25] However, the Admiralty did not have enough escorts to continue operations in the Mediterranean, conduct transatlantic escort-of-convoy operations, and defend the passage of Anglo-American Lend-Lease convoys on the new North Russia route from Iceland to Murmansk.[26] The president therefore authorized admirals Stark and King to prepare the Atlantic Fleet to conduct escort-of-convoy operations.[27] A shortage of American destroyers and complex negotiations with London and Naval Service Headquarters, Ottawa, concerning strategic areas, tactical command, and convoy organization and routing delayed the initiation of Atlantic Fleet escort-of-convoy operations until 17 September, when a Support Force task group rendezvoused with convoy HX 150 one

---

[24] The British asked for more destroyers, and Roosevelt considered it. Unlike the 1940 Destroyer Deal, however, the Navy opposed additional destroyer transfers. DirWPD to CNO, 14 Mar 1941, A3-1/DD, CNO Secret Records, RG 80, NA. A brief summary of the Atlantic Fleet plan to join the transatlantic convoy system appears in [Secretary of the Navy Frank] Knox to Roosevelt, 20 Mar 1941, Box 1, King Mss, OA, NHC. See also Entry, 25 March 1941, Stark Diary, Box 4, Stark Mss, NHC; F.B. Low, "Report on Ocean Escort in Western Atlantic," 1 April 1941, Box 1, King Papers, OA, NHC; and Abbazia, *Mr. Roosevelt's Navy*, 174.

[25] Barnett, *Engage the Enemy*, 276-77.

[26] Robert W. Love, Jr., "U. S. Naval Strategy and the Murmansk Run," paper presented at an international conference on the "North Russia Convoys in World War II," sponsored by the Center for Military History and the RoskomArchiv, Moscow, Russia, 17-20 February 1993.

[27] Waldo Heinrichs, *Threshold of War* (New York: Oxford University Press, 1988), 146-79.

hundred and fifty miles south of Newfoundland.[28] Before the Japanese attacked Pearl Harbor, Atlantic Fleet ocean escort groups defended the passage of several large, fast convoys steaming between Halifax and the Mid-Ocean Meeting Point (MOMP) south of Iceland. Building on British and Canadian experience, Atlantic Fleet and OpNav's Convoy and Routing Division assembled a formidable body of information on a wide variety of topics.[29] Thus, when the U.S. declared war on Germany in December, the navy possessed a remarkably detailed escort-of-convoy doctrine.[30]

Having lost confidence in the CNO Stark as a result of the Pearl Harbor debacle, Secretary of the Navy Frank Knox proposed that Admiral King become the Washington-based Commander in Chief of the U.S. Fleet (CominCh); Stark would remain as CNO. CominCh would plan and conduct fleet, joint, and combined operations, and CNO would superintend the shore establishment, logistics, and shipbuilding, and deal with the British. Although Knox had failed to specify whether CominCh was subordinate to CNO or vice versa, Roosevelt quickly agreed to this confusing arrangement on 14 December, and King arrived in Washington a week later to assume his new duties.[31] During 1941, Commander, North American Coastal Frontier [CNACF], Vice Admiral Adolphus Andrews, had reported to CinCLant as a task force commander. Headquartered in New York, CNACF was responsible for the seaward defenses of the East

---

[28] Heinrichs was the first historian to observe that Roosevelt instructed the Navy to inaugurate escort-of-convoy operations in July, but that locating enough destroyers and integrating Atlantic Fleet escort groups into an existing transatlantic convoy system delayed the implementation of the plan. Waldo Heinrichs, "President Franklin D. Roosevelt's Intervention in the Battle of the Atlantic, 1941," *Diplomatic History* 10 (Fall 1986): 311-32.

[29] For a detailed history of the development of Atlantic Fleet doctrine between September and December 1941, see Brian Hussey, "The Neutrality Patrol, the Atlantic Fleet, and Escort-of-Convoy Operations, 1939-1941," TRIDENT Scholar Paper, 305 pp., Special Collections, Nimitz Library, U.S. Naval Academy, Annapolis MD.

[30] This argument conflicts with the traditional assertion that the British had the "answer" and spoon-fed the Americans. See, for example, ComDesLant "Anti-Submarine Bulletins," first issued on 24 Nov 1941, Box 254, RG 38, NA. Also see "Escort of Convoy Bulletin[s]," Box 254, RG 38, NA. ComTF Four to TF Four, 2 Jan. 1942, "COM Task Force 24", Box 6, Series II, Rear Admiral Paul R. Heineman Mss, OA, NHC; King, "Subj: ASW Tactics," File A16-3(20), Box 324, CinCLant Flag Files, RG 313, NARA (Suitland, MD).

[31] At times King complained about the lack of differentiation between the two jobs. See King to Cooke, 7 Jan. 1942, Cooke Papers, Hoover Institution, Stanford, CA (hereafter Cooke Mss.); King to Stark, 20 Jan. 1942, Box 1, King Mss, NHC. Some years later, however, King told the co-author of his memoirs, Walter Muir Whitehill, that he and Stark "were in good agreement. 'I stayed on my own side of the job, but we met almost every day. Sometimes went down to see him and sometimes he came up to see me.'" Whitehill, "Admiral Stark," 4 July 50, Box 4, Whitehill-Buehl Mss, Naval War College, Newport RI (hereafter NWC).

Coast from Maine to Florida; for his operating forces, he looked to the commandants of the 1st, 3rd, and 5th Naval Districts, administrative commands — whose main business was industrial, shipyard management, and training. On 1 February, CNACF was renamed Commander, Eastern Sea Frontier, and new Gulf Sea Frontier and Caribbean Sea Frontier command were activated; the Gulf Sea Frontier drew its operating forces from the 7th and 8th Naval Districts, the Caribbean Sea Frontier, from the 10th Naval District.[32] The approaches to the Panama Canal were defended by the Panama Sea Frontier, which drew its operating forces from the 15th Naval District.[33] The Naval Districts, in turn, organized Local Defense Forces to conduct offshore patrols, minelaying, minesweeping, and search and rescue operations. Admiral King shifted CNACF to CominCh when he moved to Washington, but the Naval Districts continued to report to CNO. Because no minelaying work had been undertaken while the United States was neutral, the Naval Districts' Local Defense Forces hurriedly identified safe entrances to harbors, ports, bays, and inlets, erected net and boom defenses at those entrances, and laid antisubmarine minefields.[34]

The appearance of U-boats off the East Coast in January 1942, known as Operation *Roll of Drums*, scarcely surprised navy leaders who had already been wrestling with the Battle of the Atlantic for over a year.[35] The War Plans Division had expressed concern as early as March 1941,

---

[32] "Naval Coastal and Local Defense Vessels," 7 February 1942, Folder No. 169: VCNO, Box 1942, CominCh-CNO Double Zero Records, NHC.

[33] Commander Robert W. Morse to Rear Admiral R. K. Turner [Director, WPD], 14 Jan. 1942, subj: Antiaircraft Defenses of Panama Canal, 15th Naval District (Navy Yard), Box 104, vol. 1: 1919-1947, Strategic Plans Collection, OA, NHC.

[34] [Rear Admiral Richard] Edwards [Deputy Chief of Staff, CominCh] to CNO, 12 Jan. 1942, File F-30, Captain F. S. Low, Box 25, RG 38, NA.

[35] Their seeming inaction, however, is often criticized. Michael Gannon, in *Operation Drumbeat: The Dramatic True Story of Germany's First U-Boat Attacks Along the American Coast in World War II* (New York: Harper and Row, 1990), asserts that Admiral King concentrated Support Force destroyers along the Atlantic seaboard but then failed to send them out to intercept *U 123* (Hardegan). "Ernest King's irresolution in the face of Reinhard Hardegan's ruthlessness," says Gannon, "laid American open to the greatest maritime massacre in her history." See Gannon, *Drumbeat*, 189, 237, 240. British historian Martin Middlebrook, wrote that "the way the American autorities reacted [to Operation *Roll of Drums*] seems, in retrospect, to be almost criminal. Despite the fact that there had been an American Naval Mission at the Admiralty since August 1940 and that the members of the Mission had studied every development of Britain's U-boat war, the United States Navy seemed determined not to follow British methods. No attempt was made to form convoys, and the few available antisubmarine vessels were sent on offensive sweeps that the British had found such a waste of time." See Martin Middlebrook, *Convoy* (New York: Morrow, 1976), 16.

and Admiral King specifically warned in December that enemy submarines would appear soon off the Atlantic seaboard.[36] On 9 January 1942, CominCh informed CNACF that Ultra intercepts provided "strong indications that 16 German submarines are proceeding to the area off the southeast coast of Newfoundland," but admitted that "the object of this operation is not understood."[37] Meanwhile, Churchill, Admiral Pound, and a large British military delegation had arrived in Washington to discuss grand strategy and Lend-Lease with the president and his service chiefs at the Arcadia Conference.[38] Concern about the imminent arrival of U-boats off the East Coast did not overshadow the naval discussions at Arcadia.[39] Broad strategic and industrial policy, the collapse of the Allied position in Southeast Asia and the Western Pacific, and a proposal to land an Anglo-American army in French North Africa occupied most of their time.[40] Decisions made by the president and prime minister to

---

[36] Indeed, Rear Admiral Richmond K. Turner, the Director of the War Plans Division, argued against an additional transfer of destroyers to the Royal Navy owing to his concern for the defense of Atlantic coast shipping. DirWPD to COO, 14 Mar 1941, Box 81, Strategic Plans Collection, OA, NHC.

[37] Cominch to ComESF, 7 Jan. 1942, msg in the War Diary of the Eastern Sea Frontier, p. 62, Navy Department Library, NHC.

[38] Most of the purely naval talks among Pound, Stark, and King concerned allocations to the Royal Navy under the Lend-Lease program of ships of several types, including Destroyer Escorts, and various types of naval aircraft. The result of these negotiations revised downward the numbers of warships, including escorts, and auxiliaries being built on "British account" under the U.S. Navy's portion of the September 1941 "Victory Program" and the January 1942 "1799 Ship Program." See R.N. Dorling, "The Supply Mission: History of the British Admiralty Delegation in Washington," p. 24, ADM 199/1236, Public Record Office (hereafter PRO), Kew, London, United Kingdom; and FDR to Knox, c. 10 Jan 42, Box 5, "Navy," President's Safe File, Franklin D. Roosevelt Mss, Roosevelt Library, Hyde Park, NY (hereafter PSF, FDR Mss).

[39] Many historians criticized prewar navy leaders for not building a large force of austere escorts prior to 1941. See, for example, Nathan Miller, *The U.S. Navy: An Illustrated History* (New York: American Heritage Publishing, 1977), 332. However, austere escorts lacking antiaircraft defenses could not operate within range of enemy land- or sea-based air, and therefore seemed to have limited utility in a conflict in which the daylight would be dominated tactically by air forces. The Royal Navy's experiences off Dunkirk in 1940 and Crete in 1941 confirmed this assessment. Once Roosevelt committed the fleet to Atlantic escort operations, only conflicting demands delayed the Destroyer Escort program. Indeed, contrary to postwar critics who claimed that the Navy opposed building escorts, Admiral Dorling of the British Admiralty Delegation admitted that the "Navy Department had, however, in the main accepted that a large escort program was vital if the US were to play their full part in the European war . . . ." Dorling, "Report on the British Admiralty Delegation in Washington," PRO ADM 199/1236, p. 34.

[40] For a discussion of the navies' differences on Allied grand strategy, see Robert W. Love, Jr., "Anglo-American Conflict during the Second World War: the U.S. Navy View," at the Annual Meeting of the Conference of Contemporary Historians, Institute for Historical

adopt a "Germany-first" grand strategy, to send U.S. Army troops to Northern Ireland, and to establish a large U.S. Army Air Force in Britain underlined the importance of defending the ongoing transatlantic convoys. Moreover, Roosevelt and Churchill told the service chiefs "that it was highly important that there be no indication of reductions in the shipments to Russia" by the PQ convoys to Murmansk.[41] These decisions effectively increased the call on the Atlantic Fleet's hard-pressed destroyer pool.[42] Within days, the Admiralty asked CominCh to deploy Atlantic Fleet escorts to defend the PQ convoys on the North Russia route. The American declaration of war also meant that the Atlantic Fleet might escort convoys along the length of the transatlantic route, and arrangements for this new system were concluded.

ABC-1 envisioned the creation of an Atlantic Fleet Gibraltar Support Force consisting of three battleships, their screens, and supporting destroyers, but the demand for U. S. Navy destroyers was now so great that Stark and King told Pound they could not implement the plan. The transfer of Pacific Fleet destroyers to the British Eastern Fleet, discussed in several prewar Anglo-American forums, was also abandoned.[43] In accordance with ABC-1, an Atlantic escort group was to be based at Londonderry in Northern Ireland, and this led the First Sea Lord to propose a transatlantic system under which the defending escort groups would remain with the convoys during most of the passage.[44] When the discussions turned to *Roll of Drums*, Pound offered to lend the U.S. Navy ten older, coal-burning trawlers which had been refitted for limited antisubmarine work, but he also wanted to redraw the areas of strategic responsibility, asking that the Atlantic Fleet assume responsibility for all

---

Research, University of London, 10 July 1976, Author's Files.

[41] [General George C.] Marshall [Chief of staff of the Army] to [Colonel Thomas] Handy [Army War Plans Division], 13 Jan. 1942, copy in King Mss, OA, NHC.

[42] Captain B. Belben, R N, to Commander McDowell [U.S. Secretary for Collaboration], 18 Jan. 1942, File A14-1 Convoys, etc., Box 254, RG 38, NA; Pound to Stark, c. 1 Jan. 1942, File No. 31, VCNO, Box 39, Double Zero Files, CominCh-CNO Records, OA, NHC.

[43] There were other, unexpected calls on American destroyers. For instance, shortly after Pearl Harbor the State Department asked for ships' visits to several Latin American capitals. See CominCh to CinCLant, 6 Jan. 1942, File F-30, Captain F.S. Low, Box 25, RG 38, NA.

[44] Basing on Londonderry eliminated the need to transfer convoys from one escort group to another at MOMP, a cumbersome arrangement. These negotiations were very complex, and continued well into January. On the 12th, King noted that the "intention to use Londonderry as eastern terminal for the US (Canadian) escort units - in connection with 'through' convoys - now under discussion." King, note, dtd 16 Jan. 1942, on "Use of Projected U.S. Bases in U.K. by British," 12 Jan. 1942, File A21, Box 261, RG 38, NA.

Allied operations in the South Atlantic.[45] At the time, the Admiralty had also "requested that the CNO might give . . . escort for the [January] PQ convoy" to Murmansk.[46] Finally, Pound proposed a "unified strategic control of the trans-Atlantic convoys under CinCWA [Commander-in-Chief, Western Approaches, Admiral Sir Percy Noble]."[47] Although the Americans rejected this scheme, Pound was not unhappy with the Arcadia talks. "I must say that I hoped to return to London with more 'loot' in the way of flying boats," he told King, "but I do realise your difficulties . . . . I have greatly enjoyed our discussions and feel that we really do understand our mutual problems."[48]

The navy's prewar plan for the Atlantic theater, WPL-46, provided for the defense of the East Coast against an enemy offensive and listed one hundred vessels and craft, large and small, necessary to deal with the threat. When Congress declared war, however, this force was largely on paper. Admiral King was fully aware that Admiral Andrews' entire command operated only thirty-eight vessels of various pedigrees capable of open-ocean steaming, that the seagoing and materiel condition of many of these units was poor, and that the Eastern Sea Frontier simply could not conduct escort-of-convoy operations without additional ships.[49] As for supporting air coverage, Eastern Sea Frontier operated nine patrol planes and six blimps. The Army Air Force's 1st Bomber Command and 1st

---

[45] Meeting minutes, USN-RN, 4 Jan. 1942, PRO ADM 205/19. Admiral King promised to examine the proposal. Later that month he asked Admiral Ingersol to "comment on practicability your TF 3 taking over patrol in Western South Atlantic to which now allocated 2 British cruisers which would thus become available for British use elsewhere and serve to decrease urgent requests being made on US for allocations in other areas." King to Ingersoll, 28 Jan. 1942, Msg 281811, Map Room Messages, FDR Mss.

[46] Belben to McDowell, 18 Jan. 1942, File A14-1, Convoys, etc., Box 254, RG 38, NA.

[47] Pound to King, 29 Jan. 1942, copy in ACNS (T) to Pound, 14 June 42, in PRO ADM 205/21.

[48] Pound to King, 14 Jan. 1942, Memos to/from British - 1942, Box 40, Double Zero Files, CominCh Records, OA, NHC.

[49] As of 7 February 1942, the Eastern Sea Frontier operated a Coastal Force consisting of thirty-one vessels: two PG Gunboats, eight 165-foot PC Subchasers, five PY Yachts, three PE Eagle Boats, and thirteen PYc Coastal Yachts. The Naval Districts reporting to the Eastern Sea Frontier operated a total of seven larger patrol vessels: the 1st Naval District operated a single 110-foot PC Subchaser; the 3rd Naval District operated one 110-foot PC Subchaser; and the 5th Naval District operated five 110-foot PC Subchasers. "Naval Coastal and Local Defense Vessels," 7 February 1942, Folder No. 169: VCNO, Box 1942, CominCh-CNO Double Zero Records, NHC. As to their materiel condition, the Eastern Sea Frontier War Diary pointed out that "few were fit for operations, fewer still for combat." Robert H. Freeman, ed., *The War Offshore: War Diary, Eastern Sea Frontier, January to August 1942* (Ventnor, NJ: Shellback Press, 1988), 15. According to Morison, the World War I-era Eagle Boats were "almost completely useless." Morison, *Naval Operations* 1: 229.

Support Command of the First Air Force were instructed to conduct antisubmarine patrols, but they operated few aircraft, the gear was inadequate for the mission, the air crews were untrained for antisubmarine work, and coordination between the Army Air Force commands and the Naval Districts was weak.[50]

The sinking of the steamer *Cyclops* three hundred miles off Cape Cod on 12 January brought *Roll of Drums* to the fore. Informed navy leaders did not mince words about what their forces faced. "Until the new [coastal escort] PCs begin to get in service," concluded Admiral Royal Ingersoll, who relieved King as commander in chief of the Atlantic Fleet, "I think we are in for a beating from the subs."[51] On the evening of 13 January, Pound and King discussed transferring British escorts to the Eastern Sea Frontier, and the following day the First Sea Lord made a proposal. "Firstly, in view of the United States' needs for the smaller convoy escorts, ten single screw corvettes will be made available to the United States Navy," but the Admiralty wanted to "do this on a basis of" a trade for *Greer*-class destroyers.[52] King was willing to accept the two hundred-ton trawlers and corvettes, but he had no spare destroyers to transfer to the British, and the concept of a unified Atlantic command embodied unacceptable political implications. The matter was thrashed out at a "Convoy and Routing Conference" in Washington on 22 January with Admiral Sir Charles Little, the head of the British Admiralty Delegation. The British "agreed in principle" to CominCh's many suggestions — one of which was to reorganize the transatlantic merchant convoys so as to release "10 U.S. short-legged destroyers" for the "Protection of Atlantic Seaboard Shipping" — except for the "unified

---

[50] According to the Army's official history, Army Air Force "defenses set up in January along the east coast were scanty and improvised." Stetson Conn, *Guarding the United States and Its Outposts* (Washington D.C.: GPO, 1964), 97. The shortage of Navy patrol planes, Army Air Force bombers, and the Army's refusal to endow Admiral Andrews with command authority over the 1st Bomber Command or to allow local cooperation contributed to the success of *Roll of Drums*. However, Admiral King pointed out to Secretary Knox that "how easy it is to underestimate the difficulties of successful air attack on U-boats." King to Knox, "Memorandum on Visit of Air Vice Marshall G. R. Bromet and Captain G. E. Creasy, RN; Naval and Air Co-operation in A/S Warfare," 25 Feb. 1942, Box 1, King Mss, OA, NHC. This helpful document lists air strength on the East Coast and assesses its readiness.

[51] Ingersoll [CinCLant] to [Vice Admiral Arthur] Bristol [Commander, Task Force 4 [Support Force], Atlantic Fleet, 20 Jan. 1942, in "CinCLant Administrative History," No. 138, 1946, *Administrative Histories of World War II*, 1: 279-80.

[52] Pound to King, 14 Jan. 1942, Memos to/from British - 1942, Box 40, Double Zero Files, CominCh Records, NHC.

command" plan, which the Navy Department could not accept.[53] However, releasing these destroyers from the Atlantic Fleet to the Eastern Sea Frontier so that they might form the backbone of a coastal escort-of-convoy system supposed that there would be no additional, unexpected calls on Admiral Ingersoll's Atlantic Fleet destroyer pool and that the British and Canadians would maintain the strength of their ocean escort groups.[54]

By mid-January at the latest, Admiral King was preparing to organize coastal escort-of-convoy operations, but the escorts simply were not available.[55] One week after the "Convoy and Routing Conference," he instructed representatives from the Atlantic Fleet and the sea frontiers to meet at the Navy Department and study the problem. The resulting report was unequivocal. Until the new transatlantic escort-of-convoy plan was implemented, the Atlantic Fleet could not transfer any destroyers to the Eastern Sea Frontier.[56] New constructruction of patrol craft and subchasers, transfers of destroyers from the Atlantic Fleet, and the arrival of the British trawlers and corvettes were the only source of vessels for the necessary coastal escort groups. There was "no prospect of providing extra protection on the [Atlantic] coast except by new construction," King told Admiral Pound in early February.[57]

---

[53] "Memorandum, Conference" 23 Jan. 1942, Box 254, RG 38, NA. See also copy of BAD to Admiralty, 23 Jan. 1942, File A16-1, Cominch Mss, NHC; and ALUSNA, Ottawa, to OpNav, 30 April 1942, "Summary of Naval War Effort," File 2-4-6 Convoy General, Box 257, Convoy and Routing Records, 10th Fleet, OA, NHC. In his reply to Pound's message of 29 Jan. 1942, King reaffirmed they they were in agreement on everything "except for unified command." King to Pound, 2 Feb. 1942, msg 022335, World War II Messages, OA, NHC.

[54] The "redistribution" and more efficient use of escorts, achieved by organizing escort groups capable of defending merchant convoys across most of the transatlantic passage and by adopting more southerly routes, promised to release between ten and sixteen Atlantic Fleet destroyers "for the Atlantic seaboard." ALUSNA Ottawa to ONI, "Canada Naval Operations," 30 April 1942, based on "Summary of Naval War Effort, January 1 to March 31, 1942," issued by RCN NSHQ, File 2-4-6 Convoy General, Box 257, Convoy and Routing Records, 10th Fleet Records, NHC; and King to Pound, 24. Jan 1942, copy in ACNS [T] to Pound, 14 June 1942, PRO ADM 205/19.

[55] See, for instance, Walter Muir Whitehill, "Atlantic Fleet Matters, 1941, Notes on Conversation with Admiral King," 29 Aug. 1949, Whitehill Mss, NHC.

[56] Maurice Matloff and Edwin Snell, *Strategic Planning for Coalition Warfare: 1941-1942* (Washington: GPO, 1960), 1: 146.

[57] King felt that the "antisubmarine vessel program must be given the highest priority and must be maintained in that priority, even if it is necessary to reduce or postpone the construction of 'Liberty ships' or similar vessels to accomplish this end." King to JCS, 15 june 1942, File: FF1/A1-3, Serial 00497, CominCh NHC. See also King to Pound, 7 Feb. 1942, msg 071705, CominCh, World War II Messages, OA, NHC; copy in "Memo on Control of Shipping in North Atlantic, Jan-June, 1942," ACNS(T) to FSL, 14 June 1942, PRO ADM 205/21.

Grand strategy and military emergency now confounded theater naval strategy owing to this shortage of escorts. Plan Dog envisioned an Allied return to the continent, and ABC-1 provided for the deployment of U.S. Army and Army Air Forces to the United Kingdom soon after Congress declared war. In addition, the army had promised to relieve the marine garrison on Iceland, which had to be supplied in any case. Roosevelt and Churchill agreed to these dispositions at the Arcadia Conference and directed that a large Army Air Force be established in the British Isles; General Marshall identified the first large army troop movements to Iceland on New Year's Day. A few days later, army and navy planners scheduled convoy AT. 10, the first large transatlantic army troop convoy.[58] Knowing it to be "politically unwise not to send U.S. troops to Ulster," the president told the Joint Chiefs on 3 February to ship another 5,200 soldiers to Iceland and 9,000 men to Ireland in convoy AT. 12, scheduled to sail in mid-February. More transatlantic troop movements to Iceland and Ireland were planned, but complications quickly emerged.[59] Atlantic Fleet Task Force 15, a heavily-screened, powerful battleship-carried formation, defended the passage of AT. 10 to the Mid-Ocean Meeting Point, but only three British destroyers plus a handful of RAF Coastal Command patrol planes escorted the transports on the inbound leg of the voyage. "The necessary forces to maintain your scale of escort do not exist in the Eastern portion of the Atlantic," Admiral Pound confessed.[60] King, holding to the World War I-era policy that the navy-first responsibility was to defend army troop shipping, soon decided that the Atlantic Fleet would have to escort all American troop transport convoys during the entire transatlantic passage.

Emergency overseas troop movements also played a role in the shortage of escorts. Only hours after Pearl Harbor, General Marshall laid plans to ship troops, antiaircraft regiments, and Army Air Force units to a large number of exposed, outlying bases from Hawaii to Panama to the West Indies and Newfoundland. Often the navy received little advance

---

[58] Matloff and Snell, *Strategic Planning* 1: 146. AT.10 consisted of five transports carrying 8,000 Army troops to Iceland and five transports containing 14,000 troops destined for Belfast, Northern Ireland. The escort, Task Force 15, consisted of the battleships *Texas* and *Arkansas*, the cruisers *Quincy* and *Vincennes*, the auxiliary carrier *Long Island*, two destroyers from Atlantic Fleet Task Force 2; DesRon 11 less *Meredith*, *Grayson*, *Kearny*, and *Roe* from Task Force 1; and 5 destroyers from Task Force 4. AT.10 was scheduled to leave New York on 15 January 1942. CinCLant to Rear Admiral A. Sharp [ComBatDiv 5] 6 Jan. 1942, Lant Area File, Box 16; CinCLant, Strategic Plans Collection, NHC.

[59] Marshall to Handy, 13 Jan. 1942, copy in Box 1, King Mss, OA, NHC; and "ABC-4/7: Establishment of United States Forces in North Ireland," 11 Jan. 1942, ABC-4/1 to ABC-4/9, Box 37, ComInCh-CNO Records, Double Zero Files, OA, NHC.

[60] Pound to Ghormley, 22 Jan. 1942, PRO ADM 205/19.

notice of these sailings, although the fleet had to provide strong escorts for all troop shipping.[61] King complained to Marshall, pointing out that "my resources are limited," but the Chief of Staff did little other than to cite the "urgency" of the situation and beg for "favorable consideration" of more "emergency requests."[62] The result was that navy escorts often arrived at army ports of embarkation days before the troop convoys were ready to sail, an awkward waste of invaluable steaming time. Admiral Ingersoll bitterly criticized this on 7 March, pointing out the link between the efficient use of Atlantic Fleet escorts and the plan to transfer destroyers to the Eastern Sea Frontier for coastal convoys.[63] King had already made the same point, pleading with Marshall to "consider the possibility of reducing the need for special convoys in the Atlantic." The army's "emergency convoys" were "costly in that they result in reduced protection to coastwise sea lanes."[64] Hard upon this plea, Secretary of War Henry L. Stimson privately asked Navy Secretary Knox "to send out from the Panama Canal an escort vessel to meet a ship [carrying radar gear] sailing from New Orleans" a few days later. This straw may have broken the camel's back. "This sort of thing cannot go on," King told Marshall soon thereafter. "We simply do not have the means to conduct multifarious expeditions."[65] At length, Marshall agreed, admitting that he "appreciated" the "embarrassment to the navy in providing the necessary escorts for the overseas movements requested by the army."[66] They negotiated an agreement under which the transatlantic and transpacific sailings were regularized, and the army agreed to give the navy one

---

[61] For instance, on 31 December 1941, the "Army had requested from him the following five ships to accomplish a movement in the immediate future which had the approval of the president" consisting of five ships. OpNav complained that "no arrangements were made with Naval Transportation Service except that the urgency of this movement was expressed to this writer by Colonel Gross of the Army, who also mentioned that an escort would be required, sailing from New York about 5 January." Rear Admiral S.A. Taffinder, "Memorandum for the Chief of Naval Operations," 31 Dec. 1941, File A14-1, File #1, Arming Merchantmen, Convoys, etc., Box 254, RG 38, NA.

[62] King to Marshall, 24 Feb. 1942, Box 1, King Mss, Manuscript Division, Library of Congress, Washington D.C., (hereafter LC); Marshall to King, 3 March 1942, "Navy Escorts for Army Transports," ibid.

[63] CinCLant to Cominch only, 7 March 1942, msg 071855, WWII Message Traffic, OA, NHC.

[64] King to Marshall, 3 March 1942, Memos from Gen. Marshall, Box 38, Double Zero Files, CominCh Records, NHC.

[65] Knox to Stark, 7 Mar 1942, File: A14-1, File No. #1: Arming of Merchantmen, Convoys, etc., Box 254, RG 38, NA.

[66] Chester Wardlow, *The Transportation Corps: Movements, Training, and Supply*, pt. 1, ch. 4; and Richard M. Leighton and Robert W. Coakley, *Global Logistics and Strategy, 1940-1943* (Washington D.C.: GPO, 1955), 208.

month's notice prior to troop convoy sailings. "Every effort will be made to reduce the demands for escorts and to use to greater advantage those that are available," General Marshall promised at the end of March.[67]

The British, too, had frequently asked the navy for special escorts, and Admiral Little understood the relationship of the troop and emergency shipments issue to Eastern Sea Frontier convoys. He told London on 18 March of the navy's "difficulty in finding sufficient escorts" owing to "large numbers of occasional requirements for escorts such as British transports to Bermuda to coast and supply ships for Australia."[68] Moreover, King might be forgiven for being confused as to London's strategic priorities; on 6 February, Admiral Pound asked CominCh to send four American destroyers the new Singapore-based ABDA [Australian-British-Dutch-American] unified South Pacific command to replace five Royal Navy destroyers so that they might retire to the Eastern Fleet in the Indian Ocean.[69]

No responsible navy leader believed that a strategy other than escort-of-convoy would defeat the U-boat offensive, but shifting Atlantic Fleet escorts to the Eastern Sea Frontier offered the only immediate means to check *Roll of Drums* in February and March owing to the material condition of the Naval Districts' few ocean-going vessels and the slow pace of new PC patrol craft and SC subchaser construction.[70] Moreover, no one

---

[67] Marshall to King, 30 March 1942, File A14-1 (M61), RG 38, NA. For the problems attending one of these convoys, see CNO [Rear Admiral Metcalf, OpNav Convoy and Routing Division] to Com8thNavDist, 17 Feb. 1942, File 2-2-13 Atlantic Convoy [Coastal], Convoy and Routing Records, 10th Fleet, NHC.

[68] BAD to Admiralty, 18 March 1942, PRO ADM 205/13.

[69] Pound to King, 6 Feb. 1942, ibid.

[70] As late as 12 May, however, the War Production Board told King that "in spite of the vital importance of an adequate coastal patrol, production of submarine chasers has been discouragingly slow; less than half of the ships scheduled for completion by May first are actually completed." Moreover, the destroyer escort program was far behind schedule. Minutes, WPB Mtg XVII, 12 May 1942, King Mss, OA, NHC. When Roosevelt increased the priority of munitions and the merchant shipbuilding program at the expense of Destroyer Escort construction, King cautioned that "fully equipped air and land forces . . . are now in excess of the shipping capacity to carry them. Furthermore, as our merchant ship tonnage is being sunk by Axis submarines it is imperative that the construction of destroyers and patrol vessels be unimpeded, if not substantially increased." King to Roosevelt, 26 March 1942, File: SC, L-3/(12), Secret Files, RG 38, NA. Rear Admiral Dorling reported that the First Landing Craft "had been allocated a priority so high as to threaten the escorts." Dorling, PRO ADM 199/1236, p. 33. Nonetheless, most accounts of the Battle of the Atlantic ignore the U.S. Navy's expensive Destroyer Escort, Escort Carrier, Patrol Craft, and Subchaser building programs altogether. For instance, British historian John Terraine claimed that "as the Pacific war gained momentum, the USN found no occasion to be other than a 'Big Ship navy'." John Terraine, *The U-Boat Wars*, 450.

disputed Admiral Andrews' assessment that most of the vessels assigned to the Eastern Sea Frontier were "incapable of going to sea and maintaining a patrol." Andrews also correctly predicted "increased submarine activity on this coast in the coming Spring."[71] He had considered and rejected the concept of organizing a coastal convoy system and defending the convoys with weak, understrength escort groups. "All experience had shown that the effectiveness of the method [an escort-of-convoy strategy] depended directly upon the strength of the forces engaged in implementing it." Unlike the transatlantic convoys, convoys steaming along the Atlantic seaboard proceeded along long-established shipping lanes, had little searoom, and therefore could not exploit a strategy of evasive routing. As a result, Andrews reasoned, "unless convoys are adequately defended the hazards to merchant vessels gathered together in large and insufficiently protected concentrations are increased, rather than diminished."[72] No responsible navy leader disputed this contention, nor, at the time, did any informed British official. Inasmuch as the British plan to loan the U.S. Navy the twenty-four trawlers and corvettes was intimately connected to the reorganization of the transatlantic convoy system and related negotiations over naval boundaries, King was by no means certain, until about 12 February, if or when these vessels would arrive on the East Coast.[73] That day he informed the Sea Frontiers that he had "accepted" the offer of the trawlers "for sea frontier operations," that "these ships will report to you for duty," and that the commands should "submit a plan for a convoy system to protect coastal shipping."[74]

Another scheme to release destroyers from the Atlantic Fleet was to reduce the strength of the individual transatlantic ocean escort groups, a proposal the Admiralty raised on 9 February when Pound pointed out that a reduction from five to four ships in each of the five American ocean escort groups would free five destroyers "for coastal escort."[75]

---

[71] Andrews to Stark, 7 Feb. 1942, File A16-1, Box 254, RG 38, NA. According to historians John Gooch and Eliot Cohen, "the issue did not focus on the abstract merits of convoy. The difficult questions were: Under what conditions? How large? What kinds of escorts?" Eliot A. Cohen and John Gooch, *Military Misfortunes: The Anatomy of Failure in War* (New York: Free Press, 1990), 80.

[72] Entry for c. 5 Feb. 1942, Eastern Sea Frontier War Diary, p. 141, Library, NHC. Associated problems with bringing unescorted shipping under Naval District control are outlined in CNO to AllComNalDist, 28 Jan. 42, File A14-1, Box 152, RG 38, NA, and ComNANCF to ComNavDist 1,2,4, and 5, 1 Feb. ibid.

[73] On the complex Atlantic theater boundary negotiations, see, for instance, King to Little, 12 Feb. 1942, Box 1, King Mss, LC.

[74] CominCh to ComESF, 12 Feb. 1942, File F-30, Captain F.S. Low, Box 25, RG 38, NA.

[75] Admiralty to CominCh, 9 Feb. 1942, copy in "Memo on Control of Shipping in North Atlantic, Jan-June, 1942," ACNS(T) to FSL, 14 June 1942, PRO ADM 205/21.

Mid-ocean sinkings had declined, but U-boats still stalked these convoys. On 22 February, convoy ON 67, defended by an ocean escort group of only four American destroyers, was attacked in mid-Atlantic with three ships lost and one damaged. Nonetheless, Ingersoll suggested that "so long as enemy submarines are not more numerous and active along mid-ocean convoy routes, consider some U.S. destroyers may be withdrawn" from Atlantic Fleet to the Eastern Sea Frontier, "provided escort groups composed of destroyers and corvettes are not less in strength than equivalent of 4 or 5 destroyers," and that this would "be considered as a temporary measure." He was concerned that "our stake and corresponding influence in North Atlantic convoys should not be reduced below that agreed upon in new system," which had to be "gradually" implemented owing to the Admiralty's inability to commit more escorts to the transatlantic route.[76] King, who believed that only greatly strengthened ocean escort groups could successfully fight their way through large, mid-ocean U-boat concentrations, was reluctant to spread his escort pool more thinly. Indeed, soon after making the suggestion, Ingersoll reconsidered. "No decrease in [the] strength [of] individual escort units should be made especially since better weather may bring increased submarine activity against trade convoys," he announced.[77] The immediate tactical commander, Rear Admiral Arthur Bristol, insisted that "mixed groups of destroyers and corvettes can not provide reasonable protection to large ocean convoys with less than five ships."[78] King was trying to organize coastal convoys, he told Pound, but there were simply not enough escorts for the moment.[79] Not everyone in the Admiralty wholly understood the dimensions of the problem, for only three days later the Director of Anti-Submarine Warfare assured the First Sea Lord that the arrival of the British trawlers and the release of the ten Atlantic Fleet destroyers "should allow East Coast convoys to be established." And, despite substantial losses to the U-boats in the Eastern Sea Frontier in February, the Admiral told the Navy Department in early March that "a substantial proportion of [the] U-boats have withdrawn from U. S. coast and may now be operating in areas outside [the] range of

---

[76] CinCLant to CominCh, 11 Feb. 1942, msg 111755, World War II Message File, OA, NHC; and Pound to King, 4 Feb. 1942, cited in ANCS(T), 14 June 1942, PRO ADM 205/15.

[77] CinCLant to CominCh "only", 7 March 1942, msg 071855, World War II Messages, OA, NHC.

[78] CTF 24 to OpNav, 7 March 1942, msg. 070404, File A14-1, File #1, Arming Merchantmen, Convoys, etc., Box 254, RG 38, NA.

[79] King to Pound, 13 Feb. 1942, cited in "Memo on Control of Shipping in North Atlantic, Jan-June, 1942," ACNS(T) to FSL, 14 June 1942, PRO ADM 205/21, and Dir ASW to FSL, 16 Feb. 1942, ibid..

shore-based aircraft." According to Admiral Little, "this shows that the steps which have been taken to combat the submarines in the vicinity of the coast have been at least temporarily successful."[80] Those measures, which included occasional, irregular patrols off the mouths of major bays and shipping lanes and *ad hoc* escorts for freighters carrying special cargoes, were accepted by Admiral Andrews as expedient, temporary steps, not as substitutes for escort-of-convoy operations.[81]

Although sinkings increased in March, the shape of a solution to *Roll of Drums* soon appeared. For one thing, Admiral King relieved Admiral Stark, who had threatened to resign, in mid-month, thus consolidating into a single command responsibility for fleet, Sea Frontier, and Naval District operations. In short order, King directed the Naval District commandants to assign their chiefs of staff to operations rather than industrial or yard business. In addition, the first British trawlers arrived on the East Coast on 4 March, and the remainder were expected to appear by mid-April.[82] Moreover Rear Admiral R. Ghormley, the Special Naval Observer in London, reported that he and Pound had discussed opening out the transatlantic convoy cycle from six to seven days.[83] Admiral Ingersoll calculated that this measure, when combined with the earlier reorganization, might make twenty ships "available from mid-ocean escorts when all British vessels to be allocated are ready." The opening out of the cycle would require an agreement with the civilian shipping authorities and the president and prime minister because it would result in a reduction of Lend-Lease imports to Britain by at least 30,000 tons monthly. Furthermore, "mid-April seem[ed] [the] earliest date when all [the necessary] adjustments could be made."[84] Admiral Bristol agreed that "seaboard losses justify reinforcement of coastal escorts from mid-ocean escort forces" and concurred "in principle that opening convoy sailing interval to 7 days should effect a saving of escorts," but he added that the Canadians and "British have so far apparently been unable to meet their mid-ocean commitments." He cited instances when he had to augment British ocean escort groups with Atlantic Fleet destroyers owing to the failure of London or Ottawa to supply the necessary ships. While loudly advocating the establishment of Eastern Sea Frontier merchant convoys, Bristol recommended that only "when all midocean units are

---

[80] BAD [Admiral Little] to CNO, 6 March 1942, Box 1, King Mss, OA, NHC.

[81] For these operations, see File A14-1, Convoys, Etc., Box 254, RG 38, NA. Few disputed the contention that these expedient operations would not counter *Roll of Drums*.

[82] Andrews to Roosevelt, 6 March 1942, Navy Department, PSF, FDR Mss.

[83] SpeNavO to CominCh, 7 March 1942, msg 051716, File A14-1, File No. 1, Arming Merchantmen, Convoys, etc., Box 254, RG 38, NA.

[84] CinClant to CominCh, 7 March 1942, msg 071855, Box 1, King Mss, OA, NHC.

assured of having five ships each then should [CominCh] divert [the] excess to eastern seaboard."[85] "The British and Canadians must carry their part of the load" before Admiral Ingersoll could release any destroyers.[86] While negotiations about the convoy cycle got underway, King instructed OpNav Convoy and Routing Division and the sea frontier commanders to submit plans for escort-of-convoy operations.

Roosevelt occasionally complained about the sinkings, but he took little hand in solving the problem.[87] His confidante, Harry Hopkins, who seldom involved himself in naval affairs, was asked by Churchill on 6 February to "make sure that the president's attention has been drawn to the very heavy sinkings by U-boats in the Western North Atlantic."[88] Owing to his brief to superintend Lend-Lease assistance to the Soviet Union, Hopkins discussed the issue with King. When Churchill raised the issue with the president on 12 March, Hopkins replied, pointing out that the British had failed to make good on their commitments to the transatlantic ocean escort groups, that "most of the trawlers . . . have only recently arrived or are approaching," and that "not until the Admiralty have met their commitments will we be able to transfer more destroyers to coastal work unless you are prepared to accept correspondingly less protection for transatlantic trade convoys." Speaking for FDR, he agreed "to opening the cycle of such convoys to seven or preferably eight days," and promised that the loss of tonnage would be made up "when available later. " The results would not come quickly, he added, for "the increased coastal strength will not immediately accrue."[89] Even so, there was no

---

[85] CTF 24 to OpNav, 7 March 1942, msg. 070404, File A14-1, File #1 Arming Merchantmen, Convoys, etc., Box 254, RG 38, NA.

[86] ConCLant to CTF 24, 14 March 1942, msg. 142110, World War II Messages, OA, NHC.

[87] For example, when Stark informed him that only seven vessels were on patrol in the Eastern Sea Frontier, Roosevelt complained to Navy Secretary Knox that the situation was "a real disgrace." Roosevelt to Knox, 26 Feb. 1942, "Navy Department, February 1942," PSF, Roosevelt Mss. Rather than advancing an escort-of-convoy strategy however, the President favored a strategy of offensive "[local Naval] district hunting patrols" by swarms of small craft. FDR to Knox, 26. Feb 1942, ibid. Other evidence suggests that neither Roosevelt nor Churchill placed a high priority on the defense of East Coast merchant shipping. For instance, in April they arranged for a squadron of antisubmarine B-24 Liberators fitted with scarce ASV antisubmarine radar systems to be flown out to India. "This will prove a great help in reconnaisance missions over the Bay of Bengal or the Indian Ocean," the president assured the prime minister on 21 April 1942. Roosevelt to Churchill, 21 April 1942, in Warren F. Kimball, ed., *Churchill and Roosevelt: The Complete Correspondence* (London: Collins, 1984), 1: 464. At the time, the Eastern Sea Frontier operated only two antisubmarine patrol planes fitted with ASV radar.

[88] Churchill to Hopkins, 6 Feb. 1942, PRO ADM 199/1935.

[89] Hopkins to Churchill, 16 March 1942, Box 1, King Mss, LC.

shortage of criticism of navy strategy, even among Admiral King's own CominCh staff. "In view of the shipping losses on this coast . . . and the mounting, justified criticism of our methods of combatting the submarine menace," Captain Francis S. Low announced on 7 March, "I do not feel we are on firm ground in continuing to counter all criticism by the simple formula that Sea Frontier forces are not available."[90]

The Admiralty once again issued conflicting signals. On 18 March, Pound formally agreed to "open out temporarily" the convoy cycle from six to seven days, which was what King wanted, but the First Sea Lord added that he was "convinced that the starting of convoys should not be delayed until stronger escorts are available."[91] That same day, however, Pound admitted to the Prime Minister that "part of our difficulty is [a] lack of information as to the precise employment of their units" and confessed that "the U.S. commitments for escorting troop carriers are heavier than expected."[92] Pound's message to King provoked a surprisingly immediate clarification from Admiral Little in Washington, who reminded the Admiralty that CominCh "recognized the need . . . for coastal convoys." The "need for troop convoy escorts" and the "large number of occasional requirements for escorts," he explained, coupled with Admiral King's conviction that "inadequately escorted convoys are worse than none" meant that it was "unlikely" that the Eastern Sea Frontier would begin escort-of-convoy operations "before autumn at the earliest."[93] Little, this message suggests, was well informed on some aspects of the problem, poorly prepared on others. He knew that a "coastal convoy plan [had been] approved, that Atlantic Fleet could "spare no more," and that implementation "await[ed] 60 escorts. " On the other hand, Little was far off the mark as to when King intended to order the plan into effect. The Admiralty's analysis suggests that, owing to its own commitments elsewhere, London was not eager to reorganize the transatlantic convoys or provide the small escorts promised in February. "In light of" Admiral Little's message, the Assistant Chief of Naval Staff [Trade] told the First Sea Lord, "I do not consider there is any prospect of inducing the Americans to produce sufficient escorts to obviate our

---

[90] Low to DepCoS CominCh [Edwards], 7 March 1942, File F-30, Captain F. S. Low, Box 25, RG 38, NA. In May 1943, King turned to Rear Admiral Low to be his 10th Fleet Chief of Staff.

[91] Pound to King, 18 March 1942, PRO ADM 205/13.

[92] Pound to Churchill, 18 March 1942, ibid. Whereas most accounts of *Roll of Drums* repeat Pound's 18 March message to King, none attempted to explain this letter, also dated 18 March, to the prime minister.

[93] BAD [Little] to Admiralty, 18 March 1942, ibid.

sending reinforcements."[94] Only two weeks later, however, Admiral Pound urged an entirely opposite line. "I do not think we should encourage the Americans to leave their new ships in the Atlantic," he told Churchill, "or they will never build up a strong Pacific Fleet."[95]

By now King had instructed the Atlantic Fleet and the Commander, Caribbean Sea Frontier, to submit plans to escort convoys on routes connecting Trinidad, Bermuda, and Halifax. Acknowledging that this hinged on the transatlantic convoy cycle being "opened to 7 days which was eventually to make some of TF 24 ships available," and that the "escort for a time will be meager," he nonetheless intended to have a plan ready to implement.[96] Once the British agreed to open out the convoy cycle, Admiral King ordered his subordinates to convene a second Coastal Convoy Board in Washington on 27 March. This board "recognized that the strength of the [coastal] escorts [groups] may have to be meagre," but insisted that "effective convoying depends upon the escorts being in sufficient strength to permit their taking the offensive against submarines, without their withdrawal for this purpose resulting in unduly exposing the convoy to other submarines while they are on this mission. Any protection less than this simply results in the convoy's becoming a convenient target for submarines."[97] This consideration was hardly abstract. How long and under what circumstances to allow an escort to prosecute a sound or sight contact before directing her to regain her station on the perimeter of a convoy vexed British, Canadian, and American escort group tacticians throughout 1941-42.[98] Twenty-six destroyers and thirty-nine corvettes, trawlers, patrol craft, subchasers, "or equivalents" would be needed under the plan.[99] The Board also stressed the "importance of developing complete air coverage," and primitive questions of whether and when to institute coastal escort-of-convoy

---

[94] ACNS(T) to FSL, 19 March 1942, ibid.

[95] Pound to WSC, 8 April 1942, PRO ADM 208/15,. This letter makes meaningless the staple argument that the British advanced a "Germany-first" grand strategy whereas Admiral King's gaze was focused solely on the Pacific.

[96] CominCh to CinClant and CaribSeaFront, 20 March 1942, msg 201305, Map Room Messages, Roosevelt Mss. See also [Rear Admiral Richard] Edwards [Deputy Chief of Staff, CominCh] to CominCh, 15 March 1942, ASW File, Box 245, RG 80, NA.

[97] Informal Board to Organize Gulf-Caribbean-Halifax Convoy System to CominCh, 27 March 1942, File 2-2-13 Atlantic Convoy [Coastal], Convoy and Routing Records, 10th Fleet Records, OA, NHC.

[98] See, for instance, ComTF4 to Task Force Four, 24 Feb 1942, "Escort of Convoy Bulletin ST No. 5-42," Box 254, RG 38, NA.

[99] Informal Board to Organize Gulf-Caribbean-Halifax Convoy System to CominCh, 27 March 1942, File 2-2-13, Atlantic Convoy [Coastal, Convoy and Routing Records, 10th Fleet Records, OA, NHC.

operations. The air coverage controversy was intimately related to long-standing army-navy disputes over doctrine and tactics, Lend-Lease allocations, and broad questions of Allied grand strategy and global air strategy.[100] Assuming four-vessel coastal escort groups, Metcalf figured that fifty-two escorts were needed as "a minimum," and that "additional protection should be afforded as suitable escort vessels become available."[101]

The Convoy Board's report supposed that Admiral Ingersoll could release the long-planned ten destroyers from the Atlantic Fleet, but in early April only three had arrived on the Eastern Sea Frontier.[102] German operations against the North Russia convoys had moved Pound to ask King to reinforce the Royal Navy's Home Fleet, and in early April the Atlantic Fleet's new fast battleship *Washington*, two heavy cruisers, the attack carrier *Wasp*, and a destroyer squadron crossed the Atlantic. Inasmuch as the long-awaited 173-foot PCs would not appear in any numbers on the Eastern Sea Frontier until mid-May, King agreed to Andrews' proposal to inaugurate a partial daylight convoy system in mid-April and delay implementing the entire Convoy Board plan for another month.[103] Meanwhile, negotiations between the Admiralty and CominCh concerning escort strength for American and Canadian transatlantic troop movements reached a predictable climax. General Marshall had visited London early that month, and he returned with Admiral Pound on the 18th for a week of difficult talks about Lend-Lease, aircraft allocations, and *Roll of Drums*. Pound assured King that the British would "improve [their] destroyer strength in their [merchant convoy] escort units and agreed that the Atlantic Fleet should "take over

---

[100] For one explanation of these issues, see Morison, *Naval Operations* 1: 243. The background to King's directive is explained in CominCh to CNO, 15 March 1942, File A14-1, Convoys, etc., Box 254, RG 38, NA.

[101] DirC&R [Metcalf] to CNO, 9 March 1942, File 2-2-13, Atlantic Convoy (Coastal), Convoy and Routing Records, 10th Fleet Records, OA, NHC.

[102] Admiralty to OpNav, 4 April 1942, PRO ADM 205/21. Ingersoll issued a lengthy explanation on 22 March, and asked King to give him the "earliest practicable information - thirty days if possible - regarding special `must tasks' during May such as Panama and African convoys, additional North Atlantic convoys, or special escort jobs." Ingersoll to King, 22 March 1942, msg 212325, World War II Messages, OA, NHC.

[103] Thirty-six Patrol Craft were scheduled to be built by 1 May 1942. J.W. Powell, Office of Procurement and Management, to Knox, 2 April 1942, Box 2, King Mss, LC. For details on the complete Eastern Sea Frontier escort-of-convoy plan, see CominCh to VCNO [Admiral Horne], 3 April 1942, File 2-2-13, Atlantic Convoy [Coastal], Convoy and Routing Records, 10th Fleet, OA, NHC; CominCh to VCNO, c. 9 April 1942, File F-30, Captain F. S. Low, Box 25, RG 38, NA; and ComESF to ComNavDists and ComGulfSeaFrontier, 1 May 1942, File 1-1-14, Eastern Sea Frontier, Box 218, Convoy and Routing Records, OA, NHC.

[all transatlantic] troop escort" duties.[104] Coupled with the implementation of the earlier arrangement to open out the convoy cycle to seven days, this meant that, when all the transfers were effected, only one reinforced Atlantic Fleet ocean escort group would continue to defend the transatlantic merchant convoys. No one was happy with this outcome, but Admiral Edwards felt it was "the only way to get this thing [coastal convoys] started."[105] Details of the new arrangement were hammered out at a conference in Ottawa of all three Allied navies.[106] Admiral Andrews had already instituted a successful partial daylight escort-of-convoy system exploiting protected anchorages in mid-April, and King now ordered that the Eastern Sea Frontier implement the Convoy Board plan in mid-May.[107]

The initiation of the daylight convoys in April and the full coastal convoy system the following month produced immediate results. Sinkings fell off, U-boats found it more difficult to locate unescorted shipping, and the Germans shifted their forces to the Gulf of Mexico and the Caribbean in a new operation codenamed "Newland." Plans to deal with this campaign had already been crafted, although once again competing operational demands from other theaters and the president's refusal to put a priority on escort construction delayed the inauguration of a full convoy system until July.[108] The defeat of the Japanese Fleet at the Battle of Midway reduced the need to escort shipping between the West Coast and Hawaii and so made easier the task Admiral King confronted in allocating escorts to deal with competing threats.

Operation *Roll of Drums* off the Atlantic coast in early 1942 succeeded largely because the U.S. Navy was already committed to other tasks: transatlantic escort-of-convoy operations, defending troop transports, and maintaining powerful, forward-deployed Atlantic Fleet striking forces to prevent a breakout by heavy German surface forces. Navy leaders, especially Admiral King, were unwilling to risk troop shipping to provide escorts for coastal merchant shipping. Unscheduled, emergency

---

[104] Edwards to King, 13 April 1942, File F-30, Captain F. S. Low, Box 25, RG 38, NA.

[105] Edwards to King, 13 April 1942, and Edwards to King, 18 April 1942, both in File F-30, Captain F.S. Low, Box 25, RG 38, NA; also see Minute, "Atlantic Convoys," Admiralty, 16 April 1942, PRO ADM 205/21.

[106] CominCh to Admiralty, 24 April 1942, msg. 231901, File 1-1-14, Eastern Sea Frontier, Box 218, 10th Fleet Convoy and Routing Records, OA, NHC.

[107] As of 29 April, Eastern Sea Frontier expected to organize nine destroyers, seven gunboats, nine 175-foot patrol craft, four Coast Guard cutters, and twelve British trawlers into five coastal escort groups. ComESF to CominCh, 29 April 1942, File 2-2-13, Atlantic Convoy [Coastal], Convoy and Routing Records, 10th Fleet, OA, NHC.

[108] Edwards to King, 30 April 1942, File F-30, Captain F. S. Low, Box 25, RG 38, NA.

deployments of Army units also created repeated disruptions to navy plans, as did other occasional, unexpected tasks. Contrary to the traditional historiography, neither Admiral King's unproven yet widely alleged Anglophobia, an equally undocumented navy reluctance to accept British advice, nor a preference for another strategy caused the delay in the inauguration of coastal escort-of-convoy operations. Nor did the British adopt a consistent line of policy on the question. The delay was due to a shortage of escorts, and that resulted from understandably conflicting priorities, a state of affairs that dictated all Allied strategy until 1944.

8

Squaring Some of the Corners: The Royal Canadian Navy and the Pattern of the Atlantic War

Marc Milner

Canadian historians have always insisted that the Royal Canadian Navy's contribution to the Battle of the Atlantic was a key to Allied victory.[1] The basis for that claim is the scale of the Canadian commitment and the importance of the tasks undertaken. As the RCN's official histories remind us, by the crisis period of the Atlantic war, 1942-43, approximately half of the close escorts of the main trade convoys between North America and Britain were Canadian.[2] Yet the general accounts of the Atlantic war published in the forty years after 1945 scarcely mention the RCN as an institution.[3] Such histories occasionally distinguish Canadian warships from their British counterparts, but as often as not the ships, the men, and the institution are treated as an amorphous part of the larger Royal Navy. In the last few years that has begun to change. Recent general works on the Battle of the Atlantic have used new Canadian scholarship to attempt to assess the RCN's role and integrate

---

[1] See for example, Joseph Schull, *The Far Distant Ships: An Official Account of Canadian Naval Operations in the Second World War* (Ottawa: King's Printer, 1950).

[2] Gilbert Tucker, *The Naval Service of Canada: Its Official History*, vol. 2, *Activities on Shore During the Second World War* (Ottawa: King's Printer, 1952) points out (p. 405) that by the end of 1942 the RCN and Royal Navy controlled about 98 percent of trade escort forces in the North Atlantic north of New York. Schull mentions a figure of 48 percent RCN, 50 percent RN, and 2 percent U.S. Navy for early 1943 (p. 167).

[3] See, for example, John Costello and Terry Hughes, *The Battle of the Atlantic* (New York: The Dial Press, 1977), an excellent synthesis of the literature up to the mid-1970s which devotes only two paragraphs to the RCN on page 233.

it into their accounts, but such integration has been only partially successful.[4] What follows is an attempt to illustrate more pointedly where and how the RCN made a significant contribution to the pattern of the Atlantic war and to suggest how a closer look at the Canadian experience sheds important light on some enduring issues.

The importance of the RCN to the Battle of the Atlantic lies in its rapid wartime expansion and its assumption of key tasks in that battle. In 1939 the fleet numbered only six relatively modern destroyers and five coal-fired minesweepers, with a total professional compliment of about 1,800 all ranks.[5] The RCN's ostensible task was defense of Canada, but this was clearly predicated on the preponderance of Anglo-American seapower. Its equipment, uniforms, organization, doctrine, training, and the ensign flown astern were all British, as were some of its key officers. RCN officers were borne on the Royal Navy's *Navy List*, where a combined seniority listing for the Empire and Commonwealth was maintained, and Ottawa's naval intelligence and naval control of shipping establishments were part and parcel of the British system. Although the Canadian government of 1939 was deeply mindful and assertive of its independence from the Old Country, the RCN clearly saw itself as part of the larger British Imperial and Commonwealth Navy.[6]

By 1945 virtually all of that had changed. In a little over five years the RCN expanded fifty-fold — more than any other Second World War navy — reaching a strength of over four hundred warships and about 100,000 personnel (roughly the size of the prewar RN).[7] In doing so, the RCN became the third largest Allied navy and the one primarily responsible for the close escort of the main North Atlantic trade convoys

---

[4] Dan van der Vat's *The Atlantic Campaign* (London: Hodder and Stoughton, 1988) notes in particular its use of recent Canadian material, but the main thrust of the storyline remains unaffected by it. John Terraine's *The U-Boat Wars 1916-1945* (New York: G.P. Putnam & Sons, 1989) does a better job of integrating the Canadian material into the account, but the storyline too remains unaffected.

[5] Schull, *Far Distant Ships*, 1.

[6] The RCN had hoped that when war came its destroyers could be sent to serve alongside the RN while defense of the Canadian coast would be subsumed largely under general British command of the sea. However, the Canadian government ordered the RCN to keep its ships home. See "Development of Canadian Naval Policy," Plans Division memo, 9 December 1943, Directorate of History, National Defence Headquarters, Ottawa (hereafter DHist, NDHQ), NS 1440-5.

[7] Maximum wartime strength was reached in December 1944 at 96,000 all ranks. For a breakdown of personnel figures, see M. Milner, *Canadian Naval Force Requirements in the Second World War*, Ottawa, DND, Operational Research and Analysis Establishment, Extra-Mural paper, no. 20, December 1981, p. 47, which is drawn from "Summary of Information Respecting Departmental Activities," January 1945, W.L.M. King papers, National Archives of Canada (hereafter NAC), MG 26, J4, vol 265, f.C180727.

between North America and Europe. One of the Atlantic's theaters of war, the Canadian Northwest Atlantic, was under the operational control of a Canadian admiral, and a large portion of the offensive ASW forces operating under the RN in European waters in the last months of the war were Canadian. In addition, the RCN used the war to develop plans for, and to acquire some of the key components of, a balanced force of cruisers, aircraft carriers, and fleet destroyers: a true Blue Water Navy.[8] One of these cruisers, HMCS *Uganda*, served with the British Pacific Fleet in the Okinawa campaign in early 1945. No other Canadian service achieved this level of importance or national autonomy in its operations against the Axis. By the end of the war in Europe, the RCN was a large, assertive, and independent-minded player in the Allied naval camp.

The vast majority of the RCN's war effort was devoted to protecting Allied merchant shipping in the Atlantic, a task characterized by two things: a high degree of organization and administration of intelligence, shipping, and escort forces by shore staffs, and a large number of small ships to make the system work. On both counts the RCN made important and lasting contributions to the shape of the Atlantic war.

Geography made Canada a key partner in the organization of shipping from the outset. Indeed, Canada was a part of the British Empire and Commonwealth naval intelligence and naval control of shipping (NCS) system throughout the interwar years. When war came in 1939 those systems were ready to go.[9] The tentacles of this enormous and elaborate command and control system stretched around the world and, at the regional level, through a system of agents and officers in every major port. Ottawa served as the regional center for the organization and management of these tasks for most of North America — including U.S. east and west coast ports (the Gulf coast was run from Jamaica). The system either dispatched ships independently or routed them to convoy assembly ports for transatlantic crossings. To support this work, the RCN developed and maintained an enormous bureaucracy in Ottawa and throughout North America and constructed new communications and intelligence facilities in Canada, Newfoundland, and Bermuda.

Although this Anglo-Canadian system operated clandestinely in the U.S. until December 1941, its existence was actually well known to the U.S. Navy. Following the signing of the Lend-Lease agreement in March

---

[8] For a discussion of the wartime planning for the postwar navy, see W.A.B. Douglas' seminal article "Conflict and Innovation in the Royal Canadian Navy," in G. Jordan, ed., *Naval Strategy in the Twentieth Century* (New York: Crane Russack, 1977), 210-230.

[9] The development of Canadian naval control of shipping is discussed in Milner, *Canadian Naval Force Requirements*, passim.

1941, the U.S. Navy was actively drawn in. By then U.S. naval liaison officers tasked to study and coordinate trade matters had been appointed to Ottawa and Halifax, and a Canadian liaison officer with a similar task was on duty in Washington. All of the British confidential books and special publications related to NCS were distributed to the newly appointed U.S. Navy "Port Directors" from Ottawa, and the British "Consular Shipping Agents" — retired naval officers called back to active service in mufti — had made contact with their opposite numbers in American ports by mid-1941. When The United States finally entered the war the system was "unmasked." Then while OPNAV in Washington scrambled to get on its feet during the first six months of 1942, Ottawa acted as the conduit for daily intelligence summaries from London to Washington, and the Canadians controlled the movements of merchant shipping in the western Atlantic north of the equator.[10]

Two final points need to be made about the importance of the RCN's role in naval control of shipping to the Battle of the Atlantic. First, it was evident at the time — at least to the British and Canadians — that the infrastructure necessary for the establishment of a convoy system was in place in the U.S. prior to 7 December 1941. This, in combination with the sharing of their hard-won operational experience with the U.S. Navy, seemed to indicate the singular importance of establishing a system of convoys, supported by airpower, along the U.S. Atlantic coast on the outbreak of war. The failure of the U.S. Navy to institute such a scheme until the middle of 1942, following truly horrendous losses in U.S. waters, remains one of the great enigmas of the war. The RCN story reveals that the delay in instituting convoys along the U.S. east coast in 1942 owed nothing to organizational or administrative shortfalls. Second, the RCN's contribution to naval control of shipping, communications, and intelligence were sufficient by early 1943 to warrant the establishment of a separate Canadian theater of operations in the Northwest Atlantic. Indeed, when the Americans raised the issue of Canadian competence to operate a theater of war as a reason why the RCN should not be permitted to do so, senior RCN officers commented bitterly — and with some truth — that the U.S. Navy had learned about convoy escort and naval control of shipping from the RCN in the first place.[11]

---

[10] Ibid.

[11] During the debate over the establishment of the Canadian command, Rear Admiral L.W. Murray, RCN, the Commanding Officer, Atlantic Coast, observed that the two U.S. Navy Commanders of Task Force 24 had learned about convoy organization and escort from him. See W.G. Lund, "The RCN's Quest for Autonomy in the North West Atlantic," in J.A. Boutilier, ed., *The RCN in Retrospsect* (Vancouver: University of British Columbia Press, 1982), 138-57, esp. 155.

Small ships were the backbone of the RCN for most of the war. The most important were the Flower Class corvettes, two of which are framed here by the dinghy and davit of a third sometime in 1943. HMCS *Sherbrooke* is on the left. Photo courtesy of the National Archives of Canada.

Until substantial work is undertaken on NCS in British and American records, it will be impossible to assess accurately the significance of the RCN in easing the U.S. Navy into the war. For the moment, it seems clear that the Canadian role as the organizational and administrative lynch-pin in the Anglo-American naval alliance is missing from the literature on the Atlantic war.

At the operational level, the RCN made a major contribution to the pattern of the Battle of the Atlantic. This was possible because of two things. First, the nature of the defense against U-boats was largely organizational and structural. Ships were organized into convoys, provided with air cover when and where possible, and routed clear of known enemy dispositions by naval intelligence. To make the system work required general command of the surface of the sea and the air over it, good intelligence (which the Allies enjoyed even in the absence of Ultra), and enough escorts to establish and run a system of convoys. It bears emphasizing here that the principal means of defending shipping in the Second World War was avoidance of the enemy: convoys, intelligence, and routing allowed that to happen. Close escorts were the last line of defense. They did not have to be powerful or particularly efficient; for most of the war they just had to be there. The second key element in Allied success in the Atlantic was, therefore, enough small escorts to make the system work.

Largely by accident, the RCN was in the midst of a large construction program of Flower Class corvettes — initially seventy-nine oceangoing ships — just as the main threat in the Atlantic turned from a mix of ships (including the *Bismarck*) to U-boats alone.[12] The very month that *Bismarck* was sunk, May 1941, the RCN agreed to send its burgeoning fleet of corvettes to Newfoundland to close the last remaining gap in antisubmarine escort of convoys between the limits of British escorts based in Iceland and those operating from Canadian ports. By the end of 1941, nearly seventy RCN corvettes, plus about a dozen destroyers, were operating as part of this "Newfoundland Escort Force." How the gap in continuous antisubmarine escort of North Atlantic convoys would have been closed in 1941 without those RCN ships is a moot point: even large navies find it hard to pull seventy warships, fully manned, from a hat.

By September 1941, as a result of Anglo-American agreement, the U.S. Navy had moved into the Newfoundland-to-Iceland convoy escort business as well. Indeed, from September 1941 until February 1942, the RCN and the U.S. Navy shared responsibility for convoy escort between Newfoundland and Iceland, an area of significant U-boat activity in the fall of 1941. The Canadians, in the throes of their first major wartime expansion, escorted the slow convoys with the corvettes and a few destroyers of the Newfoundland Escort Force, while the destroyers of the U.S. Navy's Task Force 24 escorted the fast convoys. The basic division of labor was the result of a larger scheme, arranged in August 1941 between Churchill and Roosevelt, that gave the neutral U.S. strategic control over the western Atlantic and committed the U.S. Navy to oceanic escort of trade in the area, while the belligerent nations — including Canada — fought the hot war in the eastern Atlantic.[13]

---

[12] The RCN had ordered a large number of corvettes in 1940 as part of a scheme in which they would be bartered to the British for Tribal Class destroyers. When the deal fell through, the orders were allowed to stand, in part to keep shipyards busy. For a discussion of RCN ship procurement, see Tucker, *Naval Service of Canada* 2, chapters 2 and 3.

[13] For a discussion of the story of NEF and the U.S. Navy in the fall of 1941, see M. Milner, *North Atlantic Run: The Royal Canadian Navy and the Battle for the Convoys* (Toronto, University of Toronto Press and Annapolis, MD: Naval Institute Press, 1985), chapter 2. For some comments on the nature of the RCN-USN link early in the war, see also M. Milner, "RCN-USN 1939-45: Some Reflections on the Origins of a New Alliance," in William B. Cogar, ed., *Naval History: The Seventh Symposium of the U.S. Naval Academy* (Wilmington, DE:

The RCN had to contend with severe weather between the gulf of Maine and Iceland, where the Labrador Current produced arctic conditions comparable only to those on the Murmansk convoy route. The corvette *Brantford*, seen here in the winter of 1944-45, illustrates what winter on the North Atlantic could mean. Photo courtesy of the author.

The U.S. Navy, therefore, had much firsthand experience of U-boats and convoys through late 1941. It proved, in the end, a difficult time for both North American navies. The U.S. Navy discovered just how vile the North Atlantic was, had its first taste of convoy battles, and suffered its first casualties of the war.[14] Alongside them the RCN's weakly escorted slow convoys were decimated by wolf pack attacks during September and October. British historians, themselves neglectful of the Canadian story, fail to assess this U.S. Navy experience alongside the struggling Canadians when criticizing the Americans for not establishing coastal convoys in early 1942. The U.S. Navy, which was not up to speed on the

Scholarly Resources, Inc., 1988), 276-83.

[14] For a superb account of this U.S.Navy "prewar" activity, see Patrick Abazzia, *Mr. Roosevelt's Navy* (Annapolis, MD: Naval Institute Press, 1975).

constitutional history of the British Empire, apparently saw the RCN as part of some Imperial Fleet.[15] Americans might then be excused if they saw a difference between what the British said about the importance of convoys and what they witnessed of Canadian convoy battles in late 1941. It was not surprising that the U.S. Navy's Board on the Organization of East Coast Convoys reported in March 1942 that weakly escorted convoys were worse than none at all.[16]

The Canadians therefore probably had a pernicious influence on the U.S. Navy's attitude towards convoys and its handling of the 1942 crisis. The issue of air support and proximity to coastlines, both central to the defense of weakly escorted convoys, was also probably obscured for the U.S. Navy by its 1941 experience east of Newfoundland. Benefitting from the almost perpetual fog off the Grand Banks, German wolf packs operated right up to the Newfoundland coast in October. Indeed, poor weather allowed U-boat packs to operate well inside the range of Newfoundland-based airpower until the final demise of packs themselves in 1943.[17] Historical debate on the particular problem of convoys on the U.S. east coast in 1942 therefore requires some discussion of the "message" being passed to Washington from the North Atlantic, and there is little evidence of that kind of historical assessment in the present literature.[18]

There is a tendency among American historians to narrow the focus onto purely national experience when looking at the development of the

[15] The U.S. Navy's *Filing Manual*, in use in 1941, lists Canada under British Empire and Commonwealth, although since the Statute of Westminster of 1931 Canada had been a fully independent nation.

[16] "Board on the Organization of East Coast Convoys, Report to CinC, US Fleet," n.d., ADM 205/19, Public Record Office, Kew, England (herafter PRO).

[17] Problems of air support for convoy operations in the North Atlantic are discussed at length in section four of W.A.B. Douglas's *The Creation of a National Air Force: The Official History of the Royal Canadian Air Force*, vol. 2 (Toronto: University of Toronto Press, 1986). Douglas's important book is virtually unknown outside of Canada, while the role of the RCAF in the Battle of the Atlantic (roughly a quarter of the air squadrons and a further quarter of the aircrew in the RAF's Coastal Command) remains equally obscure.

[18] None of the recent works on the U-boat campaign on the U.S. east coast in 1942 — including Eliot A. Cohen's thoughtful "Failure to Learn: American Antisubmarine Warfare in 1942," in Eliot A. Cohen and John Gooch, *Military Misfortunes: the Anatomy of Failure in War* (New York: The Free Press, 1990), 29-58, and the more narrative accounts of action by Homer H. Hickman, *Torpedo Junction* (Annapolis, MD: Naval Institute Press, 1989) and Michael Gannon, *Operation Drumbeat* (New York: Harper and Row, 1990) — have drawn on the records of TF-24 (found in Record Group 313 of the U.S. National Archives, Washington D.C.). Nor, for that matter, have these American writers demonstrated awareness of the burgeoning literature in Canada on a common battle.

campaign off the American coast in 1942.[19] However, the tides of the war at sea did not respect national frontiers, and the Germans were a common enemy. Recently an irate Canadian veteran complained about a passage in Professor Michael Gannon's book *Operation Drumbeat* which claimed that the U.S. Navy could expect no help in early 1942 from the Canadians because their navy was in a disastrous state.[20] The old salt protested to the History Department at the U.S. Naval Academy, where a member of the department supported Gannon's position. Both missed the point. The RCN *did* provide the U.S. Navy with an enormous amount of assistance during 1942, not least of which was assuming responsibility for U.S. Navy convoy escort responsibilities north of Maine. According to the agreement reached by Roosevelt and Churchill at Argentia the previous August 1941, oceanic escort of convoys west of Iceland was a U.S. Navy responsibility. In early 1942 as U.S. Navy destroyers departed the North Atlantic for the Pacific and points south, the RCN simply picked up the slack. One of the reasons why the Canadian Navy was in no position to offer much help along the U.S. coastline was precisely because the RCN staff made a conscious decision to run the fleet to its limits in order to free U.S. Navy warships for more important duties and to permit convoy systems to be established.[21] Indeed, Professor Gannon's book focuses discussion on the controversy over the employment of U.S. Navy destroyers from northern waters in early 1942 because the RCN had assumed their tasks.[22]

In addition, the RCN did operate off the American coast very early in the 1942 campaign, and did so with complete success. American historians date the inauguration of regular convoys in their Eastern Sea Frontier from 14 May 1942, when KS 500 left Hampton Roads for Key West, but these were only the first *American*-escorted convoys in U.S. waters. The RCN — at the request of Admiral E.J. King, the U.S. Navy's commander in chief — began the first regular convoys in the Eastern Sea

---

[19] This tendency is not limited to discussion of the Atlantic war. See John Hattendorf's review of Robert W. Love, Jr., *History of the United States Navy*, 2 vols., (Harrisburg, PA: Stackpole Books, 1992) in U.S. Naval Institute *Proceedings*, 119 (August 1993): 99-100, in which Hattendorf comments on the American tendency to view its naval experience in isolation.

[20] Don Sedgewick, Deland, Florida, to the author, 27 January 1991, in reference to Michael Gannon, *Operation Drumbeat*. Sedgewick enclosed a copy of his correspondence with the U.S. Naval Academy, to whom he had protested Gannon's observation.

[21] A memo from Plans Division, NSHQ, in January 1942 assessing the potential impact of the expanding war on the RCN observed: "Relieving the RN and the USN of duties and the loan of ships depends on circumstances outside the control of the RCN." NAC, RG 24 3844, NSS 1017-10-39, vol. 1, as quoted in Milner, *North Atlantic Run*, 96.

[22] See especially his chapter 12, "The Navy Stirs."

Frontier between Halifax and Boston on 18 March 1942: they sailed throughout the war without loss.[23]

About the time the first U.S. convoy was assembling in Hampton Roads, the Canadians were also preparing their own series of oil convoys between Halifax and the Caribbean. Thirteen of these convoys sailed through the Eastern Sea Frontier from May to September during the height of the U-boat onslaught, bringing 110 tankers safely to port without loss. At a time when tanker losses off the U.S. coast were particularly severe, these RCN convoys were a signal success. Once the U.S. coastal convoy system was in place, the Canadian oil convoys were stopped and the escorts were assigned to the U.S. Navy's New York to Guantanamo Bay convoys.[24]

The Canadian Naval Staff, itself the subject of well-deserved criticism in the early years of the war, at least understood from the outset that getting the convoy and escort system in place was more important than the quality of the escorts themselves. The German U-boat logs from early 1942 speak of a dearth of shipping in Canadian waters, which is testimony to the effectiveness of the convoy system in clearing the seas of numerous easy targets.[25] That, and the bitter winter weather off eastern Canada from January to May, encouraged the U-boats to move south faster than they might otherwise have done in early 1942. Convoys in the broad ocean off Nova Scotia and Newfoundland enjoyed remarkable success during 1942 in part because the pickings were so good elsewhere. Only one ship was lost from an ocean convoy off Nova Scotia in 1942 (*Pacific Pioneer*, sunk from ON 113 in July).[26] All of these convoys were routed within that broad band of land-based airpower reaching seaward some four hundred miles, which gave tremendous scope for evasive

---

[23] This system was later expanded in mid-1942 when the assembly point for transatlantic convoys shifted from Nova Scotia to New York. Halifax-based escort groups, known was Western Local Escort Force, guarded the ocean convoys from New York northward for the balance of the war. For a table of RCN and RN convoys, including starting and end dates, see Tucker, *Naval Service of Canada* 2, appendix 10 and for the U.S. Navy appendix 11.

[24] The existence of the Canadian oil convoys in 1942 has, of course, been well known to students of the RCN's war, but until recently there has never been a thorough, scholarly analysis of them. Fortunately, that gap has been filled by Robert C. Fisher in his excellent article, "'We'll get our own': Canada and the Oil Shipping Crisis of 1942," *The Northern Mariner* 3, no. 2 (April 1993): 33-40.

[25] For a detailed assessment of U-boat reaction to Canadian waters in early 1942, see Michael Hadley, *U-Boats Against Canada: German Submarines in Canadian Waters* (Kingston and Montreal: McGill-Queen's University Press, 1985), chapter 3.

[26] There may well have been more, but this author is unaware of them. Losses to convoys in the St. Lawrence River and Gulf are a different matter.

routing and made individual U-boat's search problems extremely difficult. The one anomaly in the Canadian inshore convoy experience in 1942 was the Gulf of St. Lawrence convoys, where twenty-two ships were sunk. There the problem was a combination of constriction of routing in the river itself, which made it impossible to avoid the U-boats, and the very difficult layering of sea and river waters which baffled sonarmen and favored submariners. Heavy commitments to the main convoy routes prevented reinforcing the escorts of these convoys, so the RCN recommended closure of the Gulf of St. Lawrence to ocean shipping in the early fall.[27]

Why American historians of the Atlantic war ignore — completely and utterly — the Canadian experience with U-boats inshore during 1942 remains a mystery. National myopia accounts for it in part. There is, as well, a tacit assumption that what happened off the U.S. coast was inherently more important than what happened — or might have — off Canada. There is no gainsaying that the U.S. was the focal point of transatlantic shipping. But much of that shipping had to pass through Canadian waters to get there, and the object of Admiral Karl Dönitz's strategy in the Atlantic war was sinking shipping wherever that could be done with the greatest facility. The reason why there was no disaster of global proportions off Canada's coast was not because the area was strategically insignificant, but because the existing system of convoys made finding shipping and attacking it much less profitable than operations off the U.S. coast. The Canadian experience in 1942, therefore, provides a window on America's problems. The trick is to get someone to look through it.

Action in the latter half of 1942 shifted to the mid-ocean, where wolf packs renewed their depredations on convoys as they passed through the mid-Atlantic air gap. British and American historians of the Battle of the Atlantic tend to skim over events in the mid-ocean in the last half of 1942, preferring to concentrate on the more dramatic crisis which follows in early 1943. But the latter is incomprehensible without a more thorough analysis of the July to December 1942 period — and the role of the RCN.

---

[27] The case for the distinction between inshore and ocean attacks on convoys, the importance of routing, and the difference these imposed on A/S forces are discussed in M. Milner, "Inshore ASW: The Canadian Experience in Home Waters," in W.A.B. Douglas, ed., *The RCN in Transition* (Vancouver: University of British Columbia Press, 1988), 143-158. The American debate over what to do with a few destroyers obscures — from an Anglo-Canadian perspective — the essential issue, which was that the convoy system itself, supported by aircraft, was the key to stopping the Germans on the U.S. coast in 1942: the convoys could be escorted by almost anything.

By August 1942, when wolf pack attacks began again in earnest, four of the eleven escort groups protecting transatlantic shipping through the air gap were RCN — roughly 35 percent. However, between July and the end of 1942, fully 80 percent of all shipping lost from transatlantic convoys to U-boat action fell from Canadian-escorted convoys. Buried in the Admiralty's *Monthly Anti-Submarine Report* for January 1943 is the comment that, for the previous six months, the *RCN* had borne the brunt of U-boat attacks in the Atlantic: an observation which completely escaped historians for forty years.[28] This historical oversight has obscured the significance of the relationship of the fall 1942 battles to the crisis which followed in 1943. Tying the two together indicates that the RCN was more than a benign influence on the course of the Atlantic war.

At issue here is the significance of that alarming loss rate to RCN-escorted convoys in late 1942. The British argued at the time, and subsequently,[29] that the RCN failure was due to poor training, poor leadership, and lack of skill as a result of its too-rapid expansion. As a result, Canadian-escorted convoys were a disaster waiting to happen and the war simply caught up to them in late 1942. There is a strong element of truth in this: the RCN was badly stretched by late 1942, and its group leadership was uneven. But in the end, expansion and overwork were not the underlying causes of those terrible losses to RCN convoys in late 1942. The RCN argued at the time that the losses were largely due to the poor state of equipment in the fleet, especially the almost total lack of modern 10cm radar and shipborne High Frequency Direction Finding (HF/DF). The latter was essential for preventing the assembly of the pack around the convoy, while modern radar allowed the escort to detect

---

[28] This period is analyzed in depth in Milner, *North Atlantic Run*, chapters 5 and 6.

[29] The British were never very pleased with Canadian operational efficiency and carped about it for most of the war — indeed, it became habitual and obscured some essential issues, such as the role of equipment and speeds of convoys being escorted. The situation got so bad by the end of 1943 that CinC, Western Approaches Command issued an order expressly forbidding criticism of the RCN except from his office. The notion that the RCN were well intentioned but bungling permeated the postwar British literature and affected the British interpretation of the Atlantic war. In particular, in late 1942 Canadians argued that lack of modern equipment caused their exceptional loss rate. The Official British historian Captain S.W. Roskill addressed the point obliquely in his discussion of the period by arguing that training and leadership counted for more than modern equipment in late 1942. He cited the example of two aged British destroyers, *Viscount* and *Fame*, which performed sterling work with B.6, each sinking a U-boat in late 1942. The point that Roskill missed — wilfully or otherwise — was that both ships and their groups were well equipped with modern sensors and weaponry: the age of hulls was immaterial. See Roskill *The War at Sea*, vol. 2 (London, HMSO, 1957), 357.

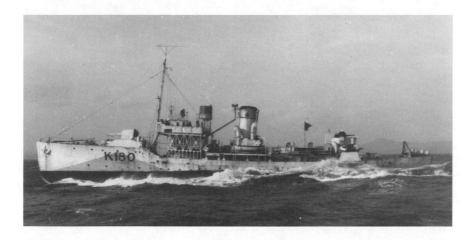

RCN corvettes remained unmodernized throughout the crucial period of the war, as evidenced by *Collingwood* seen here in 1943. She still has a short forecastle and outdated bridge, although the lantern just aft of the bridge contains type 271 ten-centimeter radar. Photo courtesy of the National Archives of Canada.

U-boats as they closed to attack at night. Virtually all RN mid-ocean escorts were fitted with modern radar and each of their destroyers had HF/DF in the fall of 1942. With this equipment, and with a minimum of two destroyers per group (while the RCN often labored with only one), British groups possessed the resources, including the tactical intelligence, to organize and successfully fight a battle with a wolf pack.

In contrast, RCN groups in the mid-ocean fought blind. The famous British operational scientist P.M.S. Blackett described convoy battles as unstable equilibriums.[30] The first blow set the pace, and if it was made successfully by the U-boats, the escort was forced to respond to the tempo set by the attacker. This is what typically happened in Canadian convoy battles. In the absence of HF/DF, wolf packs assembled around Canadian-escorted convoys with ease. Furthermore, since the 1.5m radar carried by RCN escorts could not detect the attack before it took place, the U-boats usually struck first and set the tempo of the battle.

Moreover, there was another, perhaps more important, reason for the difference between RCN- and RN- escorted convoys in the mid-Atlantic

---

[30] Blackett's assessment is contained in his report on the importance of air cover to convoy battles, submitted by the Air Officer Commanding, Costal Command to the Anti-U-Boat Warfare Committee, British Cabinet, 22 March 1943. PRO, ADM 199/1787.

in late 1942: the RCN still escorted the bulk of the slow convoys. These took appreciably longer to transit the air gap, contact with them was more easily re-established by U-boats after it was lost, and they were incapable of any effective evasive action. Of the twenty-five fast eastbound convoys (the famous HX series) escorted across the mid-ocean between July and the end of the year, only five were Canadian-escorted (nineteen had an RN escort). Over the same time period, Canadian ships escorted the majority (fourteen of twenty-four) of the slow eastbound convoys, the SC series. Some balance was achieved on westbound convoys, with sixteen of twenty-eight fast and only three of twenty-one slow convoys coming under RCN escort. This ought to have helped the RCN, but the Germans gained contact with nine of the RCN's nineteen westbound convoys (47 percent). The interception rate for British-escorted westbound convoys was only 20 percent. It should also be noted that the distinction in speeds of westbound convoys, traveling in ballast against prevailing westerly winds, was nominal. In sum, although the RCN amounted to only 35 percent of MOEF strength in late 1942 and escorted only about 38 percent of convoys transiting the air gap, the Germans concentrated fully half of their operations against them (fifteen contacts out of twenty-nine for the period).[31]

Most of the RCN losses came from two major convoy battles involving SC 107 in November (fifteen ships) and ONS 154 in December (sixteen ships). Both were slow convoys intercepted early and forced to endure an ordeal of fire through the air gap. At the end of December 1942, the British lobbied successfully for the withdrawal of Canadian groups from the mid-ocean, claiming that expansion had created a training problem that would take some time to solve. The Canadians protested that they escorted the bulk of the slow convoys and that their groups lacked of modern equipment and enough destroyers. The acid test of the Canadian and British cases for the high RCN loss rate in late 1942 was actually the lone U.S. Navy group in the mid-ocean, A.3. It was everything the British claimed the Canadian groups were not: A.3 enjoyed steady composition, highly regarded and steady leadership of two U.S. Coast Guardsmen, and frequent pre-sailing training. Unfortunately, its loss rate during late 1942 was comparable to that of the RCN groups — and so too was the state of its equipment.[32]

---

[31] These figures are drawn from M. Milner, "Canadian Escorts and the Mid-Atlantic 1942-1943" (unpublished Masters Thesis, University of New Brunswick, 1979), appendix 6, Summary of North Atlantic Convoy Operations, July-December 1942.

[32] These issues are discussed at length in Milner, *North Atlantic Run*, especially chapters 6, 7, and 8. The British wanted to removed A.3 from the air gap as well, but for some reason decided not to press the issue. Figures for A.3's record from July to December 1942 can be

The British managed to have the RCN groups removed from the transatlantic route for additional training in early 1943 and took over the whole task — save for A.3 — themselves. Their experience with slow convoys in the air gap was no better than that of the Canadians. After the disaster of SC 118 in early February, major changes in the organization of escort forces were forthcoming: the Canadians could have told them as much. As part of those changes, the Canadian groups were returned early to mid-ocean escort duty, outfitted with much new equipment, augmented by more fast escorts, and provided with RN senior officers. They were, however, kept well clear of the action, and the victory over the U-boats that came in April and May was overwhelmingly British.

The Canadian contribution to the Allied victory of early 1943, when over one hundred U-boats were destroyed in the North Atlantic and the wolf packs soundly beaten, is a metaphor for the RCN's contribution to the Atlantic battle as a whole. Although half of the escorts in the theater were Canadian, they claimed only two and a half of the hundred subs sunk by naval and air escorts. This enormous discrepancy reflected in large measure a British belief that their better trained, better led, and better equipped groups ought to be put in contact with the enemy while those of the RCN ought to concentrate on safe and timely arrival of the convoys. It was a logical division of labor. As the chief of the Canadian Naval Staff opined in late 1943 — as he was about to be sacked for the navy's failure to sink enough submarines in 1943 — had it not been for the RCN's concentration on making the system work and supporting the larger navies, the efficiency and flexibility evident in the RN's escort fleet in the victory of 1943 would not have been possible.[33] The RCN went on to success in the latter stages of the war, assuming responsibility for the close escort of all major transatlantic trade convoys north of New York and providing eight to ten support groups for the offensive phase of the ASW campaign. Indeed, the RCN was such a force in the Atlantic ASW and escort world by late 1944 that the British thought of handing it all over to them and concentrating their own forces in the Pacific. In the end, the danger of a renewed offensive by the radically new type XXI German submarine and the inability of the RN to support its large number of

---

found in appendix 6 of Milner, "Canadian Escorts and the Mid-Atlantic." Ironically, the best "British" group in the mid-ocean during late 1942, B.6, was actually built around a core of Norwegian-manned corvettes.

[33] The sentiment was expressed in a memo from Admiral P.W. Nelles, the CNS, to A.L. Macdonald, the Naval Minister, when the issue of the fleet's efficiency came to a head in late 1943. Indeed, Nelles claimed that the RN had worked on the principle of fleet modernization "to the detriment of the RCN." CNS to Macdonald, 4 December 1943, A.L. Macdonald Papers, Public Archives of Nova Scotia, f 276/39.

American-built escorts in the Indian Ocean kept a large portion of the RN A/S fleet close to home in the final months of the war.[34]

A former U.S. Coast Guardsman who joined the RCN, and spent the grimmest years of the war in command of a Canadian corvette, claimed in early 1943 that the Battle of the Atlantic up to that point ought properly to be called "The Battle of Canada." Lt. Phillip C. Evans, RCNVR, commanding officer of HMCS *Trillium*, sensed that the building resources of the U.S. would soon sweep the Canadian contribution aside — both in practice and in memory. Pinching a line from another American naval officer, Alfred Thayer Mahan, Evans wrote that "those far flung, storm tossed little ships" of the RCN had stood between Hitler and the domination of the world since 1940.[35] Despite the hyperbole, Evans had a point. The escorts that the RCN threw into the Atlantic war by 1941 were a major windfall for the Allies. Moreover, Canada built the ships and provided the rudimentary armament, the crews, and just enough professional skill to keep it all going. It was more than the Allies had asked or expected, and it was enough to help shape one of the major campaigns of World War II.

---

[34] The RCN's role in the final two years of the antisubmarine war is detailed in the author's forthcoming book, tentatively entitled *To Kill a U-Boat: The Royal Canadian Navy and the Offensive Against Germany's Submarines* (Toronto: University of Toronto Press, 1994).

[35] "Battle of Canada," Lt. P.E. Evans, RCNVR, March 1943, Heineman Papers, box 4, ONS 166, additional information, Naval Historical Center, Operational Archives Branch, Washington, D.C.

9

The Battle of the Atlantic, 1941-1943: Peaks and Troughs

J. David Brown

By early 1941, three events had advanced the British assault on the German naval ciphers: the captures of the *Krebs* in the Lofotens, the *München* north of Iceland, and the submarine *U 110* to the south of Iceland. Cipher keys and the internal settings of the Enigma machine captured from the first gave the Government Code and Cipher School (GC&CS) at Bletchley Park all the February 1941 "Heimisch" traffic. The insight enabled the mathematicians there to practice their black art to such effect that they worked out for themselves the April traffic and by May the delay between interception of German signals and their decryption had been reduced to between seven and ten days.

While this was a formidable achievement, it did not approximate to the near real-time needs of the mobile war in the Atlantic — a seven-knot convoy could cover 1,100 miles in a week, while a ten-knot U-boat athwart its track could reach Iceland from the Azores in the same time. A vivid example of the effects of the lag was provided by the eastbound convoy HX 126. On 15 May, BdU (U-boat command) ordered a seven-boat pack to take up a patrol line to the south of Greenland, across the track of the convoy, which was escorted only by an armed merchant cruiser, provided for protection against disguised surface raiders. Unaware of the U-boat deployment, the Admiralty made no attempt to divert the convoy or to reinforce its escort, for not until two days after the pack struck, on 19 May, was Bletchley Park able to pass the decrypt.

Within days, however, Bletchley Park was reading the Enigma decrypts currently — usually within an hour of their transmission. Not only that, but they were reading virtually everything to and from the U-boats. The capture of the weather trawler *München* on 7 May, a deliberate trap made possible by the cryptanalysts' previous successes, provided June's cipher settings. At least as valuable was the acquisition of the U-boat "*Kurzsignale*" code-book and the settings for the navy's "officer only" cipher which came from the *U 110,* briefly captured on 9 May by convoy escorts; her commanding officer, Fritz-Julius Lemp, had compounded his original gross error in sinking the *Athenia* (thereby persuading the Admiralty to institute a general convoy system from the outset of the war) with a final negligence which gave his enemies a priceless advantage.

The capture of the weather ship *Lauenburg* at the end of June — a repeat of the *München* operation which provided the July 1941 keys — consolidated GC&CS's grip on the naval Enigma. Thereafter, no more captures were necessary as long as the German signals authorities did not introduce fundamental technical changes. To the in-house talent, derived from familiarity with Enigma procedures, the provision of a "bombe" computer for purely naval purposes, and sheer hard experience were added two German contributions. The naval weather cipher was discovered to carry reports which had originally been transmitted by U-boats in Enigma cipher. Not only did this provide a useful "crib" to breaking the current keys, but it gave the reporting submarines' positions, which were carefully re-enciphered for security! The other source was the seemingly unlikely *Werft* dockyards and harbor approaches hand cipher; broken originally because it was discovered first that some of these signals were repetitions of deciphered Enigma signals, it was then found that some of its output was re-transmitted in the Enigma cipher. *Werft* was of negligible operational value, but it brought incalculable cryptanalytical benefits. From August 1941 through May 1945, only two days' worth of the three-rotor Home Waters naval traffic was not read by Bletchley Park.

Bletchley Park's achievement was formidable, but so was the organization to which the deciphered signals were passed. The Admiralty was unique, in Britain at least, in that as well as providing the political and administrative direction of the navy, it also exercised direct executive command, not only over operational headquarters but even over squadrons and individual ships at sea, and it did so not as an exceptional measure but as part of the routine of the conduct of the war. Such centralization was made possible only by the provision of a network of worldwide communications which radiated from Whitehall itself. It also required the concentration of all available intelligence, whose relevance would be assessed by the Naval Intelligence Division (NID) before it was forwarded to the Operations and Trade Divisions and, where necessary, to RAF Coastal Command operational headquarters.

Bletchley Park passed decrypts as "raw material" direct to the Operational Intelligence Centre (OIC), the NID section responsible for assessing, filtering, and channelling all forms of intelligence to the operations staffs. OIC had, however, realized at an early stage that the cryptanalysts could make valuable contributions to the assessment process, recognizing patterns and, as important, deviations in not only the content but also the form of the signals traffic; the marriage of the OIC and GC&CS talents was, in general, an extremely happy and fruitful one. Armed with information that was as up-to-date as that available to the BdU and the U-boat commanders, in the summer of 1941 the Admiralty was able to take immediate steps that were, for the first time, to weight the balance against the submarines.

Of these, perhaps the most important were devised to minimize the U-boats' opportunities for sinking ships. Evasive routing, to keep convoys clear of enemy concentrations, had been attempted with varying degrees of success since the outbreak of war; the shore Direction-Finding stations, the only source of current information, were of less and less value as the "front line" moved westwards across the Atlantic, and although shipborne HF/DF equipment was under development, it did not go to sea until July 1941. Enigma decrypts of the command orders and of U-boats sighting and homing signals replaced the crystal ball with a two-way mirror, enabling the Admiralty to divert convoys to avoid the known patrol lines or to strip the escorts from unthreatened convoys to reinforce convoys which could not be rerouted in time to avoid attack.

Unrelated to the state of the communication campaign was the necessary decision to provide "end to end" antisubmarine escort. The U-boats' success against HX 126 had occurred well to the west of the radius of action of the escort vessels based in Ireland and Iceland, and it was this action that provoked the Admiralty to develop an escort force base at St. John's, Newfoundland, early in June, and to introduce convoy oilers to enable escort vessels to remain continuously with their charges. Active defense complemented passive evasive routing, for while the latter reduced the submarines' opportunities for intercepting, the presence of the escorts reduced their chances of being successful when they did so.

The extension of the antisubmarine forces' reach and the availability of prompt signals intelligence produced an immediate tactical victory. On 20 June, Bletchley Park passed a BdU order to form a patrol line to the southeast of Greenland. Two westbound convoys were routed around the line, but the eastbound HX 133 could not be diverted in time. Instead, its escort was reinforced from the two unthreatened convoys so that the ten U-boats which made contact were eventually faced with thirteen escorts. Five ships were lost during the ensuing five-day battle, but so were two of the U-boats.

The westward extension of U-boat operations had necessitated the stationing of a German tanker to the southwest of Greenland; other ships were at sea to provide middle and South Atlantic replenishment for submarines and raiders. By 25 May, the Operational Intelligence Centre knew from decrypts that there were eight supply ships at sea and had exact patrol positions for half of them. The first to be eliminated was the "Greenland gas station," sunk by a pair of cruisers on 3 June; two more supply ships were intercepted and sunk on 4 June and a fourth the next day. Ten days later, yet another U-boat supply tanker was sunk, a victim, like the others and the two ships earmarked to support the *Bismarck*, of the Royal Navy's exploitation of Bletchley Park's success. The U-boats were now faced with an insoluble logistical problem just as the British had overcome theirs. Coinciding as it did with the reduction in sightings to the south and west of Greenland, this reverse led to an eastward move of the U-boat force, to areas within the reach of shore-based aircraft from Iceland and the United Kingdom.

The background to one of the most important decisions taken after the real break into the Enigma is obscure. On 18 June 1941, the Trade Division raised the speed limit for ships which *had* to be sailed independently from thirteen to fifteen knots. One of the linchpins of the journalistic approach to history is the leap to conclusions, epitomized by the formula "must have," to bridge the gaps in sequences of events or steps in reasoning which cannot be filled from available records; the equivalent for the historian teetering on the brink of legitimacy is "it is tempting to believe that."

In the absence of the missing link, however, this author is tempted to believe that, in this instance, the exploitation of decrypts did not provide the spur. Independently-sailed shipping losses had doubled from sixteen in March 1941 to thirty-two in April and had increased again to forty-three in May; twenty-eight independents had been lost in June up to the raising of the speed limit. The reasoning behind lowering it — it had been considered that U-boats would have difficulties in locating dispersed shipping — was plainly faulty: during the second quarter of the year, only thirty-nine ships had been sunk while in convoy or straggling, compared with 120 lost proceeding independently. The effect of raising it was even more dramatic for, during the second half of 1941, it nearly reversed the situation: forty-nine independents were sunk, compared with 113 convoyed ships and stragglers.

The introduction of a new concept of operations by Coastal Command's antisubmarine aircraft antedated the major cryptanalytical breakthrough but appears to have been stimulated by anticipation of success. From 9 May 1941, with Admiralty agreement, the Royal Air Force suspended routine air escort of convoys and independents: only those known to be threatened would be given protection by direct escort or sweeps. Furthermore, no night escort missions would be flown, these having proved to be particularly fruitless so far. The emphasis on Coastal Command antisubmarine operations was to be offensive, not defensive, and aircraft would seek out the U-boats and destroy them instead of waiting for the U-boats to come to the convoys.

Offensive air antisubmarine doctrine is tailor-made for the exploitation of current signals intelligence but totally flawed in its absence. In practice it failed completely in 1941. Lack of adequate numbers of long-range aircraft — fewer than fifty could operate more than 500 miles from base — and indifferent weapons and tactics meant that many valid opportunities for offensive action were missed and little significant attrition was inflicted by the attacks that were delivered. Of twenty-five Axis submarines lost in the Atlantic during the second half of 1941, RAF Coastal Command was responsible for only one outright "kill" (captured) and two shared with surface ships, out of 139 sighted. Despite claims to the contrary, aircraft continued to serve primarily as scarecrows for many months to come.

Mention has already been made of the technical advances made by the British. The fitting of centimetric radar or of HF/DF in individual ships, or the introduction of the "snowflake" illuminant as a means of "turning night into day" around a convoy did not, of themselves, have an immediate effect at the lowest tactical level. What was needed was an adequate number of escorts with a relatively simple doctrine, consisting of standard operating procedures (to borrow a 1950s term) based on hard experience, and the experience itself.

New construction and the modification of older fleet ships met the first requirement. In June 1941, Western Approaches Command had ten numbered and "special" escort groups which, with "unallocated" ships and loans, totalled 108 ocean antisubmarine escorts; by November, the Command had nineteen numbered groups with 134 ships, with twenty-six others on loan or not allocated to groups, while a dozen others were operating from Newfoundland in parallel with the Royal Canadian Navy's local forces. From 1 September, these were supplemented by the U.S. Navy's "neutrality patrol" convoy escort task groups, which the British and Americans alike believed to enjoy immunity from attack, thanks to decrypts of repeated orders, emanating from Hitler himself, to avoid action with U.S. Navy units.

Doctrine was left to the Western Approaches Command — an example of the Admiralty's decentralizing policy. The curiously named "Tactical Table Unit" at Liverpool devised and played out countermeasures to meet the U-boat tactics reported by the escort commanders and improved upon them as the U-boat commanders, in turn, modified their methods; as time went by, the TTU was able even to anticipate a new

German tactic and have the counter in hand. Operational research analysts studied the available technical intelligence and the attack reports to work out ideal convoy and escort dispositions, depth-charge patterns, and even camouflage schemes. Between them, the tacticians and analysts provided the seagoing teeth of this organization with standard operating procedures which were subject to continuous modification.

Experience came from success, measured not only in terms of "safe and timely arrival" of the convoys but in actual scalps: by the end of the year, twelve of Western Approaches' numbered groups and thirty-two individual ships had a solo or shared "kill" under their belts from the previous six months' operations. All attacks, successful and unsuccessful, were fed back as grist to the tacticians' and analysts' mill, to be added to the mass of knowledge which was promulgated routinely, and occasionally as a matter of urgency, to all those, at sea and ashore, who were waging the campaign.

The U-boats moved back to the eastern Atlantic in late July 1941. The *B-Dienst* was providing, from its decrypts of the British ciphers, details of convoy movements, but this source of information alone was unable to bring the boats into contact with the shipping. Three convoys were intercepted and roughly handled in July and August, but these were not transatlantic sailings but rather were on the north-south route between the United Kingdom and Gibraltar and West Africa. This route took the ships within range of the *Luftwaffe* long-range patrol aircraft based in southwest France, and, alerted by agents overlooking Gibraltar from neutral Spain, it was they who located the convoys and homed the U-boat packs which would otherwise have been wrong-footed by the Admiralty's evasive measures. The U-boats themselves reported that the efficiency of the escorts had increased "to an astonishing degree"; in particular their ability to deal with shadowing submarines was stressed — whereas a few months previously only a single U-boat was needed for maintaining contact, now it was a task for an entire group.[1]

The improved tactics minimized losses by depriving the U-boats of firing opportunities — during the first two Gibraltar convoy operations, only one of the dozen boats making contact had been able to deliver a second attack — but it provoked BdU into ordering attacks on the escorts at every opportunity. The third convoy action thus began and ended with

---

[1] Günter Hessler, *The U-Boat War in the Atlantic*, 2 vols. (London: HMSO, 1989) 1: 82. Sources consulted in the preparation of this paper include Public Record Office, ADM 119/2058-60 and ADM 234/51. Original research by Mr. R.M. Coppock of the Naval Historical Branch, MoD, and Mr. A.H. Hague, of the World Ship Society, into, respectively, causes of U-boat loss and individual convoy passages, has been of the utmost value and is gratefully acknowledged.

the sinking of a British escort, but even then only one of the six U-boats which delivered one successful attack managed a re-attack.

The U-boats operating between Iceland and the United Kingdom had meanwhile been experiencing a lean time, not least because Coastal Command's new patrol policy appeared to flood that area with aircraft. In early September, with more submarines at sea than ever before (an average of thirty-six each day), BdU decided to push the groups further west once more to form mobile patrol lines which would search for convoys between Greenland and the Azores and as far afield as Newfoundland. Within three days, the redeployment had fully justified itself: a "wolf pack" found convoy SC 42 off Greenland and, although the boat which made the initial contact was promptly sunk, the seven boats which followed this up sank fourteen ships and damaged two others in fifty-four hours. Four made successful re-attacks but these cost the pack another of its number.

This defeat, like the attacks on three subsequent convoys, was due in part to the introduction by BdU in September of enciphered "Quadrat" positions,[2] but there were other reasons for subsequent difficulties experienced by the OIC's Tracking Room during the month, not least being atmospheric conditions, affecting H/F wireless reception, which also affected Dönitz' handling of his U-boat packs. The latter certainly hindered a U-boat concentration against SC 44 ten days later. As for the other two convoys which sustained significant loss in September 1941, both were on the north-south route and were initially sighted by submarines on passage and relocated and shadowed by aircraft.

Depressing as the figures for September 1941 may have been, with forty-five convoyed ships and an escort sunk, there were nevertheless encouraging developments. From 1 September, the U.S. Navy had begun escorting some convoys as far east as Iceland (and four days later *U 652* had fired "defensive" torpedoes at USS *Greer*), relieving the strain on the British and Canadian escort groups. Late in the month, the entry into service of the first escort carrier, the *Audacity*, at last provided a counter to the *Luftwaffe* shadowers on the Gibraltar route.

The most unlooked-for reprieve came from Hitler himself when, early in September, he ordered six of the Atlantic U-boats to the Mediterranean, where the war at sea was going badly for the Axis. The numbers available for Atlantic operations were made up (including replacements for the two boats sunk during September) by new arrivals from German home waters, but this meant that the defenses faced no more submarines

---

[2] F.H. Hinsley, et al., *British Intelligence in the Second World War*, 2 vols. (London: HMSO, 1981) 2: 173.

in October than they had in the two preceding months, while their own strength continued to increase.

After one more notable success, against SC 48 in mid-October 1941, the U-boat offensive effectively collapsed. This convoy was sighted by chance by one of a group of submarines in transit from one area to another, but although the nine COs involved made up a "star team," so efficient and aggressive were the defenders, reinforced by a U.S. Navy group diverted from another convoy, that only four of them reached firing positions on the merchant ships, ten of which were sunk. Two British escorts were sunk and, by an act of understandable folly, the U.S. destroyer *Kearny* was damaged.

Apart from this battle, and a lesser action against a northbound convoy from Gibraltar, the OIC had the upper hand throughout October, keeping the shipping out of harm's way. Only thirty merchant ships under allied control were lost in total, thirteen of them independents. The escorts were handled more roughly, for five were torpedoed and sunk; besides the two lost with SC 48, two Royal Navy vessels were sunk on the Gibraltar run and the USS *Reuben James* was lost southwest of Iceland while escorting HX 156. As in September, two U-boats and two Italian submarines were destroyed.

If October had been unprofitable for the U-boats, November was worse and December a calamity. Only eleven merchant ships were sunk in the North Atlantic during the former month, nine of them from the four convoys which were attacked. December saw sinkings reduced to ten ships (six in convoy) while Atlantic U-boat losses reached a new high, no fewer than six being sunk by convoy escorts, all on the Gibraltar route and five while attempting to get to grips with one convoy — HG 76.

Towards the end of November, the German Naval Staff had assessed a build-up of merchant shipping at Gibraltar as indicating that amphibious landings were intended in Vichy-controlled North Africa. Besides despatching yet more boats from the Atlantic into the Mediterranean during that month and the next, the U-boats patrolling the gaps between the convoys in the mid-Atlantic and southwest of Greenland were ordered to operate in the approaches to Gibraltar. Both decisions were taken against BdU's advice and, as it transpired, better judgement.

The OIC was aware of the Mediterranean reinforcement and of the general abandonment of the Atlantic, and it took appropriate steps not merely to protect shipping but also to sink U-boats. In November, permanent surface antisubmarine patrols and a night barrier air patrol[3]

---

[3] Radar-equipped Swordfish "stranded" by the loss of the carrier *Ark Royal* provided this patrol.

were instituted in the approaches to the Straits of Gibraltar to stop the U-boats heading for the Mediterranean. By the modest late-1941 standards, the results were spectacular: of twenty-six U-boats ordered between 11 November and 19 December to pass into the Mediterranean, four were sunk, by mine, surface ship, and air attack, and six were damaged by air attack and forced to return to France. Arrival in the Mediterranean provided no sanctuary, for during the last five weeks of the year another four U-boats were sunk there.

The sailing of HG 76 from Gibraltar was delayed (thereby provoking the German Naval Staff's belief in an impending assault on North Africa) until mid-December, when a sufficiently strong escort could be gathered. The week-long defense of this convoy against the waiting U-boat group and against shadowing aircraft provides the classic example of the convoy as a killing ground, with the escorts as the "wolf pack" — the converse of the hunted flock of vulnerable merchant ships, as portrayed by opponents of the principle. Just two merchant ships were lost, one needlessly when it was prematurely abandoned, and two escorts: unfortunately, one of the latter was the Royal Navy's only escort carrier, the *Audacity*, which had more than proved her worth during the battle.

By any standards, the Royal Navy and its allies had achieved victory on the North Atlantic convoy routes by December 1941. The U-boats had never even closely approached the 800,000 tons-per-month sinking rate that the German Naval Staff had established as necessary for winning this campaign, and they were sustaining losses out of all proportion to their meager successes — one Atlantic submarine was lost for every three convoyed ships during the last quarter of 1941, compared with the preceding quarter's ratio of 1:8.

There can be no doubt that this trend would have been at least partly reversed without the diversion provided by the entry into the war of the Unites States, for in spite of losses and deployments to the Mediterranean and Arctic theaters, the number of operational U-boats leaving the Baltic training schools was increasing rapidly. Only twenty-five German submarines had undertaken North Atlantic patrols in December 1941; forty-two would do so in January 1942 and fifty in the following month.

The events of early 1942 are well known, and three statistics illustrate the grounds for criticism of U.S. antisubmarine policy and doctrine. Of nearly 550 ships sunk by U-boats during the first half of the year, only one in thirteen was in convoy; in March 1942, three U-boats were sunk by convoy escorts and the latter conceded no losses to the enemy; in the same month, of the eighty-six independently-routed merchant ships sunk, mostly in U.S. waters, fewer than a third were U.S.-flagged.

The relative immunity of the convoys owed very little to the British cryptanalysts after 1 February 1942. Certain combinations of events had led BdU's communications security branch to the conclusion that the Admiralty had foreknowledge of the movements of U-boats and their supply ships; instead of seriously doubting the Enigma machine as the source of these leaks, however, BdU tightened internal security, first by introducing re-enciphered positions in September 1941 then by adopting modified settings exclusive to the U-boats at the beginning of November. These GC&CS broke soon after introduction, but this was not possible with the ultimate measure of adding a fourth rotor wheel to the Enigma machine.

From 1 February 1942, Bletchley Park's Naval Section was neutralized by this one stroke, which was intended to exclude *German* personnel with no "need to know," not to deny the cryptanalysts, whose success was unimagined at the time and unknown for another thirty years. GC&CS continued to read the German Home Waters traffic and the lesser naval ciphers currently, but these provided little more than indications of U-boat arrivals and departures at the bases. Even with over three years of experience, access to the peripheral ciphers, wireless traffic analysis, the "fingerprinting" of individual operators, and shore-based HF/DF, GC&CS and OIC were unable to substitute for decryption of the primary U-boat communications cipher as a reliable, let alone accurate, source of U-boat movements and intentions.

The scale of shipping losses off the Americas between February and May 1942 can not be ascribed to lack of Enigma-based intelligence. As the corresponding period in 1941 bore witness, heavy independent sinkings could be expected from heavy independent traffic, which could not be given detailed instructions for evasion. The coastwise traffic off the United States concentrated the unprotected merchant ships into identifiable lanes which could be raided by the U-boats until the latter ran out of torpedoes and fuel.

The relief provided by the U-boats' concentration in American waters did not provide a sufficiently long respite for the Allied cryptanalysts, and when in late May 1942 a single group returned to the Atlantic convoy routes, the copious signals traffic remained impenetrable. On the other hand, the *B-Dienst* was currently reading the latest British "routine" convoy cipher, introduced in 1941 for Anglo-U.S.-Canadian cooperation, having completed reconstruction in February 1942, just as GC&CS "lost" Enigma.

The pendulum would have swung in completely the opposite direction when U-boat operations against the convoys resumed had the respite not granted the escort forces the opportunity to fit the latest equipment, weapons, and sensors, and to become proficient in their use. This was specifically true of HF/DF and centimetric radar. At the same time, the Western Approaches Tactical Unit, as the "Tactical Table Unit" had become, had been given the leisure to re-examine procedures. The result was that when, in July 1942, the U-boats began to return in force, the escorts were able to exact a toll which should have acted as a deterrent, for the dozen escorted merchant ships lost from North Atlantic convoys that month cost six U-boats, while as many more were sunk by patrols.

It was inevitable that such a favorable rate of exchange could not be sustained. "Only" seventy U-boats were on patrol in July 1942; this rose to eighty-six in August and their effectiveness was out of proportion to the small increase, for losses in convoy more than doubled. Twenty-two ships were sunk from seven ocean convoys and twenty-one from thirteen convoys intercepted in the Caribbean and Gulf of Mexico; escorts destroyed five U-boats. Independent and straggler losses rose only slightly, with fifty-two ships sunk north of the equator in August. For the first time in the war, more than half-a-million gross tons of Allied merchant shipping was lost to U-boats in a single month.

While it might have been expected that a further increase in the number of active submarines to one hundred in September would have been matched by a corresponding increase in the number of merchant ship losses, this was not the case, for the U-boats managed to intercept only twelve convoys, compared with the fifteen which had been sighted in August. More boats made delivered attacks, but their scale of success was much reduced. For example, in the previous month, forty-eight direct contacts had resulted in the sinking of twenty-two ships in convoy and three stragglers in mid-ocean; in September, however, the sixty contacts sank only thirteen ships in convoy and six stragglers from the ten transatlantic convoys which were actually attacked.[4] The only saving grace from BdU's point of view was that this slight success was achieved without loss and independents were still about in large numbers, fifty-one being sunk in this one month.

The last quarter of 1942 followed September's pattern, with one important difference. Six transatlantic convoys were intercepted in each month, 120 U-boats approached sufficiently close to attack or to be prevented from doing so by the escort, and these sank sixty-three ships in convoy, nine stragglers, and two escorts. The difference was that they paid dearly for these sinkings, thirteen submarines being destroyed by

---

[4] Figures for U-boat sightings have been obtained from the BdU War Diaries and correlated with Jürgen Rohwer's "Die U-boot-Erfolge der Achsenmachte 1939-45," which has in turn been compared with manuscript abstracts from the "Convoy Packs" held at the Public Record Office, Kew, prepared by Arnold Hague.

the escorts. Elsewhere, proportionately more was achieved by fewer U-boats at less cost: twenty-four contacts with five north-south ocean convoys resulted in eighteen sinkings for the loss of two boats. Perhaps the most important statistics of the many available were that three out of every four ocean convoys reached their destinations without loss as did ninety-seven out of every one hundred ships that sailed in these convoys.

Without doubt, chance played a hand in this long game. The North Atlantic weather was particularly severe during the winter of 1942-43, and the succession of gales affected the U-boats as badly as they did the convoy and the escorts. Thus, although as many as twenty-seven U-boats were ordered to concentrate against a single convoy in October, only eight managed to make contact and two of those were sunk before reaching an attacking position. The merchant ship masters and escort group commanders had also learned the lessons of previous winters and knew the dangers of dispersal and straggling under stress of weather: of ninety ships lost in the North Atlantic, only ten were stragglers, compared with thirty-four out of eighty-eight in the last quarter of 1940.

Although signals intelligence was of little assistance to the Allies during this phase, by the standards of the similarly Enigma-less winter of 1940-41 the convoy escorts were actually winning, for they were fending off far larger numbers of U-boats while exacting a steady toll, not simply of the Atlantic U-boat fleet as a whole but of those who were able to intercept convoys — fewer than a third of the number of boats at sea in any one month.

BdU acknowledged the increased expertise of the defenses by modifying tactics and introducing technical countermeasures of varying effectiveness. Of these, the most successful was the "Metox" UHF-band radar intercept gear, which began to enter service during the summer of 1942 and gave a useful measure of immunity against aircraft search radar and substantially reduced losses in the transit areas. Against most surface escort groups its use was limited, for the majority of Royal Navy and U.S. Navy ships were now fitted with undetectable centimetric radar sets. New anti-escort weapons, notably the acoustic homing torpedo, were under development, but these would not be ready until the summer of 1943. In the meantime, the U-boats' best defense proved to be its ability to dive deeper than the Allies imagined. The Type VIIC had a "normal" limit of 660 feet, but in emergency it could go safely to 1,000 feet.

To extend the endurance of the U-boats operating off the Americas, BdU had in March 1942 introduced the "U-tanker," originally a modified operational boat but latterly a custom-built "Milch Cow" capable of supplying fuel oil, lubricants, provisions and even torpedoes to the fighting boats. Although the front line had moved closer to the bases in France by late 1942, the U-tankers had proved to be so successful that they were retained as a force multiplier, enabling the operational groups to be redeployed at their best sea speeds without regard to the individual boats' fuel states. Replenishment at sea in the winter Atlantic was by no means a relaxing pastime. Taken with the increasing difficulty of penetrating the convoys' defenses, BdU could not expect more than two or three active group operations — successful or unsuccessful — per U-boat sortie, even when the boats failed to make contact, because of the strain on the crew.[5]

Hindsight may be the curse of the historian but it is crucial to the analyst. A definite pattern had emerged from the renewed convoy campaign — a pattern which should have been apparent to the Allied trade divisions, if not to Dönitz, who had to rely on his COs' inflated claims for his analyses. Despite increasing numbers, superior intelligence, and the Allied cryptanalysts' continuing lack of success, between July 1942 and the end of January 1943 the U-boats managed to "win" only one major convoy battle per month.

The optimistic convoy situation belied the actual state of affairs, although it reflected "what might have been" had more ships been in convoy. In October 1942 the losses again fell upon the independents, particularly in the more distant waters of the central and South Atlantic, outside the interlinking convoy system. Altogether, fifty-four independents were sunk, compared with only twenty-three convoyed transatlantic ships; perhaps the worst aspect was that while the latter was compensated by the sinking of five U-boats, the independents represented completely "free hits."

November 1942 was the worst month of the war in terms of tonnage sunk, with over 720,000 tons lost worldwide. The transatlantic losses were actually marginally less than in October, with twenty-eight ships sunk in convoy and forty-seven independents lost in the Atlantic areas, of which twenty-three were off the coasts of the Americas, where antisubmarine measures had been steadily improving since the bad days of the summer. The contemporary inability to read the U-boat cipher had little real effect on independent losses, but these continued to bite deep into the Allies' deep-water shipping resources. Every ship lost represented a loss of capacity, either to sustain the war effort of the nations closest to the front line (and therefore fighting a campaign of survival) or to develop and sustain an offensive against the Axis. The remarkable facility with which the United States shipbuilding industry responded, first to make good losses and then to expand the Allied carrying capacity, should never blind historians to the problem of manning those ships. The merchant crews lost by policies which ignored all previous lessons were as much

---

[5] Hessler, *U-Boat War in the Atlantic* 2: 51.

assets as the ships themselves and were absolute losses to the Allied cause.

December 1942 appeared to bring a ray of long-term hope. GC&CS' unremitting efforts against the four-rotor Enigma were at last making substantial progress, thanks to yet another windfall — cipher material retrieved from the sinking wreck of the *U 559* off Haifa.[6] This was sufficient to lead Admiral Sir Dudley Pound, the First Sea Lord, to pass on the qualified good news to Admiral Ernest J. King. In this message, sent on 13 December,[7] Pound re-emphasized the need for complete security, saying that: "It would be a tragedy if we had to start all over again on what would undoubtedly be a still more difficult problem." It was a somewhat cloudy dawn. Bletchley Park's successes were spasmodic during the first three months of 1943, sometimes reading the U-boat traffic currently, usually within three days, but occasionally not at all for a period of over a week.

The escorts fought on, unaware of this backroom battle. Ninety-seven U-boats were at sea during December, but the weather again favored the convoys and the escorts. Up to Christmas Day, only five transatlantic convoys were located, and fourteen contacts had resulted in just six sinkings while three of the U-boats had been destroyed. On 26 December, the weather gods smiled on BdU when the westbound convoy ONS 154, diverted far to the south to avoid storms in the Iceland area, was sighted by the southernmost boat of a patrol line. During the next five days, thirteen of the eighteen U-boats ordered to intercept made contact and sank thirteen ships from the convoy and two stragglers. Only one U-boat was lost. Even with this success, BdU could scarcely be satisfied with December's results, for besides the twenty-one ships sunk from transatlantic convoys and two sinkings from chance encounters with north-south convoys, the Allies had lost only twenty-four independents in all North Atlantic areas.

ONS 154 was, furthermore, merely a "blip on the graph." Marginally fewer U-boats were at sea (ninety-two) in January 1943, and they managed to intercept only three convoys bound for the United Kingdom, from which one convoyed ship and three stragglers were sunk with the loss of a single submarine. The *B-Dienst*'s decrypts had revealed the extent of the direct traffic between the United States and the Mediterranean, and by redeploying an existing group nine hundred miles southwards and redirecting boats on passage, BdU assembled a force of a dozen submarines to intercept the first major eastbound tanker convoy,

---

[6] David Kahn, *Seizing the Enigma* (Boston: Houghton Mifflin, 1991), 223-227.
[7] Cited in Hinsley, *British Intelligence*, 233.

TM 1, to the west of the Canaries. Eight actually made contact, and thanks to a weak and inexperienced escort, they sank seven of the nine ships. Those U-boats which had sufficient fuel loitered in the area during the rest of the month but succeeded only in sinking four stragglers from two other U.S. Mediterranean convoys.

The most striking statistic of the month, however, was that for the first time since the outbreak of war in September 1939, independent losses in the Atlantic were fewer than those in convoy. Only nine ships were sunk in all, and of those only one was in the waters of the Americas, where fifteen had been sunk in December. February proved to be even less costly, with only six independents lost, but this success was seen only in negative terms in some quarters, where the reasoning ran that, when put to the test, convoy was proving to be more expensive than independent sailings. There were, of course, two underlying reasons for the trend: fewer independent ships were being sailed, reducing the opportunities for chance encounters in areas of heavy traffic, and BdU had recognition that large concentrations of ships presented the best opportunity to sink the necessary monthly tonnage.

In early February 1943, the British convoy cipher and information from a rescued merchant seaman enabled BdU to set up the first interception in force of a U.K.-bound convoy since the beginning of November. Out of twenty-one U-boats deployed, twenty made contact with the fifty-four-ship convoy in mid-Atlantic. They ran into a most determined escort (EG B.2 — four old escort destroyers and four corvettes, later joined by three U.S. Coast Guard Cutters and supported by Liberator aircraft from Iceland) and only five submarines managed to deliver torpedo attacks, sinking nine ships out of the main body of SC 118 and one straggler. Every U-boat was attacked, fifteen by the ships and five by aircraft, four were damaged and forced to return to base, and three were sunk.

With over one hundred U-boats at sea, BdU could call upon fresh groups to intercept the next convoys, but it was distracted from the key eastbound convoys by excellent positional information provided by the *Luftwaffe*, whose DF stations were able to intercept transmissions made by the Coastal Command aircraft escorting the convoys. This real-time intelligence coincided with a loss by GC&CS of current Enigma settings which had kept the eastbound convoys away from the waiting U-boat groups. Three successive westbound (and therefore strategically "empty") convoys were intercepted, the first by four U-boats, the next by fifteen and the last by a single boat, attempts at concentration having failed. Inevitably, the largest group enjoyed the greatest success, sinking fourteen out of the eighteen merchant ships lost, but the series cost another four U-boats destroyed and several damaged. Although the U-boats had grossly overclaimed, neither the sinkings-to-contact rate nor the sinkings-to-loss ratio could be regarded as satisfactory.

From the Allied point of view, February's losses in convoy — thirty-one ships in convoy and six stragglers — were alarming, the more so as all had occurred on the transatlantic routes and they far exceeded the independent losses. The Allies could not have known that the air and sea escorts of the eleven ocean convoys intercepted or encountered had despatched twelve U-boats out of the fifty-nine individual boats which had made contact, but it should have been evident that each major effort was followed by a lull which permitted succeeding convoys to pass either scot-free or at least without serious loss.

For this, the intermittent Bletchley Park successes can take some of the credit, providing sufficient information to the OIC for effective evasive routing. But it was noticeable that, hitherto, even with several large groups at their disposal for interception and decrypts to give warning of convoy movements, the U-boat headquarters staff had seldom been able to coordinate simultaneous major operations, possibly because the sheer number of submarines at sea was growing unwieldy. They were to be more successful in March.

One hundred and sixteen U-boats operated against Atlantic shipping in March 1943, making ninety-six individual contacts with convoys, but not until the end of the first week was the first convoy sighted. SC 121 was unlucky, for it had been skillfully rerouted between two waiting groups only to be sighted by a U-boat in transit. Twenty-eight submarines were redeployed to overhaul or cut off the convoy, but in indifferent weather only eleven made contact, sinking five ships from the main body and seven stragglers. The general movement of U-boat groups put another dozen boats in the grain of HX 228, just as the Enigma traffic became indecipherable again, but the defending escort group kept losses down to four merchant ships and sank two U-boats.

The battle which followed four days after the last shots of HX 228 was a complete disaster for the Allies, but it should be seen in its true context. The Admiralty made a fundamental mistake in sending a "fast" convoy with a weak and indifferently led escort, HX 229, up the track of the "slow" SC 122 (the difference was, in fact, a knot and a half). The official history[8] implies that lack of current decryption was behind the inability to provide effective rerouting and states that evasion on the basis of DF bearings proved ineffective, but the fact is that HX 229 was located by accident, a U-boat astern of the convoy sighting a detached

---

[8] Hinsley, *British Intelligence* 2: 561-62.

escort and making the report which led to the first actual contact being made by a group which was not looking for HX 229. The two groups which were lying in wait ahead ran into SC 122, 120 miles to the east, while HX 229 continued to close from astern. Eventually, forty U-boats were ordered to operate against what became a confused gaggle of shipping, but of these only nineteen made attacks, which resulted in the loss of twenty-three ships out of eighty-seven in the two convoys.

Nearly simultaneously, twenty U-boats of three other groups made a copybook interception of a U.S. Mediterranean convoy, UGS 6. This convoy's track was known in detail, thanks to the efforts of the *B-Dienst*, but unfortunately for the submarines, the six U.S. Navy destroyers of the escort conducted a copybook defense, and only five U-boats got within firing range to sink four of the ships. One U-boat was destroyed.

The 1943 end-of-year summary by the Naval Staff's Anti-U-boat Division stated that the heavy losses up to 20 March 1943 (i.e., from HX 229/SC 122) had led the Admiralty to believe ". . . that it appeared possible that we should not be able to continue convoy as an effective system of defence against the enemy's pack tactics."[9] This paints a picture of an imminent change of policy, which was not the case. The intermittent failures of Bletchley Park were becoming fewer, although there was always the risk that another blow, like the introduction of the fourth rotor had been, would cause the complete loss of all U-boat intelligence derived from cryptanalysis. But just as up-to-date signal intelligence had not been wholly responsible for all the successes in the North Atlantic, so its absence was by no means the main cause of some of the worst reverses.

The Admiralty still had a number of measures which were even more imminent and which were based wholly upon the doctrine of convoy. More very-long-range aircraft were already appearing far out into the mid-Atlantic (they had supported the later stages of the passage of HX 229/SC 122), but as important were the "support groups," homogeneous squadrons of sloops or destroyers which had worked up together in the antisubmarine role and which were to reinforce threatened convoys. The concept of these independent antisubmarine units dated back to the autumn of 1942, and while the lack of escorts and the demands of the North African campaign had prevented more than a brief trial, the Western Approaches staff had kept the idea alive, to the extent

---

[9] "Monthly Anti-Submarine Report," December 1943 (dated 15 January 1944), 3, PRO ADM 199/2060. This summary does not include Roskill's ringing phrase about "disrupting communications between the New World and the Old . . ." but employs this much more mundane phraseology.

of playing out a paper exercise on the Tactical Table as HX 228 was fighting a real battle.[10]

Two support groups, one British, the other American, took the field in late March with an escort carrier attached. The USS *Bogue*'s first convoy was SC 123, while the first to benefit from a Royal Navy carrier support group was HX 230. The former was not threatened, but one ship was sunk, in exchange for the U-boat responsible, from the latter. The full impact of "organic air" as a mid-ocean U-boat killer was not to be felt until after May 1943, but its defensive benefits were immediately apparent, adding an extra dimension to the U-boats' already considerable tactical problem.

Total losses for March 1943 amounted to forty-seven ships, of which ten were stragglers, from eight transatlantic convoys; four independents were also sunk in the North Atlantic. Elsewhere, on the north-south route and off the Americas, twenty-one ships were sunk from eight convoys attacked, as well as just two independents; as before, the sinkings per submarine contact were higher in these areas — despite the achievements of the wolf packs which had attacked HX 229/SC 118, the U-boats had still not achieved a one-to-one rate against the east-west shipping. Over half the U-boats at sea found convoys, but seven were lost to the escorts and five were sunk by patrols. They themselves had sunk just over half a million tons of Allied shipping.

On the other hand, during the first three months of 1943, 270 more convoyed merchant ships had reached their destinations safely than during the last quarter of 1942, even though the number of convoys intercepted had increased as had the number of ships sunk. Only one convoy escort had been lost, as against three in late 1942, while the toll taken of U-boats around the convoys had risen from fourteen to twenty-four, an exchange rate of one submarine for every five ships.

Most of the U-boat losses were made good in April, from new construction and by re-allocating submarines from West Africa and the South Atlantic, but although seventy U-boats were sailed from Germany, Norway, and France to operate against the convoys, bringing the total on patrol to 111 for the month, they achieved little of significance. Over fifty individual U-boats came close enough to convoys to attack or be sunk by the escorts, and they sank just twenty-four ships in convoy and six stragglers from seventy-six contacts in all areas; nine were destroyed by escort vessels and aircraft and six by patrols or mines in the transit areas.

The lack of success was not for want of opportunity. Although GC&CS had broken back into the Enigma settings after the mid-March

---

[10] MS notes by the late Captain H.N. Lake, RN (staff, Western Approaches, 1942-43).

catastrophe and could provide timely evasive routing intelligence, the *B-Dienst* was just as active and successful in decrypting the alterations of route and, in fact, the U-boats intercepted one more convoy in April than they did in March and in sufficient strength to achieve reasonable results. Weather, strong defenses, and inexperienced commanding officers were considered to be the main causes, and all three were certainly present when, towards the end of the month, the twelve U-boats in contact with HX 234 managed to sink only two ships.

The U-boat command staffs appear to have taken some comfort from the fact that losses in the second half of 1942 and the first quarter of 1943 were proportionately lower than those suffered during the first twenty-seven months of the war when expressed as a percentage of the submarine force at sea on operations. In March 1943, replacements were still coming forward faster than the Allies could sink them. But what the German navy's statisticians overlooked was the *cumulative* effects of the losses and the special nature of the COs: the fifty-odd U-boats destroyed by convoy escorts during the nine most recent months represented a loss of experienced manpower needed for rapid expansion — their First and Second Watch Officers, who would have expected to get their own boats after a successful apprenticeship, were a lost generation. The boats also represented much of the potentially most effective element of the U-boat fleet, for they were an appreciable percentage (nearly 20 percent) of the minority which actually found a convoy.

The end of March 1943 was, perhaps, not the best moment for any measured analysis by BdU's staff. Dönitz had replaced Gross-Admiral Raeder at the head of the German navy in January 1943 but was not ready to delegate the U-boat war to his capable Chief of Staff, Kapitän Godt. Instead, in the last days of March, he pulled back the operations staff from Paris (whither it had been withdrawn from Kerneval following the British Commando raid on St. Nazaire a year before) to Berlin, where it became functional on 31 March.

Quite apart from the discontinuity caused by the move, the overall commander had more than physically distanced himself and his group of talented veterans from the front-line crews. Once totally immersed in every aspect of U-boat activity, Dönitz now had the entire navy to supervise, and even the BdU staff could be regarded as "them" — the remote, rear-area warriors. Whether or not the move to Berlin reduced efficiency and morale, 31 March 1943 is a symbolic date, for it marked the beginning in the decline of the fortunes of the U-boat arm.

The Royal Navy's escort commanders certainly noticed a lack of expertise, or of determination, on the part of the U-boats during the weeks that followed HX 229/SC 122, but no great comfort was derived from the lull. As April drew to a close, the initial contact was made between the escorts of convoy ONS 5 and the first of four groups, totalling sixty U-boats, which BdU had assembled for a great set-piece battle. This proved to be one of the epic encounters of the Battle of the Atlantic and has been regarded ever since as a turning point. The victory of the escorts, by six U-boats to thirteen merchant ships, was, however, a triumph for tactical and technical expertise, won mainly by the ships and aircraft involved. In this sense, it was another step on the "knock down, drag out" road shown by the defenders of HG 76, SC 118, and UGS 6.

Dönitz had held fast to a very clear aim for the past year: Britain and her allies were to be brought to their knees by the submarine blockade in the North Atlantic. He resisted every fresh initiative by the Naval Staff (the *Seekriegsleitung*) and even by Hitler himself if it appeared to lead to the weakening of the U-boat fleet in the Atlantic. One can sympathize with the Skl, whose only major maritime contribution to the wider war could be the submarine arm, which they wished to deploy to the Mediterranean to bolster a flagging ally, to the Indian Ocean to reassure the Japanese, and to the Arctic, where they were not only to interdict supplies to Russia but also to deter an invasion of Norway. Dönitz remained adamant and his philosophy coincided with his operational doctrine: "Strategic pressure alone is not sufficient, only sinkings count."[11] The North Atlantic convoys provided the potential numbers of victims and were, besides, the critical link in Allied strategy. Increased sinkings increased the pressure to the point where the stresses began to show at the highest level, but, thankfully, not in the commands, the groups, or the men in the line of battle.

The end finally came on 24 May 1943, after a week in which the fifty-odd U-boats had attempted two major set-piece battles, only to be thwarted by evasive routing and by veteran defenders. Dönitz acknowledged a defeat which he believed to be only temporary. He would resume the campaign with new weapons and equipment, as well as a new generation of commanding officers, who would hold the ring until the new types of U-boat could enter service and achieve the victory which he believed had been so close.

---

[11] BdU War Diary, 13 August 1942.

Appendix
Quarterly Balance Sheets - Winter 1942-43

October-December 1942

A total of 99 convoys consisting of 2,992 ships sailed in both directions on transatlantic and UK-Gibraltar and West African (North-South) ocean routes.

	Transatlantic	North-South	Americas
convoys intercepted	18	5	3
convoyed ships lost	63	17	7
stragglers lost	9	1	-
escorts sunk	2	1	1
independents sunk	18	17	56
U-boat contacts[a]	73	14	4
U-boats sunk by escorts	13	1	-
contact: convoy sinking	0.99	1.29	1.75
exchange rate[b]	5.54	18.0	-

January-March 1943

A total of 3,233 ships sailed in 105 ocean convoys.

	Transatlantic	North-South	Americas
convoys intercepted	24	7	6
convoyed ships lost	77	13	12
stragglers lost	23	-	-
escorts sunk	1	-	-
independents sunk	12	7	2
U-boat contacts[a]	112	11	7
U-boats sunk by escorts	16	4	2
other U-boat losses[b]	2	4	-
contact: convoy sinking	0.89	1.18	1.71
exchange rate[c]	5.55	3.25	6.00

[a]U-boats known to have delivered an attack or been sunk by convoy escorts.
[b]U-boats lost in the area of convoys, for which no Allied claims have been proven.
[c]Escorted merchant ships or stragglers sunk for every U-boat lost near convoys.

10

The U-Boat War off the Outerbanks

James T. Cheatham

During the early months of World War II, North Carolina Outerbanks residents were the most susceptible of any along the Atlantic seaboard to rumors and misinformation. The isolated villages at Hatteras and Ocracoke on these barrier islands were without means of receiving current news of the war. Picture yourself living under those conditions and waking up at night with the windows rattling from concussions of ships being torpedoed and looking out on the horizon of the ocean to see as many as five ships burning at one time.[1] Most Outerbanks residents earned their living fishing and many were without formal education, and as far as they were concerned, invasion was imminent and their lives were severely threatened. Rumors ran amuck. These people were witnessing the war firsthand much more graphically than the west coast Americans, who the country seemed to think were at great risk. For many, a mail boat several times a week was all the news they received, except what they heard on the radio. As we know, the U.S. government censored all radio broadcasts in the early part of the war once it learned that the Germans were able to pick up the names of ships being sunk and weather information from local radio stations along the coast. During the first few months of 1942, over sixty ships were sunk off the North Carolina Outerbanks between Cape Lookout and the Virginia border.[2]

Now it is quite a contrast to compare the news coverage that we saw in the Persian Gulf War. We were able to sit by our television and watch the actual initial bombing of Baghdad and hear all the commentators,

---

[1] Interview with Jack Willis, Ocracoke Island, December 20, 1987.
[2] David Stick, *Graveyard of the Atlantic* (Chapel Hill: The University of North Carolina Press, 1952).

generals, admirals, the President and Saddam Hussein give the status of the war. Conversely, these Outerbanks residents were completely in the dark in World War II.

When I vacationed at Atlantic Beach or Morehead City, North Carolina, early in World War II, I remember hearing rumors of German spies being caught with theater tickets from the Morehead City theater in their pockets. these were never proven true; in fact, between January 1942 and May 1943, the FBI investigated over 500 reports along our coasts of such spies signalling to submarines, or other vessels, but each one was a false alarm.[3]

The only spies put ashore by submarine were at Long Island, New York, and Ponte Vedra, Florida. These were caught because of one spy who surrendered and revealed their identies.[4]

I recall houses on the coast whose windows were covered with blackout curtains at night and cars whose headlights were painted so only a small amount of light would be emitted.

During those early months of 1942, most of the sinkings along the coast were caused by submarines on the surface at night. They were much faster on the surface, making seventeen to eighteen knots against seven knots, underwater. They usually fired only one torpedo at a target because there were so many and they wanted as many hits as possible. This practice usually saved lives on the stricken ships since it allowed the crew an opportunity to disembark before the U-boat finished off the ship with its deck gun. Conversely, U.S. submarines in the Pacific had a standard procedure of firing three initial torpedo salvos. Obviously, if all three were accurate and the ship was not too large, there was not much left of the ship or crew.

Experiences of the Coastal Residents

On Harker's Island, a small island between Beaufort, North Carolina, and Cape Lookout, Paul Tyndall (former member of the N.C. House of Representatives) remembers well the early months of World War II.[5] He was the principal of the local school at Harker's Island. The residents of the island at that time consisted of many families who had moved over from a whaling village at Cape Lookout after the hurricane of 1899. The

---

[3] Quote by J. Edgar Hoover, Director, Federal Bureau of Investigation, *American Magazine*, (October 1943): 110.

[4] Interview with Professor Dr. Jürgen Rohwer, German naval historian, 20 October, 1989, Annapolis, Maryland.

[5] Interview with Paul Tyndall (former member of North Carolina House of Representatives), 13 February 1988.

island was isolated, with no telephones, and at that time a bridge connecting the mainland had not been completed.

Soon after the war started, passes were required for citizens to go over on the Outerbanks to fish. Tyndall remembers seeing the many ducks and loons washed ashore covered in oil from tankers that were sunk off the coast. At night, he recounted that windows would occasionally be blown out from the vibrations caused by ships exploding off shore. In this atmosphere rumors got started early about German spies and the possibility of signals from shore being given to U-boats. At Tyndall's school there was a teacher of German descent who was immediately suspected of being a spy and even followed by well-intentioned natives who suspected him of foul play. When this teacher began to leave his home early in the morning to cross over to the mainland, the citizens immediately suspected he was collaborating with the enemy. As it turned out he was only going to get milk for his children. However, by the end of the school year he was forced to leave the island and seek employment elsewhere.

One day the principal noticed that many of the boys in school who usually came barefooted were wearing new Florsheim shoes. Investigation revealed that these had washed up on the Outerbanks from a merchant ship that was sunk by a U-boat. The fathers of these children who were fishermen had quickly commandeered these shoes and the children wore them proudly.

During the spring of 1942, Tyndall's wife had to be transported to the Morehead City Hospital with a serious appendicitis, and while she was a patient there he visited the hospital daily and saw the many burn victims being treated. These were seamen who had been rescued off the coast from burning tankers. Tyndall even assisted the nursing staff in caring for these patients since they were shorthanded and the hospital was overflowing at the time. The public was not made aware of this for fear of panic along the coast.

In fact, on 1 April 1942 the navy, after nearly three months of bad news, announced that twenty-eight Axis submarines had been sunk in the Atlantic.[6] This was good news for the beleaguered coastal residents, but absolutely false. The navy did not sink an enemy submarine on the East Coast until 14 April.

On the sound near Salter Path, North Carolina, a small fishing village west of Atlantic Beach, lived Mrs. Alice Hoffman, whose niece married Theodore Roosevelt, Jr. She had purchased approximately a nine-mile

---

[6] Michael Gannon, *Operation Drumbeat: The Dramatic True Story of Germany's First U-Boat Attacks Along the American Coast in World War II* (New York: Harper & Row, 1990), 378.

portion of Bogue Banks in the early 1900s. Her name, of German origin, spurred many rumors that she was aiding the enemy. One such rumor had Mrs. Hoffman refuelling submarines from the dock of her home. Since the water was only a few feet deep in the sound, even I, at six years of age at the time, could figure out that this was impossible. After the war, I visited Salter Path (at that time still accessible only by boat or a dirt road) and talked to fishing families who were quick to tell of windows being blown out by exploding ships just off the coast, much debris and oil on the beach, and suspicious persons seen about during the spring of 1942.

Further up the coast at Ocracoke Island, Jack Willis, who was then in his late teens and later served in the navy, remembers seeing as many as four or five ships burning at one time off the coast at night. Both he and long-time native Thurston Gaskill adamantly refute the rumors among vacationers that native fishermen assisted German submarines off the coast.[7] In fact, further investigation through the German Military Historical Research office has proved their contentions correct. German historian, Captain Werner Rahn, in an interview in September, 1987, emphatically stated that he had read all the U-boat logs concerning East Coast activity and there was absolutely no evidence of islanders selling supplies to U-boats and he does not believe it happened either on the East Coast or in the Caribbean area later on.[8]

German Admiral Dönitz introduced large U-boat tankers called "Milch-Cows" by April of 1942 which allowed the submarines further cruising limits. Some, including *U 123* captained by Reinhard Hardigan, moved further south off Florida and in the Caribbean where the "turkey shoot" continued unabated. In one incident, Hardigan showed compassion for Florida residents watching from shore when he brought his submarine around between a burning tanker and the beach so that shells from his deck gun would not fall ashore.

On 11 March the American freighter *Caribasca* was sunk near Ocracoke. Survivors were tossed about on life rafts all day until their use of a metal can as a reflector attracted one steamship, *Norlindo*, bound for Baltimore. One of those lost was James Gaskill from Ocracoke whose brother, Thurston Gaskill, still resides on the island. The ship's nameplate is said by island residents to have floated through the Ocracoke inlet and washed ashore near where Gaskill lived. Marvin Howard found it and

---

[7] Interview with Thurston Gaskill, Ocracoke Island, North Carolina, July, 1986.

[8] Interview with Captain Werner Rahn, German Military Historical Research Office, 25 September 1987, Annapolis, Maryland.

made a cross which can be seen today in the Methodist church located on the island.[9]

It was not until the fall of 1945 that the Fifth Naval District released the number of merchant seamen and guncrews lost off the coast due to Axis submarines in World War II. In this district's waters, which extend halfway to Bermuda and include the shores of Maryland, Virginia, and North Carolina down south to Onslow Bay, 843 men lost their lives.[10]

The Bedforeshire Incident[11]

Alarmed by the large number of ships sunk off the eastern coast of the United States, in February 1942, the British government agreed to loan the U.S. Navy twenty-four antisubmarine corvettes. These ships were about one half the size of a World War II-type destroyer, at 170 feet long, with a crew of four officers and thirty-three enlisted men. Their armament consisted of a four-inch quick-fire deck gun and a 303-caliber Louis machine gun. They also carried approximately 100 depth charges and were equipped with sonar.

It seems ironic that only two years after the United States gave (through its Lend-Lease program) fifty destroyers to the British the Americans would need some of their ships to combat the U-boat menace.

Among the twenty-four corvettes leaving England in early March was the HMS *Bedfordshire*. The ships travelled through the North Atlantic to Newfoundland, then Halifax, Nova Scotia and New York. At least one ship was lost during the winter gales on this trip, and the others arrived in New York in much need of repairs. Among the officers on board the *Bedfordshire* was Sub-Lieutenant Thomas Cunningham. The *Bedfordshire* spent April and part of May patrolling off the North Carolina coast between Morehead City and Norfolk, with Morehead City its home port. These ships were coal burners and required frequent refuelling.

In early May, a naval intelligence officer visited the ship to obtain British flags to use in the burial of British seamen at Cape Hatteras who lost their lives in ship sinkings. Sub-Lieutenant Cunningham was the officer who procured these flags for the U.S. Navy. The *Bedfordshire* then refuelled at Morehead City and left to check out a submarine siting report.

On the night of 12 May, *U 558*, captained by Gunther Krech, was cruising between Cape Hatteras and Cape Lookout. Its mission to date

---

[9] Interview with Jack Willis, Fall, 1989, Ocracoke Island, North Carolina.

[10] Fifth Naval District Press Releases, September, 1945.

[11] L. Vanloan Narisawald, *In Some Foreign Field: The Story of Four British Graves on the Outerbanks* (Winston-Salem, North Carolina: John F. Blair, Publisher, 1972).

had been uneventful, and the captain was beginning to wonder if he would have as successful a patrol on the American coast as his fellow commanders. Suddenly, the noises of a ship's screw were heard on the submarine's listening device, and a lookout saw the HMS *Bedfordshire*.

Visibility was limited. Krech decided to attack while surfaced because submarines can move much faster on the surface. The first torpedo fired by *U 558* missed but the second torpedo hit the *Bedfordshire* squarely amidships, catapulting the ship into the air and sinking it almost immediately. No one survived this sinking.

The U.S. Navy, to which the British ships were attached, was not diligent in keeping track of these patrol craft, as evidenced by the fact that the navy did not know for several days what happened to HMS *Bedfordshire*.

On 14 May, while patrolling the shore at Ocracoke Island, a Coast Guardsman discovered the bodies of Sub-Lieutenant Thomas Cunningham and telegraphist Stanley Craig. later, two other bodies, unidentifiable, were recovered. These were removed to a small plot next to a local cemetery at Ocracoke Village and, with Coast Guard assistance and Protestant graveyard services, they were given proper burial. Ironically, the flag used for Cunningham's funeral was one of the very ones given by him to the navy about ten days earlier.

In subsequent years, with the cooperation of the United States government and the citizens of Ocracoke Island, this small plot was deeded to the British government and is now an official cemetery of the United Kingdom. It can be viewed today on Ocracoke Island. Permanent grave markers are present and a British flag flies continuously over the site to remind all who see it of the brave men who fought and died off American shores in World War II.

Cape Lookout

Cape Lookout, with its fine natural harbor, is located five miles east of Beaufort, North Carolina. It was an ideal sanctuary for pirates in the colonial era. The Cape was a beautiful, isolated barrier with only a lighthouse until early World War II when again it became a "haven" for desperate seafaring men. The German submarine menace on the North Carolina coast in the winter of 1942 forced the navy to form a "bucket brigade." This brigade consisted of a group of ships that set out submarine nets, mined harbors, and performed other defensive tasks. They only sailed during daylight hours and spent their nights anchored in harbors such as Charleston, Cape Lookout, and the Chesapeake Bay. These vessels tended buoys which marked submarine nets. Many years after the war these buoys could be found rusting on the coastal beaches.

Early Mined Harbor

One of the "bucket brigade" harbors was a specially mined harbor in the ocean between Hatteras Inlet and Ocracoke Inlet. The idea was to put U.S. merchant ships in the harbor at night because it was protected by Mark 6 contact mines.

In theory this sounded good, but as a practical matter several of our own ships were sunk by the mines when they failed to enter the harbor properly. In 1943, a navy minesweeper was dispatched from Norfolk to clear this minefield as the harbor was no longer used. The Mark 6 contact mines were considered "unsweepable" because instead of a cable they were anchored to the bottom with chains. This proved an interesting and exciting time for the minesweepers, but after several months most of the mines were swept.[12]

Many years after the war, one of these mines was snagged in a trawler's net. It was taken to the dock at Jack's Store in Silver Lake on Ocracoke Island. Apparently, the fishermen did not know what it was and hammered on it for several days, thinking it might be a treasure from Blackbeard's time. When the Coast Guard heard about it, they carried the mine to the northern end of the island to be detonated. On the way it fell off the truck, but still did not detonate. Finally, with the aid of a bomb squad from Norfolk, who determined it was still live, the mine was exploded with a single shot. The explosion left a crater 150 feet across, caught the marsh on fire and the Ocracoke Fire Department had to be called out. Needless to say, if the mine had gone off in Ocracoke Harbor, there would have been little left of Jack's Store and the surrounding area.[13]

Some seamen who were on ships torpedoed during World War II still reside in Snug Harbor, a seamen's retirement home on the Outerbanks about thirty miles north of Morehead City. They can recite their experiences with the U-boats and subsequent rescue at sea. While I was visiting there, an old sailor sitting in the lobby was overheard saying, "that young author believes all these stories they are telling him."

---

[12] Interview with Armistead J. Maupin, Executive Officer of the minesweeper, 15 August 1990, Raleigh, North Carolina.

[13] Interview with Norman Miller, waterman, Ocracoke Island, North Carolina, December, 1990.

Conclusion

Hitler's refusal to heed his U-boat commander's recommendation to send more than six submarines to the East Coast in early 1942 probably saved America an oil and sugar crisis. These products were rationed and Britain' s ability to stockpile war materials for pending operations against the Axis was curtailed. While all such postponements and setbacks cannot be directly linked to the success of the German U-boats off the American coast, Dönitz's submarine offensive unquestionably restricted Allied operations. During the early part of 1942, the U-boats made their mark and the Americans repeated just what happened in World War I; that is, instead of instituting escorted convoys, to better protect merchant shipping, some antisubmarine ships were randomly dispatched to hunt the U-boats. President Woodrow Wilson had a saying for this action in World War I which was equally applicable for the first months of 1942, "They despaired of hunting the hornets all over the farm."[14]

---

[14] T.J. Belke, "Roll of the Drums," U.S. Naval Institute *Proceedings* (April 1983).

PART THREE

Turning the Tide

11

"Situation Extremely Dangerous": Three Atlantic Convoys in February 1943

David Syrett

In the middle of February 1943, the situation in the North Atlantic appeared to be generally favorable for German U-boat operations as they had just scored a major victory over the Allies in the battle for Convoy SC 118.[1] Although the Germans enjoyed a number of advantages in the Battle of the Atlantic, as demonstrated in their recent victory, the *Befehlshaber der Unterseeboote* (BdU) did not at this time have adequate intelligence, if indeed any, on the movements and locations of Allied convoys. As a result, the U-boats were stationed or were being deployed across several possible Allied convoy routes in the North Atlantic.[2]

Thus, group *Haudegen*, consisting of thirteen U-boats,[3] was stationed in an arc some three hundred miles northeast of Cape Race, Newfoundland. Two other groups of U-boats, *Ritter* and *Neptun*,[4] were deployed into two patrol lines running north-south along 25° and 30° west. The *Ritter* and *Neptun* patrol lines overlapped and were able to sweep an area of the North Atlantic 450 miles wide. This deployment had a further advantage, for the Germans thought the area to be beyond the range of

---

[1] David Syrett, "German U-Boat Attacks on Convoy SC 118: 4 February to 14 February 1943," *The American Neptune* 44 (Winter 1984): 48-60.

[2] Ministry of Defence (Navy), *The U-Boat War in the Atlantic, 1939-1945*, 3 vols. (London, 1989), 2: 77.

[3] U 606, U 69, U 201, U 226, U 525, U 303, U 383, U 607, U 358, U 186, U 223, U 403, U 707.

[4] *Ritter* consisted of U 468, U 377, Faatz, U 225, U 653, U 628, U 623, U 616, U 332, U 92, U 753. *Neptun* included U 759, U 405, U 448, U 638, U 359, U 35, U 608, U 376, U 566, U 659.

range of shore-based Allied anti-U-boat aircraft.[5] Allied intelligence knew the location of the U-boats of the *Haudegen* group east of Newfoundland, but the Allies believed that these U-boats were short of fuel and that a number of the German craft would be ordered to return to base. Allied intelligence had a less clear picture of the deployment of the *Ritter* and *Neptun* groups, however, and thought that the area north of 50°30'N southeast of Greenland, known as the "Air Gap" or to the Germans as the "Black Hole," was "heavily stocked" with U-boats.[6]

At 1550 on 15 February, the BdU ordered the *Haudegen* group to disband, eight U-boats to return to base, and the remaining U-boats to be formed into the *Taifun* group.[7] Several hours after receiving these orders, at the beginning of the voyage back to her base in France, the *U 607* encountered and sank the American tanker *Atlantic Sun*. The U-boat picked up several men from the American ship, who told the Germans that the *Atlantic Sun* had left an Allied convoy "some nights ago."[8] The *Atlantic Sun* belonged to convoy ONS 165 and had been forced to part from the Allied formation by heavy weather.[9] Upon receiving the *U 607's* sinking report, BdU concluded that the *Atlantic Sun* belonged to "a extra-schedule fast convoy."[10] However, the situation in the North Atlantic remained obscure at best for the Germans until 1541A on 17 February, when the *U 69* sighted the main body of ONS 165.[11]

ONS 165 was a slow westbound convoy, consisting of thirty-six merchant ships which sailed from the Clyde at 1900 on 2 February. The convoy had proceeded west across the Atlantic at an average speed of 4.5 knots until it reached 53°48'N 36°50'W on 15 February, where the Allied formation encountered gales and fog that scattered the ships and forced ten merchant vessels to part company with the convoy.[12]

When the BdU received the *U 69's* sighting report, it thought that

---

[5] BdU War Diary, 15 Feb. 1943. Microfilm edition of the English translation of this source, original is at the Naval Historical Center, Washington, D.C.

[6] U-boat Situation week ending 15.2.43, ADM 223/1, U-BOAT TREND Replacing report delivered on 15/2, ADM 223/17, Public Record Office, Kew (hereafter PRO).

[7] *U 525, U 175, U 226, U 606, U 607, U 69, U 383, U 201* returned to base; *U 358, U 186, U 223, U 403, U 707* formed *Taifun.* See PRO, DEFE 3/7/711, intercepted 1550/15/2/43, decoded 1655/16/2/43; intercepted 1601/15/2/43, decoded 1356/17/2/43.

[8] PRO, DEFE 3/711, intercepted 2319/15/2/43, decoded 1725/16/2/43.

[9] PRO, ADM 199/583, f. 191.

[10] BdU War Diary, 15 Feb. 1943.

[11] German Navy/U-boat Message Translations & Summaries 02 Feb 1941 - 09 July 1945, ff. 11492, 11498, SRGN-001/49668, Record Group 457, National Archives, Washington D.C. (hereafter RG 457, NA).

[12] PRO, ADM 199/583, ff. 194-197. There are almost no records in the PRO concerning the passage of ONS 165 except for a very brief report by the convoy's commodore.

ONS 165 was some five hundred miles east of Newfoundland and steering a course of 225 degrees. The BdU wanted to mount a mass wolf pack attack on ONS 165, but the U-boats were too scattered to use this tactic because of the earlier disbanding of the *Haudegen* group.[13] In the end the U-boats of the *Taifun* group and those U-boats of the former *Haudegen* group returning to base were ordered to "operate on the *U 69*'s convoy to the very limit of your fuel supply." At the same time, the U-boats were informed that they would be refueled at sea from the U-boat tanker *U 460*.[14]

There was almost three hundred miles of sea room to the westward in which the U-boats could chase and attack ONS 165. Even though there were almost continuous sightings of Allied ships by the U-boats in the next two days, both the weather — heavy seas and poor visibility — and a lack of fuel in the U-boats[15] conspired to blunt the attack on ONS 156. Only two stragglers from the convoy were sunk[16] and the *U 69* and *U 201* were lost to counterattacks by the convoy's escorts.[17] In the early hours of 20 February, those U-boats still chasing ONS 165 were ordered by the BdU to end the operation and to move east to be refueled by the *U 460* for the return voyage to their bases in France.[18] The BdU judged the operations against ONS 165 to be less than successful because the U-boats could not concentrate against the convoy owing to a lack of fuel and poor weather conditions.[19]

On 18 February the *Luftwaffe* in France located an Allied convoy by means of DF bearings. The BdU thought the convoy was ONS 167 and believed it to be about three hundred miles west of the North Channel, steering approximately west.[20] To intercept this convoy, which was in fact ON 166, the BdU ordered the *Neptun* group to form a patrol line running from 56°45'N 30°24'W to 56°45'N 30°12'W and for the *Ritter* group to take station in a patrol line running from 56°27'N 30°12'W to 52°45'N 30°05'W.[21] At the same time, the BdU formed another patrol line south

---

[13] SRGN f. 11499.

[14] BdU War Diary, 17 Feb. 1943.

[15] See for example, SRGN ff. 11540, 11545, 11607, 11634, 11640, 11646, 11649, 11657, 11658, 11682. For weather, see SRGN ff. 11585, 11594; for U-boat fuel supplies, see SRGN ff. 11656, 11663, 11671, 11672, 11676.

[16] The stragglers were the merchant ships *Zeus* and *Rehurst*. PRO, ADM 199/583, f. 195. See also Jürgen Rohwer, *Axis Submarine Successes* (Annapolis, MD, 1983), 149.

[17] S. W. Roskill, *The War at Sea, 1939-1945*, 3 vols. (London: HMSO, 1956), 2: 357.

[18] SRGN ff. 11687, 11741.

[19] BdU War Diary, 19 Feb. 1943.

[20] Ibid., 18 Feb. 1943.

[21] SRGN ff. 11622, 11623.

and east of the *Ritter* patrol line, consisting of four U-boats which had just sailed from France, code named *Knappen*; this third line would run from 53°03'N 28°05'W to 52°03'N 27°05'W.[22] The U-boats were to be in position by 0800A on 20 February to intercept the expected Allied convoy. The next day, on the basis of additional information obtained by the *Luftwaffe* from DF fixes, the Germans deduced that the Allied convoy was on a southwesterly course.[23] Therefore, the BdU ordered the *Neptun* and *Ritter* patrol lines, beginning at 1000A on 20 February, to steam on a course of 130 degrees and for the *Knappen* patrol line to steer at the same time a course of 90 degrees. All three groups of U-boats were to carry out these movements at a speed of six knots.[24]

Although the Allies had broken the German codes and had been reading the U-boat command radio communications since December 1942,[25] there were lags and delays in their decoding process. Thus it was not until 1035, 1044, and 1045 on 20 February and 1815 on 22 February that the orders for the deployment of the *Neptun*, *Ritter*, and *Knappen* patrol lines were decoded and read by the Allies.[26] Just before they had decoded and read the orders to the three U-boat patrol lines, however, the *U 604* heard on her hydrophones the noise of ships at 52°45'N 27°45'W.[27] Shortly afterward, the *U 604* reported sighting three corvettes and a steamship proceeding "slowly" on a "south-westerly course."[28] This was convoy ON 166. Upon receipt of the *U 604*'s sighting report, the BdU ordered fourteen U-boats to operate against ON 166.[29]

Convoy ON 166 was formed north of Ireland at the entrance of the North Channel on 12 February and consisted of sixty-three merchant ships escorted by seven Allied warships of Escort Group A.3 under the command of Captain P. H. Heineman, USN.[30] For the first nine days of its voyage, ON 166 made slow progress westward across the North

---

[22] The U-boats in *Knappen* were *U 92*, *U 604*, *U 91*, *U 600*. See also SRGN f. 11628.

[23] BdU War Diary, 19 Feb. 1943.

[24] SRGN f. 11689.

[25] F.H. Hinsley, et al., *British Intelligence in the Second World War*, 3 vols. (London: HMSO, 1981), 2: 548-553.

[26] PRO, DEFE 3/711, intercepted 2315/18/2/43, decoded 1035/20/2/43; intercepted 2244/18/2/43, decoded 1044/20/2/43; intercepted 2237/20/2/43, decoded 1815/22/2/43.

[27] SRGN f. 11748.

[28] PRO, DEFE 3/711, intercepted 1111/20/2/43, decoded 2254/20/2/43.

[29] The fourteen were *U 600*, *U 91*, *U 603*, *U 454*, *U 332*, *U 753*, *U 621*, *U 623*, *U 628*, *U 653*, *U 225*, *U 377*, *U 468*, and *U 383*. See also SRGN f. 11754, 11755.

[30] The escort consisted of USCGC *Campbell*, USCGC *Spencer*, and the corvettes HMS *Dianthus*, HMCS *Chilliwack*, HMCS *Rosthern*, HMCS *Dauphin*, and HMCS *Trillium*. PRO, ADM 237/96, Commander Task Unit 24.1.3 to Commander Task Force Twenty Four, 28 Feb. 1943.

Atlantic in the face of heavy northwest gales, and the escorts intercepted a number of radio transmissions which were thought to be from U-boats attacking another convoy. On 20 February the weather moderated, and at 1605A on 20 February Heineman received a radio message from the Admiralty stating that "DF bearings on 6675kc/s at 1219Z indicate U-boat in your vicinity may have reported you."[31] This information was most likely based on a combination of shore-based DF and decryption intelligence.[32]

At 2340Z on 20 February the USCGC *Campbell* obtained a radar contact on the starboard beam of the convoy which upon investigation produced no results. Shortly afterwards, at 0015Z on 21 February, the USCGC *Spencer* obtained another radar contact and then sighted what appeared to be the conning tower of a U-boat off the starboard bow of ON 166. The American warship ran towards the enemy vessel, which submerged at a range of 5,000 yards. The Coast Guard cutter gained sonar contact and delivered an unsuccessful depth charge attack.[33] The U-boat was most likely the *U 604*, for she reported to the BdU that she had been driven away from the convoy twice by a destroyer and had lost contact. However, the *U 454* then gained contact with ON 166.[34] At 0110Z Heineman radioed Commander in Chief, Western Approaches that he believed four U-boats to be contact with his convoy.[35]

Indeed, there were numerous contacts between the escorts of the convoy and the U-boats during the daylight hours of 21 February.[36] From Heineman's radio report and, most likely also from communications intelligence, it was becoming clear to Commander in Chief, Western Approaches that ON 166's escort needed reinforcement. At 0923Z Heineman received word that the convoy's escort would be reinforced by the destroyer ORP *Burza*[37] and that three VLR B-24 Liberator aircraft would be dispatched to support the convoy. These aircraft, operating at more than 750 miles from their base, spent several hours in the vicinity of ON 166 and sighted several U-boats. Aircraft T/120 sighted two U-boats — the *U 623* and *U 91* — and two escorts were called to the area

[31] PRO, ADM 199/1705, Admiralty to Escorts ON 166.

[32] Cf., SRGN f. 11748.

[33] PRO, ADM 237/96, Commander Task Unit 24.1.3 to Commander Task Force Twenty Four, 28 Feb. 1943.

[34] SRGN ff. 11769, 11770, 11789, 11816, 11818.

[35] PRO, ADM 199/1705, Commander Task Unit 24.1.3 to C-in-C Western Approaches, 21 Feb. 1943.

[36] PRO, ADM 237/96, Commander Task Unit 24.1.3 to Commander Task Force Twenty Four, 28 Feb. 1943.

[37] PRO, ADM 199/1705, C-in-C Western Approaches to HMS *Harvester*, 21 Feb. 1943.

to attack with depth charges.[38] In the course of these attacks the *U 91* was damaged and was forced to withdraw to make repairs.[39] Throughout the daylight hours of 21 February there were numerous contacts between the escorts of ON 166 and the U-boats. The only Allied casualty was the merchant ship *Stigstad* which had straggled from the convoy the previous night and was torpedoed and sunk astern of ON 166 by the *U 323*.[40]

At 2050Z the convoy made an "Evasive course change from 220° to 248°" just as the *U 92* torpedoed the merchant ship *Empire Trader*. HMCS *Chilliwack* and HMCS *Rosthern* illuminated the convoy but detected no U-boats. The torpedo which hit the *Empire Trader* was thought to have been fired from a position off the port bow of the convoy outside the screen.[41] The *Empire Trader*, having been hit in "the vicinity of the forepeak and No. 1 hold," did not sink but dropped astern of the convoy with HMCS *Dauphin* and the rescue ship *Stockport* standing by. It was decided to try and save the *Empire Trader* by sailing the merchant ship to the British Isles escorted by HMCS *Dauphin*; however, the next day the Admiralty decided to abandon the merchant ship. The *Empire Trader*'s crew were taken on board HMCS *Dauphin* and the merchant ship was last seen by her master at 1900 on 22 February when the Canadian corvette began to steam to rejoin the escort of ON 166.[42]

When the *U 92* torpedoed the *Empire Trader*, the rescue ship *Stockport* went to search for survivors. In the process, the *Stockport* fell astern of ON 166, and *U 604* torpedoed and sank the rescue ship as she steamed to rejoin the convoy at 0312 on 23 February.[43] Several hours later the *U 604* reported to the BdU that she had attacked and sunk a 7,000 GRT passenger freighter![44]

U 92 also carried out the next attack on ON 166. Without warning, the *U 92* torpedoed the merchant ship *Nielsen Alonso* in her engine room. The convoy was illuminated, but nothing was seen. It seemed that the torpedo had been fired from the port quarter of the convoy from inside the screen of escorts. The *Nielsen Alonso*, dead in the water with her engine room flooded, did not sink but drifted astern of the convoy. The USCGC *Campbell* picked up the crew of the merchant ship and began to

---

[38] PRO, AIR 27/911, 21 Feb. 1943.

[39] PRO, DEFE 3/711, intercepted 0139/22/2/43, decoded 1514/22/243.

[40] PRO, ADM 199/583, f. 216; Rohwer, *Axis Submarine Successes*, 150.

[41] PRO, ADM 237/96, Commander Task Unit 24.1.3 to Commander Task Force Twenty Four, 28 Feb. 1943.

[42] PRO, ADM 237/96, Report of an Interview with the Master, Captain E.T.Baker, S.S. *Empire Trader*.

[43] Rohwer, *Axis Submarine Successes*, 150.

[44] PRO, DEFE 711/3, intercepted 0535/23/2/43, decoded 2231/23/2/43.

steam to rejoin the convoy at 1121Z, and the destroyer *Burza* later sank the wreck of the *Nielson Alonso* astern of ON 166.[45]

During the daylight hours of 22 February, the U-boats remained in contact with ON 166. At 0220 the BdU ordered the *U 92* to keep shadowing the convoy, for "contact at present is of decisive importance." At 0500, *U 92* reported that she was transmitting radio beacon signals to home in other U-boats on to ON 166; however, at 0803 she reported that she was "being driven off." Several hours later the *U 606* reported sighting four merchant ships and two escorts on a course of 225 degrees. The BdU ordered a number of U-boats, who formerly had belonged to the *Haudegen* group and who were being refueled at sea by the *U 460*, to join in the attack on ON 166. To enable those U-boats who were running short of fuel to continue the operation against ON 166, the BdU moved the station of the U-boat tanker *U 460* further to the west.[46]

At 1348A the Admiralty informed the escort of ON 166 that the convoy was being "shadowed by three or more U-boats."[47] There was no air support on 22 February for ON l66. A VLR B-24 Liberator aircraft had been dispatched, at a distance of over 1,000 miles from base, but the aircraft had failed to locate the convoy and did not sight any U-boats.[48] At sunset on 22 February the escort of ON 166 consisted of USCGC *Spencer* and the corvettes HMCS *Chilliwack*, HMCS *Trillium*, HMCS *Rosthern*, and HMS *Dianthus*. During the evening of 22 February the destroyer ORP *Burza* joined the escort of the convoy, while the USCGC *Campbell* remained some thirty-five miles astern of ON 166 and was steaming to rejoin.[49]

At 2031Z the USCGC *Spencer* obtained a radar contact about four miles ahead of ON 166 and ran down the contact. Then *Spencer* obtained a sonar contact, which she attacked with depth charges without result. The American warship then began a box search. At 2124Z "a single flash was seen on the port bow of the convoy." These were the merchant ships *Chattanooga City*, *Expositor*, and *Empire Redshank* being torpedoed by the

---

[45] PRO ADM 237/96, Commander Task Unit 24.1.3 to Commander Task Force Twenty Four, 28 Feb. 1943; Rohwer, *Axis Submarine Successes*, 150.

[46] PRO, DEFE 3/711, intercepted 0220/22/2/43, decoded 1515/22/2/43; intercepted 0500/22/2/43, decoded 1527/22/2/43; intercepted 0803/22/2/43, decoded 1308/22/2/43; intercepted 1131/22/2/43, decoded 1613/22/2/43; intercepted 0827/22/2/43, decoded 1540/22/2/43; intercepted 1820/22/2/43 decoded 2147/23/2/43.

[47] PRO, ADM 199/1705, Admiralty to Escorts of ON 166, 22 Feb. 1943.

[48] PRO, AIR 41/48, p. 36.

[49] PRO, ADM 237/96, Commander Task Unit 24.1.3 to Commander Task Force Twenty Four, 28 Feb. 1943.

U 606.[50] Heineman thought that the attack had come from the port bow ahead of the convoy, and he ordered the ships illuminated with star shells. At 2131Z HMCS *Chilliwack* sighted a U-boat on the port bow of ON 166 and attacked with gunfire followed by depth charges. At 2142Z ORP *Burza*, who had just joined the escort, gained a sonar contact at a range of 1,200 yards which she attacked two times with depth charges. At 2205Z *Burza* sighted a U-boat which she thought was *U 606* and began firing, but the boat disappeared one minute later.[51] HMCS *Rosthern* at 2301Z obtained a sonar contact off the starboard bow of ON 166 and attacked two times with depth charges; after the second attack the crew of the Canadian corvette heard a "violent underwater explosion" and concluded that "S/M [to be] at least badly damaged." However, *Rosthern* could not continue the attack, for at 2316Z her main steam line ruptured and the corvette lost all power. Repairs had to be made before she could regain her station on the screen of the convoy.[52]

When the *U 606* attacked ON 166, HMCS *Trillium* was astern of the convoy and steaming to rejoin after investigating a radar contact. As *Trillium* approached the convoy she came upon the survivors of the three merchant ships which had been torpedoed by the *U 606* and began to rescue the men from the water and lifeboats. The rescue operation was broken off for a short time when the Canadians observed ORP *Burza* in what appeared to be a gun battle with a U-boat. But as the Canadian corvette approached, the Polish warship ceased fire and HMCS *Trillium* returned to rescuing Allied merchant seamen from the torpedoed ships, picking up a total of 160 men. After completing the rescue operation, *Trillium* then attempted to sink the wrecks of the *Expositor* and *Empire Redshank* with depth charges.[53] She succeeded in sinking the *Empire Redshank*, but the Canadian corvette failed to sink the *Expositor*; later *U 303* would finish her off.[54]

After the attack on ON 166, the *U 606* attempted to escape on the surface but was forced to dive by an Allied escort. The *U 606* went deep and was attacked with depth charges, which damaged the German vessel. Shortly after the depth charge attack, the *U 606* surfaced. The vessel's

---

[50] PRO, ADM 237/96, Commander Task Unit 24.1.3 to Commander Task Force Twenty Four, 28 Feb. 1943; Rohwer, *Axis Submarine Successes*, 150.

[51] PRO, ADM 237/96, Commander Task Unit 24.1.3 to Commander Task Force Twenty Four, 28 Feb. 1943; ibid., Extract from *Burza*'s S.1203 of Attack on U-boat on 22nd February.

[52] PRO, ADM 237/96, Commander Task Unit 24.1.3 to Commander Task Force Twenty Four, 28 Feb. 1943.

[53] Report of events following torpedo attack, night of 22nd February, 1943, *Trillium*, ON 166, Directorate of History, National Defence Headquarters, Ottawa (hereafter D. Hist).

[54] Rohwer, *Axis Submarine Successes*, 150.

hydrophones were not working and the conning tower hatch was jammed and could not be opened. However, the U-boat's diesel engines and electric motors were functioning. The *U 606* was running "blindly" on the surface.[55]

When the *U 606* had attacked ON 166, the USCGC *Campbell* was astern of the convoy and steaming to rejoin. As the Coast Guard cutter approached the rear of ON 166, the Americans saw the convoy illuminated with star shells and shortly afterward obtained a radar contact at a range of 4,600 yards bearing 350 degrees. As the USCGC *Campbell* ran down the radar contact, she obtained a sonar contact bearing 40 degrees at a range of 1,700 yards. Four minutes later the Coast Guard cutter sighted a U-boat on her starboard bow. *Campbell* closed with the U-boat, which was the *U 606*, passing along and very close to the port side of the enemy vessel. When the U-boat's conning tower was on the beam of the Coast Guard cutter, *Campbell* dropped two depth charges which exploded under the *U 606*. She then took the U-boat under gunfire before stopping dead in the water with her engine room flooded from water entering through a fifteen-foot-long, four-inch-wide tear in her side, which occurred when she ran up on the hydroplane of the *U 606*. When the American gunfire stopped, about fifteen members of the U-boat's crew jumped into the water.

The USCGC *Campbell* was thus dead in the water with a flooded engine room while the *U 606* was sinking. *Campbell* sent a boat to the *U 606* and took five crewmen off, and the ORP *Burza*, which Heineman had sent to assist the *Campbell*, rescued seven other Germans. The rest of the Germans were left in the water to die or went down with the *U 606*, which sank shortly afterwards leaving the disabled Coast Guard cutter screened by ORP *Burza* astern of ON 166. *Burza* stood by the *Campbell* until 24 February, when HMCS *Dauphin* arrived to stand by the disabled American warship. Two days later, HMS *Salisbury* and the tug *Tenacity* reached the USCGC *Campbell* and began towing the American warship to St. John's, Newfoundland, where she arrived on 3 March.[56]

HMCS *Trillium*, astern of ON 166 and steaming to rejoin the convoy after picking up the survivors from the three torpedoed Allied merchant ships, obtained a sonar contact at 0236 on 23 February and attacked with

---

[55] U.S. Department of the Navy, *Report of Interrogation of Survivors from the U-606 Sunk on February 22, 1943* (Washington, D.C., 1943), 1415. The author wishes to thank the Directorate of History, National Defence Headquarters, Canadian Armed Forces, for providing this publication.

[56] Commanding Officer *Campbell* to Commander in Chief U.S. Atlantic Fleet, 11 March 1943, and Lt. (jg) Barring Coughlin to Commanding Officer, *Campbell*, 8 March 1943, Operational Archives, Naval Historical Center, Washington, D.C.

depth charges. As the corvette was turning to make a second depth charge attack, she obtained a radar contact. Shortly afterwards the Canadian warship sighted "a large boiling wake." She gave chase and opened fire with her main armament and a 20mm Oerlikon. At 0250 the U-boat dived and was attacked with depth charges. HMCS *Trillium* then ran out, turned, gained sonar contact, lost sonar contact, and did not attack. No further contact was obtained, and HMCS *Trillium* continued hunting the U-boat until on 0315 when she obtained a radar contact. The target disappeared and sonar contact was gained only to be lost. The hunt was continued, and at 0442 another radar contact was obtained, then lost, at a range of 2,000 yards; a sonar contact was subsequently picked up but was also lost. HMCS *Trilllium* remained in the area hunting for the U-boat until 0923 when the corvette set course to rejoin ON 166.[57]

After the *U 606* torpedoed the *Expositor, Empire Redshank,* and the *Chattanooga City,* ON 166 made two evasive alterations in course in an attempt to throw off the pursuing U-boats. However, at 0625Z and 0630Z the *U 628* succeeded in torpedoing the tankers *Winkler* and *Glittre.*[58] The escorts of the convoy, now reduced to one Coast Guard cutter and three corvettes,[59] counterattacked. The USCGC *Spencer* obtained a radar contact, ran down the bearing, attacked a U-boat with gunfire and depth charges, and then obtained a sonar contact which she attacked with depth charges. This U-boat was most likely the *U 628.*[60] Both the *Winkler* and the *Glittre* were hit on the port side and dropped astern of the convoy; they would later be sunk by the *U 223* and *U 603.* Within minutes of the torpedoing of the *Winkler* and *Glittre,* the *U 186* torpedoed the merchant ships *Hastings* and *Eulina.* The *Hastings* sank in seven minutes and the *Eulina* remained afloat drifting astern of the convoy; she was later sunk by a torpedo from the *U 186.*[61] Heineman thought that the attack had been carried out by "at least four U-boats, two from ahead, and one from the port bow and one from astern." After the action, 135 merchant seamen from the four ships were rescued by HMS *Dianthus* and HMCS *Chilliwack.* During the rescue operation, HMS *Dianthus* fell astern of the convoy and was so short of fuel that she could not rejoin ON 166. The British corvette

---

[57] Report of events following torpedo attack, night of 22 February 1943. *Trillium,* ON 166, D. Hist.

[58] PRO, ADM 237/96, Commander Task Unit 24.1.3 to Commander Task Force Twenty Four, 28 Feb. 1943; Rohwer, *Axis Submarine Successes,* 150.

[59] USCGC *Spencer,* HMCS *Rosthern,* HMCS *Chilliwack,* and HMS *Dianthus.*

[60] PRO, ADM 237/96, Commander Task Unit 24.1.3 to Commander Task Force Twenty Four, 28 Feb. 1943. See also SRGN f. 12032.

[61] Rohwer, *Axis Submarine Successes,* 150, 151.

had just enough fuel remaining to reach St. John's, Newfoundland, on one boiler.[62]

Just before midnight on 22 February, Heineman radioed Commander in Chief, Western Approaches requesting assistance for the damaged USCGC *Campbell* and reported that "ON 166 critically short of escorts. U-boat situation extremely dangerous." Several hours later he received word that HMS *Salisbury*, HMCS *Montgomery*, and HMS *Witherington* would sail to reinforce ON 166. Heineman also informed the Allied command authorities in Newfoundland that the escort of ON 166 had been reduced to three escorts with two others astern of the convoy, either chasing U-boats or rescuing survivors, and he requested air support "If at all possible." Several hours later Heineman was told by radio that HMS *Salisbury* would be sent to assist the USCGC *Campbell*. And at 2147Z the American officer was further informed that there were at least eight U-boats in the vicinity of ON 166 and possibly three other U-boats "closing" on the convoy.[63] On this bleak note the remaining ships of Escort Group A.3 prepared to defend ON 166 during another night of U-boat attacks. However, no attacks materialized.

Throughout 23 February, the *U 707* maintained contact with ON 166 and transmitted radio beacon signals to home in other U-boats to the convoy.[64] However, a number of U-boats had lost contact with the convoy, or had been damaged, or were running low on fuel. The *U 628* reported being attacked by an escort and having lost contact.[65] The *U 403* requested permission to break off the operation and go to the *U 460* to be refueled. At 1039 the *U 189* reported having lost contact with ON 166 and later that she was going to the *U 460* for fuel. The *U 454* radioed that she was ending the operation because of battle damage and returning to base. And the *U 358* dropped out of the operation because of the need to refuel.[66] However, even with these setbacks, seven other U-boats, in addition to the *U 707*, were in contact with ON 166.[67]

On 23 February, the BdU instituted a measure designed to prolong

---

[62] PRO, ADM 237/96, Commander Task Unit 24.1.3 to Commander Task Force Twenty Four, 28 Feb. 1943.

[63] PRO, ADM 199/1705, CTU 24.1.3 to C in CWA, 22 Feb. 1943; Comtask 24 to CMO ETU 24.1.5, 23 Feb. 1943; FONF to Mid Ocean ETU 24.1.3, 23 Feb. 1943; COM ETU 24.1.15 to Comtask 24, 23 Feb. 1943; Comtask 24 to *Salisbury*, 23 Feb. 1943; NSHQ Ottawa to Ships Escorting ON 166, 23 Feb. 1943.

[64] SRGN ff. 12039, 12099, 12129.

[65] PRO, DEFE 3/711, intercepted 0115/23/2/43, decoded 1952/23/2/43.

[66] SRGN ff. 11986, 12022, 12057, 12098.

[67] *U 621*, *U 358*, *U 653*, *U 468*, *U 92*, *U 600*, and *U 628*. See BdU War Diary, 23 Feb. 1943.

the ability of the U-boats to remain in contact with ON 166. It ordered another U-boat tanker, the *U 462*, to take station at 45°09'N 33°15'W with the possibility of moving west, if required, to support the operations against ON 166.[68] Even before this U-boat tanker had taken up her station the *U 454* was directed to be refueled from the *U 462*.[69]

Just after sunset on 23 February, ON 166 made an 80-degree turn to port while the USCGC *Spencer* conducted a series of high speed sweeps ahead of and off the port bow of the convoy in an attempt to throw off the U-boats. The radio frequency employed by the Allied ships was also changed at this time, but the U-boats remained in contact. At 0021Z the Allied ships saw two white flares. As nothing else was seen nor heard in the convoy, the escorts took no action other than to conduct a limited search. The flares were probably from the merchant ship *Madoera*, which had been torpedoed in the bow by the *U 653*. The *Madoera* dropped astern of the convoy without being noticed and was later towed to St. John's, Newfoundland.[70]

At 0405Z the escort of ON 166 was strengthened when HMCS *Trillium* rejoined from astern of the convoy. At 0650Z the USCGC *Spencer* obtained a radar contact followed by a sonar contact which was attacked off the starboard bow of the convoy. Shortly afterwards HMCS *Rosthern* reported that the merchant ship *Ingria* was showing two red lights and dropping astern of the convoy. The *Ingria* had been torpedoed by both the *U 600* and the *U 628* and sank shortly afterwards. *Rosthern* rescued the survivors of the *Ingria*. A confused battle between the escorts of ON 166 and the U-boats folowed, ending at 0900Z with a U-boat being sighted astern of the convoy and being taken under gunfire by several merchant ships. According to Heineman it was the "aggressive action of the escorts" in this action which held down the Allied losses to one merchant ship.[71]

There were no attacks on ON 166 during the daylight hours of 24 February. The BdU ordered that six U-boats[72] be refueled from the *U 460* and the *U 462* before beginning the voyage back to their bases in France. The *U 603*, sending radio beacon signals to home in other U-boats to the convoy, remained in contact with ON 166 during the daylight hours of

---

[68] PRO, DEFE 3/711, intercepted 1759/23/2/43, decoded 2347/23/2/43.

[69] SRGN f. 12127.

[70] PRO, ADM 237/96, Commander Task Unit 24.1.3 to Commander Task Force Twenty Four, 28 Feb. 1943; Rohwer, *Axis Submarine Successes*, 152.

[71] PRO, ADM 237/96, Commander Task Unit 24.1.3 to Commander Task Force Twenty Four, 28 Feb. 1943; Rohwer, *Axis Submarine Successes*, 152.

[72] *U 223, U 303, U 186, U 358, U 454*, and *U 707*.

24 February.[73] Just before sunset the *U 621, U 600,* and *U 628* were in contact with the convoy.[74] However, in the late afternoon a RCAF PBY Catalina aircraft appeared over ON 166. It spent three hours in the area and was able to attack the *U 604*.[75]

At dusk the USCGC *Spencer* conducted a high speed sweep on the port bow of ON 166 to drive away any U-boats that might be in contact with the convoy. The escorts reinforced by the arrival of HMS *Witherington*, attacked several radar and sonar contacts without results. Just after dark ON 166 made an evasive turn of 80 degrees to starboard returning to base course after midnight. At 0200Z HMCS *Montgomery* joined the escort of ON 166. However, in the early hours of 25 February a number of HF/DF bearings indicated that a number of U-boats were attempting to approach the rear of the convoy.[76] The U-boats had some difficulty, in the first hours of darkness before the moon rose at 0300, in gaining visual contact with ON 166.[77] They maintained hydrophone contact with the convoy, however, and at 0725Z the *U 628* successfully torpedoed the merchant ship *Manchester Merchant*, which sank in "about 90 seconds."[78] HMCS *Montgomery* and HMCS *Rosthern* rescued thirty-two men from the water and the USCGC *Spencer* and HMCS *Chilliwack* both attacked sonar contacts without results. The sinking of the *Manchester Merchant* was the last U-boat attack on ON 166.[79]

On 25 February both the U-boats and ON 166 encountered fog. The *U 468* reported, for example, that visibility was "about 800 metres." Even though there were several contacts between the escorts of ON 166 and the U-boats[80] on 25 February, the fog and the resulting poor visibility made it virtually impossible for the U-boats to maintain contact with the convoy. The BdU as a result ordered the operation to end at first daylight on 26 February.[81]

To the eastward and behind ON 166 was Convoy ONS 167. This was a slow convoy bound to North America consisting of twenty-five

[73] SRGN ff. 12220, 12199, 12205, 12206.

[74] BdU War Diary, 24 Feb. 1943.

[75] PRO, ADM 199/538, f.222; PRO, DEFE 3/712, intercepted 1653/24/2/43, decoded 1953/25/2/43.

[76] PRO, ADM 237/96, Commander Task Unit 24.1.3 to Commander Task Force Twenty Four, 28 Feb. 1943.

[77] BdU War Diary, 24 Feb. 1943.

[78] SRGN ff. 12284, 12300; Rohwer, *Axis Submarine Successes,* 152.

[79] PRO, ADM 237/96, Commander Task Unit 24.1.3 to Commander Task Force Twenty Four, 28 Feb. 1943.

[80] PRO, DEFE 3/712, intercepted 1350/25/2/43, decoded 044/26/2/43; intercepted 1618/25/2/43, decoded 0157/26/2/43.

[81] SRGN f. 12411.

merchant ships escorted by six warships. On 19 February the Admiralty warned the escort of ONS 167 that a "U-boat [is] estimated to be in your vicinity."[82] However, it is clear that the BdU had no knowledge of the whereabouts of ONS 167 until 21 February[83] when the *U 664*, outward bound from her base in France, sighted the convoy by chance and reported to the BdU that the convoy was at 50°49'N 24°15'W.[84] Within an hour the BdU ordered four other U-boats that had just sailed from France to operate against ONS 167.[85]

Shortly after the *U 664* made her sighting report, the Admiralty warned ONS 167 that a "U-boat [is] estimated to be in vicinity of convoy, and may have possibly reported it."[86] This warning was too late, however, for the *U 664* had already managed to torpedo and sink two merchant ships — the *Rosario* and *H.H. Rogers*.[87] The escort then counterattacked, forcing the *U 664* to lose contact with the Allied formation. Several hours later the *U 758* obtained contact with ONS 167,[88] then at 0945 on 22 February the *U 664* regained contact,[89] but both U-boats again lost contact. The *U 758*'s report, at 1035, stated that she had been driven off by the escorts and that ONS 167 was at 49°33'N 26°05'W steering a course of 230 degrees and steaming at between seven and eight knots.[90] This was the last contact the U-boats had with the main body of ONS 167.

The BdU did not give up attempting to intercept ONS 167. U-boats sighting Allied escorts provided several clues as to the course and location of the convoy[91] At 2125 on 22 February, the BdU formed the five U-boats assigned to operate against ONS 167 into the *Sturmbock* group and ordered the boats to make high speed sweeps along "courses of from 230 to 250 degrees." The next day the BdU warned the U-boat tanker, *U 460*, that ONS 167 might pass near her station. Later the BdU radioed to the U-boats of the *Sturmbock* group the arrangements for being

---

[82] The escort included the destroyers HMS *Harverster*, HMS *Escapade*, and ORP *Burza* (later detached to reinforce ON 166), corvettes FFS *Roselys*, FFS *Renoncule*, and FFS *Aconit*. There are no after-action reports and very few other papers in the PRO which deal with this particular convoy. However, see PRO, ADM 199/1705, Admiralty to Escorts of ONS 167, 19 Feb. 1943.

[83] BdU War Diary, 21 Feb. 1943.

[84] SRGN f. 11832.

[85] These were *U 758, U 84, U 591*, and *U 432*. See also SRGN f. 11835.

[86] PRO, ADM 199/1705, Admiralty to Escorts of ONS 167, 21 May 1943.

[87] Rohwer, *Axis Submarine Successes*, 150.

[88] SRGN ff. 11860, 11872.

[89] PRO, DEFE 3/711, intercepted 0945/22/2/43, decoded 1350/22/2/43.

[90] SRGN f. 11905.

[91] BdU War Diary, 22 Feb. 1943.

refueled at sea from the *U 462* and informed them that the group was to be reinforced by three additional U-boats.[92]

There was still no contact by the U-boats with ONS 167, but the BdU did not give up the effort. Just before midnight on 22 February, it ordered the U-boats of the *Sturmbock* group to set up by 1000 on 24 February a patrol line running from 48°27'N 38°45'W to 46°03'N 37°45'W. At the same time the U-boats were informed that the "group will be reinforced." The Allies decoded this order at 0417 on 24 February.[93] The BdU ordered this deployment of the *Sturmbock* U-boats even though it thought that most of the U-boats "are probably already behind the enemy."[94] Besides, due to the distances involved, three U-boats could not carry out the deployment order.[95] On 24 February the BdU made one last attempt to intercept ONS 167. It assumed that the convoy had altered course to the northward to avoid the battle taking place around ON 166 and ordered at 1219 on 24 February that the *Sturmbock* patrol line, now reinforced to eleven U-boats,[96] be moved northward to run from 49°57'N 38°35'W to 46°21'N 38°45'W. The Allies decoded this order at 1620 on 25 February.[97] By this time the BdU's directive to the *Sturmbock* U-boats would be mostly of academic interest to Allied intelligence, for the prompt decoding of the order setting up the first *Sturmbock* patrol line provided the Allies with enough information to route ONS 167 around the German formation. In any case, the *Sturmbock* group was dissolved on 25 February without ever having gained contact with ONS 167.[98]

The battles for Convoys ONS 165, ON 166 and ONS 167 were Allied defeats. The major Allied objective was the safe and timely arrival of merchant ships, but out of the three convoys the U-boats sank eighteen ships against the loss of only three U-boats.[99] There are several reasons for the failure of the Allies and for the success of the U-boats. Of great importance to both the Allies and the Germans in these three convoy battles was communications intelligence. From such intelligence the Allies

---

[92] PRO, DEFE 3/711, intercepted 2125/22/2/43, decoded 1845/23/2/43; intercepted 1129/23/2/43, decoded 2215/23/2/43; intercepted 1759/23/2/43, decoded 2347/23/2/43; intercepted 2201/23/2/43, decoded 0441/24/2/43.

[93] PRO, DEFE 3/711, intercepted 2344/23/2/43, decoded 0417/24/2/43.

[94] BdU War Diary, 23 Feb. 1943.

[95] The three were *U 84*, *U 753*, and *U 664*. See also SRGN f. 12150.

[96] *U 332*, *U 753*, *U 383*, *U 84*, *U 378*, *U 432*, *U 226*, *U 758*, *U 646*, *U 544*, and *U 607*.

[97] PRO, DEFE 3/711, intercepted 1219/24/2/43, decoded 1620/25/2/43.

[98] BdU War Diary, 25 Feb. 1943.

[99] The eighteen ships sunk were *Atlantic Sun*, *Zeus*, and *Redhurst* from ONS 165; *Stigstad*, *Empire Trader*, *Nielson Alonso*, *Empire Redshank*, *Chattanooga City*, *Expositor*, *Winkler*, *Glittre*, *Hastings*, *Eulima*, *Ingria*, *Manchester Merchant*, and *Stockport* from ON 166; *Rosario* and *H.H. Rogers* from ONS 167. The U-boats lost were *U 69*, *U 201*, and *U 606*.

knew the general location to the east of Newfoundland of the *Haudegen* group of U-boats and had been able to route ONS 165 south of them, but because of bad luck — a storm that scattered the convoy — the U-boats were able to intercept and sink three merchant ships. However, the same heavy weather, the proximity of the Allied air bases in Newfoundland, a lack of intelligence about the location and course of the convoy, and a general shortage of fuel among the U-boats prevented the Germans from gaining contact with the main body of the Allied ships and bringing them to battle. In the case of ON 166, foreknowledge of the convoy's route obtained from communications intelligence enabled the U-boats of the *Knappen* group to be deployed so as to intercept and bring to battle the convoy. At the same time, the Allies were unable to decode the German orders for the deployment of the *Knappen* group of U-boats quickly, which precluded ON 166's route from being altered so as to avoid the U-boats. The U-boats' interception of ONS 167 was also by chance. The BdU did not have from communications intelligence any foreknowledge of the route or location of ONS 167, nor did the Allies have knowledge of the location of the U-boats which intercepted the convoy. However, communications intelligence gave the Allies the knowledge of the deployment of the *Sturmbock* patrol line and enabled ONS 167 to escape quickly from the U-boats.

It was the deployment of the U-boat tankers, *U 460* and *U 462*, which enabled the Germans to conduct operations against ONS 165, ON 166, and ONS 167. Without the possibility of being refueled at sea, the U-boats of the *Haudegen* group would not have been able to operate against ONS 165 and the U-boats of the *Knappen* group would not have been able to pursue ON 166 across 1,000 miles of the North Atlantic. The Allies, on the other hand, owing to a series of equipment failures and mistakes, had great difficulty in refueling ON 166 at sea. HMS *Dianthus* almost ran out of fuel, and several other corvettes would have run out if it had not been possible to obtain small amounts of fuel on an *ad hoc* basis from several tankers, who were not escort oilers, within the convoy.[100]

Air support by Allied aircraft could have most likely reduced the number of ships lost to the U-boats. However, bad weather precluded the use of aircraft based in Newfoundland to support ONS 165. Furthermore, neither ON 166 nor ONS 167 received any air support after 22 and 23

---

[100] PRO, ADM 237/96, Commander Task Unit 24.1.3 to Commander Task Force Twenty Four, 28 Feb. 1943. In the Pacific, the Americans had perfected the techniques of refueling at sea. However, they were not yet used by the ships of the British Commonwealth in the Atlantic. Cf., Thomas Wildenberg, "Chester Nimitz and the Development of Fueling at Sea," *Naval War College Review* 46 (Autumn 1993): 52-62.

February, respectively. It is most likely that, in the case of ON 166 especially, air support would have greatly reduced, if not totally prevented, the large loss of merchant ships from that convoy. However, in February of 1943 the Allies, for a number of reasons, simply did not have deployed in support of North Atlantic convoys a sufficient number of aircraft which were capable of operating in the "Greenland Air Gap." Nevertheless, VLR B-24 Liberator aircraft based in Iceland and Newfoundland could have supported, with great effect, convoys in the "Air Gap" southeast of Greenland. But owing to a series of mix ups and mistakes in the allocation and deployment of aircraft, the Allies were not capable in February of 1943 of supporting with aircraft convoys in the "Greenland Air Gap".[101]

A bright spot for the Allies in the battle for ONS 166 was shipborne HF/DF.[102] While he only mentioned it once in the narrative section of his after-action report, Heineman cited HF/DF as being of "tremendous value . . . in determining strength and movements of U-boats near convoys." The USCGC *Spencer*, USCGC *Campbell*, and the rescue ship *Stockport* were equipped with HF/DF during the battle for ON 166. These ships obtained bearings on 137 radio transmissions made by U-boats in the vicinity of the convoy.[103] There can be no doubt that information from HF/DF was of great assistance to the escorts of ON 166 in anticipating attacks and the deployments of U-boats near the convoy.

The battles for Convoys ONS 165, ONS 167, and especially ON 166 showed that the Allies, if they were going to be the victors in the Battle of the Atlantic, had to increase the number and effectiveness of the surface and air escorts of convoys and perfect a number of techniques such as refueling at sea. Communications intelligence had also to be available in a more timely fashion so that convoys could be routed around U-boat patrol lines. Perhaps most important of all, Allied anti-U-boat aircraft had to be deployed in support of convoys in the North Atlantic throughout their passage from North America to Britain. Had these precautions been taken, the course of the battles for Convoys ONS 165, ON 166, and ONS 167 might have been different and certainly their losses would have been greatly reduced.

---

[101] Cf., David Syrett and W.A.B. Douglas, "Die Wende in der Schlacht im Atlantik: Die Schliebung des 'Gronland-Luftlochs', 1942-1943," *Marine-Rundschau* 83 (Jan.-Feb., March-April, May-June, 1986): 2-11, 70-73, 147-149.

[102] Cf., Kathlene Williams, "HUFF DUFF: High-Frequency Direction Finding and the Battle of the Atlantic" (Ph.D. diss., City University of New York, 1993).

[103] PRO, ADM 237/96, Commander Task Unit 24.1.3 to Commander Task Force Twenty Four, 28 Feb. 1943; ibid., [ON 166] HF/DF Reports.

12

Ultra, Air Power, and the Second Battle of the St. Lawrence, 1944

Roger Sarty

The five U-boats that struck into Canadian waters in the late summer of 1944 failed in their hopes of renewing the success of the *Roll of Drums* (*Drumbeat*) offensive of 1942, even though Canada's home naval forces were still weak and thinly stretched and the maritime air forces in the region had been considerably reduced.[1] The official history of the Royal Canadian Air Force's coastal commands, published in 1986, demonstrated that air power directed by naval intelligence was the key to the ultimate success of the defense in late 1942 and all through 1944.[2] In particular, the history revealed that the instant availability of British and American Ultra decrypts to Canadian naval operational intelligence in 1944 helped the air force to continue to suppress U-boats that were now equipped to evade Allied aircraft. This official work was one of the first studies to apply in detail freshly opened Ultra material on maritime operations late in the war. Sources subsequently released and recent research now make it possible to fill in both the details of the story and its broader context.

The growth of the RCAF's coastal commands in 1939-45 was as remarkable as the better-known expansion of the Royal Canadian Navy. The two stories are inextricably intertwined, for it was the strength of the RCAF Eastern Air Command in the northwest Atlantic that allowed the

---

[1] The author thanks Alec Douglas, Michael Hadley, Doug McLean, and Marc Milner who, as always, generously shared their research and expertise.

[2] W.A.B. Douglas, *The Creation of a National Air Force: The Official History of the Royal Canadian Air Force, Vol. 2* (Toronto and Ottawa: University of Toronto Press in cooperation with the Department of National Defence and the Canadian Government Publishing Centre, 1986), chapters 13-17.

RCN to maintain only minimal forces there and lend substantial assistance to both U.S. and British escort forces.

Eastern Air Command had been established at the end of 1938. When war broke out in the following year, its meager order of battle included only seven reconnaissance aircraft — biplane Supermarine Stranraer flying boats — that could by any stretch of the imagination be considered modern. Although well down the priority list behind the British Commonwealth Air Training Plan in Canada that recruited and trained personnel for the Commonwealth air forces overseas, Eastern Air Command underwent considerable expansion in 1939-41. As a result of Churchill and Roosevelt's agreements on American assistance to Britain in the Atlantic theater, U.S. Army and U.S. Navy squadrons joined the command in Newfoundland during 1941 to share in coverage of ocean convoys eastward of that giant island but not back into the Canadian coastal area.

The onset of *Roll of Drums* in January 1942 accelerated the expansion of Eastern Air Command to some one hundred patrol bombers by the end of that year, but it was by no means possible to complete or perfect the organization during these months of intense operations. Nevertheless, Canadian policy, learned from Britain, of immediately organizing coastal shipping into convoys allowed the thinly stretched defenses to keep losses to a low level while also maintaining and expanding commitments elsewhere. The RCN, for example, provided a growing share — nearly 50 percent by late 1942 — of the escorts for North Atlantic convoys from the vicinity of Newfoundland to the United Kingdom. Moreover, it extended further assistance as the U.S. withdrew ships to the Pacific by taking nearly full responsibility for the escort of those convoys from their new western terminus at New York up to Newfoundland.[3]

The one area where the Anglo-Canadian policy of rigorous application of coastal convoy failed was in the Gulf of St. Lawrence. There, twenty-one ships, including two Canadian escorts and the U.S. Army transport *Chatham*, were destroyed between May and October of 1942. This vast waterway, reaching some six hundred miles west from the Straits of Canso to the mouth of the St. Lawrence River and some four hundred miles north to the Strait of Belle Isle, proved to be a submariner's paradise and a defender's hell.[4] Because of the contours of

---

[3] See, for example, Marc Milner, *North Atlantic Run: The Royal Canadian Navy and the Battle for the Convoys* (Toronto: University of Toronto Press, 1985), chapters 4-6.

[4] In addition to Douglas, *Creation of a National Air Force*, ch. 13, see Michael L. Hadley, *U-Boats against Canada: German Submarines in Canadian Waters* (Kingston and Montreal: McGill-Queen's University Press, 1985). The latter draws on both the full range of German

the surrounding land masses, convoys had to follow closely fixed routes where it was easy for the U-boats to locate them and take up attacking positions, but the broad, deep waters and sinuous coasts enabled the boats to evade escorts easily. In addition, sonar performance was poor in the Gulf. The mixing of frigid arctic waters, warmer water from the Grand Banks, and fresh water from the river produced salinity and temperature layering that deflected sonar sound waves and allowed the submarines to hide, immune, even as escorts were swarming overhead.[5]

Still, conventional submarines had to make extended runs on the surface to chase down shipping and to recharge the relatively inefficient batteries that powered their underwater propulsion systems. When in late September and October 1942 Eastern Air Command, adopting effective British tactics, used the navy's direction finding bearings on U-boat radio reports to saturate German operating areas with air searches, the German submarine command (BdU) soon concluded that the Gulf was no longer a promising hunting ground. As it happened, the RCN had already decided to close the Gulf to ocean shipping in order to free the many escorts tied down there for service in the Mediterranean in response to British appeals for assistance in that theater. The Gulf restriction was gradually loosened in 1943, as the extent of the dislocation to shipping became evident and there were no further German incursions. The slowing of the movement of trade must be counted an important German victory that resulted rather paradoxically from the failure to realize how impressed the enemy had been by the eleventh-hour reform of air operating methods.

After the defeat of the German wolf pack offensive against the main convoys in mid-ocean in the spring of 1943, single U-boats began to return to the Canadian coast regularly. Their return was part of an effort by Admiral Dönitz, commander in chief submarines, to maintain some presence in the Atlantic to tie down Allied forces and to gather vital weather and shipping intelligence. The RCAF, aided by Ultra decrypts of U-boat signal traffic that were now available to complement DF bearing intelligence, kept on the tails of these boats, compelling them to operate with such caution that their only victims were the few unfortunate ships

---

documentation and extensive interviews with German naval veterans. It is probably the definitive account of the "Canadian" U-boats, including all of those discussed in this chapter.

[5] Hachey, MacVeigh and Barber, National Research Laboratories, Division of Physics and Electrical Engineering, "Asdic Ranging Conditions in the River and Gulf of St. Lawrence in Late Summer," 17 Nov. 1944, file "Official Memoranda," National Archives of Canada, Record Group 24, (hereafter NAC, RG 24) vol. 11463. Significantly, this study was made immediately after the failure of RCN ASDIC hunts for U-boats in the gulf and river described in this chapter.

that happened onto their hiding places.[6] In a review of June 1944, U-boat headquarters noted:

> Coast of North America, Newfoundland: Traffic, apart from a few fast single ships entirely in convoy, which were extremely difficult to approach on account of strong enemy air patrol.[7]

What Dönitz did not know was that these results had been achieved with modest forces. After the defeat of the wolf packs in 1943 the U.S. air squadrons in Newfoundland had been withdrawn, and the RCAF's Eastern Air Command, after reaching a peak strength of eleven reconnaissance squadrons (approximately 150 aircraft) in mid-1943, had been cut by a third to seven squadrons (100 aircraft) by the spring of 1944.[8]

Soon after the rather gloomy assessment of possibilities in North American waters, the mood at U-boat headquarters lightened. Boats equipped with schnorkel breathing tubes that had attempted the English Channel in the face of the crushingly dense Allied defenses for the Normandy invasion bridgehead were not only surviving but making attacks. Schnorkel, which allowed boats to cruise at periscope depth while drawing in enough air to run their main diesel engines and recharge the batteries for the submerged drive system, had been intended primarily to enable conventional boats to escape Allied air power. In the Channel it became evident that the system also afforded excellent protection against sonar-equipped warships because the boats could hide, without ever showing anything more than the almost invisible head of the schnorkel mast, amid the sea-bottom clutter and under the pronounced temperature density layers of coastal waters.[9]

Admiral Dönitz immediately thought of the earlier victories in the Gulf of St. Lawrence. As he explained to his submarine commanders:

> 1) [This]Operational area has not been occupied since 1942. Great surprise successes are possible as area has abundant traffic. Area was evacuated in 1942 in view of appearance of a/c [aircraft] and location

---

[6] Jürgen Rohwer and Roger Sarty, "Intelligence and the Air Forces in the Battle of the Atlantic 1943-1945," in International Commission of Military History, *Acta No. 13: Helsinki 31.V.—6.VI. 1988* (Helsinki: Finnish Commission of Military History), part 2, 135-161.

[7] BdU (*Befehlshaber der Unterseeboote*, that is, commander in chief submarines), War Diary, "Submarine situation 1.6.1944," filed after entry for 15 June 1944, Canada, National Defence Headquarters, Director General History (hereafter DG Hist) 79/446.

[8] Douglas, *Creation of a National Air Force*, 376, 395, 558.

[9] Great Britain, Ministry of Defence, Naval Historical Branch, *The U-Boat in the Atlantic, Vol. 3: June 1943-May 1945* (BR 305[3]: German Naval History Series, 1977), 57-8, 67-72.

[anti-submarine radar], which impeded battery charging. But area is easily navigable with "Schnorchel" (see also English Channel experiences). . . .

4) Countermeasures: situation in 1942
    Medium to strong air with and without location [radar], especially after being observed. Sea [naval] countermeasures relatively slight and unpractised. Location [sonar] conditions very unfavourable to the enemy, as there is marked underwater density layering. Find out about this density-layering, even for considerable depths, before a depth-charge hunt starts.
    In General: main defense by a/c. Sea defenses little to be feared. Situation thought to have altered little since 1942.[10]

Dönitz did not have much choice but to wax optimistic about the Gulf. The Allied armies were poised to retake France's Atlantic ports, and the Canadian coast was virtually the only overseas theater within practicable range of alternate bases in Norway.

In late July and August a total of five schnorkel-equipped Type IX boats set out for Canadian waters. Of these, two were to occupy the area off Halifax which, as two recent and otherwise unproductive missions by early schnorkel boats had confirmed, was still the major shipping center in the region.[11] The other three boats were to push deep into the Gulf of St. Lawrence. This effort in the Gulf matched the maximum of 1942.

On 17 July 1944 Allied intelligence already knew that a boat they code-named *Love Easy* (*LE*) had sailed from Lorient, France the preceding day.[12] This was *U 802*, under the command of KapitänLeutnant Helmut Schmoeckel. Schmoeckel and his boat had returned on 2 May from a three-month mission to the Canadian coast on which it had achieved the

---

[10] ZTPGU 31873, time of origin [TOO], Central European Time, 1339/1459/ 1855/2005/2058 23 Sept. 1944, to IDG8 (i.e., the plain text despatched to the Operational Intelligence Centre), 1755 (Greenwich Mean Time) 27 Sept. 1944, Great Britain, Public Record Office (hereafter PRO), DEFE 3/736. This long signal was dispatched to each of the three boats tasked for the Gulf of St. Lawrence as they approached North American waters, but the Allies appear to have succeeded in decrypting it for the first time in the transmission cited here, to *U 1223*, the last of the boats in this wave.

In all following references to decrypt material, the time and date of the transmittal of the plain text will be mentioned only if it is more than twenty-four hours after the time of origin.

[11] BdU War Diary, 27 May, 16 and 30 June 1944, DGHist 79/446.

[12] BdU War Diary, 16 July 1944, DGHist 79/446; Admiralty to CominCh, 171642Z July 1944, Record Group 457, National Archives, Washington D.C., (hereafter RG 457, NA), SRH 236, pt. 3.

meager record of a single coastal vessel destroyed.[13] The crew were thus "Canadian" veterans, but familiar with the limited capabilities of conventional submarines in the face of Allied air power. During her layover, *U 802* had been fitted with schnorkel, and on 20 July, when she was four days out of port, BdU assigned the submarine to spearhead the new offensive into the Gulf of St. Lawrence, approaching from the south of Newfoundland on a course along about 45° north latitude (a line that runs through the center of Nova Scotia). Within less than twenty-four hours (the speed with which Allied intelligence decrypted most U-boat signal traffic throughout this period), the Allies had the tasking information.[14] During the first part of August, the commander in chief U.S. Atlantic Fleet (CinCLant) assigned the escort carrier (CVE) USS *Bogue* and her destroyer screen (Task Group 22.3), then northwest of the Azores, to hunt westward for *LE* as the boat crossed the central ocean.[15]

Meanwhile, Rear Admiral L. W. Murray, commander in chief Canadian Northwest Atlantic, was laying on a gamma search about five hundred miles to the east of Newfoundland to catch the boat as it came in towards the approach point BdU had ordered. British forces had developed this tactic to trap U-boats transitting to or from their bases on courses that intelligence had detected with fair certainty. A minimum of five escorts were repeatedly to sweep "to and fro" along a fixed sixty-mile section of the U-boat's estimated course in line abreast at a distance of three to five miles between ships, thus creating a band of fifteen to twenty-five miles in width of overlapping ASDIC and radar coverage.[16]

Murray had little to spare for the operation. The RCN had assigned sixty escorts to support the Normandy landings while at the same time accepting total responsibility for the close escort of transatlantic convoys all the way from New York to the United Kingdom in order to release additional British warships for the offensive in European waters.[17] Only a single support group ("hunter killer" in U.S. parlance), the recently organized and inexperienced EG 16 of five newly commissioned frigates, was available. Aside from EG 16's need for a considerable period of

---

[13] BdU War Diary, 29 Jan., 9 April, 2 May 1944, DGHist 79/446; Douglas, *Creation of a National Air Force*, 576-7.

[14] ZTPGU 28278, TOO 1215, 20 July 1944, PRO, DEFE 3/733.

[15] *U 802* log, 12 Aug. 1944, DGHist 85/77 (all U-boat logs cited are collected in this file; extracts were translated by Mr. David Wiens); "CVE Dispositions," 4 Aug. 1944, "TF Composition," NA, Washington National Records Center (WNRC), RG 313 Red, box 143.

[16] Flag Officer Newfoundland (FONF) War Diary, Aug. 1944, and enclosed papers, NSC 1926-102/3 pt 1, DGHist.

[17] Hodgson, "The First Year of Canadian Operational Control in the Northwest Atlantic," 18 Aug. 1944, file 8280A pt. 1, DGHist 81/520/8280 Box 1.

"shake down" before it became truly effective, this was much less than what was needed. Because the broad ocean approaches to the Canadian coast offered an infinitely wide range of possible courses as compared to the confined waters off the German submarine bases in France, Murray's staff oriented the gamma search perpendicular to the estimated course, rather than along it, meaning that the density of coverage — and the possibility of locating the boat — would be a small fraction of what a gamma was designed to produce. What was more, as a result of supply problems three of the ships had the undependable Canadian RXC radar and only two the more trustworthy British type 271.[18]

To overcome these weaknesses, Murray, as was by now the habit in the Canadian area, turned to his strong arm, the RCAF. Beginning on the evening of 9 August, when EG 16 was in its gamma position and *U 802* was estimated to be approaching, Liberators from Gander, Newfoundland and Canso A's (the RCAF variant of the PBY5A) from Torbay near St. John's began to sweep an area 150 miles north to south and 120 miles east to west immediately seaward of the frigate line with patrols of up to fourteen hours' length. In accordance with the estimated advance of the U-boat, on the night of 11-12 August EG 16 moved its gamma line about 240 miles back towards the southeast tip of Newfoundland. The RCAF search area to the seaward of the surface escorts similarly fell back, after heavy fog which is so common on the Grand Banks shut down flying late on the 11th and much of the 12th. On 9 to 13 August the RCAF carried out thirty missions or more, of which at least twenty-two were completed, and substantially achieved the goal of sweeps over every part of the probability zone every two hours, particularly at night when the schnorkel boat was most likely to be on the surface.[19]

During the Canadian hunt the *Bogue* group, coming in from its chase across the Atlantic, closed into the area where the Canadians were searching. This was not the result of a carefully laid plan to trap the submarine between the Canadian and American forces. When Admiral Murray was establishing his hunt, he had signalled his plan to CinCLant and queried if *Bogue* might also be operating in the probability area. CinCLant, who never handed off control of the CVE groups, opened communication between *Bogue* and the Canadians so that they could coordinate.[20] The close proximity of the forces was actually evidence of

[18] DWT/Tactics to DWT and ACNS, 4 Oct. 1944, DGHist Naval Historical Section papers (hereafter NHS) 8440-EG 16.

[19] Nixon to ACNS et al., 28 Sept. 1944, enclosing "Summary of Operation 'Perch'," 25 Sept. 1944, "Official Memoranda" file, NAC, RG 24, vol. 11, 463.

[20] CinC CNA to CinCLant, 1936Z 8 Aug. 1944, NSS 8910-166/10, NAC, RG 24, vol. 6901.

the full extent to which the submarine trackers in Ottawa, Washington, and London who plotted U-boats had joined their efforts.

Allied estimates of *U 802*'s advance were very good, so good they closely matched BdU's own.[21] But they were only estimates, and they were wrong. *U 802* had last signalled on 27 July,[22] after she had cleared the Bay of Biscay and broken into the eastern Atlantic. Since that time, the boat's Tunis search receiver had picked up what were apparently aircraft radar emissions on several occasions, leading Schmoeckel to report later "Remarkably active air surveillance over the whole outward-bound route. Apparently my whole route was followed by enemy DF [i.e., radar]." Worse, the Tunis was prone to break down.[23] Instead of running fast on the surface through the night, Schmoeckel came up for only a couple of hours and made a scant sixty to seventy nautical miles a day instead of the usual one hundred or more. Further, no doubt to keep clear of Newfoundland-based aircraft, he ran far to the south, down to 40° (the latitude of New York), as he approached North America.[24] Even so, Schmoeckel was certain that he had been precisely located when during his brief run on the surface during the night of 11-12 August the Tunis warned of nearby airborne radar and he had to crash dive. Now that the Allies apparently knew where he was, in accordance with standard procedures he took the opportunity to make a short report signal the next night, 12-13 August.[25]

No Allied aircraft or vessel had in fact located *U 802* on the night of 11-12 August, but the boat's subsequent signal was accurately DFed. Initially the submarine trackers concluded that a second boat was following *LE*. Within twelve hours, however, they realized that *LE* was some four days behind and 250 miles to the south of her expected line of advance.[26] Admiral Murray called off his operation in the north, and *Bogue*'s group hunted to the south. One of the great advantages of carriers was that they could outrun or maneuver around the weather

---

[21] On 12 Aug. 1944, for example, BdU estimated *U 802* to be in quadrant BC 75, approximately 4345 to 4445 degrees north by 4900 to 5030 degrees west (BdU War Diary, 12 Aug. 1944, DGHist 79/446). The Canadian estimate was "within 75 miles 4440 N 5030 W" (Naval Service Headquarters, Ottawa [NSHQ] Daily U-boat Estimate, 1420Z 12 Aug. 1944, NSS 8910-7 pt. 1, NAC, RG 24, vol. 6895).

[22] BdU War Diary, 27 July 1944, DGHist 79/446.

[23] Schmoeckel, "Final Remarks," 23 Nov. 1944, *U 802* log.

[24] *U 802* log, 10-15 Aug. 1944.

[25] *U 802* log, 12-13 Aug. 1944.

[26] NSHQ daily U-boat estimate, 1435Z 13 Aug. 1944, NSS 8910-7 pt 1, NAC, RG 24, vol. 6895; NSHQ "Otter" signals, 0615Z, 0927Z, 1426Z 13 Aug. 1944, NSS 8910-20 pt. 2, NAC, RG 24, vol. 6896. "Otter" was the code name for U-boat probability areas which NSHQ promulgated each day primarily for the direction of air sweeps.

fronts that so often shut down flying from shore bases, especially on the Canadian coast. On 14-19 August, the RCAF could make only three sorties into the new probability zone, while the CVE, dodging the weather, kept up the chase. *Bogue* unwittingly came so close on 16 August that the carrier narrowly escaped coming under torpedo attack. On the night of 18-19 August, one of *Bogue*'s TBMs sighted the surfaced submarine about three hundred miles south of St. John's and made a depth charge attack that was wide of the mark. Meanwhile, on 17 August Admiral Murray had ordered the RCN's EG 16 to begin a gamma search across the U-boat's new estimated line of advance, about halfway between the position of the attack and the Cabot Straits entrance to the Gulf of St. Lawrence. On the 19th, when *Bogue*'s continued hunt for the boat that had been attacked was coming up empty handed, Murray placed EG 16 under the American carrier's orders, and the Canadian group headed southeast with three Canso A's from Torbay flying in support. During broad daylight on 20 August, before the Canadian group arrived, one of *Bogue*'s TBMs was startled to sight a fully surfaced U-boat and made a rocket and bomb attack that severely damaged her. Two hours later, the crippled boat lurched to the surface again and the swarming U.S. aircraft polished her off.[27]

The Canadian coast was apparently clear, and Murray cancelled the air-sea barrier patrols in the approaches to the Gulf. By 22 August, however, interrogation of the sunken U-boat's survivors had revealed that the submarine had not been *U 802 (LE)* but *U 1229*. Allied intelligence had known that *U 1229* — or *LT* as the trackers had labelled her — was at sea, and had correctly surmised from the absence of radio traffic that she was on a secret mission, but her destination had remained a mystery. The boat had in fact been going to put agents ashore on the coast of Maine and then operate off Halifax, and it had the bad luck to stumble into the hunt for *U 802*.[28]

Murray immediately reclosed the coast to independent shipping and

[27] *United States Fleet Anti-Submarine Bulletin* (Sept. 1944), 15-21; Commander-in-Chief, Canadian Northwest Atlantic (CinC CNA) War Diary, Aug. 1944, file 30-1-10 pt. 35, NAC, RG 24, vol. 11054; EAC proposed operations and operations summary signals, 14-20 Aug. 1944, DGHist 181.003(D3254); Signals, Aug. 1944, DGHist NHS 8440, "EG 16 Signals"; *U 802* log, 16 Aug. 1944.

[28] CinC CNA War Diary, Aug. 1944, file 30-1-10, pt. 35, NAC, RG 24, vol. 11054; Admiralty to CominCh, 2236Z 15 July 1944, 1031Z 15 Aug. 1944, 1800Z 17 Aug. 1944, SRH 236, pt. 8, pp. 31, 84, 87, RG 457, NA; CominCh to Admiralty, 1945Z 21 Aug. 1944, 1227Z 22 Aug. 1944, SRH 208, pt. 4, pp. 84-5, RG 457, NA; BdU War Diary, 2 Dec. 1944, DGHist 79/446.

restarted coastal convoys.[29] On the evening of 22 August, the RCAF again began intensive sweeps (flights over every part of the area every two hours at night and every four hours by day) in a probability zone from 120 miles seaward of the 100-mile wide Cabot Straits back 120 miles into the Gulf. The next day, EG 16 sailed to establish a gamma search outside the Cabot Straits, and on the 25th, Fairmile antisubmarine launches began a gamma within the straits. This heavy coverage of the straits and its immediate approaches continued until 28 August, when the focus of the search, although still including the Cabot Straits, began to shift into the Gulf. By the end of 30 August, the RCAF's Liberators and Cansos had flown more than sixty missions in the probability zone and additional missions in support of coastal convoys in the vicinity.[30] Already in the early part of August the command's squadrons had deployed additional Cansos to Newfoundland in anticipation of extended operations against *U 802* when she was thought to be following the northern route; now Cansos and Liberators moved into Sydney to sustain the new hunt. Aircraft would continue to move back up into the Gulf stations as the probability zones followed *U 802*'s estimated track.[31] This flexibility in rapidly moving aircraft and immediately dispatching them on operations over the vast, barren Canadian coastal areas (it is nearly 1,000 miles from Gaspé on the central Gulf to St. John's, Newfoundland) had not been possible in 1942, and the relative ease with which it was achieved in 1944 was a credit to the enormous effort that had been devoted to the development of bases, communications, and logistics.

The Canadian submarine trackers had estimated that *U 802* might pass through the Cabot Straits on 26 August and then, by 28 or 29 August, push up to the Gaspé Passage and the mouth of the St. Lawrence River, where the 1942 boats had enjoyed their greatest success.[32] This time, the Canadian estimates were better than BdU's; Dönitz's headquarters had *U 802* through the Cabot Strait as early as 24 August.[33] Again, both German and Allied plots were wrong.

Schmoeckel had understandably been terrorized by the encounter

---

[29] CinC CNA War Diary, Aug. 1944, file 30-1-10 pt 35, NAC, RG 24, vol. 11054.

[30] "Summary of Operation *Perch*," 25 Sept. 1944, "Official Memoranda" file, NAC, RG 24, vol. 11, 463; EAC Proposed Operations and Operations Summary Signals for 22-30 Aug. 1944, DG Hist 181.003(D3254); 10 Squadron RCAF Operations Record Book (hereafter ORB), 22-30 Aug. 1944, DGHist; CinC CNA to NOIC Sydney, 1701Z 24 Aug. 1944, NSS 8910-166/10, NAC, RG 24, vol. 6901.

[31] EAC Weekly Intelligence Reports for Aug. 1944, DGHist 181.003(D4863).

[32] NSHQ Daily U-boat Estimates 26-29 Aug. 1944, NSS 8910-7 pt. 1, NAC, RG 24, vol. 6895.

[33] BdU War Diary, 24 Aug. 1944, DGHist 79/446.

with *Bogue*'s group south of Newfoundland. "[P]ure Bay of Biscay conditions," he later reported, referring to the nightmare density of air and sea barrier patrols off the French coast where the British and Canadian maritime forces had concentrated their main effort.[34] He had therefore crept along, constantly submerged, daring to raise his schnorkel only at night. His progress slowed to as little as thirty nautical miles a day and never more than sixty.[35] In the end, he passed through the straits on 31 August, three days after the main naval forces had begun to move into the Gulf, and only hours after the RCAF had reduced the density of its patrols in the straits.[36] "The defenses of the entrance to the Gulf appear to me to be extraordinarily weak," he commented.[37] He continued to have a quiet run — always submerged, always two to three days behind the concentration of the Canadian searches — and finally reached the mouth of the St. Lawrence River on 6 September, where he lurked to try to locate shipping coming down into the Gulf.[38] By that time the situation had become more complicated for the defenders of the Gulf.

Allied intelligence had been able to follow, again with a delay of no more than twenty-four hours, the final fitting out of *U 541* (Kapitän-leutnant Kurt Petersen) with its new schnorkel for departure from Lorient on 6 August.[39] The submarine trackers were privy to BdU's tasking signal of 10 August that directed the boat, known as *JS* (Jig Sugar) in the Allied bigram identification code, to an approach point off Nova Scotia. They also promptly had a decryption of a further signal of 25 August that assigned *JS* to the Gulf.[40] On 28 August *Bogue*'s group, having refuelled at the U.S. Navy base at Argentia, Newfoundland, departed to hunt for *JS* then estimated to have recently crossed 40° west, in mid-ocean about 1,000 miles east of Newfoundland.[41] On the night of 28-29 August, *U 541* was overflown by an aircraft and Petersen made a short radio report that

---

[34] *U 802* log, "Final Remarks," 23 Nov. 1944.

[35] *U 802* log, 20-31 Aug. 1944.

[36] "Summary of Operation *Perch*," 25 Sept. 1944, "Official Memoranda" file, NAC, RG 24, vol. 11, 463; CinC CNA to NOIC Gaspé, 1222Z 28 Aug. 1944, NSS 8910-166/10, NAC, RG 24, vol. 6901; EAC Proposed Operations Signals for 30 and 31 Aug. 1944, DGHist 181.003(D3254).

[37] *U 802* log, 31 Aug. 1944.

[38] *U 802* log, 1-6 Sept. 1944.

[39] ZTPGU 29116, TOO 1917 6 Aug. 1944, ZTPGU 29019, TOO 1621 5 Aug. 1944, PRO, DEFE 3/734.

[40] BdU War Diary, 10 Aug. 1944; CominCh to Admiralty signal 1945 21 Aug. 1944, SRH 208, pt. 3, RG 457, NA; ZTPGU 30532, TOO 1453 25 Aug. 1944, PRO, DEFE 3/735.

[41] "CVE Dispositions," 2 Sept. 1944, "TF Composition," WNRC, RG 313 Red, box 143, NA; NSHQ "Otter" Signal, 0712Z 27 Aug. 1944 for 28 Aug. 1944, NSS 8910-20, pt. 2, NAC, RG 24, vol. 6896.

the Allies. This fix placed *U 541* at about 44°30'N by 44°30'W, on the approach route BdU had ordered, and just beyond the furthest on limits of the Allied estimates.[42] RCAF Liberators from Gander, Newfoundland, made three long sorties over the probability area on the night of 29-30 August, but for the next two days fog interrupted operations.[43]

Encouraged by the lack of opposition, Petersen forged ahead with long surface runs during the nights, making 132 to 146 nautical miles on each of three days. He thus arrived off the Cabot Straits early on 3 September, some 150 miles ahead of the furthest-on point of the Allied probability zone where aircraft were searching, and some six days before BdU plotted him into the area. He arrived, moreover, just as the Canadians were further reducing coverage of the straits in order to concentrate against *U 802*'s estimated position in the western Gulf. Indeed, the Canso A that had carried out the last straits patrol on 2 September was landing at about the time *U 541* surfaced off Cape Breton, and weather was closing in that would force cancellation of the patrol scheduled for the early hours of the next day. The boat was able to proceed towards the straits on the surface and had the further good luck to locate and sink the unescorted steamer *Livingstone* before dawn on the 3rd, about 110 miles east of Sydney, Cape Breton, in the southern approaches to the straits. Word of the sinking did not reach shore authorities until some eight hours later when a convoy happened upon the lifeboat carrying the steamer's survivors. By the time aircraft could take off in the unfavorable conditions and warships — the close escort group C 6, the frigates of EG 16, and motor launches — could establish gamma barriers in the straits, *U 541* was well away on a submerged run through these broad waters.[44]

The submarine trackers credited the destruction of *Livingstone* not to the newcomer *JS* but to *LE (U 802).*[45] The sinking had, after all, occurred

---

[42] *U 541* log, 28-9 Aug. 1944; CinC CNA War Diary, Aug. 1944, pt. 2, file 30-1-10, pt. 35, NAC, RG 24, vol. 11054; NSHQ "Otter" Signal 0829Z 28 Aug 1944 for 29 Aug. 1944, NSS 8910-20, pt. 2, NAC, RG 24, vol. 6896.

[43] 10 and 160 Squadron ORBs, 30 Aug.-1 Sept. 1944, DGHist.

[44] *U 541* log, 31 Aug.-3 Sept. 1944; EAC Proposed Operations and Operations Summary Signals for 3 Sept. 1944, DGHist 181.003(D3254); NSHQ "Otter" signal 0705Z 2 Sept. 1944 for 3 Sept. 1944, NSS 8910-20, pt. 2, NAC, RG 24, vol. 6896; BdU War Diary, 8-9 Sept. 1944, DGHist 79/446; CinC CNA War Diary, Sept. 1944, file 30-1-10 pt 37, NAC, RG 24, vol. 11054.

[45] CominCh to Admiralty, signal 1827Z 7 Oct. 1944, SRH 208, pt. 4, p. 94, RG 457, NA.

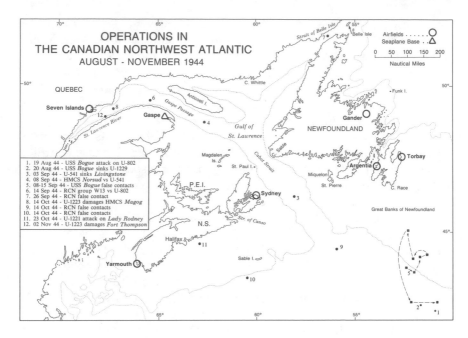

OPERATIONS IN
THE CANADIAN NORTHWEST ATLANTIC
AUGUST - NOVEMBER 1944

Airfields . . . . . . O
Seaplane Base . . △

0   50   100   150   200
Nautical Miles

1. 19 Aug 44 - USS *Bogue* attack on U-802
2. 20 Aug 44 - USS *Bogue* sinks U-1229
3. 03 Sep 44 - U-541 sinks *Livingstone*
4. 08 Sep 44 - HMCS *Norsud* vs U-541
5. 08-15 Sep 44 - USS *Bogue* false contacts
6. 14 Sep 44 - RCN group W13 vs U-802
7. 26 Sep 44 - RCN false contact
8. 14 Oct 44 - U-1223 damages HMCS *Magog*
9. 14 Oct 44 - RCN false contacts
10. 14 Oct 44 - RCN false contacts
11. 23 Oct 44 - U-1221 attack on *Lady Rodney*
12. 02 Nov 44 - U-1223 damages *Fort Thompson*

well to the west of the furthest-on estimate for *JS*, and that estimate was
a firm one given the confirmation by DF only a few nights before. *U 802*,
not heard from since 19 August, had evidently never undertaken her Gulf
mission or had abandoned it after a lack of success in favor of the Cabot
Straits. It thus seemed that there might be two U-boats on the shipping
lanes outside the straits. Canadian antisubmarine motor launch flotillas
and aircraft from the Gulf stations maintained searches of the western
Gulf, but the main offensive was in the seaward approaches to the Cabot
Straits. The Canadian strike force, EG 16, ran gamma patrols close in,
while *Bogue*'s group hunted about 250 miles to the southeast, at the outer
edge of the probability zone, and RCAF aircraft swept the probability
area between the naval forces. What was more, the light defenses that
continued in the Gulf were greatly hampered by weather that closed
down flying in the area on 5-7 September. Both U-boats had a quiet time
as *U 802* reached the mouth of the St. Lawrence River and *U 541*
traversed the central Gulf.[46]

[46] NSHQ "Otter" Signals for 4-5 Sept. 1944, NSS 8910-20, pt. 2, NAC, RG 24, vol. 6896;
EAC Operations Proposals and Summary Signals for 3-7 Sept. 1944, DGHist 181.003(D3254);
10 and 116 Squadron ORBs, 4-7 Sept. 1944, DGHist.

Firm evidence that at least one boat was in the Gulf came to hand on the night of 7-8 September. Surfacing to attack what appeared to be an unescorted steamer about twenty miles south of the southeastern tip of Anticosti Island, *U 541*'s captain was shocked to see a "destroyer" (actually the corvette HMCS *Norsyd*) closing at speed, pouring Oerlikon fire into the conning tower. The boat crash-dived and fired a torpedo. Petersen heard noises like a ship breaking up and claimed a victory, but it was just an end-of-run detonation. Together with another escort from the convoy and aircraft, *Norsyd* began an expanding hunt to exhaustion. Within ten hours of the attack they were reinforced by three frigates of EG 16, rushed up from the Cabot Strait. Motor launch flotillas and additional aircraft established barrier patrols at a distance across possible escape routes. Searches at this full intensity continued for ten days. After the initial forty-hour expanding hunt (ultimately five Canso A's simultaneously swept the whole probability circle), the emphasis was on the key narrow passages from the Cabot Strait up to the mouth of the St. Lawrence. Meanwhile, after the attack *U 541* had made a quiet submerged run north into shallower water off Anticosti and rested on the bottom through the night of 8-9 September before continuing, submerged, towards the mouth of the St. Lawrence.[47]

U 802, already on station in the river estuary, decided to get out. Because radio reception had been virtually blacked out by poor atmospheric conditions, Schmoeckel had not been privy to the dispatch of *U 541* into his area and assumed he himself was the focus of the searches:

> The difference in surveillance, as compared to the first four days which were completely quiet, is remarkable, even though no shipping traffic has been detected during the last two days either. It appears that the enemy may after all have picked up some indication of my presence. After all, there hasn't been any other boat in this area for the last two years. Perhaps he was able to pick up my schnorkel with his land-based equipment. It strikes me as odd that the aircraft are always flying back and forth over the area on a north-south course, while I have also been standing to and off land on north-south courses for the last seven days.[48]

On 13 September, Schmoeckel began to creep back towards the central Gulf. The next day he was run over by the Canadian frigates of W 13, a

---

[47] *U 541* log, 8-10 Sept. 1944; CinC CNA War Diary, Aug. 1944, pt. 1, file 30-1-10, pt. 35, NAC, RG 24, vol. 11054; EAC Proposed and Operations Summary Signals, 8-18 Sept. 1944, DGHist 181.003(D3254).

[48] *U 802* log, 13 Sept. 1944.

temporary scratch group put together to relieve the hard-pressed EG 16, and let fly a torpedo that exploded in HMCS *Stettler*'s wake. Encouraged by the quick detonation of the torpedo at a short-range target, Schmoeckel took credit for the sinking of a "destroyer," but no damage had been done to the warship. As before, the frigates found their ASDIC blinded by the miserable water conditions, and their counter attacks were wide of the mark. Schmoeckel made for shallower water towards the shore and bottomed the boat, where he intended to hide for twenty-four hours, but after twelve it became clear that the submarine was on a ledge and beginning to slide deeper. As he rose to periscope depth after daybreak on 15 September, he was relieved to see thick fog. Still, whenever he attempted to schnorkel on the following day, aircraft appeared. When he reached the Gaspé Passage on 18 September, the defenses seemed to be so strong that he stopped his engines for twenty-four hours and let the current carry him silently.[49]

Petersen, *U 541*, who arrived at the mouth of the St. Lawrence River on 13 September just as *U 802* was leaving, also noted the increased defense activity. Having stirred things up five days before, he was less alarmed than Schmoeckel, but no less cautious and no more successful.[50]

The submarine trackers had no way of knowing that the encounters on 8 and 14 September had been with separate U-boats. They in fact had reason to believe that both contacts were with the same one, for at this very same time, beginning 8 September, USS *Bogue*'s aircraft and destroyer escorts began to pick up convincing radar and sonar returns far out on the ocean routes, about two hundred miles south of Cape Race, the southeastern tip of Newfoundland. Here was confirmation of the earlier appreciation that *Livingstone*'s destruction showed that at least one of the submarines was making an extended patrol in the ocean approaches to the Cabot Straits. The RCAF squadrons in Newfoundland lent strong support to *Bogue* in a week-long hunt.[51] As the days passed without anything definite turning up, the submarine trackers downgraded the plotting of *Bogue*'s submarine to "not considered definitely located."[52] It was, in the words of Samuel Eliot Morison, the semi-official historian of the U.S. Navy, "probably the most frustrating time of the

---

[49] *U 802* log, 14-19 Sept. 1944; DWT/Tactics to DWT and ACNS, 14 Nov. 1944, DG Hist, NHS 8440-"W 13."

[50] *U 541* log, 13-18 Sept. 1944.

[51] FONF War Diary, 8-11 Sept. 1944, NSC 1926-102/3, pt. 1, DGHist; 10 and 160 Squadron ORBs, 9-14 Sept. 1944, DGHist.

[52] NSHQ "Otter" Signals for 8-14 Sept. 1944, NSS 8910-20, pt. 2, NAC, RG 24, vol. 6896.

war for . . . the *Bogue* group."[53] The constant false radar returns from the flotsam on the Grand Banks and the tricks the shallow water and cluttered seabed played with sonar — all too familiar to the Canadian forces — were an unwelcome new experience for the Americans.

As *Bogue* gratefully left the Canadian area, the escort carrier USS *Core*'s group arrived to begin a hunt for a new intruder. On 30 August the submarine trackers had had a clear version of BdU's routing signal of the 29th for *U 1221* (Oberleutnant P. Ackermann) to head for the vicinity of 45°N 50°W, southeast of Newfoundland.[54] Ackermann made a series of weather reports on 14-15 September, which the Allies evidently DFed, and he also flashed his position in a signal that was decrypted by late on the 15th.[55] This unusually specific information boosted the plot to top grade and priority.[56] When *Core*'s group rushed out from refuelling at Argentia on 17 September, the RCAF squadrons in Newfoundland had already launched an all-out effort the day before: up to twelve aircraft swept the probability area each day for most of the following week.[57]

The destination of the boat was initially unclear. On 15 September BdU had assigned Ackermann to the Halifax approaches, with latitude to "Approach focal point [the area within about fifty miles of the entrance to the port] according to defense situation." The signal gave the codebreakers some difficulty, and it was only on the 18th they were able to give operational intelligence a clear text.[58]

Meanwhile, the boat had begun to pick up radar emissions and hear distant explosions as the Canadian and American searching forces attacked false contacts. *U 1221* did not take such extreme precautions as *U 802* had but was soon running behind Allied plots and arrived in the southern approaches to Halifax on 30 September, four days later than the submarine trackers and five later than U-boat headquarters estimated.

---

[53] Samuel Eliot Morison, *History of United States Naval Operations in World War II, Vol. 10: The Atlantic Battle Won, May 1943-May 1945* (Boston: Little, Brown, 1956), 328; see also William T. Y'Blood, *Hunter Killer: U.S. Escort Carriers in the Battle of the Atlantic* (Annapolis: Naval Institute Press, 1983), 248-9.

[54] ZTPGU 39793, TOO 1256 29 Aug. 1944, PRO, DEFE 3/735.

[55] *U 1221* log, 14-15 Sept. 1944; ZTPGU 31435 TOO 0448 14 Sept. 1944, PRO, DEFE 3/736.

[56] NSHQ "Otter" Signal 0845Z 16 Sept. 1944 upgraded the plot for *U 1221* from "B" to "A", and then 1236Z, same date, sharpened up the estimate by shifting it somewhat to the west and south, NSS 8910-20, pt. 2, NAC, RG 24, vol. 6896.

[57] FONF War Diary, 16 Sept. 1944, NSC 1926-102/3, pt. 1, DGHist; EAC Proposed Operations and Operations Summary Signals, 16-23 Sept. 1944, DGHist 181.003(D3254); 10 and 160 Squadron ORBs, 16-23 Sept. 1944, DGHist.

[58] ZTPGU 31469, TOO 1216 15 Sept. 1944, plain text to ID8G 0006Z 18 Sept. 1944, PRO, DEFE 3/736.

as the probability area neared the coast, continued heavy coverage over the boat's assigned operational area until dense fog rolled in on 7 October for the better part of a week; on one day, 5 October, there were sixteen sorties, including support for convoys passing through the danger zone. The probability area was large, extending one hundred miles out to sea from Halifax and one hundred miles to the south, the submarine trackers evidently having taken account of the freedom BdU had given Ackermann to use his judgement in closing within fifty miles of the port. The trackers had made the right guess, for Ackermann held back, fifty to one hundred miles south of Halifax, on the route to the United States. All shipping he located was in convoy, and he saw enough signs of an active defense that he continued to lie low.[59]

The submarine trackers knew that another boat, in fact *U 1223* (Oberleutnant Albert Kneip), had followed *U 1221*. Kneip revealed his presence at about 36°W 49°N with short reports on 21-22 September.[60] On the 22nd U-boat headquarters, in a message the allies decrypted within twenty-four hours, allocated an approach point south of Newfoundland.[61] By the 27th, after the codebreakers had worked for four days, the submarine trackers also had the clear text of the tasking signal for the Gulf of St. Lawrence.[62] Because *U 1223*'s log has not survived, it is not possible to describe her passage, but she likely suffered little harassment owing to extraordinarily good fortune. When the RCAF in Newfoundland began long-range patrols against the boat on 25 September, only two missions were flown because a promising schnorkel sighting by another RCAF aircraft off the Avalon Peninsula warranted an extended hunt to exhaustion. The single mission against *U 1223* on the 26th was curtailed by weather, and on that same date an extraordinarily convincing sighting by a warship of a U-boat submerging in the Strait of Belle Isle drew in

---

[59] *U 1221* log, 15 Sept.-10 Oct. 1944; BdU War Diary, 25-6 Sept. 1944, DGHist 79/446; NSHQ "Otter" Signals for 18 Sept.-10 Oct. 1944, NSS 8910-20, pt. 2, NAC, RG 24, vol. 6897; EAC Proposed Operations and Operations Summary Signals, 26 Sept.-7 Oct. 1944, DGHist 181.003(D3254); EAC Intelligence Report for week ending 12 Oct. 1944, DGHist 181.003(D486).

[60] ZTPGU 31672, TOO 0605 22 Sept. 1944, PRO, DEFE 3/736; CinC CNA War Diary Sept. 1944, pt. 2, file 30-1-10, pt. 37, NAC, RG 24, vol. 11054; NSHQ "Otter" Signal, 1326Z 23 Sept. 1944, NSS 8910-20, pt. 2, NAC, RG 24, vol. 6896; Knowles, "U-Boat Intelligence Summary," 23 Sept. 1944, SRMN 037, p. 475, RG 457, NA.

[61] BdU to Kneip, 1534/22 Sept. 1944, ZTPGU 31687, PRO, DEFE 3/736.

[62] BdU signal in five parts, 1339/1459/1855/2005/2058/23 Sept. 1944, ZTPGU 31873 to ID8G 1755Z 27 Sept. 1944, PRO, DEFE 3/736.

many of the group's aircraft for a three-day hunt. Foul weather then moved in and virtually shut down flying for the next two weeks: a total of only fifteen missions could be flown to cover *U 1223*'s estimated track up to the mouth of the St. Lawrence River. This left the defense almost solely to the weak RCN forces, which aside from the close escorts for convoys, included only EG 16 and the antisubmarine motor launches.[63]

The contacts southeast of Newfoundland and in the Strait of Belle Isle that had drawn aircraft from the initial hunt for *U 1223* also sent astray searches for the other two Gulf boats, the long-silent *U 541* and *U 802*. The submarine trackers changed their plots to show that one boat had left the Gulf by the northern route and the other by the southern.[64] They were probably predisposed to accept the contacts, both of which were false, because they had a decryption of an order by BdU on 20 September for the boats to report, and that was clear evidence that Dönitz himself expected they would shortly begin their homeward runs.[65] Actually, both boats had crept submerged through the southern exit, the Cabot Straits, on 23-24 September. *U 802* gingerly made its way well to the south, approximately 41°, to avoid Newfoundland-based aircraft as it began the transatlantic voyage. *U 541* lingered in the eastern approaches to the straits, to the south of Newfoundland, hoping to repeat her success of 3 September. Petersen made two attacks — both were so wide of the mark they were unnoticed by the crews of the vessels — before cutting short his stay in order to reach safer ocean waters and signal in response to U-boat headquarters' increasingly insistent demands for reports from the North American submarines.[66]

The Allied intelligence picture began to clear on the night of 2-3 October, when shore stations DFed a short position report from *U 541* as she began the homeward trip from south of Newfoundland. The heavy weather that had saved *U 1223* from harassment also prevented a hunt for *U 541*; even warships dispatched towards the position were forced to return to port. An air search guided by bearings on the boat's further reports finally got underway on the fifth and pursued the submarine into mid-ocean during the following week; on four occasions *U 541* was

---

[63] CinC CNA War Diary, Sept. 1944, file 30-1-10 pt 37, NAC, RG 24, vol. 11054; EAC Operations Summary Signals, 25 Sept.-13 Oct. 1944, DGHist 181.003(D3254); 10 and 160 Squadron ORBs, 25 Sept.-13 Oct. 1944, DGHist; EAC Intelligence Reports for weeks ending 5, 12, 19 Oct. 1944, DGHist 181.003(D4863).

[64] NSHQ "Otter" Signal 0730Z 27 Sept. 1944, NSS 8910-20, pt. 2, NAC, RG 24, vol. 6896.

[65] ZTPGU 31524 TOO 1140 20 Sept. 1944 to ID8G 0255Z 22 Sept. 1944, PRO, DEFE 3/736.

[66] *U 541* and *U 802* logs, 22-28 Sept. 1944.

forced to dive when the search receiver detected radar transmissions from the aircraft. The U.S. CVE *Guadalcanal* and her group (TG 22.7) later joined in the chase.[67]

The Allies decrypted *U 541*'s full report, which Petersen broadcast on the night of 6-7 October, within less than forty-eight hours. Although transmission had been garbled, the essential point was clear: there was little traffic to be found within the Gulf of St. Lawrence, but "good chances" of success in the eastern approaches to the Cabot Strait, south of Newfoundland.[68] On 9 October, U-boat headquarters broadcast permission for the submarines still in the Canadian area "to transfer your operational area in accordance with [*U 541*'s] situation report," and within a few hours the submarine trackers had a clear version of the signal.[69] Canadian intelligence therefore allowed for the possibility that *U 1223* was outside the Cabot Strait, where *U 541* had patrolled, and Eastern Air Command assigned aircraft to cover both this area and the Gulf.[70]

It soon became clear that *U 1223* had not left the Gulf. Freed from harassment by weather that prevented or curtailed air operations on most days during the first two weeks of October, the boat had penetrated through the Gulf to the mouth of the St. Lawrence River. In broad daylight on the morning of the 14th, an inward-bound convoy passed close by her hiding place. She let fly two torpedoes, one of which blew sixty feet off the stern of the escorting frigate HMCS *Magog*. Although the warship remained afloat and was towed to port, she proved to be damaged beyond economical repair given the pressure of more urgent new construction work on available shipyards. The convoy escort had been greatly reinforced because of *U 1223*'s suspected presence in the Gulf; *Magog* had been part of EG 16 which had been providing support. The rest of the group and the Canso A flying close cover responded quickly, but the temperature gradients and the layering of salt and fresh water at the river mouth protected the submarine from sonar detection.

---

[67] CinC CNA War Diary, 3,7 Oct. 1944, file 30-1-10 pt 37, NAC, RG 24, vol. 11054; FONF War Diary, 9 Oct. 1944, NSC 1926-102/3, pt. 1, DGHist; 10 and 160 Squadron ORBs, 5-11 Oct. 1944, DGHist; U541 log, 3-9 Oct 44; "CVE Dispositions," 10 Oct. 1944, "TF Composition," WNRC, RG 313 Red, box 163, NA; Knowles, "U-Boat Intelligence Summary," 27 Oct. 1944, SRMN 037, p. 498, RG 457, NA.

[68] ZTPGU 32303A, TOO 0106 7 Oct. 1944, PRO, DEFE 3/737.

[69] ZTPGU 32347, TOO 1104 9 Oct. 1944, PRO, DEFE 3/737.

[70] NSHQ "Otter" Signal 0815Z 10 Oct. 1944 for 11 Oct., NSS 8910-20, pt. 2, NAC, RG 24, vol. 6896.

The forty-eight-hour hunt to exhaustion by warships and aircraft also came up empty handed.[71]

The submarine trackers had meanwhile revised their estimates. If *U 1223* had not taken advantage of BdU's encouraging signal about the Cabot Strait approaches, then perhaps the U-boat plotted into the Halifax approaches, *U 1221*, which had enjoyed no success there, might have done so. Some evidence, admittedly tentative, suggested as much. During the night of 13-14 October there had been two separate submarine reports by warships — a torpedo track in the vicinity of Sable Island and a radar and sonar contact about 250 miles to the northeast towards Newfoundland. Hunts of twelve to forty-eight hours had turned up nothing, and the distance between the two incidents showed that one must be false in light of the fact only one boat could possibly be in the area.[72] Still, both, and especially the encounter near Sable Island, were compatible with an attempt by *U 1221* on the Cabot Strait approaches. On 15-18 October, the Canadian trackers allowed that *U 1221* might still be off Halifax or, alternatively, out on the ocean route to the Cabot Straits. Then, on 19 October, the assessment changed to a firm estimate that *U 1221* was in fact homebound, about five hundred miles southeast of Newfoundland.[73] The abrupt change in the Canadian plotting leaves no doubt that some fresh intelligence came to hand. British and Canadian records available are silent as to the source, but it seems likely that it was an uncertain DF of 16 October mentioned in American records as having been analyzed as a possible weather report by a boat southeast of Newfoundland. The Americans had paired this with the earlier Canadian torpedo track report from the vicinity of Sable Island to conclude that *U 1221* was homebound, complying with BdU's urgent calls for weather reports from the North American boats as soon as they had cleared the coast.[74]

---

[71] EAC Proposed Operations and Operations Summary Signals, 14-17 Oct. 1944, DGHist 181.003(D3254); EAC Intelligence Report week ending 19 Oct. 1944, DGHist 181.003(D4863); CinC CNA War Diary, Oct. 1944, file 30-1-10 pt 37, NAC, RG 24, vol. 11054; "Magog," DGHist NHS 8000.

[72] CinC CNA War Diary 14 Oct. 1944, file 30-1-10, pt. 37, NAC, RG 24, vol. 11054.

[73] NSHQ "Otter" Signals, 15-19 Oct. 1944, NSS 8910-20, pt. 2, NAC, RG 24, vol. 6896.

[74] Knowles, "U-Boat Intelligence Summary," 27 Oct. 1944, SRMN 037, p. 498, RG 457, NA. See also RCN Operational Summary No. 504, 18 Oct. 1944, which quotes the U.S. CominCh's "U-Boat Trends" for October as stating that the Sable Island incident on the 14th "fixed" a submarine in that location, and that it was "likely to start homeward shortly." Daily Operational Summary July to December 1944, DGHist. CinClant to CTG 22.5 [*Croatan*], 1952Z 19 Oct. 1944, ordered the group to "Proceed when ready" to hunt the phantom homebound boat. (NSS 8910-166/10, NAC, RG 24, vol. 6901). *Croatan's* group was then exercising off Bermuda, and it seems they never undertook this mission. ("CVE

U 1221 had actually continued the patrol off southern Nova Scotia until 17 October and only then pressed north to locate the traffic *U 541* had identified. Moreover, the boat did not attempt to move out onto the ocean route or close the Cabot Strait but merely crept up to the immediate northern approaches to Halifax. There the submarine might well have claimed a rich prize, the troop ship *Lady Rodney* who, with her two escorts, crossed the submerged boat's track in daylight on 23 October. The spread of three torpedoes missed, but so convinced were Canadian naval authorities that *U 1221* had departed that they attributed the explosions to mines and dispatched sweepers to the scene.[75]

Ten days later the errors in the U-boat plot that had begun with the too-literal interpretation of the German headquarters advisory signal of 9 October resulted in an actual casualty. After the failed attack on *Lady Rodney*, *U 1221* returned to the waters off southern Nova Scotia and then struck out for Norway. Because the submarine trackers believed that only *U 1223* remained in the Canadian zone, they interpreted bearings on *U 1221*'s homebound report, transmitted on the night of 30-31 October, to mean that the whole coast was clear.[76] Aircraft began to depart from the Gulf of St. Lawrence stations and the Gulf was reopened to independently sailed shipping.[77] On the afternoon of 2 November, SS *Fort Thompson*, one of the vessels that had set off on its own through the mouth of the St. Lawrence River, was struck by a torpedo from *U 1223* who was still lurking there. Buoyed by its cargo of grain, the ship did not sink and was later salved.[78] Although the submarine remained in the Gulf for at least two weeks longer, Kneip laid low and maintained radio silence until he reached mid-Atlantic on 26 November.[79]

The first concentrated wave of U-boats to strike in Canadian waters since 1942 had achieved little, even though the U.S. Navy and RCN had only four firm contacts, and the RCAF none at all. During extended patrols of five to six weeks each within the coastal area, five submarines had, in exchange for the loss of one of their number, damaged an escort, sunk a single merchant vessel, and damaged another. The main reason for this slight success was the limited mobility of submerged boats. They

---

Dispositions," 10-30 Oct. 1944, "TF Composition," WNRC, RG 313 Red, box 143, NA.)

[75] *U 1221* log, 14-23 Oct. 1944; CinC CNA War Diary, 23 Sept. 1944, file 30-1-10, pt. 37, NAC, RG 24, vol. 11054.

[76] CinC CNA War Diary, 31 Oct. 1944, file 30-1-10, pt. 37, NAC, RG 24, 11054; amended "Otter" Signal 0614Z 31 Oct. 1944 for same date, NSS 8910-20, pt. 2, NAC, RG 24, vol. 6896.

[77] FONF War Diary, 31 Oct. 1944, NSC 1926-102/3, pt. 1, DGHist.

[78] Saul to Scott, 5 Nov. 1944, NSC 8341-3995, NAC, RG 24, vol. 6791.

[79] BdU War Diary, 26-7 Nov. 1944, DGHist 79/446.

located shipping but could not maneuver into attacking positions. As one commanding officer later complained: "I feel like a tethered mine which has to wait for something to hit it."[80] For its part, U-boat headquarters brooded about the opportunities *U 1223* had missed: had she been one of the new Type XXI boats being developed for fast submerged speed, multiple attacks on all three convoys and three independents she had contacted would have been possible rather than only a single shot at one convoy and one independent.[81]

In this light, the central point is that, with the exception of *U 541*'s two attack runs, none of the boats dared surface to make fast runs in pursuit of shipping during the whole time of their patrols in Canadian waters. Naval escorts, according to the reports of the U-boat captains, were weak and inexperienced;[82] the great danger was of sudden attack by aircraft. Although extended submerged runs and radio silence had deprived the Allies of the sightings and DF bearings essential to contact boats, high quality and timely Ultra intelligence enabled air forces to harass them during their approach to the coast and in their initial operations area. The clearest case was that of *U 802*, whose experienced captain was entirely cowed by the encounter with USS *Bogue*'s aircraft and the subsequent RCAF patrols over the Gulf of St. Lawrence. The captain of *U 1221*, another boat that returned empty handed, also commented upon the "efficient" air defenses,[83] and upon analyzing the report headquarters concluded that there was the "usual well-trained day air patrolling, [and] when a convoy was passing day and night air patrols were strengthened."[84] Headquarters took even *U 1223*'s report of her successful cruise in the Gulf as confirmation that "It is only possible to operate there with schnorkel."[85] Significantly, every one of the successful attacks and the best missed opportunity, *U 1221*'s chance at *Lady Rodney*, occurred after misinterpretations of intelligence or weather conditions had prevented air operations in the area.

Still, schnorkel had indeed undercut the killing power of the Ultra - air forces combination. At best, the decryptions gave the approach course and destination of the submarine, and that was not enough information to gain contact with the U-boat or even to assure suppression. The submarine, as we have seen, was often several days — and several hundred

---

[80] *U 1231* log, 23 Dec. 1944.

[81] BdU War Diary, 25 Dec. 1944, DGHist 79/446.

[82] Report of *U 1222*, BdU War Diary, 27 May 1944, DGHist 79/446; report of *U 1223*, ibid., 26 Nov. 1944; report of U-541, ibid., 8 Oct. 1944.

[83] *U 1221* log, 5 Nov. 1944 (text of radio report to U-boat headquarters).

[84] BdU War Diary, 5 Nov. 1944, DGHist 79/446.

[85] ZTPGU 33697, TOO 1851 27 Nov. 1944, PRO, DEFE 3/738.

miles — ahead of or behind the rate of advance BdU itself anticipated. The three cases in which suppression worked best — *U 802* and *U 1221* during their approach runs, and *U 802* and *U 541* in the Gulf — resulted from the submarines having broadcast signals that allowed accurate location by Allied DF networks or from making an attack in the presence of forces that could rapidly respond and supply full information to shore authorities. Equally significantly, USS *Bogue's* tough, experienced, and superbly equipped team succeeded in finding *U 802* only when she surfaced, and it made a kill solely because *U 1229* had had the bad luck and judgment to run surfaced into the follow-up hunt for *U 802* after the initial attack. When *U 802* and the following boats took care to keep their heads down, *Bogue* and other first rate CVE groups found themselves blind and powerless, even with the help of top-grade Ultra and DF fixes. The CVE hunter killer groups first ran headlong into the riddle of the schnorkel boat during that frustrating autumn in Canadian waters.

Dönitz, in his larger goal of tying down Allied antisubmarine forces so that they would not be available to strike directly at Germany, could derive little satisfaction from developments in the Canadian area. The cut in Eastern Air Command of late 1943 and early 1944 to only seven squadrons had not been reversed. Furthermore, since early 1944 Eastern Air Command had begun to dispatch its most experienced crews overseas, to feed bomber and maritime reconnaissance squadrons serving under the Royal Air Force in the European theater. Similarly, the Royal Canadian Navy maintained and expanded the increased commitments it had shouldered for mid-ocean escort and operations in European waters.

The ability to sustain support for the British forces overseas was particularly important for interallied relations. For reasons of national interests and to rationalize confused command arrangements, after the spring of 1943 the United States had withdrawn from the direction of and substantial participation in trade defense on the north Atlantic routes to the United Kingdom, leaving this area to Britain's and Canada's closely integrated forces. In 1944 there was no urgent requirement to reintroduce major U.S. forces or readjust command structures because of Canada's ability to meet Britain's increased needs arising from the invasion of northwest Europe. U.S. CVE groups afforded great assistance in the Canadian theater in 1944, but the CVEs were simply following their roving commission under CinCLant. Canada had not called for help: the CVEs had gone to where the hunting was most promising.

Certainly the endless, unproductive searches in the unpleasant conditions off Newfoundland, Nova Scotia, and in the Gulf seemed fruitless misery to the Royal Canadian Air Force and United States Navy air crews who flew them. These patrols, however, assured an adequate, economical defense of North American waters and in so doing directly supported the offensive on the other side of the Atlantic.

13

Operation *Teardrop* Revisited

Philip K. Lundeberg

Allen's Law, to wit, "Nothing is as simple as it may appear," applies with singular force to the tale of Operation *Teardrop,* the last and largest Allied hunter-killer group operation in the Atlantic during World War II. While it is not possible to recount the complex history of this operation in full detail, it is necessary to focus on several aspects that significantly modify earlier narratives of this concluding and in many respects tragic drama in the long North Atlantic struggle. Earlier surveys of *Teardrop* have been limited in their intelligence perspectives for security reasons and lacked adequate insight from the German side, owing to the fact that the War Diary of the U-boat Command, an indispensable source on the Atlantic battle, fell silent in mid-January 1945 amid the growing collapse of the Third Reich.[1] Writers in the early 1950s, moreover, were enjoined to avoid discussion of communications intelligence and indeed knew nothing of the German Enigma coding system or of Bletchley Park's decoding activities. Also unknown was the Anglo-American "Special Intelligence" collaboration that had provided Admiral Ernest J. King's secret antisubmarine command, Tenth Fleet, and Jonas Ingram's Atlantic Fleet not only with prompt HF/DF fixes on operating U-boats but also with timely decrypted text and analysis of their wireless communications to and from Konteradmiral Eberhard Godt, Grossadmiral Dönitz's operational deputy at U-boat Command headquarters. Relevant U-boat war diaries found in the Tambach Archives proved little more than

---

[1] Samuel Eliot Morison, *History of United States Naval Operations in World II,* vol. 10, *The Atlantic Battle Won, May 1943-May 1945* (Boston, 1956), 344-356; Philip Karl Lundeberg, "American Anti-Submarine Operations in the Atlantic, May 1943-May 1945," 2 vols. (unpublished Ph.D. diss., Harvard University, 1954) 2: 421-439.

enigmatic postmortems; the surviving *Kriegstagebuch* of *U 805* was not yet available; data on U-boat prisoner-of-war interrogations was limited (as indeed it still remains); and there was no inkling of Fregattenkapitän Günther Hessler's authoritative inside history of the U-boat Command, written after the war for the British secret staff history series.[2]

Deeper insight into Operation *Teardrop* must therefore begin with the U-boat Command's actual intentions in launching its last major venture in the North Atlantic, which proved the effective trigger for the Allied operation. As Hessler recounts, Admiral Godt's prime objective was simply to re-establish the campaign against North Atlantic convoys, possibly to be strengthened by high underwater speed Type XXI boats:

> In an attempt to tie down enemy forces in the Atlantic, six boats bound for the American coast were formed into Group Seewolf on 14 April, for a westward sweep along the great circle convoy routes. It was thought that Atlantic convoys were less strongly protected at this time and that a surprise against one of them might induce the enemy to transfer some of his hunter groups from British coastal waters into the open ocean, thereby weakening, to some extent, his A/S [antisubmarine] concentration in the former area.[3]

Voluminous National Security Agency files of decrypted U-boat traffic show what the Tenth Fleet knew then,[4] that this last convoy assault, as originally projected on 28 March 1945, involved *seven* Norwegian-based 1140-tonners, including *U 881*, which had departed Kristiansand South two days earlier and subsequently returned to port with schnorkel damage. *U 881* would play catch-up thereafter, again departing Kristiansand on 7 April, evading British air patrols, torpedo

---

[2] Lundeberg, "American Anti-Submarine Operations," 2: 421-439; Patrick Beesly, "Special Intelligence and the Battle of the Atlantic: The British View," in Robert W. Love, Jr., ed., *Changing Interpretations and New Sources in Naval History: Papers from the Third United States Naval Academy History Symposium* (New York, 1980), 413-419; Jürgen Rohwer, "Radio Intelligence and Its Role in the Battle of the Atlantic," in Christopher Andrews and David Dilks, eds., *The Missing Dimension: Governments and Intelligence Communities in the Twentieth Century* (Urbana, 1984), 159-168; Günter Hessler, *German Naval History: The U-Boat War in the Atlantic, 1939-1945,* 3 sections (London: Ministry of Defence - Navy, 1983), hereafter cited as Hessler, *U-Boat War,* section and page.

[3] Hessler, *U-Boat War,* 3: 97. Compare *U 805* (Bernardelli) Kriegstagebuch, 29 March 1945, in microfilm, Manuscript Division, Library of Congress (hereafter LC).

[4] Kenneth A. Knowles, "ULTRA and the Battle of the Atlantic: The American View," in Love, *Changing Interpretations and New Sources,* 444-449; German Navy/U-Boat Messages, SRGN 47205, Record Group 457 (National Security Agency), National Archives, Washington, D.C. (hereafter RG 457, NA).

boats, submarines, and mines along the Norwegian coast and seeking to rejoin the outbound sextet as they headed west-southwest, cruising submerged by day and at schnorkel depth by night.[5] Owing to the U-boat Command's continued insistence on outbound passing reports,[6] Bletchley Park, the Admiralty, and Tenth Fleet secured early confirmation of the transients' position and westward progress, beginning on 30 March when Oberleutnant G. Schötzau of *U 880* reported passing longitude 22°W, due south of Reykjavik.[7] That night Admiral Godt was monitored encouraging his southwest-bound boats: "Make ruthless use of chances for attack, once they present themselves. You must sink ships."[8]

British and United States U-boat analysts received a critical bonus from the flow of Ultra decrypts on 2 April, when the six lead boats were ordered to form reconnaissance line "Harke" (Rake) to intercept convoys believed proceeding east-northeast from Flemish Cap between latitudes 47° and 49°N. In addition to defining the initial and subsequent patrol line positions for "Harke" — information of inestimable value for CinCWA headquarters in Liverpool and Tenth Fleet's Submarine Plotting Room and Convoy and Routing Section — the U-boat Command concluded with an ominous advisory: "Following that, release for occupation of [by] boats individually of attack areas in American coastal zone."[9]

Admiral Godt's reference to subsequent coastal operations proved a red flag for CominCh and CinCLant Fleet headquarters, bringing into urgent focus a variety of earlier reports from the continent that suggested a possible German V-1 rocket bombing strike against East Coast cities launched by U-boats, disguised merchant ships, or even very long-range aircraft.[10] Accordingly, the Tenth Fleet Submarine Tracking Room intensified its concentration on the transient wolf pack, which was designated on 12 April as "Gruppe Seewolf" by the U-boat Command and included *U 518* (Offermann), *U 546* (Just), *U 805* (Bernardelli), *U 858* (Bode), *U 880* (Schötzau) and *U 1235* (Barsch), the laggard *U 881* (Frischke) being temporarily out of consideration.[11] Tension inevitably

---

[5] SRGN 47133, 27229, and 47677, RG 457, NA.

[6] SRGN 45063, 45457, and 45558, RG 457, NA.

[7] SRGN 47205, 47268, and 47456, RG 457, NA.

[8] SRGN 47275 and 47291, RG 457, NA.

[9] SRGN 47404 of 2030/2 April 1945, RG 457, NA.

[10] See SHAEF message to AGWAR of 1 November 1944 in SHAEF AG files (1944), 370-3 (Crossbow), Record Group 331, National Archives (hereafter RG 331, NA); Ladislas Farago, *The Tenth Fleet* (New York, 1962), 5-15, 290-291; Ira Wolfert, "The Silent, Invisible War Under the Sea," *Reader's Digest* (November 1945): 125.

[11] U-Boat Messages, SRGN 47863 of 2338/12 April 1945, RG 457, NA.

emerged between long-standing Allied concern for the safety of Atlantic convoys and the apparent threat of U-boat rocket attacks on the East Coast, notably the New York and Washington D.C. areas. Bomb-battered London would have a more measured view than skittish New York. Admiral Godt's pivotal instruction of 2 April, transmitted even as German armed forces radio reported the fall of Danzig and American seizure of the Remagen bridgehead on the Rhine, had been accompanied by detailed tactical instructions from U-boat Command for the anticipated convoy operation, advice which CinCWA and Tenth Fleet doubtless also found most instructive.[12] Transit records of North Atlantic convoys during this storm-wracked period reveal that Godt's initial U-boat reconnaissance line was envisioned well north of the tracks actually followed by eastbound HX and SC convoys, as well as westbound ONS convoys, currently being routed along the 43rd and 44th parallels of latitude, both to mitigate the iceberg hazard and to take advantage of long-range Coastal Command patrols based on the Azores. British and Canadian close-escort groups, typically mustering a handful of warships, were hard pressed to keep the merchantmen together in the prevailing late winter gales. Subsequent diversions, first apparent on 24 April with westbound ONS 47, would route the convoys north of the well-defined "Seewolf" patrol line.[13] Meanwhile, Godt's *U-bootfahreren*, proceeding westward barely a hundred miles daily at schnorkel depth or submerged, were heading for a devastating surprise.[14]

Operation *Teardrop*, formulated at CinCLant headquarters in New York early in January 1945, had its genesis in a mounting accumulation of Allied intelligence reports which indicated that U-boats had been observed at German naval bases mounting what appeared to be rocket launchers. The factual kernel of these emerging rumors and estimates had been sown as early as June 1942, when scientists at the German Army experimental station at Peenemünde had carried out a series of test launchings of small artillery rockets from the submerged *U 511* with the cooperation of its commander, Kapitänleutnant Fritz Steinhoff. Development of this weapons system was abandoned early in 1943 by the Naval

---

[12] SRGN 47376, 47404, 47411, 47417, and 47422, RG 457, NA.

[13] Ibid., SRGN 47404. Compare CominCh Headquarters Daily Location Plot, U.S. Naval Units, Atlantic, 15 March-10 May 1945, and track charts and messages, CominCh Tenth Fleet Convoy and Routing Section message files, 15 March-10 May 1945, both in Operational Archives Branch, Naval Historical Center, Washington, D.C. (hereafter OA, NHC).

[14] *U 805* Kriegstagebuch, 20 March-17 April 1945, LC.

On 10 December 1944, some two weeks after this view of wartime Manhattan was recorded from the escort carrier *Bogue* (CVE-9), Mayor Fiorello LaGuardia alerted New Yorkers to the likelihood of German long-range missile attacks on their city. One month later, Vice Admiral Jonas Ingram publicly announced plans, later designated Operation *Teardrop*, to ward off any attempted V-weapon attack, whether by sea or air. Photo courtesy of the National Archives, Washington, D.C.

Ordnance Office *(Marine-waffenamt)*, however, on the rationale that the cumbersome topside armament would decrease the seaworthiness of the U-boat.[15] Not surprisingly, given increasing employment of rocket ordnance by Allied and Axis air, sea, and land forces both in the Atlantic and Pacific, the idea acquired a life of its own, surfacing in September 1944 when one Oscar Mantel, a survivor of the *U 1229* (Zinke), sunk while on a special mission off the Maine coast, was apprehended. Discovered to be a spy, Mantel reported under interrogation by the Federal Bureau of Investigation that a task force of missile-equipped U-boats was being readied for a buzz-bomb attack on the United States. Subsequent Tenth Fleet analysis of photographs of suspicious mountings

[15] *U 511* Kriegstagebuch, 30 May–5 June 1942, Roll T-7-F, Record Group 242, National Archives, (hereafter RG 242, NA); Erik Bergaust, *Wernher von Braun* (Washington, 1976), 222-228.

on U-boats at bases in occupied Norway determined that these structures were simply wooden tracks used in loading torpedoes, but rumors from the continent resurfaced, including a report from Sweden via SHAEF headquarters that four U-boats based on Bergen were designated for a missile strike at New York.[16] CominCh headquarters received measured Admiralty appraisals of these rumors in November and again late in January 1945, acknowledging that the Germans might be capable of installing V-1 launchers on Type IX-C boats but considering it doubtful that they would devote considerable resources to such a peripheral venture. In London and Liverpool, the early entrance of Type XXI U-boats in the Atlantic struggle was now of prime concern. For CinCLant headquarters, as well as CominCh Tenth Fleet, however, the bare possibility of vengeance attacks on major East Coast cities — a final *Paukenschlag,* as it were — could not be dismissed, particularly after repeated press references to this highly plausible threat.[17]

The monstrous rumor would not die, being reignited early in December 1944 when two more German spies, landed by *U 1230* on 29 November in Frenchman's Bay on the Maine coast, were trailed to New York and apprehended by FBI agents with telltale weapons, cash, cameras, and radio transmitters. The account of their intended sabotage mission given by Erich Gimpel and William C. Colepough included further detail on a group of rocket-equipped U-boats expected to create panic in East Coast urban areas. Public awareness of these developments was reflected in the warning issued by Mayor Fiorello LaGuardia on 10 December that the Germans were contemplating a long-range rocket attack on New York, leading *Life* on Christmas Day to report on a 12-ton "ocean-crossing rocket" of the V-2 type propelled by successive booster elements, postulated by American rocket specialists. Scientists of the Tenth Fleet's ASWORG branch had meanwhile grappled with the problem of anti-missile defense, contributing important elements to CinCLant's Operation *Teardrop* (originally *Bumblebee),* promulgated by

---

[16] *The New York Times,* 2 January 1945; *Life,* 22 January 1945, 33; Farago, *Tenth Fleet,* 5-15; Lundeberg, "Anti-Submarine Operations," 2: 392-395, 411. See also Op-16-Z Fort Hunt Log, 28 August-18 September 1944, Subject File 1942-1945, Special Activities Branch (Op-16-Z), CNO Office of Naval Intelligence, Record Group 38, National Archives (hereafter RG 38, NA.

[17] CinCLant Fleet Operation Plan "Teardrop" (originally "Bumblebee"), 6 January 1945, OA, NHC; *The New York Times,* 9 January 1945; SHAEF outgoing message to AGWAR, 5 November 1945, in SHAEF AG files (1944), 370-3 (Crossbow), RG 331, NA; CinCLant, *Administrative History of the U.S. Atlantic Fleet in World War II,* 9 vols. (Washington, 1946), 1, part 4: *Commander in Chief, U.S. Atlantic Fleet,* 763-765; CominCh File of U-boat Intelligence Summaries, 16 February 1945, NSA/USN SRMN-037, RG 457, NA.

Vice Admiral Ingram on 6 January 1945. The plan, encompassing a wide range of United States antisubmarine forces, included Army Air Corps squadrons and anti-aircraft units charged with defense against transatlantic aerial raiders and robot missiles actually encountered in flight. The ebullient Ingram, who roused the New York press corps on 8 January with a public announcement of the anticipated missile threat, mandated a full commitment of Eastern, Gulf, and Caribbean Sea Frontier air and surface forces against seaborne missile launchers. Much more was available for coastal defense than in the grim early months of 1942. The offensive heart of Operation *Teardrop*, it proved, was the unannounced creation of two major mid-ocean barrier task forces, drawn from several escort carrier hunter-killer groups, based on the East Coast and staged from the strategic American advance base at Argentia, Newfoundland.[18]

The ensuing North Atlantic operations of CinCLant's unprecedentedly large barrier forces, each composed of two escort carriers and twenty or more destroyer escorts, have frequently been recounted. The size of forces deployed by Ingram reflected not only the supposed missile threat but more fundamentally a growing CominCh concern over the possible appearance of Type XXI high submerged speed U-boats in the mid-Atlantic.[19] This critical element of Operation *Teardrop* began with the departure of escort carriers *Mission Bay* and *Croatan* and their consorts from Hampton Roads on 25-27 March, following confirmation by Special Intelligence of the sortie of Atlantic-bound U-boats from Norway. The Northern (First) Barrier Force, commanded by Captain John R. Ruhsenberger in *Mission Bay*, proceeded to Placentia Bay, replenished at Argentia, and rendezvoused on 11 April east of Cape Race, well north of the current Atlantic convoy route. Deploying on a broad 120-mile search line, backed by the flattops and their screens, this force encountered heavy seas that made air search operations extremely hazardous but not impossible during the ensuing week.[20] Concurrent Ultra intercepts of

[18] Regarding *U 1230*'s mission, see Op-16-Z memorandum "Interrogation of Agents Landed in Maine" of 12 January 1945, CNO/ONI Op-16-Z, box 6, RG 38, NA; *The New York Times*, 14 December 1944 and 9 January 1945; *Life*, 25 December 1944, 46-48; CinCLant Operation Plan "Teardrop," OA, NHC; Lundeberg, "Anti-Submarine Operations," 2: 414-423.

[19] Lundeberg, "Anti-Submarine Operations," 2: 414-423; Morison, *Atlantic Battle Won*, 345-347, 376-379; William T. Y'Blood, *Hunter-Killer: U.S. Escort Carriers in the Battle of the Atlantic* (Annapolis, MD, 1983), 251-272.

[20] Commander Task Group 22.1 (Captain J.R. Ruhsenberger), Report of Operations of Task Group 22.1 for Period 27 March to 27 April 1945, OA, NHC. All related action reports and war diaries hereafter cited are located in OA, NHC, unless otherwise indicated.

Allied carrier airmen in the North Atlantic frequently faced flying conditions like the ones seen from the after flight deck of the escort carrier *Core* (CVE-13), which saw extensive round-the-clock flight service during Operation *Teardrop* off the Newfoundland Banks in April and May 1945. Photo courtesy of the National Archives, Washington, D.C.

U-boat Command transmissions to the new "Gruppe Seewolf" between 2 and 19 April, which designated a dozen successive standing (scouting) lines intended to intercept east and westbound convoys, provided Tenth Fleet and Ruhsenberger's barrier force with invaluable data on the prospective locations of the wolf pack's southwesterly moving patrol line and, remarkably, the positions of individual boats in that line *(U 546, U 1235, U 805, U 858, U 880* and *U 518,* from north to south).[21] Although shipboard HF/DF operators had detected U-boat transmissions far to the northeast as early as 8 April, the "Seewolf" transients fell silent as they approached their initial stations in the storied Black Pit, east of the Newfoundland Banks, unaware of the massive American barrier force, which had also moved into position under strict radio silence.

Round-the-clock air patrols from the pitching decks of *Mission Bay*

---

[21] U-Boat Messages, SRGN 47863, 47932, 48000, 48030, and 48130, RG 457, NA.

and *Croatan* produced but a single doubtful sighting on these elusive schnorkel boats. Late on the foggy night of 15 April one of *Croatan*'s screening escorts, USS *Stanton*, suddenly acquired a suspicious radar contact which her skipper, Lieutenant Commander John C. Kiley, Jr., promptly attacked with hedgehogs at 2347 as *U 1235* belatedly submerged, over five hundred miles north of Flores in the Azores. Assisted by USS *Frost*, *Stanton* gained sound contact on the 1140-tonner and carried out three additional ahead-thrown attacks, producing violent underwater explosions at 0033, followed by an oil slick that evidently marked the end of Oberleutnant Franz Barsch and his crew, none of whom survived.[22] The identity of this first "Seewolf" victim remains uncertain. Scarcely forty minutes later, *Frost* obtained radar contact on another westbound transient, later estimated by Tenth Fleet to have been *U 880*, attempting to clear the area quickly on the surface amid heavy rain squalls. Shortly after midnight, *Frost*'s skipper, Lieutenant Commander Andrew E. Ritchie, opened fire with star shell, illuminating the 1140-tonner with searchlight at 650 yards and attacking at 0209 with 40-mm gunfire. Oberleutnant Gerhard Schötzau rang his diving alarm belatedly, being picked up on sonar and tracked by *Frost* and *Stanton* for over an hour before being attacked in succession by their hedgehog crews, laboring on rain-swept decks. *Stanton* secured direct hits on the U-boat at 0404 that were followed three minutes later by a powerful underwater concussion which staggered all hands.[23] As reported by Commander Frank D. Giambattista, Commander, Escort Division 13, "These explosions are terrific. I don't really know how to explain them; they may have something new." The *Croatan*'s escorts, alert for possible boarding and rescue operations that might shed light on CinCLant's robot missile enigma, were confronted, as in the case of *U 1235*, with no evidence of *U 880*'s destruction save the strong scent of oil.[24]

For Tenth Fleet, the apparent violent destruction of these first two "Seewolf" boats provided sobering validation of Admiral Ingram's massive barrier deployment, while strengthening apprehensions of a V-1 missile attack on the East Coast. Any inclination to write off that threat

---

[22] CTG 22.1 Operations Report, 27 March–27 April 1945; USS *Stanton* (DE-247) Anti-Submarine Action Report, 15-16 April 1945; USS *Frost* (DE-144) Anti-Submarine Action Report, 15-16 April 1945.

[23] *Frost* Anti-Submarine Action Report; *Stanton* Anti-Submarine Action Report.

[24] CTG 22.5 dispatch to CinCLant of 1751/16 April 1945; ComCortDiv 13, TBS message to CTG 22.5 at 0410/16 April 1945, in *Stanton* Anti-Submarine Action Report. Cf. British Admiralty, *German, Italian and Japanese U-Boat Casualties during the War* (London, 1946), 24; and Naval History Division, *U.S. Submarine Losses, World War II*, 2nd ed., including Axis submarine losses (Washington, 1963), 173.

as a diversionary hoax would have been further shaken by Ultra intercepts indicating that among subsequent U-boat departures from Norway early in April had been *U 873*, commanded by Kapitänleutnant Fritz Steinhoff, a participant in the earlier submerged rocket trials at Peenemünde.[25] Thus on 16 April Ingram signaled his hunters: "Well done. I expect you to bring the score up to six before you return. Let nothing get by. You will be backed up by a second strong task force by the 21st."[26] First Barrier Force meanwhile continued the search, briefly assisted by Azores-based patrol bombers. On the nights of 18 and 19 April, Leigh-light Liberators of the U.S. Navy VPB-114 twice surprised *U 805* on the surface, some 420 miles north of Flores and only fifty miles from the *Mission Bay* group. Uncertain of their target's identity as they roared overhead, both pilots were unable to return on bombing runs before Korvettenkapitän Richard Bernardelli submerged, twice making good his escape before Lagens managed to alert the barrier force.[27]

Time had seemingly run out for the First Barrier Force as it maneuvered slowly westward under Tenth Fleet guidance, but more elements of "Gruppe Seewolf" were indeed in their waters east of Cape Race. The detailed memoir of Kapitänleutnant Paul Just, seasoned commander of *U 546*, discloses that his 1140-tonner, driven down repeatedly by airborne and shipboard radar activity, encountered an unsuspecting escort on the night of 20 April and attacked it unsuccessfully with a torpedo, the only known offensive action taken against Ruhsenberger's force.[28] On the following night, as the *Croatan* group undertook a final air-surface sweep before retiring to Argentia for replenishment, USS *Mosley* made radar contact on *U 805*, which dove deep and escaped sustained sonar probing and depth charging by *Mosley*, assisted by USS *Lowe* and *J.R.Y. Blakely*, for more than two hours.[29] Meanwhile, shortly before midnight on 21 April, USS *Carter* made sonar contact on yet another "Seewolf" transient, *U 518*, some one hundred miles south on the barrier line. Joined by USS

---

[25] The Interrogation Report on *U 873* outlines Steinhoff's career but contains no reference to the Peenemünde rocket trials or indeed his suicide on 19 May 1945. Op-16-Z Report on Interrogation of the Crew of *U 873*, dated 26 June 1945, in CNO/ONI Op-16-Z file on *U 873*, box 37, RG 38, NA.

[26] CinCLant message to CTG 22.1 and CTG 22.5, of 2236/16 April 1945.

[27] The USN Patron 114 was attached to RAF Coastal Command Group 247, based on Lagens. Cf. *U 805* Kriegstagebuch, 11-19 April 1945, LC; and RAF Coastal Command U-Boat Sightings Summary, January-May 1945, in AIR 15/142, Public Record Office, London.

[28] Paul Just, *Vom Seeflieger zum U-Boot-Fahrer* (Stuttgart, 1979), 157-162.

[29] *U 805* Kriegstagebuch, 22 April 1945, LC; USS *Mosley* (DE-321) Anti-Submarine Action Report, 21-22 April 1945.

Neal R. Scott, the escort's skipper, Lieutenant Commander F. J. T. Baker, coached in his consort on an initial hedgehog run, following up with one of his own that scored a succession of violent underwater explosions, marking the sudden end of Oberleutnant Hans Offermann and his crew, with no survivors.[30]

In scoring this third kill on the murky Grand Banks against "Gruppe Seewolf," hard-hitting *Carter* had virtually snatched her victim from the jaws of Captain George Dufek's Second or Southern Barrier Force, through which *Croatan* and company steamed that same afternoon en route to Argentia. The fog-enshrouded trap in which Gruppe "Seewolf" had been virtually immobilized — through round-the-clock radar patrols by Ruhsenberger's tireless airmen and Admiral Godt's requirement that his boats maintain their successive reconnaissance lines — was suddenly sprung. On the night of 22-23 April, as the carriers *Bogue* and *Core* cruised eastward with twenty-two destroyer escorts, forming a 105-mile barrier along the Forty-Fifth Meridian, a U-boat Command signal was monitored that dissolved "Seewolf" and ordered its survivors to patrol stations between Halifax and the waters off New York, once again reheating the robot missile menace.[31] Scarcely six hours later, Tenth Fleet had received a second Ultra intercept, indicating that three more North Atlantic transients, *U 889*, *U 1229*, and the laggard *U 881*, had been ordered to operate between New York and Cape Hatteras.[32]

For Tenth Fleet and CinCLant analysts, nothing in a month's harvest of Ultra intercepts had provided substantive confirmation of the robot missile threat, yet the possibility of a final German vengeance attack remained, given credibility by the desperate tenor of propaganda emanating from the dying Nazi regime.[33] The violent convulsions of the first three ill-fated "Seewolf" boats were indeed tantalizing, and it appeared that only the capture of survivors from one of that pack's remaining transients, now dispersing, might clarify the issue. Shortly before noon on 23 April, Lieutenant Commander William W. South, the skipper of VC-19, sighted a surfacing U-boat, now believed to be *U 881*,

---

[30] USS *Carter* (DE-112) Anti-Submarine Action Report, 22 April 1945; Naval History Division, *Submarine Losses*, 173.

[31] U-Boat Command instructions for these coastal operations contained no allusions to U-boat missile launchings. U-boat message SRGN 48237 of 2154/22 April 1945, RG 457. NA.

[32] U-boat message SRGN 48472 of 0348/23 April, RG 457, NA, also made no reference to missiles, though such reticence might have been prearranged.

[33] Farago, *Tenth Fleet*, 13-15.

Photographed by Chief Sonarman Roger Cozens of the USS *Flaherty* (DE-135), this creeping attack on 24 April 1945 occurred during the ten-hour hunt for *U 546*, which had just sunk USS *Frederick C. Davis*. USS *Hubbard* (DE-211, in foreground) and USS *Nuenzer* (DE-150) assisted *Flaherty* in the attack. Photo courtesy of Sonarman Cozens and Captain Howard Duff of USS *Flaherty*.

some seventy-four miles northwest of the *Bogue*.[34] Spotting the Avenger, Kapitänleutnant Karl-Heinz Frischke hurriedly crash-dove, escaping fatal damage as a brace of depth bombs straddled his submergence swirl.[35] During the ensuing stormy night, ships of Commander Frederick S. Hall's Escort Division Four conducted retiring searches in the vicinity, then being traversed by *U 881*, *U 546*, and *U 805*. At daybreak on 24 April, Kapitänleutnant Just of *U 546* sighted a distant carrier, subsequently discovering Dufek's advancing escort line, some five hundred miles northwest of the Azores. Intent on reaching the carrier, Just gambled on penetrating the barrier line at periscope depth, taking advantage of the morning haze. Venturesome *U 546* had nearly slipped past the USS *Frederick C. Davis* when Sonarman Andrew A. Barnak reported a moving sound contact, leading the escort's watch officer, Lieutenant (jg) John F. MacWhorter, to swing about, alert his standby hedgehog crew, and prepare to attack. Observing his detection, Just forgot the carrier and loosed an acoustic torpedo at his approaching stalker, firing at barely 650

---

[34] LCdr. South's sighting was made at 1507. Escorts did not reach the scene until 1910. CTG 22.3 Report of Operations, 10 April to 11 May 1945.

[35] Ibid. Neither the experienced *U 546* nor the elusive survivors of Gruppe "Seewolf," *U 805* and *U 858*, can be documented as having surfaced in daylight in these waters on 23 April and sustained a surprise air attack. See Just, *U-Boot-Fahrer*, 155-158, confirmed in a personal communication to the author, 20 November 1993.

yards, virtually point blank range. The *Davis*, struck amidship in her forward engine room, jack-knifed in five minutes, going down in the shark-infested waters with the loss of 126 of her 192 crewmen, including her young skipper, Lieutenant James R. Crosby.[36] The *Davis* sinking opened a classic hunt in which Dufek's escort divisions employed every joint creeping attack and retiring search in the CominCh tactical manual. The German commander, adept at throwing out knuckles and bubble slugs, employing last minute bursts of speed, and diving deep to hide under thermal layers, maneuvered through repeated attacks for nearly ten hours, finally sustaining massive damage forward at 1710 from a pattern of hedgehogs launched by Lieutenant Commander Howard C. Duff of USS *Flaherty*. Just blew tanks and managed to bring the stricken 1140-tonner to the surface, where it came under heavy fire from *Flaherty* and other approaching escorts. Hall's hunters, who, led by USS *Hayter*, had at great risk rescued sixty-six *Davis* crewmen, lost no time in picking up thirty-three exhausted crewmen from *U 546*, five including Just being recovered by *Flaherty*.[37] Nearby *Varian*, skippered by Lieutenant Commander Leonard A. Myhre, rescued nine Germans, from three of whose unwary remarks and waterlogged diary Myhre established the boat's identity, torpedo armament, and details of its thirty-hour ordeal.[38] Unknown to Hall's escorts, another "Seewolf" boat, *U 805*, lurked in the offing, near enough for Bernardelli to log the thunderous ten-hour barrage over *U 546* as he cautiously cleared the area and headed north. Shades of *Aboukir, Hogue,* and *Cressy!* A chilling thought in retrospect for the survivors and their rescuers.[39]

---

[36] Ibid., 158-189; Ensign Robert E. Minerd, Senior Survivor, Preliminary Report of the Torpedoing of the USS *Frederick C. Davis* (DE-136), no date, Enclosure (A) in USS *Hayter* (DE-212), Report of the Rescue of Survivors of the USS *Frederick C. Davis*, 17 May 1945.

[37] Fourteen of the *U-546* survivors were rescued by USS *Pillsbury*, nine by *Varian*, five by *Flaherty*, four by *Keith*, and one by *Neunzer*. *Hayter* Report, 17 May 1945; Just, *U-Boot-Fahrer*, 173-179; USS *Flaherty* (DE-135), Narrative Account of Engagement with *U 546*, 24 April 1945; USS *Pillsbury* (DE-133), War Diary, 23 April 1945, NA.

[38] USS *Varian* (DE-798) War Diary, 23-24 April 1945; USS *Varian*, "Information from Prisoners of War from *U 546*, taken aboard the USS *Varian* (DE-798), April 24th, 1945," dated 25 April 1945, to which are appended notes on POW remarks and an anonymous diary, 10 March-23 April 1945, all contained in Op-16-Z Interrogation file on *U 546*, CNO/ONI Op-16-Z U-Boat Interrogation files, box 24, RG 38, NA.

[39] Bernardelli's dead reckoning position estimates for *U 805* on 24 April effectively bracket the location of *U 546*'s hunt and destruction. Cf. *U 805* Kriegstagebuch, 24 April 1945, LC, and Naval History Division, *Submarine Losses*, 173.

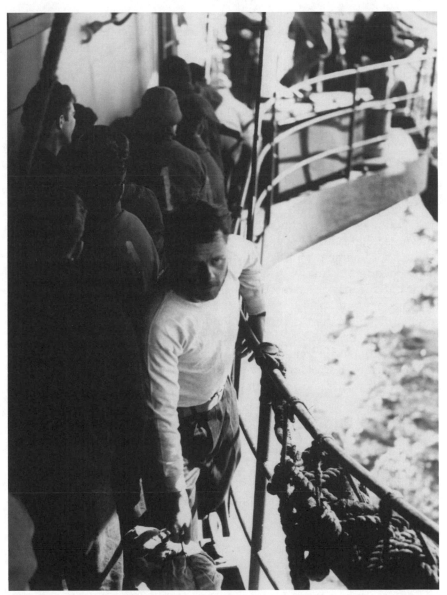

Kapitänleutnant Paul Just, commanding officer of *U 546*, comes on board the USS *Bogue* after being rescued on 24 April 1945. A former naval airman who had flown during the invasion of Poland and the Battle of Britain, this veteran submariner remained non-committal during brief questioning on the carrier. With thirty-two fellow survivors, Just was taken to Argentia, Newfoundland, for interrogation, particularly about the supposed V-1 threat. Photo courtesy of the National Archives, Washington, D.C.

The survivors of *U 546*, the first of "Gruppe Seewolf" to fall into American hands, represented a potential intelligence coup, offering CinC-Lant the prospect of resolving the protracted V-1 missile rumor — now an urgent matter as the surviving U-boats were within days of possible launchings against the East Coast — and thereby redefining the mission of the barrier forces. But Kapitänleutnant Just and his men would provide minimal satisfaction on that critical point. Briefly interviewed in *Bogue's* wardroom, the veteran submariner identified himself as "deutsche Offizier" and decline comment on military matters. Just and his crew would not be further troubled — afloat. At CinCLant direction, the *U 546* survivors were transported to the USNOB, Argentia, Newfoundland. Arriving on 27 April, they were met by the base security detachment, hustled to the navy brig, mustered and screened for interrogation, twenty-five being subsequently transferred to prisoner of war camps in the United States. Eight specialists, including two officers, were placed in solitary confinement and treated not as prisoners of war but as recalcitrant offenders.[40] Just was subjected to what has been described as a "shock interrogation" preceded by exhausting physical exercise and beatings, a treatment also inflicted on his seven shipmates, that is recalled in vivid detail in the veteran commander's postwar memoir.[41] The naval interrogators of Just's crew, pressed by time constraints that mitigated against routine cell monitoring, were clearly influenced by knowledge of the death camp horrors recently discovered in Germany, possibly also by the heavy loss of life on *Frederick C. Davis*. As an Atlantic survivor, Just ignored his captors' challenges to a boxing match, absorbed another one-sided beating and may have avoided a fatal incident seriously damaging, in retrospect, to Canadian-American relations. On 30 April, following a second interrogation in which he collapsed unconscious,[42] Just's interrogators reported to Tenth Fleet that *U 546's* commander was "now cooperative and believed entirely reliable." Their dispatch thereupon provided brief detail on the composition and mission of "Gruppe Seewolf," known to Washington through Ultra since early April, and data on the types of *U 546's* torpedoes, similar to that disclosed on board *Varian* a week earlier. No timely comment could be secured from Just or his men

---

[40] CinCLant message to CTG 22.3 of 1633/25 April 1945 and CTG 22.3 dispatch to CinCLant of 2305/25 April 1945, CominCh Chart Room Atlantic Dispatches, March-May 1945, box 38, RG 38, NA; Just, *U-Boot-Fahrer*, 179-183, 192-194.

[41] Kaptlt. Just records being beaten eight successive days following his crew's arrival at Argentia on 27 April 1945. *U-Boot Fahrer*, 192-204; Farago, *Tenth Fleet*, 20-21.

[42] Just's account indicates no electric shock coercion, only that applied with rubber truncheons. His collapse during interrogation occurred after he drew several puffs on a proffered cigarette. Farago, *Tenth Fleet*, 20-21; Just, *U-Boot-Fahrer*, 202.

regarding V-1 missile launchers, of which, ironically, they had no knowledge.[43] Following a week of relentless "prep" sessions (*Folterung*, as Just termed them) at remote Argentia, Just and his seven crewmen were flown to Washington shortly after V-E Day. For reasons still unknown, the submariners received renewed solitary treatment at Fort Hunt, near Mount Vernon, where they again confronted their Argentia interrogators. Four days after V-E Day, Just finally managed to halt the traumatic proceedings by agreeing to write an account of *U 546*'s history, a document still missing that may well have provided most of the data in the interrogators' final report.[44]

There would be no early end to CinCLant's massive barrier operation, even as dispatches announced the collapse of the Third Reich and grim Allied discoveries at Dachau, Buchenwald, and Auschwitz. The U-boat harvest was far from complete, for upwards of a half dozen boats, any of which might conceivably have been fitted with V-1 missile launchers, were still estimated south of the Grand Banks, headed west. As the Second Barrier Force moved southwest on the evening of 24 April, Commander Hall slowed his escort line to five knots, hoping to flush

---

[43] In the second of two messages from Argentia on 30 April to Tenth Fleet, the two Op-16-Z interrogators, Agent J.H. A____ and Lcdr. S.R. H____, reported: "Following from Commanding Officer U-546 now cooperative and believed entirely reliable X U-546 operated as part of Group Seewolf with U-Rodde U-Bartsch U-Aufhammer U-Schotzau and one other on patrol line crossing Atlantic from East to West x On 17 April Group received long message ordering proceed to American coast to operate from Newfoundland Banks to Florida x Carried 13 torpedoes as follows four T-5 nine Luts X Torpedo fired at Davis was T-5 X U-546 not attacked prior to attack on Davis." No mention is made of V-1 missiles in the Op-16-Z agents' dispatches to Tenth Fleet of 0015/30 April or 1217/30 April, found in CNO/ONI, Op-16-Z *U 546* Interrogation file, box 24, RG 38, NA, or indeed in their "Preliminary Report on the Interrogation of Survivors of U-546, Sunk on 24 April 1945," dated 3 May 1945, also in the aforementioned *U 546* file. Just indicates that the V-1 missile question, of which he had no knowledge, was raised at his first Argentia interrogation session, at which he was also queried on the names of six "Seewolf" commanders. Just, *U-Boot-Fahrer*, 196. Regarding earlier information on "Seewolf" and the armament of *U 546*, cf. the aforementioned *Varian* Report on *U 546*; U-boat message SRGN 47404 of 2 April 1945, RG 457, NA, and CTU 22.7.1 dispatch to CominCh of 25 April 1945.

[44] LCdr. Leonard A. Myhre, whose USS *Varian* had brought the *U 546* survivors to Argentia on 27 April, was invited by the security force commander to observe one of Kaptlt. Just's "exercise" sessions and immediately protested when beating ensued. The author's telephone conversation with Captain Myhre of 15 March 1992 confirms an earlier statement to the author in 1952 by the late RAdm. Jack F. Bowling, Jr., who was Cdr Cort Div 62 in 1945, that the crew of *U 546* had received the "third degree" at Argentia. See Morison, *Atlantic Battle Won*, 355. Regarding Fort Hunt, cf. Just, *U-Boot-Fahrer*, 210-213; Op-16-Z Fort Hunt Log, 4-15 May 1945; John Hammond Moore, *The Faustball Tunnel: German PWs in America and Their Great Escape* (New York, 1978), 34-41, 48-54; Timothy P. Mulligan, *Lone Wolf: The Life and Death of U-Boat Ace Werner Henke*, (Westport, CT and London, 1993), 1-4, 203-218.

another westbound transient. Shortly thereafter, at 1912, USS *Swenning* secured a radar contact that sent the relieved hunters gyrating through the night in retiring searches.[45] Captain Dufek's barrier continued its search south of the Newfoundland Banks for nearly a week before he split the force on 2 May to secure greater barrier depth.[46] Meanwhile, CinCLant had dispatched the replenished *Mission Bay* group from Argentia in a howling blizzard to reinforce the Second Barrier Force, bringing the total of American hunters in those waters to three carriers and thirty-one escorts, ample indeed for the final mop-up. Late on 5 May, one of *Mission Bay*'s Wildcat pilots reported a promising radar contact, which her escorts investigated and subsequently diagnosed as an iceberg.[47] Shortly before daybreak, however, Sonarman Charles W. Hoeftman on board USS *Farquhar* alertly detected a sharp, metallic contact moving rapidly through the patrol line submerged, evidently headed for the carrier, much the same situation as when the *Frederick C. Davis* had flushed *U 546*.[48] *Farquhar*'s watch officer, Lieutenant Lloyd R. Borst, took action, swinging right and planting at 0616 an urgent pattern of shallow depth charges that claimed the *U 881*, yet another of Admiral Godt's unlucky Norway seven. Kapitänleutnant Karl-Heinz Frischke and his crew of fifty-three men never reached the surface. They were the last U-boat crew to be lost to United States forces in the Atlantic.[49]

On 6 May, as the hour of victory approached in Europe, CinCLant's combined hunter forces established their final barrier along the sixtieth meridian, subsequently receiving the surrender at sea of the two surviving "Seewolf" boats, Richard Bernardelli's elusive *U 805* and Thilo Bode's equally low-profile *U 858*.[50] Subsequent interrogations of their

---

[45] USS *Swenning* (DE-394) War Diary, 24-25 April 1945. See also SRMN-032, CominCh File on Memoranda Concerning U-boat Tracking Room Operations, 2 January-6 June 1945, U.S. Navy Records Relating to Cryptography, Records of the National Security Agency, and SRMN-030, COMINCH File on U-boat Trends, 1 May 1945, both in RG 457, NA.

[46] CTG 22.5, Report on Operations of Task Group 22.5 for the Period 25 March to 14 May 1945, dated 14 May 1945.

[47] Ibid.; USS *Mission Bay* (CVE-59) War Diary, 1-5 May 1945: CinCLant dispatch to CTG 22.1, of 2246/01 May 1945.

[48] USS *Farquhar* (DE-139) Anti-Submarine Action Report, 6 May 1945.

[49] Aside from an outbound passing report on 19 April, *U 881* had not been heard from prior to her destruction. See U-boat messages SRGN 48103 and 48272, RG 457, NA. See also First Endorsement to *Farquhar* Anti-Submarine Action Report by ComCortDiv 9, dated 14 May 1945; and USS *Farquhar* Deck Log, 6 May 1945, NA.

[50] Report of Interrogation of the Crew of *U 805* which surrendered to the USS *Varian* on 13 May 1945 off Cape Race, dated 20 June 1945, in CNO/ONI, Op-16-Z U-boat Interrogations, box 35, RG 38, NA. Data on the interrogation of the crew of *U 858* (Bode) is found in ibid., box 36, but no summary report is included.

crews at Portsmouth Navy Yard indicated that none of these Atlantic transients had been fitted with robot rocket launchers, nor indeed *U 873*, whose commander, Kapitänleutnant Fritz Steinhoff, commited suicide in Boston's Charles Street Prison several days after surrendering and being interrogated at Portsmouth.[51] The surviving U-boat officers were of little assistance to the Admiralty and Tenth Fleet in the final assessment and identification of those boats in "Gruppe Seewolf" that had disappeared during their last Atlantic passage. When the head of Tenth Fleet's Combat Intelligence Section, Commander Kenneth A. Knowles, departed for London late in May 1945 to sort out these and other grim accounts, he carried a full appreciation of the immense advantage that Special Intelligence had provided the Allies by making possible systematic U-boat tracking in this final chapter of the Atlantic struggle.[52]

In completing their reports on Operation *Teardrop*, American task force and escort group commanders opened an illuminating critique on that unprecedented venture. Successful as it proved in decimating "Gruppe Seewolf," the operation had been a marked disappointment for the escort carriers' airmen. As Captain Kenneth Craig, commander of the *Croatan* group, reported of his Squadron VC-55: "They flew, both day and night, under the most unfavorable weather and sea conditions in the experience of this ship, and the skill, training, and resourcefulness shown by the squadron during these flights was of the highest order."[53] Only one airman in the tireless carrier air groups had the satisfaction of carrying out an attack on the elusive schnorkel boats, yet the cumulative effect of their perilous sorties had been to deny Godt's submariners the modest option of cruising surfaced or even at schnorkel depth at night, thereby slowing their approach to the North Atlantic convoy routes and setting them up for the escorts' coordinated rooting-out tactics. In the latter regard, the Commander of Task Group 22.8, Commander Jack F. Bowling, Jr., observed that "The barrier patrol in the scouting line, once it was set

---

[51] The abusive interrogation of Kaptlt. Steinhoff at Portsmouth Navy Yard, also by the interrogators of the *U 546* crew, was the subject of a searching official navy investigation. Inspector General of the Navy letter to CominCh and CNO, dated 19 June 1945, entitled "Irregularities Connected with the Handling of Surrendered German Submarines and Prisoners of War at the Navy Yard, Portsmouth, New Hampshire," found in SecNav/CNO file A16-2(3)/EF30, Record Group 80, National Archives. See also coverage on the Steinhoff suicide in the *Boston Daily Globe*, 18-20 May 1945.

[52] ComNavEu dispatch to CominCh of 1243/29 June 1945; Knowles, "ULTRA and the Battle of the Atlantic," 444-449; K.A. Knowles memorandum for Fleet Admiral King of 7 September 1945, in NSA/USN Crypto, SRMN 040, CominCh File, "Assessment of U-Boat Fleet at the End of World War II, Box 15, RG 457, NA.

[53] CTG 22.5 Report of Operations, Task Group 22.5, 25 March-14 May 1945, to CominCh, dated 14 May 1945.

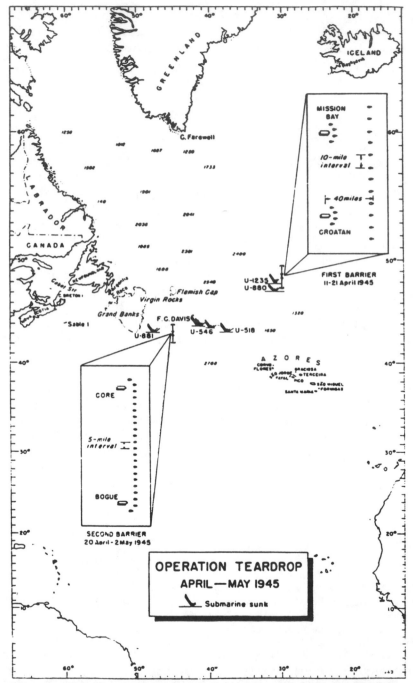

Operation *Teardrop*, April-May 1945. From Samuel E. Morison, *A History of Naval Operations in World War II*, vol. 10, *The Atlantic Battle Won, May 1943-May 1945* (Boston: Little, Brown, 1956), 347.

up in accordance with the November 1944 issue of the *U.S. Fleet Anti-Submarine Bulletin,* worked smoothly and seemed to give an efficient and thorough surface coverage." Given the spacing between patrolling ships and the often substantial distance between air contacts and the nearest ships, this experienced U-boat hunter emphasized that "A definite effort should be made in assigning stations on a barrier line, in ordering ships to the scene of a contact, and in actual contacts, to ensure that ships of the same task group work together as a team."[54] Insight into the tactics of well-proven Escort Division 13, which had claimed *U 1235* and *U 880* within less than an hour, was provided in the action report of Commander Giambattista, who disclosed that, excepting urgent situations, "This group operates on the doctrine of 'double contact', i.e., ship having contact does not attack until second ship makes sonar contact."[55] In the fog-bound, often storm-wracked setting of these operations, such deliberate coordination, as well as grim persistence, proved the key to success of the escorts' patient "rooting out" tactics, founded on sonar search and classically demonstrated in the prolonged hunt for *U 546*.[56]

Commander Theodore S. Lank, Commander of Escort Division 51, operating with the *Bogue* group, expressed dissatisfaction with the single extended-line barrier employed during Operation *Teardrop.* In his report to CinCLant, Lank observed that:

> Aircraft contacts in most instances were at great distances from nearest ship, resulting in periods of three to four hours before sonar search was started. Surface ships were operating on 7 to 10 mile scouting line which resulted in ships arriving singly at scene of contact or in further delay while they were found for search.
>
> It is felt that a single line surface ship barrier is ineffective against submarines. It is recommended that, in future operations of this nature, surface anti-submarine vessels should be concentrated in groups of three and assigned patrol areas such that at least one group would be within one or two hours steaming distance of any point covered by air search. This would also tend to reduce the amount of radio traffic (especially TBS) necessary before contact is made.[57]

---

[54] CTG 22.8 Special Operation and Action Report to CominCh, of 15 May 1945.

[55] ComCortDiv 13 Operations Report to CominCh, of 12 May 1945.

[56] Lundeberg, "Anti-Submarine Operations," 2: 429, 439; Morison, *Atlantic Battle Won,* 356.

[57] ComCortDiv 51 Operational Report, 16 April-11 May 1945, to CominCh, of 11 May 1945.

Given the bare half-dozen radar contacts and actual sightings made on Godt's "Seewolf" schnorkelers by land and carrier-based aircraft during *Teardrop*, it would appear probable, however, that more U-boats would have escaped detection during their submerged transit if they had not been confronted by Admiral Ingram's relatively tight sonar barrier during the fortnight's murky proceedings.[58] Played out during the concluding month of the Atlantic struggle, Operation *Teardrop* would remain as popularly unknown as those other pivotal Allied hunter-killer campaigns in World War II, including the decisive North Atlantic convoy battles of March-May 1943 and ensuing air-surface operations in the Bay of Biscay and on the Central Atlantic convoy route. Yet Jonas Ingram's concluding masterpiece would emerge as a classic demonstration not only of coordinated hunter tactics, derived in part from British experience, but also of the profound impact of communications intelligence in the interdiction of U-boat transit and operating areas. As such, and with due respect for the judgments of its participants, *Teardrop* clearly awaits detailed analysis through a full-blown, computerized war game, most effectively undertaken at the Naval War College in Newport, Rhode Island.

History, even at half-century, discloses its full dimension only by degrees. The events of the Newfoundland Banks, Argentia, Fort Hunt, Portsmouth, and Boston, as yet imperfectly understood, have weighed on the memory of many participants of Operation *Teardrop*, most particularly the survivors of the *Frederick C. Davis, U 546,* and their dauntless rescuers, now nearly to the grave. The full outlines of its moral lessons are not apparent, but conclusions are not far distant.

---

[58] The regularly-spaced escort barrier formation provided patrolling carrier airmen a much-needed radar baseline reference, one not recognized by the Azores-based Liberators in their sudden, frustrating encounters with *U 805*.

14

Mahan's Principles
and the Battle of the Atlantic

R. A. Bowling

According to Sir Winston Churchill — and he should have known:

> The Battle of the Atlantic was the dominating factor all through the war
> [WW II]. Never for one moment could we forget that everything
> happening elsewhere, at sea, or in the air, depended ultimately on its
> outcome . . . . The only thing that frightened me during the war was the
> U-boat peril . . . . It would have been wise for the Germans to stake all
> on it.[1]

That appraisal is supported by the sheer volume of related archival
material, published works, and even films, such as Günther Buchheim's,
Das Boot, which although historically and technically flawed, presents
some dramatic sequences of the rigors and terrifying moments of U-boat
warfare.[2]

Such a profusion of research material, however does not explain,

---

[1] Winston Churchill, *Second World War*, vol 5, *Closing the Ring* (Boston: Houghton
Mifflin, 1952), 6; Winston Churchill, *Second World War*, vol 4, *The Hinge of Fate* (Boston:
Houghton Mifflin, 1951), 107.

[2] Archival material may be found in such repositories as the Military Archives and the
Military History Research Office in Freiburg, Germany; the Public Record Office in Kew,
England; and the Naval Historical Center and the National Archives and Record
Administration in Washington D.C. Published works include Dan van der Vat's *The Atlantic
Campaign: World War II's Great Struggle at Sea* (New York: Harper & Row, 1988); Michael
Gannon's *Operation Drumbeat: The Dramatic True Story of Germany's First U-Boat Attacks Along
the American Coast in World War II* (New York: Harper & Row, 1990); and Jürgen Rohwer's
Axis Submarine Successes (Annapolis: Naval Institute Press, 1983) and *The Critical Convoy
Battles of March 1943: The Battle for HX.229/SC122* (Annapolis: Naval Institute Press, 1991).

why, after coming perilously close to losing World War I because of Germany's U-boat assault on their Atlantic sea lines of communications, the British, the Americans, and their allies again came close to defeat in World War II because of U-boats. On reflection, the poverty of explanations is probably because the answer is so simple. It was because of the influence of a single individual: Captain Alfred Thayer Mahan, U.S.N.

Mahan has had — and continues to have — more influence on naval policy and doctrine than any other naval theoretician in modern times. His first and most influential work, *The Influence of Sea Power upon History, 1660-1783*, published in May 1890, advanced principles of naval warfare that were — and continue to be — accepted as universal precepts by leading admiralties and governments worldwide, particularly in Europe, the United States, and Japan.[3] Specifically, Mahan's principles that have mostly affected naval policy and doctrine are "the superiority of capital ships"; "the decisiveness of big battles" with their resultant "command of the sea"; "the superiority of the offensive"; and "the secondary, inconclusive, indecisive nature of the *guerre de course*."

Adherence to these principles of Mahan materially affected the composition, strategy, and tactics of the navies of both the Allies and the Central Powers in World War I. By 1914, the British Government and Admiralty had adopted the Mahanian concept that in any future maritime conflict the first priority of the British Fleet would be to seek out and destroy the battlefleet of the enemy, thereby achieving "that which is the only decisive factor — command of the sea" — which, in turn, would afford the best protection for shipping. Thus, convoying would be

---

[3] Mahan's principal theories and conclusions are contained primarily in his sea-power series: *The Influence of Sea Power upon History, 1660-1783* (Boston: Little, Brown, 1890); *The Influence of Sea Power upon the French Revolution, 1793-1812*, 2 vols., (London: Sampson Low, Marston, 1892); and *Sea Power in its Relation to the War of 1812*, 2 vols., ((London: Sampson Low, Marston, 1905). For a short summary of the above works, see Margaret T. Sprout, "Mahan: Evangelist of Sea Power," in *Makers of Modern Strategy*, ed. Edward M. Earle (Princeton: Princeton University Press, 1971), 415-45. For specific references to Mahan's "capital ships" and "big battle" dictums, see his *Influence upon History*, 138, 513-14, 539; A.T. Mahan, *Lessons of the War with Spain: And Other Articles* (Boston: Little, Brown, 1899), 264-72. For his views on the *guerre de course*, see his *Influence upon History*, 31, 132-38, 196, 229-30, 329n., 400, 539-40, 540n.; *Influence upon the French Revolution*, II, 197, 203-6, 218, 223-27; *Sea Power in War of 1812*, 398. For a more complete review of Mahan's works, see *Letters and Papers of Alfred Thayer Mahan*, 3 vols., eds. Robert Seager II and Doris D. Maguire (Annapolis: U.S. Naval Institute, 1975). An accepted authority on the life of Mahan is W.D. Puleston's *Mahan: The Life and Work of Captain Alfred Thayer Mahan, USN* (New Haven: Yale University Press, 1939). Additional insights into his character and philosophy are contained in Mahan's partial autobiography, *From Sail to Steam: Recollections of Naval Life* (New York: Harper & Bros., 1907; rpt. New York: Da Capo Press, 1968).

unnecessary and therefore, was specifically ruled out in favor of "the more effective work of hunting down the enemy's destroyers."[4] But, this protection-of-shipping policy was a direct contradiction of Mahan who had concluded that convoying "will have more success . . . than hunting for individual marauders — a process which, even when most thoroughly planned, still resembles looking for a needle in a haystack."[5] This repeated misreading of Mahan would result in a period rich in disasters for allied merchant shipping in World War I and for both sides in World War II.

In Germany, Mahan found willing converts to his strategic concepts of sea power in the Kaiser and Grand Admiral Alfred P. von Tirpitz, father of the modern German Navy. This conversion resulted in a major change in German naval policy in which the existing policy that concentrated on cruiser warfare against the enemy's shipping was replaced by a policy of achieving command of the sea by building a High Seas Fleet based on battleships and then using that battlefleet as a "thunderbolt" to determine the outcome of any future maritime war in one grand action.[6] This historical change in German national and naval policy resulted in a modern German Navy that became a formidable challenger to the overbearing power of the British Navy just in time for a trial by combat of Mahan's principles in World War I.

---

[4] For the British government's acceptance of Mahan's "capital ships" and "big battles" theses, see Great Britain, Parliament, *Hansard's Parliamentary Debates (Commons)*, 4th series, vol. 16 (1893), 1233. For the Admiralty's full acceptance, see Great Britain, Public Record Office (hereafter PRO), *Admiralty Papers*, Class No. ADM 1/7422b, "Foreign Office, March 1 - March 31, 1899," N.I.D. Memoranadum, "The Effect on Commerce of the Anglo-Continental War," February, 1892, 7-8. For the full report of the Royal Commission on the Supply of Food and Raw Material in Time of War, including related Papers of the Association to Promote an Official Inquiry into the Security of Food Supply in Time of War, see Great Britain, Parliament,*Parliamentary Papers (Commons)*, 1905,vols. 39, 40 (Reports, vol. 8), "Report of the Royal Commission on Supply of Food and Raw Materials in Time of War," 3 vols. For the Admiralty's dealings with the Commission, see Great Britain, PRO *Cabinet Papers*, Cab 17/3, "Miscellaneous Collection of loose correspondence on naval matters, 1902-1912," "Protection of Ocean Trade in Wartime" of October 1905; also PRO, *Admiralty Papers*, ADM 1/7734 and ADM 116/866b, Naval Staff Memorandum, 1899-1912, Minutes of the Admiralty meeting on April 30, 1905, on the protection of ocean trade in wartime, Appendix 5, DNI Memorandum, "The Protection of Trade: Remarks on Various Methods of Stationing Cruisers for the Protection of Trade," 30 March 1905, 45-52.

[5] Mahan, *Influence upon French Revolution*, 2: 217.

[6] Sir Archibald Hurd and Henry Castle, *German Sea Power: Its Rise, Progress, and Economic Basis* (London: John Murray, 1913; rpt. Westport, CT: Greenwood Press, 1971), 174-75. For the close correlation between the views of Mahan and those of the wartime commander of the German High Seas Fleet, see Admiral Reinhaart von Scheer, *Germany's High Seas Fleet in the World War* (London: Cassell, 1920), ix, xii-xiv.

By the summer of 1914, the transition in the United States from a Jeffersonian national strategy and naval policy of coast defense and commerce raiding to one of Mahanian offensive action with a superior battlefleet of capital ships against an enemy's battlefleet was all but complete. In motion was a long-range naval construction plan to build a fleet based on forty-eight battleships in support of the Mahanian naval policy espoused by the General Board of the Navy that "the power of the fleet is to be measured by the number and efficiency of its heavy fighting units, or battleships."[7] The subject of the direct protection of shipping, *i.e.*, convoying, was not addressed. Instead, as in the case of Great Britain, the General Board, and so the Congress, placed full reliance on the Mahanian view that the defeat of an enemy's battlefleet would ensure the victor such absolute command of the sea that the safety of shipping would be automatically assured. Thus, at the outset of the first true test of Mahanian concepts of naval warfare in the "Great War," both sides unreservedly subscribed to the principles of Mahan, the "evangelist of sea power."[8]

Great Britain initially saw the conflict in classic terms of the Napoleonic Wars buttressed by Mahan's dictums. First, the Royal Navy would blockade Germany. And then, if and when the German High Seas Fleet sortied, the superior Grand Fleet would decisively defeat it in a Nelsonian Trafalgar-style battle. After which, according to Mahan, Great

---

[7] For the major change along Mahanian lines in naval policy and the U.S. Navy, see William F. Livezey, *Mahan on Sea Power* (Norman: University of Oklahoma Press, 1947), 13-14, 113-16, 218-20; Mahan, *Sail to Steam*, 285, 303, 312, 313; B. Franklin Cooling, *B.F. Tracy: Father of the Modern American Fighting Navy* (Hamden, CT: Archon Books, 1973) 74; George T. Davis, *A Navy Second to None: The Development of Modern American Naval Policy*, (New York: Harcourt, Brace, Jovanovich, 1940; rpt. Wesport, CT: Greenwood Press, 1971), 30, 37-40, 74, 86-88, 91, 93-94, 100, 140; U.S. Congress, Joint, *Report of the Secretary of the Navy*, 30 November 1889, Document no.1, Part 3, ser, 2721, 51st Cong., 1st Sess., 1889 (Washington D.C.: Government Printing Office, 1889), 4. (Tracy's argument for a battlefleet was based on Mahan' Naval War College lecture notes and the draft of his book, *Influence of Sea Power upon History*; U.S. Congress, Senate, Document no. 43, Part 3, 51st Cong., 1st Sess., 1890 (Washington, D.C.: Government Printing Office, 1890), 1; U.S. Congress, Joint, *Report of the Secretary of the Navy*, 18 November 1893, Document no. 1, Part 3, 53rd Cong. 2d Sess., 1893 (Washington, D.C.: Government Printing Office, 1893), 37-38. For Mahan's influence on both Roosevelts, see Theodore Roosevelt, *Theodore Roosevelt: An Autobiography* (New York: Outlook, 1913; rpt. New York: Macmillan, 1916), 212, 225-26, and William L. Neuman, "Franklin D. Roosevelt: A Disciple of Admiral Mahan," U.S. Naval Institute *Proceedings*, (July 1952): 713. For the shipbuilding programs, see General Board Records, Operational Archives Division, Naval Historical Center, Washington, D.C., GBR File II-177, G.B. to SECNAV, G.B. no. 58, 9 February 1903, "Composition of the Fleet;" GBR File 420-2, G.B. to SECNAV,30 September 1905, "Shipbuilding Program 1906;" GBR File IV-65, G.B. to SECNAV, G.B. no. 420-2, 28 October 1905, "Shipbuilding Program 1906;" GBR Studies (1914-1915) [microfilm and letter], G.B. to SECNAV, G.B. 420-3, 1 July 1916, "Building Program 1916."

[8] Sprout, "Mahan: Evangelist of Sea Power."

Britain would have achieved that "overbearing power" that would give her absolute "military command of the sea." This in turn would ensure not only the driving of the enemy's shipping from the sea, but also the safety of Britain's own seaborne trade.[9] Germany held exactly the same exalted dream — in reverse.

And so the two battlefleets met on 31 May 1916 off Jutland Bank in the fog-shrouded North Sea.[10] According to the principles of Mahan, the ensuing Battle of Jutland should have been a decisive victory for the British, who enjoyed a substantial superiority in capital ship numbers, particularly in dreadnoughts, 28 to 16, and battlecruisers, 9 to 5. But it was not decisive. On the contrary, it was *indecisive*. Additional refutations, but one resounding affirmation, were in the offing.

After Jutland, Germany radically changed its naval policy from the Mahanian concept of seeking a direct confrontation with, and crushing victory over, the British Grand Fleet to the historical naval policy of a weaker naval power espoused by the *Jeune École*: the *guerre de course*, twentieth-century submarine style.[11] But initially, the British persisted in the Mahanian belief that commerce destroying was a "secondary" operation that could not be decisive. And therefore, the Royal Navy continued its "cold storage" watch on the German High Seas Fleet, and bullheadedly refused to introduce convoying — as advocated by Mahan — as a counter to the U-boat war on its shipping.[12]

Belatedly and grudgingly, when faced with the political threat of Prime Minister David Lloyd George to order it directly, the British Admiralty introduced the "ancient practice of convoy" in May 1917.[13] As

---

[9] Great Britain, PRO, *Admiralty Papers*, Class ADM 137/1936, Grand Fleet Secret Packs, 1914-1918, "War Orders and Plans," M-0053, July-August 1914 (forwarded by Admiralty ltr. no. 507, 3 July 1914), Part 1, 3, 15.

[10] For the official British account, see Great Britain, Admiralty, *Narrative of the Battle of Jutland* (London: H.M.S.O., 1924), which is complete with diagrams and recounted in terse operational language in a compact 121 pages. The classical unofficial account is contained in Holoway H. Frost, Commander, USN, *The Battle of Jutland* (Annapolis: U.S. Naval Institute, 1936). Also see Geoffrey M. Bennett, *The Battle of Jutland* (London: B.T. Batsford, 1964). Admiral Scheer, the German commander, gives his account in his *Germany's High Seas Fleet*.

[11] Bennett, *Battle of Juland*, 163, 167; Scheer, *Germany's High Seas Fleet*, 246.

[12] David Lloyd George, *War Memoirs of David Lloyd George*, 4 vols. (Boston: Little, Brown, 1933-1937; rpt. in 2 vols. London: Odhams Press, 1942), 1: 694 and 2: 712.

[13] The British War Council, incensed by the continued recalcitrance of the Admiralty to even consider convoy despite the crippling merchant ship losses, authorized Prime Minister Lloyd George to visit the Admiralty on 30 April 1917 to force a decision. Whether the impending and unorthodox visit of the Prime Minister forced the Admiralty to adopt convoy is a matter of dispute. The fact is that three days before his visit the Admiralty approved a trial convoy, which was so successful that on 21 May 1917, the day after its safe arrival, the Admiralty approved universal convoying for all merchant shipping in the

predicted by Mahan, shipping losses plummeted dramatically. But the American latecomers to the fray were not enthusiastic about the alleged defensive nature of convoying. Imbued with Mahanian concepts of naval warfare, American naval leaders and President Woodrow Wilson himself made uncomplimentary demands on the British to take the offensive. This offense-mindedness was shared by many influential British government and Admiralty leaders. As a consequence, the Allies allocated disproportionately large amounts of fiscal and manpower resources and escort-capable vessels to allegedly offensive operations, such as mine barriers in the North Sea and the Otranto Straits, and hunter-killer groups which proved far less efficient than convoying.[14] In the end, it was convoying that proved to be the decisive element.

Thus, in World War I, three of Mahan's principles — the "superiority of capital ships," the "decisiveness of big battles," and the resultant "command of the sea" — failed the ultimate test of all military theory: trial by combat. Mahan was proven equally wrong regarding the "secondary" nature of the *guerre de course*. For the U-boat campaign against Allied shipping in World War I came perilously close to forcing Great Britain, and then the other entente powers, to capitulate unconditionally as early as the summer of 1917, and no later than the end of the year.[15]

Atlantic. See Lloyd George, *War Memoirs*, 1: 690-92; Stephen W. Roskill, *Hankey: Man of Secrets*, 3 vols. (London: Collins, 1970-1974), 1: 379. For additional details on Lloyd George's visit to the Admiralty on 30 April 1917, see Arthur J. Marder, *From the Dreadnought to Scapa Flow: The Royal Navy in the Fisher Era, 1904-1919*, 5 vols. (London: Oxford University Press, 1961-1970), 4: 160-65; Elting E. Morison, *Admiral Sims and the Modern American Navy* (Boston: Houghton Mifflin, 1942), 349-50; Winston S. Churchill, *Amid These Storms: Thought and Adventures* (New York: Charles Scribner's Sons, 1932), 136; John R.J. Jellicoe, *The Submarine Peril: The Admiralty Policy in 1917* (London: Cassell, 1934), 130.

[14] GBR, File 425-5, G.B. to SECNAV, ser. 778 of 24 October 1917, "Proposed measures to prevent German submarines from operating against Allied commerce in the Atlantic." For a detailed description of how the largest minefield in the history of naval warfare was planned and laid, see Reginald R. Belknap, *The Yankee Mining Squadron: Laying the North Sea Mine Barrage* (Annapolis: U.S. Naval Institute, 1920). For some of the Allied strategy involved and the results, see Philip K. Lundeberg, "Underseas Warfare and Allied Strategy in World War I." pt. 2, "1916-1918," *The Smithsonian Journal of History* (Winter 1966); Robert M. Grant, *U-Boats Destroyed: The Effect of Antisubmarine Warfare, 1914-1918* (London: G.P. Putnam's Sons, 1964), 143, 145; Marder, *Dreadnought to Scapa Flow*, 5: 119-20, 119, n. 57. For direct pressure between the Wilson administration and the British Government, see GB, PRO, ADM 116/1351, Browing [British naval attaché in D.C.] to 1st S.L [First Sea Lord], 8 October 1917, and ADM 116/1351, [Lord} Northcliffe [special emmissary to U.S.] to Geddes [First Lord of the Admiralty], 458, 30 October 1917.

[15] Temple Patterson, ed., *The Jellicoe Papers: Selections from the Private and Official Correspondence of Admiral of the Fleet Earl Jellicoe*, 2 vols, (London: Navy Records Society, 1968) 2: 149-51; Great Britain, Ministry of Defense, Naval Library, ADM 137/3050, *The Technical History*, TH 14, *The Atlantic Convoy System, 1917-1918*, 4; GB, PRO, ADM 137/1322,

But Mahan was eminently right regarding the superiority of convoying over hunting for individual marauders. The almost unanimous conclusion on both sides of the conflict after the war was that the "ancient practice of convoy" was eminently more efficient than alleged offensive operations, and the decisive factor in the defeat of the U-boat campaign against shipping in World War I.[16]

Notwithstanding, and to their great misfortune, the Allies dogmatically continued to support Mahan on the four principles where he was proven wrong, and just as mulishly ignored him on the one concept where he was proven right. Even before the war ended, the U. S. resumed building a battlefleet along Mahanian principles that would be "second to none."[17] Great Britain followed suit in January 1918 when the War Cabinet approved construction of a battle cruiser, *Anson*, which would not be completed until 1920 but would in the meantime absorb the resources equivalent to the construction of twenty-four destroyers while merchant vessels were still sailing independently for want of escorts.[18]

The United States Navy also devoted a disproportionate amount of its limited resourses to the modernization, manning, and maintenance of its battlefleet. This emphasis on capital ships was founded on an overall strategic concept of engaging the Japanese battlefleet in a decisive super-

---

41-55, 58, 77-82, 97-200; Jellicoe, *Grand Fleet*, 104-6; William S. Sims, *The Victory at Sea* (Garden City: Doubleday, Page, 1921), 10-11, 19, 106-7; Lloyd George, *War Memoirs*, 1: 687, 689; Sir Julian Corbett and Sir Henry Newbolt, *History of the Great War: Naval Operations*, 5 vols. (London: Longmans, Green, 1920-1931) 5: 8, 15-16; Churchill, *Amid These Storms*, 135-36; U.S. Congress, House, Committee on Naval Affairs, American Participation in the Great War, *Affairs of the House of Representatives on Sundry Legislation Affecting the Naval Establishment, 1927-1928, 70th Cong. 1st Sess.*, 1927, 2654-55; Arthur Marder, *The Anatomy of British Sea Power: A History of British Naval Policy in the Pre-Dreadnought Era, 1880-1905* (New York: Alfred A. Knopf, 1940), 86, 86n., 8, 87-91. Primary sources for Allied shipping losses are GB, M.O.D., Naval Historical Branch, Analysis of Statistics of Shipping Losses, 1917-1918, "Statistical Review of the War Against Shipping," 23 December 1918, Bailey & Waters, # 37; ADM 137/3050, TH 14 & TH 15, *Convoy Statistics and Diagrams*; ADM 1/11323, "Convoys or Independent Sailings." Also see Ernest C. Fayle, *Seaborne Trade*, 3 vols. (London: John Murray, 1920); Sir Arthur Slater, *Allied Shipping Control: An Experiment in International Administration* (Oxford: Clarendon Press, 1921); Corbett and Newbolt, *Naval Operations*, vol. 5; Marder, *Dreadnoughts to Scapa Flow*, 5: 87, 114-17.

[16] Sims, *Victory at Sea*, 165; Lewis Bayly, *Pull Together! The Memoirs of Admiral Sir Lewis Bayly* (London: Geaoge C. Harrap, 1939), 215; Salter, *Allied Shipping Control*, 125, 127-28; Lloyd George, *War Memoirs*, 1: 687, 689, 695; Karl Dönitz, *Memoirs: Ten Years and Twenty Days*, trans. R.H. Stevens in collaboration with David Woodward (Cleveland: World Publishing, 1959), 4; Churchill, *Amid These Storms*, 135-36.

[17] Davis, *Navy Second to None*, 238, 241.

[18] GB, PRO, ADM 116/1349, "Proposed Programme of Warship and Auxiliary Constuction for 1919," Submitted to War Cabinet on January 17, 1918 [actually submitted on 18th], 1-2.

Jutland battle in the western Pacific where battleships would be supreme.[19] Class after class at the Naval War College studied Jutland not only for the tactical lessons that might be derived, but also in terms of the Mahanian principles involved, with a view toward their application in the planning of a super-Jutland against the Japanese fleet. This Mahanian philosophy had permeated the officer corps to the point where every officer who prepared or discussed war plans followed the teachings or invoked the ideas of Mahan. As one wit put it, Jutland was a "major defeat for the USN."[20] As was Mahan.

Almost as if by agreement, the Japanese, similarly mesmerized by Mahan's principles — reinforced by their Trafalgar-like destruction of the Russian Fleet at Tsushima Straits — adopted essentially the same strategy. It envisioned a complex "attrition" and "ambush" plan that in its final stages would involve a Jutland-style grand battle wherein the Japanese super-battleships would play the dominant role in annihilating the American Fleet. As for the protection of their own shipping, they paid less attention to it before and during World War II than either the British or the Americans. As a result they paid the heaviest price.[21]

Germany also adopted essentially the same Mahanian naval strategy as the others. In September 1938, all but ignoring her near success with the submarine version of commerce destroying in World War I, she adopted the Z-Plan, a ten-year naval building program that envisioned a balanced fleet consisting of capital ships, cruisers, and submarines that would have the dual mission of fleet action against elements of the British battlefleet and commerce destroying.[22] This dual mission resulted in a distribution of resources and multiple types of warships that provided neither a strong surface fleet which could viably challenge the British battlefleet nor a strong enough underseas fleet capable of decisive results in a resumed U-boat war on shipping. Thus, the greatly

---

[19] In war plan parlance, "Orange" referred to the Japanese Fleet and "Blue" to the American. See Grace P. Hayes, LT, USN, "The History of the Joint Chiefs of Staff in World War II: The War Against Japan," Naval Historical Center, Operational Archives, Washington D.C. (1953),1: 1-7; Louis Morton, "War Plan Orange: Evolution of a Strategy," *World Politics*, (January 1959) 221-58.

[20] Samuel E. Morison, *The Two Ocean War* (Boston: Brown, Little, 1963), 9.

[21] Stephen E. Pelz, *Race to Pearl Harbor: The Failure of the Second London Naval Conference and the Onset of World War II* (Cambridge: Harvard University Press, 1974), 14-40, 220, 224-25; W.J. Holmes, *Underseas Victory: The Influence of Submarine Operations on the War in the Pacific* (Garden City: Doubleday, 1966), 52-53; Sir Arthur Hezlet, *Submarine and Sea Power* (New York: Stein & Day, 1967), 114.

[22] Eric Raeder, *My Life*, trans., Henry W. Drexel (Annapolis: U.S. Naval Institute, 1960), 200-201; Friedrich Ruge, *Der Seekrieg, The German Navy's Story, 1939-1945*, trans, Cdr. M.G. Saunders. R.N. (Annapolis: U.S. Naval Institute, 1957), 32-38; Dönitz, *Memoirs*: 37-39, 38n.

outnumbered surface forces of the German Navy were soon more tightly blockaded in World War II than had been the High Seas Fleet in the previous war. And Admiral Karl Dönitz lacked at the outset of hostilities the 300 operational U-boats that he had pleaded for as necessary to achieve decisive results in a submarine campaign against shipping, *if* the British again adopted convoying.[23]

Thus it was that on the eve of World War II the four most powerful antagonists in the forthcoming conflict — Great Britain, the United States, Germany, and Japan — had prepared for a naval war along the lines of a super-Jutland in accordance with the principles of Mahan and had placed little emphasis on exploiting the near success of the submarine campaign against shipping during World War I or defending against its resumption in the future. Although Germany did adopt as its primary naval mission the destruction of British merchant shipping, its paradoxical decision to build a balanced "fleet in being," instead of staking all on a large U-boat fleet to carry out that mission, largely vitiated the chances of achieving decisive results. In no other area did the invisible hand of Mahan have such a profound effect on World War II. For if the German Navy, instead of building a Z-Plan balanced fleet, had built the 300 U-boats recommended by Dönitz, they might very well have won the Battle of the Atlantic before the British and the Americans could have produced the necessary fast escorts.

There can be little doubt but that the renewed faith in Mahan's teachings during the interwar years accounted, in large measure, for why both sides in World War II were initially unprepared either to conduct a concerted submarine campaign against shipping or to defend against such a campaign. Such was the negative influence of Mahan on the fate of merchant shipping in World War II, in general, and in the Battle of the Atlantic, in particular.

Neither the Germans, who initiated anew the U-boat campaign against shipping, nor the British, who had to defend against it, was ready for the task. Germany had failed to rebuild her navy around a powerful underseas fleet that the lessons of World War I indicated could have achieved decisive results. Consequently, she began the war with only 57 U-boats, of which only 47 were operational, and of which only 22 were type VII's and IX's capable of extended patrolling in the open Atlantic.[24]

---

[23] Dönitz, *Memoirs*, 33, 39, 122-26; Raeder, *My Life*, 280,283; Roskill, *War at Sea*, 1: 356; Hezlet, *Sub & Sea*, 121, 162. Note the *if* qualification similar to that of the British regarding unrestricted submarine warfare.

[24] Cajus Bekker [Hans D. Berenbrok], *Hitler's Naval War*, trans., Frank Ziegler (Garden City: Doubleday, 1974), 164-65.

That was less than one-tenth the 300 U-boats Dönitz had estimated would be required to achieve decisive results. Nevertheless, Germany again came close to severing the Atlantic sea lines of communication.

Although the British government had belatedly decided in 1938 to convoy, *if* a war on shipping materialized, the Royal Navy was not prepared for the grueling task. As predicted by Admiral Jellicoe in 1934, there was a critical shortage of convoy escorts.[25]

This acute shortage of escorts was exacerbated by hunting and patrolling operations that further reduced the number of vessels available for the direct support of shipping — with little justification in view of the lessons of World War I. But the Admiralty had little choice, since the foremost champion and spokesman for hunting and patrolling was the reappointed First Lord, Winston Churchill. Adamantly opposed to what he considered a "defensive obsession [of] convoy and blockade," he pressed the Admiralty to go on the offensive against U-boats by dispatching an "independent flotilla which would work like a cavalry division on the [Western] approaches."[26]

On 6 March 1941, Churchill, now the Prime Minister, issued his "Battle of the Atlantic Directive" which explicitly reveals his predilection for the offensive.

> We must take the offensive against the U-boat and the Focke-Wulf [long range reconnaissance aircraft] wherever we can and whenever we can. The U-boat at sea must be hunted, the U-boat in the building yard or in dock must be bombed, the Folke-Wulf and other bombers employed against shipping must be attacked in the air and in their nests.[27]

---

[25] GB, M.O.D., Naval Historical Branch, "Ocean Convoys," 10-11; ADM 199/1, M/T.O. 1209/39, 10 October 1939; Roskill, *War at Sea* 1: 343, 451-52, Map 9; Dönitz, *Memoirs*, 104.

[26] Winston S. Churchill, *The Second World War*, vol. 1 (1948), *The Gathering Storm*, 362-63; vol. 2, *Their Finest Hour*, 669; Roskill, *War at Sea* 1: 134; Pt. 1, 265 n 1. The Admiralty temporarily detached the fleet carriers *Ark Royal* and *Courageous* from the Home Fleet in early September 1939 to form the nuclei of two submarine Hunter-Killer (HUK) Groups, or Striking Forces. On 17 September 1939, shortly after *Courageous* detached two of her four destroyers to investigate a reported U-boat contact some 130 miles distant, Leutnant Otto Schuhart, *U 29* (same number as Weddigen's boat, sunk by *Dreadnought*), sighted the lightly protected carrier. *U 29* penetrated the two-destroyer screen and sank the carrier with two torpedoes out of a spread of three. *Courageous* sank in fifteen minutes, taking with her the commanding officer and 518 of the crew. Although heavily counterattacked by the two screening destroyers and claimed sunk, Leutnant Schuhart successfully evaded and returned safely to port to a hero's welcome. The British immediately withdrew fleet carriers from HUK operations. See Roskill, *War at Sea* 1: 105-6; 3: 397.

[27] Churchill, *Second World War*, vol. 3 (1950), *The Grand Alliance*, 107-9; Roskill, *War at Sea*, 1: Appendix O; Hezlet, *Sub & Sea*, 171; Sir Peter Gretton, *Winston Churchill and the Royal Navy* (New York: Coward-McCann, 1969), 291-92.

Gradually, the slow but steady increase in convoy escort strength and the number of combat-experienced personnel — a 3:1 advantage over inexperienced ASW crews — began to produce results consistent with the unqualified success of convoy in previous wars. In a series of convoy battles south of Iceland during the period 17-31 March 1941, surface escorts brought the U-boats to heel and sank five. The bag included three super-star U-boat aces: Gunther Prien (*U 47*), the "Snorting Bull of Scapa Flow"; Otto Kretschmer (*U 99*), the tonnage king of the war; and Joachim Schepke (*U 100*). Thus ended the first U-boat "Happy Time."[28]

There had been a strong tendency in some American quarters to fault the British for their lack of preparedness in combating the resumption of the U-boat war against shipping. But the American Navy exhibited an even greater lack of preparedness. Like their British cousins, the American naval leaders between wars also reaffirmed their belief in Mahan by concentrating their limited resources on the modernization and maintenance of battleships and aircraft carriers to the detriment of escorts and general-purpose destroyers. And in the strategic and tactical areas, they concentrated almost exclusively on plans, preparations, and exercises for a Jutland-style "big battle" in which they would decisively defeat the Japanese battlefleet. The resultant shortage of escorts contributed significantly to the "merry massacre" of merchant shipping that occurred in American waters between January and July 1942.[29]

Particularly egregious is the fact that the Americans had the benefit of full disclosure of over two years of prior experience by the Royal Navy in countering the threat. Shortly after the beginning of hostilities in Europe in 1939, the U.S. Naval Attaché in London, Captain Alan G. Kirk, made arrangements with the Admiralty to obtain continuous reports on naval developments and operations in the areas of submarine detection,

---

[28] While attacking convoy OB.293 on 17 March 1941, *U 70* and *U 47* (Prien) were sunk by corvettes *Camellia* and *Arbutus*, and destroyer *Wolverine*; while attacking or trailing convoy HX.112 on 27 March 1941, *U 100* (Schepke) and *U 99* (Kretschmer) were sunk by the destroyers *Walker* and *Vanoc*; and before the month was out *U 551* was sunk by the trawler *Visenda*. See Roskill, *War at Sea* 1: 364-65; Stephen W. Roskill, *White Ensign, The British Navy at War, 1939-1945* (Annapolis: U.S. Naval Institute, 1960), 121; Hezlet, *Sub & Sea*, 174; Anthony Preston, *U-Boats* (London: Bison Books, 1978), 113, 116. The commanding officer of *Walker* at the time was Donald G. Macintyre, one of Britain's most decorated U-boat killers. See Donald G. Macintyre, *U-Boat Killer* (Annapolis: Naval Institute Press, 1976).

[29] Samuel E. Morison, *History of United States Naval Operations in World War II*, vol. 1, *The Battle of the Atlantic*, intro. Commodore Dudley W. Knox. USN, "The United States Navy Between World Wars" (Boston: Little, Brown, 1947), 12, 265, 200-201; "Eastern Sea Frontier War Diaries, December 1941-February 1942," NHC, Operational Archives, Washington, D.C.; Roskill, *War at Sea*, vol. 2, 95; Dönitz, *Memoirs*, 216; Robert G. Albion and Robert H. Connery, *Forrestal and the Navy* (New York: Columbia University Press, 1962), 86-87.

ASW operations, mine defense, AAW defense for both naval and merchant vessels, and, particularly, information concerning British naval combat experience. He sent almost daily messages and frequent letters to the Navy Department in Washington on this intelligence.[30]

At the Ambassadorial level, Joseph Kennedy reported frequently to the State and Navy Departments on the general developments of the war at sea. His primary source of information was Churchill, then First Sea Lord.[31] After the fall of France in June 1940, the Admiralty formed a special committee, headed by Vice Admiral Sir Sidney Bailey, to improve and expedite Anglo-American naval cooperation. As a result, an extensive system of practically unlimited exchange of information developed between the Admiralty and the U.S. Navy Department. In July 1940, Roosevelt accepted Churchill's invitation and sent a team of senior army and navy officers to London for informal discussions of the war situation.[32] This culminated in a British delegation of military staff officers meeting on 29 January 1941 in Washington with their American counterparts "to determine the best methods by which . . . the United States and the British . . . could defeat Germany . . . should the United States be compelled to resort to war." The final ABC-1 Agreement on 27 March 1941 incorporated "Germany first" as a fundamental principle of Anglo-American strategy, and the protection of shipping in the Northwestern Approaches to the United Kingdom as the focal point of the U.S. war effort. Appendix V of the agreement specifically provided that: "The Chief of Naval Operations, immediately on the entry of the United States into war, will arrange for the control and protection of

[30] Tracy B. Kettredge, "Historical Monograph: U.S.-British Naval Cooperation, 1940-1945," unpublished manuscript, NHC, D.C., I, sec. 2, 108-12, also see Chap.6, nn. 62 and 93. For more on Anglo-American rapprochement during the thirties, see Stephen Roskill, *Naval Policy Between the Wars*, vol. 2, *The Period of Reluctant Rearmament, 1930-1939* (Annapolis: Naval Institute Press, 1976). For the technical side, see James R. Leutze, *Bargaining for Supremacy: Anglo-American Naval Collaboration, 1937-1941* (Chapel Hill: University of North Carolina Press, 1977); see also James R. Leutze, "Technology and Bargaining in Anglo-American Relations: 1938-1946," U.S. Naval Institute *Proceedings* (June 1977), 50-61.

[31] Kitteredge, "Historical Monograph," I sec. 2, 112-13.

[32] Kitteredge, I, sec.2, 108-9; I, sec. 3, pt. A (Chap. 10), 207-44; Roskill, *War at Sea*, vol. 1, 454-56; vol. 2, 98-99; Morison, *Naval Operations World War II*, vol. 1, 40-41. Rear Admiral R.L. Ghormley, USN, arrived in London on 15 August 1940 and remained as Special Naval Observer (SPENAVO) until March 1942 when he became Commander Naval Forces Europe (COMNAVFOREUR). He was relieved on 28 April 1942 by Admiral Harold R. Stark, who had been relieved in March 1942 as Chief of Naval Operations (CNO) by Admiral Ernest J. King — part of the shakeup after Pearl Harbor.

shipping of United States registry or charter within United States Areas."[33]

In May 1941, Admiral John A. Godfrey, British Director of Naval Intelligence and supervisor of the Admiralty's Operational Intelligence Centre (OIC), visited Captain Alan G. Kirk, now American Director of the Office of Naval Intelligence (ONI) in Washington, and provided him with a detailed summary of experience gained at the OIC and the code-breaking center at Bletchley Park during the war against the U-boats.[34]

Then on 1 July 1941 Churchill approved a measure to provide the Americans all information, except information regarding future operations and "Most Secret" sources of information as established by the Cabinet. This enabled the American Naval Attaché, Captain Charles A. Lockwood, to attend the Fortnightly Review of U-boats sunk (FRU), which gave full information on all known and probable sinkings, German and Italian. He also was shown the latest estimates of German U-boat construction and given additional details as requested.[35]

Finally, on 12 January 1942, the British provided Admiral Ernest J. King (CominCh) early warning of a "Large concentration [of U-boats] proceeding to or already arrived on station off canadian and north-eastern United States coasts."[36] Those U-boats were the *Paukenschlag*

---

[33] "ABC-1, March 27, 1941, United States-British Staff Conversations, Report," Morison Papers, Series III, vol, 1 (14), NHC, D.C. For a narrative on the ABC-1 Staff Agreement, see Morison, *Naval Operations World War II* 1: 41; for exact working of the agreement and the level of participation, up and including President Roosevelt, see U.S., Congress, Joint, Joint Committee, *Investigation of Pearl Haarbor Attack: Hearings*, 79th Cong., 1st Sess., 1946, 39 vols. (Washington D.C.: Government Printing Office, 1946) 15: 1485-1550.

[34] Gannon, *Operation Drumbeat*, 164-65.

[35] GB, PRO, ADM 1/12784, P.D. 0115/41 of 6-16-41, 1st Sea Lord minute of 6-26-41 and his memo. to the P.M. The P.M. approved on 7-1-41.

[36] Naval Message 121716, 12 January 1942, see Gannon, *Operation Drumbeat*, 212; also see 153-66, 211 449n. 17. On 14 January 1942, Admiral Adolphus Andrews, Commander, North Atlantic Naval Coastal Frontier (ComNANCF) advised Admiral Ernest J. King, (CominCh) that submarine intelligence stated "there is a definite westward movement of enemy submarines in the North Atlantic." Although the source was not identified, we now know that it probably was Ultra. At Bletchley Park, the British were able to break some of the most highly classified and operationally sensitive messages during most of the war. This information was then "'processed' and distributed with complete security to President Roosevelt, Winston Churchill, and all the other principal Chiefs of Staff and commanders in the field throughout the war." See F.W. Winterbotham, *The Ultra Secret* (New York: Harper & Row, 1974), 11, vii. Although Ultra was used in the Battle of the Atlantic to help defeat the U-boats, it was not always available when needed the most. And the German Naval Intelligence (Beobachtungsdienst, or *B-dienst*) code-breaking Service (*xB-dienst*) had been able to read the British merchant ship and convoy signals from the beginning until 1 June 1943. Winterbotham, *Ultra Secret*, 84-85. For a cautious view of *post facto* claims of decisive sucesses and results by intelligence personnel, see David Kahn, "World War II

(Operation *Drumbeat*) group. The "merry massacre" was about to begin.

Despite the benefit of full disclosure of all that the British had learned about ASW in almost two and a half years of war, however, the U.S. Navy was completely unprepared for the onslaught on shipping off the Atlantic seaboard by Operation *Paukenschlag*. The tactical environment in which this initial U-boat blitz occurred — and went on for a protracted time — is revealed by the rueful log entry U-boat commander Kapitän-leutnant Reinhard Hardegen made on the night of 18-19 January 1942:

> It is a pity that there were not . . . ten to twenty U-boats [as Dönitz had recommended] here last night, instead of one. Altogether I saw about 20 steamships, some undarkened; also a few tramp steamers, all hugging the coast. Buoys and beacons in the area had dimmed lights which, however, were visible up to two or three miles.[37]

This situation existed in part because the Americans believed that they did not have sufficient escorts to implement the convoy plans on hand, contrary to the "lessons relearned" by the British and passed along. So the meager air and surface forces available were used for patrolling — about as effective as "looking for a needle in a haystack." In addition, Admiral King persisted in drawing down naval assets in the Atlantic to reinforce "imperative needs in the Pacific," despite the overall "Germany first" war strategy ennunciated in the ABC-1 Agreement. This contributed to the initial success of the U-boats, for most of the sinkings were made by individual U-boats against vessels proceeding independently for want of escorts. In many cases gunfire was used in preference to torpedoes. That was an option that would have been completely denied the U-boats by the mere presence of a single armed escort — a lesson of World War I already relearned by the British and likewise passed on to the Americans. They were beginning to learn, however, and one of the first lessons relearned by the Americans was that U-boats avoided convoys and concentrated on independent sailers. In the month of January 1942, only one of the few escorted convoys along the American coast was attacked.[38]

History: The Biggest Hole," *Military Affairs* (April 1975):74-76. See Patrick Beesly, *Very Special Intelligence: The Story of the Admiralty's Operational Intelligence Centre, 1939-1945* (London: Hammish Hamilton, 1977); David Kahn, *Hitler's Spies* (New York: Macmillan, 1978) David Kahn, *The Codebreakers* (New York: Macmillan, 1967); Noel F. Busch, *The Emperor's Sword* (New York: Funk & Wagnalls, 1969); William Jameson, *The Code Breakers of Room 40: The Story of Admiral Hall* [WW I] (New York: Atheneum, 1968).

[37] Quoted in Roskill, *War at Sea* 2: 95.

[38] "ESF War Diaries, December 1941-February 1942," NHC, D.C.; Wesley R. Craven and James L. Cate, *The Army Air Force in World War II*, Vol 1 (1948), *Plans and Early Operations, January 1939 to August 1942* (Chicago: University of Chicago Press, 1948-1958), 522; William

The British were appalled and rightly so not only by the lack of American preparedness but also by the slowness and apparent unwillingness of their new allies to start coastal convoys. To get the Americans started, the British provided them with a "fifty destroyers deal" in reverse. They sent twenty-four ASW trawlers to work off the eastern seaboard, handed over outright ten new corvettes to the U.S Navy, sent a British escort group and eight *Fairmile* motor launches to work in the Trinidad area, and promised the future production allocation of fifteen single-screw and two twin-screw Canadian-built corvettes.[39] In addition, the British Admiralty prepared a special review of the battle for the Americans, summarizing British ASW experience since the war began. It stressed the comparative failure of hunting forces, the great value of aircraft in convoy protection, the supreme importance of training and practice, and the value of efficient radar.[40]

Spurred on by these British entreaties and direct assistance, the Americans belatedly adopted coastal convoying on 14 May 1942 and then progressively introduced it throughout the eastern seaboard, the Gulf of Mexico, and the Caribbean. Finally, on 27 August 1942, the Interlocking Convoy System was introduced to coordinate the sailing schedules in all areas. As predicted by the British there was an immediate and sharp decline in shipping losses and a concurrent and significant rise in U-boat losses in areas where convoying was introduced. Evaluating the overall situation, Dönitz considered the meager results in the once lucrative American theater not worth the U-boat losses. So, he redeployed them back along the North Atlantic shipping routes where the final victory of the escorts would be won. Thus ended the second U-boat "Happy Time", as had been the first, by the introduction of convoying which served not only as a deterrent to attack, but also as a primary U-boat killer.[41]

D. Leahy, *I Was There* (New York: Whittlesey House, 1940), 140, 118-19; GB, PRO, ADM 1/12062, "Extracts from General Review by Director A/S Warfare Branch;" Hezlet, *Sub & Sea*, 177; "Anti-submarine Warfare, 1942-1943: Notes from British ASW Reports," January 1943 (C.C. 04050/42(1), Morison Files, Series III, vol, 1 (8), NHC, D.C.; "The Inauguration and Carrying Out of Convoy Operations and Its Effects," of December 7, 1942, by LCDR Ames, filed under "Coastal Convoy System, General Information," Morison Files, Series III, vol. 1 (19), NHC, D.C. [Ames Memo. of Dec. 7].

[39] GB, PRO, ADM 1/12130, "Memorandum by First Sea Lord on the Need for More Escort Vessels (PO 18049/1942)," 3; for additional British views on the shortage of escorts, see ADM 1/12120 (1942), "Admiralty's Views on Continued Sinking of Ships Off East coast of United States, Institution of Convoy, Ratio of Escorts (PO 17244/1942)."

[40] Roskill, *War at Sea* 2: 89-99; GB,PRO,ADM 1/12062, paras. 13, 20, 24, 29.

[41] The shifting of U-boat operating areas as convoy was introduced in American waters is depicted in the charts prepared for Morison in writing his *History of United States Naval Operations in World War II*. See Morison, *Naval Operations* 10: 12, 15, 66; Preston, *U-Boats*, 131;

These dramatic results did not satisfy everyone, however. A U.S. Atlantic Fleet study of the U-boat campaign off the North American coast from January through June 1942, when the "merry massacre" was in full swing, reveals the pervading offensive-mindedness in the U.S Navy. Ignoring its own finding that it was the introduction and gradual expansion of the convoy system that accounted for the shifting of U-boat operating areas to where ships were still sailing independently, the study deplored the time and money involved in evasive routing and the "totally defensive employment of combatant ships as escorts." It concluded:

> . . . If offensive forces such as organized killer groups had been employed in February and March just ahead of the introduction of convoys, merchant ship losses at that time would have been materially reduced and submarine activities curtailed to such an extent that, perhaps, the convoy system now required might not be necessary.
>
> Killer groups, carefully organized, even now may be employed effectively along convoy routes when the German High Command begins execution of its plan for concerted attacks on convoys.[42]

That attitude and the lack of readiness of the U.S. Navy during this period was harshly criticized by its semi-official World War II historian, Samuel Eliot Morison. He concluded that the value of convoying seemed to have been forgotten in spite of the navy's direct involvement in the U-boat campaign against shipping in World War I and the steady flow of information on previous British experience in World War II. A more accurate portrayal is that the U.S. Navy had not forgotten; it simply ignored the lessons of the previous war, even though relearned by the British and freely passed on to them. Undoubtedly, the advocates of the offensive, who looked upon convoying as a "defensive" measure, had gained the ascendancy in the naval hierarchy. As an example, early in the war an American naval officer stated that "the Navy does not like convoys. It is a purely defensive form of warfare. . . . Insofar as enemy submarine warfare forces us to use the convoy system, we unwittingly play into his hands."[43] This anti-convoy, offensive-mindedness permeated the officer ranks to such a degree that Secretary of War Henry L. Stimson, in frustration, characterized it in his memoirs as follows:

> . . . the peculiar psychology of the Navy Department, . . . frequently

---

for effectiveness of escorts, see Roskill, *War at Sea* 2: 376-77 and 3: 265.

[42] U.S. Atlantic Fleet, ASW Unit, ltr. to CinCLant, file A16-3 (9), ser.: 0462 of July 21, 1942, sub.: "Study of the U-boat Campaign," Morison Files, Ser. IV (195), NHC, D.C., 7-8, 9.

[43] Morison, *Naval Operations in World War II* 1: 265; Preston, *U-Boats*, 129.

seemed to retire from the realms of logic into a dim religious world in which Neptune was God, Mahan his prophet and the United States Navy the only true church.[44]

Morison delivered his harshest criticism of the U.S. Navy in his chapter on the "merry massacre":

> This writer cannot avoid the conclusion that the United States Navy was woefully unprepared, materially and mentally, for the U-boat blitz on the Atlantic Coast that began in January 1942. He further believes that, apart from the want of air power which was due to prewar agreements with the Army, this unpreparedness was largely the Navy's own fault. Blame cannot justly be imputed to Congress . . . nor . . . to President Roosevelt. . . . The Navy couldn't see any vessel under a thousand tons [referring to the lack of escorts] . . . the Navy had no plans ready for a reasonable protection to shipping when the submarines struck, and was unable to improvise them for several months.[45]

Morison's indictment was soundly based, except for the conclusion that "the Navy had no plans ready." On the contrary, from the time of the ABC-1 Agreement in March 1941, which specifically provided in Appendix V for convoying by the U.S. Navy, there had existed acceptance of the essential need to convoy. That acceptance was manifested in various war plans drafted by the navy in preparation for war. Further, these plans were supported by tactical publications reflecting British naval experience in World War II. Finally, the navy had experience escorting American and Icelandic convoys starting in July 1941 and Allied convoys starting in September of that year.

Therefore, it was not plans that were lacking, it was the means and the will. Of these two, it was the latter, manifested in a pervasive anti-convoy, obsession-with-the-offensive mentality — tinged with no little Anglophobia in high places (*e.g.*, Admiral King) — that is the most culpable. For had the navy objectively studied the British reports of their experience, instead of virtually ignoring them, they too most probably would have accepted the fact, without the grim tutelage of combat, that convoying, even with as few as one or two escorts, was significantly safer than independent sailing and far more effective than offensive operations such as hunting and patrolling.

---

[44] Henry L. Stimson and McGeorge Bundy, *On Active Service in Peace and War*, 2 vols. (New York: Harper, 1948), 2: 506.

[45] Morison, *Naval Operations in World War II* 1: 200-201. Also see Robert G. Albion and Robert H. Connery, *Forrestal and the Navy* (New York: Columbia University Press, 1962), 86-87, for the unprepared condition of the navy at the outbreak of the war.

Meanwhile, March 1943 saw the Battle of the Atlantic rage to a pitch that came nearly as close to disrupting communications between America and her European allies as had the U-boat campaign in the spring of 1917.[46] During the month, 64 percent of the Allied ships sunk in all theaters were sunk in convoy in the North Atlantic. Once again strong arguments were made to discard the convoy system for allegedly more effective offensive schemes. With the strong support of Admiral King, however, the Allies clung to the convoy system through the crisis. King stated his position and support clearly at the Atlantic Convoy Conference, 1-12 March 1943:

> The military must also recognize that the defeat [sinking] of the U-boat is not of itself the goal we seek. . . . Your immediate task is to protect our shippinng by what may be called defensive anti-submarine warfare [convoy]. . .
>
> I have heard something about "killer groups" which may be of great use when we get enough means, provided they are used where the "bait" is. I see no profit in searching the oceans, or even any but a limited area, such as a focal area − all else puts to shame the proverbial "search for a needle in a haystack."
>
> Let me say again, . . . that anti-submarine warfare for the remainder of 1943, at least, must concern itself primarily with the escort of convoys.[47]

Earlier, King had told General Marshall:

> . . . escort is not just *one* way of handling the submarine menace; it is the *only* way that gives any promise of success. The so-called patrol and hunting operations have time and again proved futile."[48]

---

[46] Morison, *Naval Operations in World War II* 2: 273-74; "ASW,1942-1943, Notes from British ASW Reports," Morison Files; Roskill, *War at Sea* 2: 365-67; Hezlet, *Sub & Sea*, 182; Dönitz, *Memoirs*, 182,329-30. For a more detailed account of the convoy battles in the critical monthe of March 1943, see Jürgen Rohwer, *Critical Convoy Battles of World War II* (Annapolis: Naval Institute Press, 1977); Jürgen Rohwer, *The Critical Convoy Battles of March 1943: The Battle for HX.229/SC122* (London: Ian Allan Ltd., 1977); Jürgen Rohwer, "The U-Boat War Against the Allied Supply Lines," *Decisive Battles of World War II: The German View*, eds. H.A. Jacobsen and J. Rohwer (New York: G. Putnam's Sons, 1965), 295-315; Peter Gretton, *Convoy Escort Commander* (London: Cassell, 1964); Peter Gretton, *Crisis Convoy: The Story of HX 231* (Annapolis: Naval Institute Press, 1974).

[47] "Report of the Conference [Atlantic Convoy Conference, 1-12 March 1943], (VOPNAV Op 12), A14-1, Doc. 76822," NHC, D.C., 1.

[48] King to Marshall Memo. of June 21, 1942, Papers of FADM Ernest J. King, 1878-1956, Series XI, Miscellanious Material, 1943- 1948, Memorandum for the Secretary of the Navy: "Review of the Marshall-Arnold-King Correspondence on ASW — 1942-1943" (Box 13), February 4, 1948, NHC, D.C.

By the end of March 1943, this faith in convoy was vindicated by the appearance of five support groups, with their prosecute-to-kill capability; escort carriers, with their air umbrellas; and additional very long range (VLR) land-based maritime aircraft, to close the "Black Pit" gap. The tide began to turn in April and in May 1943 the victory was won. Thirty-three U-boats were sunk in the first twenty-three days of May, with little loss of merchant vessels. Such appalling losses could not be sustained, even in the bitter no-quarter battle being fought in the stormy wastes of the North Atlantic, without destroying the U-boat arm as a viable fighting force. Dönitz soberly recognized that fact and withdrew his U-boats from the North Atlantic convoy lanes. In his memoirs he admitted defeat:

> . . . Wolf-pack operations against convoys in the North Atlantic, the main theater of operations . . . , were no longer possible. . . . Accordingly, I withdrew the boats from the North Atlantic on May 24. . . . We had lost the Battle of the Atlantic.[49]

Stephen W. Roskill, official historian for the Royal Navy in World War II, provided the victor's version:

> . . . the victory [Battle of the Atlantic] . . . marked one of the decisive stages of the war; for the enemy then made his greatest effort against our Atlantic life-line – and he failed. After forty-five months of unceasing battle, of a more exacting and arduous nature than posterity may easily realize, our convoy escorts and aircraft had won the triumph they had so richly merited.[50]

In summary, during World War I, the Allies clung to Mahan's basic tenets — except that regarding the superiority of convoy over hunting and patrolling — until it was almost too late to avoid defeat as a result of the German unrestricted submarine warfare version of the *guerre de course*. Between wars, all of the maritime nations of the world adopted Mahan's concept of the "capital ship" as the yardstick for measuring naval power and relegated commerce destroying to his category of a "secon-

---

[49] Dönitz, *Memoirs*, 341, 332; Roskill, *War at Sea* 2, 377; Hezlet, *Sub & Sea*, 183; Morison, *Naval Operations in World War II* 10: 83-84, 108, 203; Preston, *U-Boats*, 140. Post-war interrogation of U-boat officers and Rear Admiral Godt gave the following reasons for the defeat: (1) HF/DF cross bearings on U-boat radio transmissions to headquarters ashore, (2) aircraft escorts, (3) good escort radar, and (4) growth of experience and superior training among escort crews. See, GB,PRO,ADM 1/17561 (1945), "Report from Capt. Roberts, RN, on visit to Germany, May 1945, in connection with interrogation of German naval officers in U-boat operations (ASW 060/1945)."

[50] Roskill, *War at Sea* 2: 377.

dary" naval operation. As a result, at the beginning of World War II Germany had insufficient numbers of submarines to wage a decisive war against shipping, while Britain and America were initially unprepared to meet even the limited U-boat campaign. Although the latter eventually won the Battle of the Atlantic, it was in no case a "secondary" naval operation. In fact, it was "the dominating factor through the war." And in the Pacific, Japan's inflexible adherence to Mahan's dogmas resulted in the annihilation of her merchant fleet well before Hiroshima and Nagasaki — a decisive result for a war on shipping.[51]

Thus, for the second time in the twentieth century, Mahan's conclusion that commerce destroying was a "secondary, inconclusive, and indecisive" method of naval warfare proved invalid in trial by combat. On the contrary, considered in modern terms of logistics-dependent warfare, rather than in nineteenth-century terms of seaborne trade economics, the destruction of shipping in wartime has demonstrated its potential for becoming a primary, even decisive, method of naval warfare.

---

[51] U.S. Department of War, *The United States Strategic Bombing Survey* [USSBS], *The War Against Japanese Transportation 1941-1945*, Monograph 116 (Washington, D.C.: Government Printing Office, 1947), 114. For additional details on Japanese shipping losses and why their ASW efforts failed, see U.S. Department of War, USSBS, Joint Army-Navy Assessment Commitee, *Japanese Naval and Merchant Shipping Lossses During World War II by All Causes* (Washington, D.C.: Government Printing Office, 1947), iv-x; Atsushi Oi, "Why Japan's Anti-submarine Warfare Failed," U.S. Naval Institute *Proceedings* (June 1952), 587-601; Y. Horie, "The Failure of the Japanese Convoy Escort," ibid. (October 1956), 1072-81; Theodore Roscoe, *United States Submarine Operations in World War II* (Annapolis: U.S. Naval Institute, 1949), 493, 495; Morison, *Two Ocean War*, 493, 496; Hezlet, *Sub & Sea*, 223.

15

Kapitän Fred Krage: Blockade Runner

Harold D. Huycke

Before 1939 the German government made a firm decision not to repeat the mistake made in the 1914-1918 war by leaving the nation's far-flung merchant fleet in neutral ports. In 1919 the Versailles Treaty took away what was left of its merchant fleet, still anchored in neutral ports at the time of the armistice, and Germany was reduced to practically nothing by the terms of that peace settlement.

Thus it was decided by the Admiralty in 1938, and presumably earlier, that no matter what the cost, a major effort would be made to bring their ships home from foreign ports. On the one hand, it was assumed that whatever blockade the British and French might throw up for interception in the Channel approaches and North Atlantic, it would not be leakproof. What efforts the Germans made would be risky. It was assumed that some ships would be lost. Others threatened by capture were to be scuttled by their crews. But the alternative was to sit and await the unknown. The primary fact was, no matter what, no German ship was to fall into the hands of the enemy.

In 1938, fully a year before the war actually began, German merchant shipmasters were given sealed envelopes by the German Admiralty with basic instructions to run for the nearest neutral port, then to advise home offices of the name of the port of refuge, and the quantity of fuel and stores aboard. All was to be transmitted by code. Upon receipt of this data, decisions would than be made on the disposition of the ship.

The year between the Munich agreement in 1938 and the invasion date by the German army into Poland was one of apprehension for the ocean-going Germans. Hundreds of ships were at sea at all times, traversing the ocean's trade routes and it was almost like a game of musical chairs as to where each ship would be when the music suddenly stopped.

So it was that at the very end of August 1939, just a quarter century after the last hot summer which erupted in war on the European continent, that wireless messages and news broadcasts suddenly brought word to the German merchant ships that the Second World War had suddenly begun.

It was my good fortune in 1955 to meet Captain Fred Krage, one time master of the Hamburg America Line freighter *Ermland*. He was then living in a little town called Brush Prairie, Washington, a few miles from the river port of Vancouver, Washington. I was particularly interested in his sailing ship background, but it was during the course of getting to know him better, and during a few visits to his little chicken ranch in this obscure village, that his high adventures during World War II came into clear focus.

He was a blockade runner, and had commanded the first ship to break out of hibernation in Japan and make a run for it to France. He was successful and his story is probably typical of the others who made the successful break-through in the first two years of the war.

I should say at this point that there is a book available on the subject, Martin Brice's *Axis Blockade Runners of World War II* published by the Naval Institute Press in 1981. It has an impressive bibliography and fine detail of the overall story of all German ships and the successes and failures of the blockade-running business. But it does not contain the wealth of information and drama I discovered listening to Fred Krage's own recollections.

During the year 1955, Fred sent me handwritten pages of his life story, and I typed them for further use. The biography was later published in Britain in a privately printed mimeographed newsletter called *The South Spainer*. No reference to this work is found in Brice's sources.

Back to Fred Krage and his motorship *Ermland*. The *Ermland* was a 1922 vintage twin-screw freighter of 6521 gross tons, employed in Hapag's Far East trade in the late 1930s. Captain Krage had discharged his German crew in Shanghai and hired a nearly-all-Chinese-crew in the summer of 1939, then drydocked the ship in Hong Kong and began loading for Europe. The outbreak of the war on 1 September caught him at sea, and upon receipt of this news, and examination of the sealed envelope, he proceeded to Takao, Formosa and interned himself for an unknown future. Nearly a year passed before he received orders to proceed to Kobe to join a growing fleet of other German freighters in that port. Japanese officials, professed Allies of Nazi Germany, for weeks withheld permission for the departure of the *Ermland*, until a German envoy went to Takao to negotiate the release of the ship. Once in Kobe, the *Ermland* was singled out as the first ship to make the break-out for Europe. Krage regained his German crew and paid off the Chinese.

During the early part of 1940, numerous ships in neutral Atlantic ports, presumably in Africa, South America, and perhaps the United States, had made the effort to return to Europe and were more or less successful. Raw materials were in demand in the homeland, and now occupied France provided a number of more accessible Bay of Biscay ports to which the ships were directed.

Conferences with Admiral Wennecker, who was the German Naval Attaché in Tokyo and former commander of the battleship *Deutschland*, led to preparations to get the *Ermland* underway. A plan was formulated to send the ship to the Central Pacific to pick up a large number of British and French prisoners, then crowded upon a roving German commerce raider operating amongst the French and British islands. The *Ermland* sailed from Kobe at night on 28 December 1940, rendezvoused with the raider *Orion* and received 320 prisoners. Quickly, accomodations were constructed of the crudest sort in the forward hold and 'tween deck to confine the various nationalities to the forward part of the ship. Eight armed guards were detached from the *Orion* to guard the prisoners on *Ermland*. One old machine gun was mounted on a bridge wing, aimed over the foredeck.

Ermland sailed at dusk on 4 January 1941 and made a long sweeping traverse toward Cape Horn. Disguised first as a Russian ship, she now changed her disguise to a Japanese ship, avoiding the remaining peaceful sea routes and crossing through the tropics into the colder climes of the South Pacific. The prisoners were allowed as much freedom during the day as common sense would allow, being employed building life rafts out of dunnage and drums, and playing games and reading. At night they were locked up in the 'tween decks.

Colder weather created a certain restlessness amongst the prisoners and German crew alike, as Cape Horn was passed and the Falkland Islands drew abeam. Here in these dark waters twenty-seven years before, a German cruiser squadron under Admiral von Spee was caught and all but one ship was sunk by a British fleet. This time the Falklands were given a wide berth and *Ermland* entered the South Atlantic's broad reaches in comparative safety.

After a close encounter with a two-funnelled passenger ship, not identified, Captain Krage received orders to rendezvous with the tanker *Uckermark*, disguised as the *Dixie*. For ten days the two ships hove to, steaming idly in circles awaiting the arrival of the *Admiral Scheer*, the German heavy cruiser homeward bound from a raid in the Indian Ocean. In due course the ships rendezvoused, took fuel from the *Uckermark*, and the *Ermland* received fifty-six more prisoners from the cruiser.

The prisoners taken from the *Admiral Scheer* had been a rebellious lot, and these had infected the original number with an increased sense of mutiny and resistance. A few bursts of machine gun fire over their heads quieted the multitude of British, French, Australian, and Norwegian prisoners and all settled down again for the run to the North.

Now it was time to start the tortuous passage through the narrow neck of mid-Atlantic between South America and Africa. With wireless messages providing advice from the Admiralty in Berlin, *Ermland* avoided enemy ships and entered the Bay of Biscay.

Captain Krage enlisted the willing support of a prisoner, the French Captain Jego and a civilian M. Paul Vois to help identify the low profile of the land at the entrance to the Gironde River. Both were intimately familiar with the approaches, and the entry was made safely, despite the fact that after the ship arrived Captain Krage was told he had steamed right through a newly-laid minefield.

As the *Ermland* entered the Gironde and was proceeding up river to Bordeaux, word was sent to Captain Krage that the prisoners would like to see him on the 'tween deck. With the pilot in command for the time being, Captain Krage went to see them. In his words he described the following:

> When I went down to comply with their wishes and entered the tween deck, all of the prisoners, dressed in their best, had voluntarily lined up and stood at attention. They wanted, they told me, to show their gratitude for the fair treatment they had received during the whole voyage. I was deeply impressed and moved by this fine gesture, and on my part I expressed my recognition and thanks for their good behavior. When I left the tween decks after some more or less encouraging remarks to the men, a thunderous yell rang from 380 throats: "Three cheers for the captain! This indeed was the greatest honor the prisoners could bestow on their prison commander, and I felt immensely proud at the moment."

Captain Krage was soon ordered to Berlin to meet Grand Admiral Raeder. He, the second mate, and lieutenant in charge of prisoners were awarded the Iron Cross, second class. Further honors were given by the Hamburg-America line in Hamburg, and then Captain Krage returned to his ship in Bordeaux. Admiral Menche, the naval commander of Bordeaux brought a five-foot-high framed picture of Adolf Hitler aboard, personally inscribed by the Fuehrer, to be mounted in the ship's saloon. Captain Krage, incidentally, was not then nor ever was a member of the Nazi party.

With this first successful break-through voyage, other ships were ordered home from Japan and during the year 1941 many got through. *Ermland* lay idle for weeks and months. Eventually she was renamed *Weserland*. After a year of inactivity in Bordeaux the ship was overhauled and armed with anti-aircraft guns placed fore and aft, and on the bridge wings; large refrigeration lockers were built into the 'tween decks and a modern radio shack was installed. A new crew, including about thirty naval armed guard, was assigned.

During the year an elaborate trade agreement had been struck with Japan by Germany, by which critical machinery and supplies were to be traded between the allies, and a trade commission sent to Japan to implement the massive program.

Weserland sailed from Bordeaux in July 1942 but ran into heavy air attacks over the Bay of Biscay. Rather than risk continued exposure to more air attacks and perhaps surface attacks, Captain Krage ran for the Spanish port of Camarinas, near Cape Finisterre. Within hours he was ordered to return to Bordeaux. The long summer days were too hazardous for the attempt to clear the Bay of Biscay. Two months passed and as early fall days and cloudy weather approached, another attempt was made. This time *Weserland* made another run and nearly got clear before she was attacked by a Sunderland flying boat, which in turn was shot down by the *Weserland*'s gun crew. Two badly burned survivors of the airplane were picked up by the Germans, as the ship proceeded into the Atlantic.

More or less in company with the tanker *Uckermark*, *Weserland* started to Batavia as a first port of call, then to Singapore for bunkers. *Uckermark* cleared ahead with a full load of oil and arrived in Yokohama before the *Weserland*. Within days she blew up, reportedly due to a careless welder's torch in a gas-filled tank, taking the commerce raider *Thor* and the steamer *Leuthen* with her, all ships reduced to tangled wrecked steel, with heavy casualties. A big hole was blown in the Yokohama docks where the ships were moored.

The homeward passage for *Weserland* was fraught with high risks. Captain Krage loaded quickly and sailed in early January 1943. Now the full weight of the Allies with American sea power, coupled with a resurgent British effort, made the return transit very risky. *Weserland* loaded in Saigon, Batavia, and Singapore and started off on her hazardous voyage across the Indian Ocean. Three leading German freighters were caught and scuttled in the Atlantic, which caused the German Admiralty to order all other in-transit ships to return to Japan. More time was lost awaiting dirty weather in the Atlantic which would increase the chances of the Germans getting through to France. Three ships out of the Dutch East Indies made the attempt but were caught in the net and scuttled. Krage returned to Yokohama and laid up until October. There were only five ships left in Japan to run the gauntlet. Submarines were being employed to bring critical materials, in limited quantities, to Western France, but they were ineffectual.

Finally the desperate order was given for the last five ships to depart and make the dash for home. *Weserland* rounded Cape of Good Hope in December and struck out for the narrows between Freetown and Natal. January 1944 was not the same as March 1941. The Allies were everywhere and dominated all sea approaches to the Atlantic routes. Ascension Island in Latitude 11 North was the cork in the bottle in one respect, affording the American long-range bombers and search planes a permanent platform from which to scour the ocean wastes.

On New Year's Day 1944 *Weserland* approached the critical zone. At noon an American patrol plane appeared and circled the ship. The German gun crew opened up and drove the plane off. Thereafter, more planes arrived and circled out of range. Two nights later on 4 January, the American destroyer *Somers* appeared out of the dark and fired at *Weserland*. The engines stopped, demolition charges were set off and the crew took to the boats. In the melee that followed, five of the Germans were lost. The rest were taken prisoner, landed in Pernambuco and eventually transported to Arizona. Captain Krage spent the rest of the war as chief gardener for the prison camp commandant. In 1945 he returned to Europe and upon landing in Hamburg was pounced upon by the British and put in a prison camp for another few months. His recollections of the British treatment were not exactly favorable. He had been captured in the English Channel in 1915 from a Dutch ship and spent the next three years in Knockeloe, the huge British camp on the Isle of Man where thousands of Germans, Austrians, and Turks were locked up in that war.

Eventually Captain Krage was released and returned to Hamburg where he obtained a shore job and worked for American occupation forces for about four years. In 1950 he migrated to the United States to work on his brother's chicken farm in Washington, and there he stayed until the fall of 1964 when he returned to Germany to live out his years. Captain Fred Krage died in December 1974 at the age of 83.

PART FOUR

Looking Back

16

United States Merchant Marine Casualties

James E. Valle

The ships and men of the United States Merchant Marine constituted one of the smallest of the American services which saw action during World War II. They were also among the most heavily engaged, participating in every major theater of war and sustaining exceptionally heavy casualties by American standards. During the period from 1941 to 1945, approximately 6,000 civilian-manned merchant ships sailed under the American flag as part of either the Maritime Commission's War Shipping Administration (WSA) pool or the Army Transportation Service fleet.[1]

An undetermined number of additional vessels sailed as American-owned ships flying flags of convenience and were either fully or partially manned by American civilian seamen. There was also a fleet of foreign and confiscated Axis-owned ships that operated under charter by the Maritime Commission with some American personnel on board to supplement predominantly foreign crews.[2]

According to the most authoritative tabulations available, 624 of the 6,000 American flag vessels were sunk by enemy action, 130 were

---

[1] Statistics related to the size of the wartime Merchant Marine vary somewhat from source to source. I have used Eloise Engle and Arnold Lott, *American Maritime Heritage* (Annapolis, MD: Naval Institute Press, 1975), 306-307. The Army Transportation Service fleet stood at 185 seagoing ships directly controlled by the army and another 1,500 "allocated" to the army from WSA. See *Army Ships and Watercraft of World War II* (Annapolis, MD: Naval Institute Press, 1987), 3-4. Ships counted are those over 1,000 gross tons.

[2] These ships, sixty-four in all, were confiscated in early 1941. See Thomas A. Bailey and Paul B. Ryan, *Hitler vs. Roosevelt* (New York: The Free Press, 1979), 180.

damaged, 2 were captured and used by the Japanese, 27 were deliberately scuttled to form artificial harbors off the Normandy beachheads, and 82 became marine casualties.[3] Thus, statistics show that about 12 percent of American merchant ships were sunk during or just after the war and a further 2 percent were damaged but not sunk.

Approximately 290,000 civilian seafarers served in the Merchant Marine and Army Transportation Service at one time or another during the hostilities.[4] Of this number, 114,145 received the Merchant Marine combat ribbon, indicating that they had been engaged in combat action. At least 6,103 men were killed while serving on merchant vessels. This averages to 9.8 fatalities per sinking or approximately 20 percent of a typical crew of 50. A further 1,760 men were wounded, and 609 were taken prisoner, 54 of these dying in Japanese prisoner-of-war camps. These numbers indicate that the Merchant Marine and Army Transportation Service had 39 percent of their total strength engaged in hostilities and suffered 2.8 percent fatal casualties, the highest total of any service except the Marine Corps. The ratio of killed to wounded was extraordinarily high at 3.46:1.[5]

Of the 609 seamen who were detained, figures developed separately by Captain Arthur R. Moore and Charles Dana Gibson indicate that 440 were captured off of U.S. flag vessels and 169 were interned after being found ashore in ports overrun by the Japanese. Approximately 47 merchant seamen were held at Stalag Marlag and Milag Nord near

---

[3] Once again, statistics vary from source to source. I have used figures developed by Arthur R. Moore, *A Careless Word . . . A Needless Sinking,* rev. ed. (Kings Point, NY: American Merchant Marine Museum, 1985), esp. 543-546, and checked them against those presented during the hearings conducted by the House Committee on Merchant Marine and Fisheries relative to H.R. 679 on 13 August 1986. Even these are not always in complete agreement.

[4] That is, 270,000 U.S. Maritime Commission seafarers and 20,000 U.S. Army Transportation Service civilian seafarers. The only difference between them is that the USMC seafarers were unionized while the ATS men were direct employees of the federal government under civil service.

[5] See the statement of the Hon. John A. Gaughan, Administrator, Maritime Commission, *Hearing Before the Subcommittee on Merchant Marine of the Committee on Merchant Marine and Fisheries, House of Representatives, Ninety-Ninth Congress, Second Session* on H. R. 679, Serial No. 99-60 (Washington, D. C.: Government Printing Office, 1987), 31-32. It is possible that additional deaths occurred which have gone unrecorded. Some merchant seamen may have died of wounds while being treated in civilian hospitals both in the United States and overseas. There was no uniform system to account for merchant mariners admitted to civilian hospitals, and it is likely that some men died in them without any report being made to the Coast Guard or Maritime Commission. How many additional deaths could be added to the current known total from this source can only be speculated upon, but it may be a significant number.

Bremen as German POWs. The rest were captives of the Japanese, who held 233 as POWs and the remaining 329 as civilian internees. Apparently 54 of the POWs died in captivity, including 2 who were executed upon capture. A further 8 merchant seamen died in internment camps, for a total of 62 deaths among all categories of detained merchant seamen. The Japanese practice of holding two categories of merchant marine detainees was rooted in principles of international law, which held that a merchant seaman taken from on board a ship was a legitimate prisoner of war, but that one who was captured while separated from his ship or while not serving in a particular ship was a civilian and belonged in an internment camp where treatment was much less severe. To complicate matters further, the Japanese were not always consistent in applying the rules and on occasion accepted prisoners taken by German submarines and raiders operating in the Indian Ocean.[6]

The geographical spread of U.S. casualties can best be understood by an analysis of the ocean areas in which the ships were sunk (see table 1 on page 263). The American Merchant Marine had a slightly different experience than the combined Allied merchant marines, which sustained 76 percent of their losses in the North Atlantic.[7] The United States lost about 251 ships on the North Atlantic/Arctic routes, not including the 27 deliberately sunk at Normandy. Approximately 133 ships went down in the Caribbean/Gulf of Mexico area, making this a major killing ground. 42 ships were lost in the South Atlantic, including 5 to surface raiders, and 45 were lost in the Mediterranean, including a significant number bombed and sunk in port or at anchor. Forty ships were sunk in the Indian Ocean/Red Sea, including 2 by surface raiders. The Pacific Ocean accounted for 52 ships lost, including 2 to surface raiders and 2 captured.[8]

A further analysis of these figures shows that 24 percent of ship losses occurred in areas where the convoy system was absent or intermittent, such as the Pacific, South Atlantic, and Indian Oceans. Furthermore, 263 ships were lost in the North Atlantic and Caribbean/Gulf areas in the first six months of 1942 before effective convoy systems were organized throughout the Western Hemisphere. This is 44 percent of the total losses for the entire war and more than 64 percent of the losses sustained in the North Atlantic and Caribbean/Gulf areas for

---

[6] See Moore, *A Careless Word*, 495 and 528-532, and Charles Dana Gibson, "Prisoners of War vs. Internees — The Difference as Judged by the Experience of World War II," unpublished MS furnished to me by Mr. Gibson.

[7] See Terry Hughes and John Costello, *The Battle of the Atlantic* (New York: The Dial Press/James Wade, 1977), 305.

[8] These figures were compiled by a tabulation of the data in Moore, *A Careless Word*, chapter 1, section 1.

the full duration of the war. Before the advent of a full convoy system, ship losses averaged forty-five per month, but after convoying became general, losses dropped to an average of eleven per month by 1944.[9]

Obviously, the time it took to get the Merchant Marine completely "buttoned up" for war was the most costly period of all, and this process took virtually the entire year of 1942. Consequently, that year alone accounted for almost half of all ship casualties recorded, or 47 percent (see table 2 on page 263).

This pattern of losses, heavily weighted towards the early months of the war, reveals another interesting fact. It is customary to think that the Merchant Marine was a war-built fleet and that the Emergency-type ships, particularly the Liberties, bore the brunt of casualties. An examination of the casualty reports compiled by Moore, however, shows that this is not the case. During World War II there were six broad categories of ships which made up the Maritime Commission and Army Transportation Service fleets. These were, in order of age: pre-World War I ships and ships purchased from foreign sources; Emergency Fleet ships constructed between 1917 and 1922; interwar ships constructed between 1923 and 1936; Maritime Commission standard types built between 1937 and 1942; Emergency types (i.e., Liberties and Victories) built from 1941 to 1945; and Maritime Commission standard types built from 1942 to 1945. Losses among these categories were extremely uneven, reflecting the relative numbers of each type being operated and, most of all, the ships that were available to sustain maritime traffic during the crisis year 1942 (see table 3 on page 263).

This table shows that ships of the World War I Emergency Fleet program formed the mainstay of the American Merchant Marine in the first year of the war and suffered the heaviest casualties of any type in use throughout the war. They also formed the vast majority of the ships sacrificed during the Normandy breakwater operation, along with a few Liberties. It cannot be stated with complete accuracy just how many World War I ships, of the approximate total of 2,500 that were built, served in the Merchant Marine during World War II. Some were scrapped, sold foreign, or lost as marine casualties between the wars. Perhaps as many as 1,800 sailed under the American flag during the war, making them the most numerous type of vessel operated after the the Liberties, which numbered 2,710 ships. If these figures are correct, the Emergency Fleet ships suffered a loss rate of 17 percent as opposed to a

---

[9] These figures were obtained by graphing the sinkings documented by Moore and listed in *A Careless Word*, 543-546.

Table 1
Ship Losses by Sea Area[10]

North Atlantic/Arctic	278 ships	47%
Caribbean/Gulf	133 ships	23%
Pacific Ocean	52 ships	9%
Mediterranean	45 ships	8%
South Atlantic	42 ships	7%
Indian Ocean/Red Sea	40 ships	6%
Totals	590 ships	100%

Table 2
Ships Lost and Damaged by Year, 1941-1945[11]

September 1939 - 7 December 1941	6 ships	1%
December 7 - 31 December 1941	14 ships	2%
1942	373 ships	47%
1943	204 ships	26%
1944	130 ships	16%
1945 (all 12 months)	68 ships	7%
Totals	795 ships	99%

Table 3
Ship Losses by Type During World War II[12]

Pre-WWI and ships of miscellaneous origin	67 ships	11%
WWI Emergency Fleet types	306 ships	49%
Interwar construction, 1923 - 1936	18 ships	3%
USMC standard types, 1937 - 1942	34 ships	5%
Emergency types, 1941 - 1945	180 ships	29%
USMC standard types, 1942 - 1945	19 ships	3%
Totals	624 ships	100%

---

[10] Ibid., chapter 1, section 1. Percentage calculations are the author's. The Normandy breakwater ships are not included in this table, nor are seven others for which Moore does not supply data.

[11] Ibid., 543-546. All ships that Moore lists are included here.

[12] Ibid. Moore lists the builder and launch date of each ship cited in *A Careless Word*. The Normandy ships are included here, but damaged ships are not included, nor are ships for which Moore could find no data. From this data the table is compiled. The prominence of Emergency Fleet ships among the World War II casualties was a revelation to this author.

6 percent loss rate for the Liberties. The World War I era ships also suffered a higher loss rate of personnel when they were sunk because their lifesaving equipment was obsolete and often in poor condition, especially in 1942. Many of these "rustbuckets" were still operating in 1945 but were scrapped *en masse* soon after hostilities ended.[13]

Another area of interest is the number of ships damaged by enemy action. Moore lists a total of 130 American flag merchant ships that were damaged in some way during the hostilities. Comparing ships sunk to ships damaged yields a ratio of 589:130 or 4.5:1. This ratio is quite high by naval standards and indicates a much lower survivability rate for merchant vessels once hits have been scored on them. Lack of compartmentalization, smaller crews, absence of any real damage control doctrine, and the tendency of merchant marine crews to begin abandoning stricken ships almost immediately, all contributed to this ratio.

If we regard this subset of 130 damaged ships as a random sample of attacks launched by all Axis forces on American merchantmen, we can postulate that German submarines were the most deadly aggressors, followed by German mines, Japanese aircraft, German aircraft, Japanese submarines, and German shellfire. Losses inflicted by Italian forces and surface raiders were negligible[14] (See table 4 on page 266).

Additional information comes from an analysis of war losses due to marine casualties. These were vessels lost to the normal hazards of the sea and, perhaps, to some abnormal hazards imposed by wartime conditions but not directly related to enemy action. American merchant ships were obliged to run without showing normal running and range lights, to ship large numbers of green hands, to cope with blacked-out aids to navigation, and to make do with very hastily trained junior officers, some of them sailing on "emergency" tickets. Also, there was greater potential for collision because of the need to sail in convoy, and many ships were sent to sea overloaded and in doubtful condition, especially early in the war. Structural faults in some of the newly built ships were also a factor.

With so many adverse conditions to cope with, the actual number of marine casualties was surprisingly low. Approximately eighty-two ships, or 1.4 percent of those operated, became total constructive losses between

---

[13] See Glover, *Army Ships and Watercraft,* 66. This author recalls seeing a few "Laker" class freighters serving with the Olsen Lines as lumber carriers on the West Coast in the 1950s as well as a few "Arrow" class tankers carting oil for Texaco.

[14] See Moore, *A Careless Word,* chapter 1, section 2. In addition, Glover lists 171 Army Transportation Service vessels sunk along with the cause of their loss in *Army Ships and Watercraft,* 61-64. The results are very similar. Forty-four percent were lost to submarines, 18 percent to air attack and 8 percent to mines. One ship was captured, two sunk by gunfire, three by surface raiders, and one by a torpedo boat.

1942 and 1945. Of course, there were many other ships that were damaged as a result of accidental mishaps but were later salvaged and returned to service. Even vessels with catastrophic structural failures sometimes survived. Table 5 on page 266 lists the numbers lost to each major hazard.

Although they represent only a small percentage of marine casualties, the ships that were lost to structural failure gave rise to many rumors which eventually led to a full-scale congressional investigation. The Liberty ships took the brunt of criticism, although out of the huge number built, only six are known to have been lost this way.[15] Contrary to popular belief, Liberty ships were not designed to have a temporary or limited lifespan. They had all the structural components of a normal ship of their size and intended use, and the materials that went into their construction were of the customary dimensions and quality. They were, of course, built quickly, making extensive use of welding and prefabrication. In adapting the original British design for American use, Gibbs and Cox, the naval architects hired by the Maritime Commission, cut away the sheer strake to accommodate a different type of gangway, thus unwittingly creating a weak spot almost exactly amidships. Poor quality welding, done in some shipyards that paid their personnel on a piecework basis, further exacerbated the problem. Once the problems were recognized, however, corrective measures were taken and no further losses of Liberty ships due to structural failure were reported.[16]

In fact, the greatest cause of accidental loss among Liberty ships was being driven ashore in bad weather, a problem that also afflicted the Emergency Fleet ships. Both types of vessels were low-powered for their displacement, and the combination of a severe gale catching one of them with a lee shore in the offing and inexperienced officers on the bridge proved fatal on too many occasions. Inexperience may also have contributed to some of the collisions, along with crowded harbors, the need to run without lights, the difficulties of keeping station in convoys, and the general urgency of wartime operations. Given all of the difficulties that

---

[15] These were the *J. L. M. Curry, John P. Gaines, Joseph Smith, Samuel Dexter, Thomas Hooker,* and *Joel R. Poinsett.* Of course, other Liberties came close to foundering due to serious hull fractures but made port after emergency repairs had been performed by the crew. A statistical study carried out in 1944 as part of a Congressional investigation indicated that 12.5 percent of Liberties operated during 1942 and 1943 proved to have defective welding. Ten percent developed cracks, and one ship in thirty suffered a major fracture. See L. A. Sawyer and W. H. Mitchell, *The Liberty Ships* (Newton Abbot, England: David and Charles, 1970), 19.

[16] See Frederic C. Lane, *Ships for Victory* (Baltimore: The Johns Hopkins University Press, 1951), 588, and Sawyer and Mitchell, *The Liberty Ships,* 19-20.

Table 4
Causes of Merchant Ship Damage, 1941 - 1945

Torpedoed by submarines:	German	51 ships	38%
	Japanese	11 ships	8%
	Italian	0 ships	0%
Torpedoed by aircraft:	German	2 ships	1.5%
	Japanese	3 ships	2%
	Italian	0 ships	0%
Bombed by aircraft:	German	12 ships	9%
	Japanese	9 ships	7%
	Italian	0 ships	0%
Crashed by aircraft:	Japanese only	14 ships	11%
Shelled by submarine:	German only	2 ships	1.5%
Shelled (shore batteries):	German only	6 ships	4%
Mined, European waters		18 ships	14%
Mined, Pacific waters		2 ships	1.5%
Totals		130 ships	97.5%

Table 5
Non-combat Marine Casualties in World War II[17]

Grounding, stranding, and driven ashore	37 ships	45%
Collisions with other ships	26 ships	32%
Structural failures	8 ships	10%
Fire and explosion	6 ships	7%
Foundered in storms	5 ships	6%
Totals	82 ships	100%

---

[17] These figures derive from Moore, *A Careless Word*, chapter 1, section 2 and are compiled from statistics related to all ships lost. The subset of 1,706 oceangoing ships operating under Army Transportation Service orders seemed to suffer much higher marine casualties. Forty were lost, or 2.3 percent. Causes were: grounding, 21 ships (52 percent); collision, 9 ships (23 percent); fire/explosion, 6 ships (15 percent); broke up, 2 ships (5 percent); foundered, 2 ships (5 percent). See Glover, *Army Ships and Watercraft*, 61-65.

had to be overcome, it seems that the Merchant Marine operated with reasonable safety and competence throughout the war years.

In accounting for ship losses sustained by the Merchant Marine, one further category is of interest. A total of thirty-five ships went missing with all hands in such a way that their fate could not be accounted for during the war. Virtually all of these vessels had been sailing alone or straggling from convoys when they were lost. An analysis of Axis records after the end of hostilities revealed that all of them had been sunk by German or Japanese submarines or surface raiders. Apparently there were no wartime ship losses for which we cannot now account.[18]

Mine warfare had played a significant part in World War II, and not all of the devices that were planted could be recovered immediately. Twelve ships were lost and eight damaged by mines after the war ended. All but one of these losses occurred in European waters. The last ship to be a casualty of mine warfare was the *St. Lawrence Victory*, damaged by a mine in the Adriatic in 1947. This is doubly ironic because the very first American merchant ship to be lost in the war, the *City of Rayville*, had struck a mine seven years earlier off the south coast of Australia.

The losses in ships and men sustained by the American Merchant Marine and its counterpart, the Army Transportation Service, were grave and painful to bear, but they need to be put in perspective in order to achieve an objective understanding of their significance. The loss of 817 American merchant ships and 6,103 American merchant seamen contrasts with the British merchant navy's sacrifice of 2,177 ships and 30,132 seamen. British loss of life per sinking was higher as well, averaging 26 percent of a typical crew as opposed to the American 20 percent.[19] Merchant seamen of the Axis nations were even more severely tested. The Japanese merchant marine was all but wiped out, its personnel suffering 79 percent fatal casualties.[20] No figures have yet been developed to quantify the losses of the Norwegian, Danish, Dutch, and Belgian merchant marines, contingents of which served on both sides, but it is probable that they were even heavier than the British casualties.

Compared with these fleets, the American Merchant Marine actually got off rather lightly. Wartime rumors to the contrary, few ships were lost

---

[18] Moore has accounted for all the missing ships in *A Careless Word*, presumably utilizing data furnished in Jürgen Rohwer, *Axis Submarine Successes, 1939-1945* (Annapolis, MD: Naval Institute Press, 1983), esp. Appendix D. Rohwer describes the Axis and Allied records he consulted to compile his data on pp. ix-xiv.

[19] These figures are derived from Admiralty Trade Division Records and are cited in Hughes and Costello, *Battle of the Atlantic*, 304.

[20] Y. Horie, "The Failure of the Japanese Convoy Escort," United States Naval Institute *Proceedings* 82, no. 10 (October 1956): 1073-1081.

TOP: Profile of a Liberty ship underway. Armament consisted of one gun aft and a small machine gun forward. Photo courtesy of the U.S. Coast Guard. BOTTOM: Shipbuilding went on around the clock as shown here at a Baltimore yard. Assembly line methods and a heavy reliance on welding accelerated construction. Photo courtesy of the Library of Congress.

TOP: The Liberty ship *John Woolman* slides down the ways in April 1943. She was damaged by a mine in the English Channel in May 1945. Photo courtesy of the Library of Congress. BOTTOM: The freighter *Robin Goodfellow* was torpedoed in the South Atlantic on 25 July 1944 by *U 862*. Photo courtesy of the Delaware Division of Historical and Cultural Affairs.

because of structural failure, and there is no record of any ordinary trade convoy ever being completely wiped out.[21] Of the infamous Arctic convoys, the majority experienced light to moderate losses, and some had no casualties at all. PQ 17's heavy losses were due to exceptional circumstances rather than the inherent danger of the run.[22]

It is now nearly fifty years since these casualties were sustained. The time has come for wartime rumors and colorful memories to be checked against the actual record so that what really happened can be known and understood with clarity and accuracy.

---

[21] The closest instance was Convoy TM-1, a tanker convoy running from Trinidad to Gibraltar in January 1943. It lost seven out of nine ships. See John W. Waters, Jr., *Bloody Winter*, rev. ed. (Annapolis, MD: Naval Institute Press, 1984), 121.

[22] The controversy surrounding PQ 17 will probably never be laid to rest. It was the only Arctic convoy ever deliberately scattered. Contrary to wartime legend, its escort was not afraid of the *Tripitz* but rather of the German *Luftwaffe*. The British Admiralty, cognizant of the lesson learned when the *Prince of Wales* and *Repulse* were sunk, did not want to operate capital ships against the *Tripitz* without adequate air cover. They had hoped to grapple with the *Tripitz* before the convoy got beyond the range of British aircraft, but when it sailed into the region of North Cape that was no longer possible, and the heavy units withdrew. The convoy was then scattered and the individual ships decimated by U-boats and aircraft. Had the convoy been held together it probably would have been able to fight off the *Luftwaffe* much more effectively and would have suffered a more normal casualty rate.

Appendix

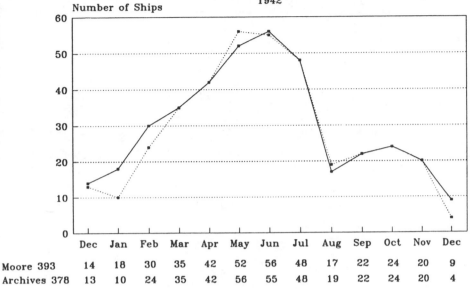

Ships Lost and Damaged
1942

Number of Ships

	Dec	Jan	Feb	Mar	Apr	May	Jun	Jul	Aug	Sep	Oct	Nov	Dec
Moore 393	14	18	30	35	42	52	56	48	17	22	24	20	9
Archives 378	13	10	24	35	42	56	55	48	19	22	24	20	4

■— Moore 393   ▪▪▪■▪▪▪ Archives 378

Both totals include six ships sunk prior to December 1941.

Ships Lost and Damaged
1943

Number of Ships

	Dec	Jan	Feb	Mar	Apr	May	Jun	Jul	Aug	Sep	Oct	Nov	Dec
Moore 204	9	22	21	37	13	18	11	22	10	14	14	6	16
Archives 193	4	18	19	32	13	17	8	24	14	15	10	5	18

●— Moore 204   ▪▪▪■▪▪▪ Archives 193

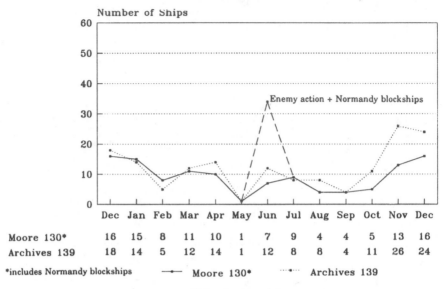

Ships Lost and Damaged
1944

Number of Ships

	Dec	Jan	Feb	Mar	Apr	May	Jun	Jul	Aug	Sep	Oct	Nov	Dec
Moore 130*	16	15	8	11	10	1	7	9	4	4	5	13	16
Archives 139	18	14	5	12	14	1	12	8	8	4	11	26	24

includes Normandy blockships   —•— Moore 130   ····•···· Archives 139

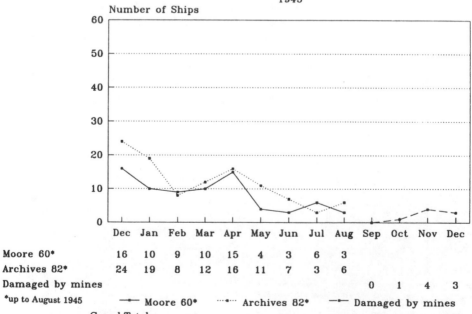

Ships Lost and Damaged
1945

Number of Ships

	Dec	Jan	Feb	Mar	Apr	May	Jun	Jul	Aug	Sep	Oct	Nov	Dec
Moore 60*	16	10	9	10	15	4	3	6	3				
Archives 82*	24	19	8	12	16	11	7	3	6				
Damaged by mines										0	1	4	3

up to August 1945   —•— Moore 60   ····•···· Archives 82*   —•— Damaged by mines

Grand Totals:
Moore: 787 - 27 = 760
Archives: 792, not including Normandy blockships, which would bring total to 819.

17

The Merchant Marine Cadet Corps

Thomas A. King

In a unique and little-known aspect of World War II, well over 10,000 young Americans participated in combat while they still were undergraduates in the U.S. Merchant Marine Cadet Corps. This program became the basis of one of the five U.S. service academies. The U.S. Merchant Marine Academy continues today, as part of its core program, the assignment of its undergraduates to working merchant ships both in peace and in war.

As one consequence of the Corps of Cadets wartime service, the Merchant Marine Academy is only one of the military academies authorized a Regimental Battle Standard. The World War II casualties, numbering 142, are commemorated upon that standard.

A war memorial prominently located upon the campus of the Merchant Marine Academy at Kings Point, New York, lists each of the 142 by name, together with those of sixty-eight young graduates who were also casualties of World War II. The sixty-eight lost their lives during what, in most cases, would have been their planned four-year undergraduate program. The desperate need for shipboard manpower resulted in their graduation and assignment to sea duty as licensed officers in as little as eighteen months.

Besides the casualties, hundreds of battle reports required from those of the Cadet Corps who survived enemy action graphically attest to the fact that torpedoing, bombings, shell fire, and harrowing days on a raft or in a lifeboat had become a very real part of an undergraduate's educational program. This was so because even in war there was a required mix of practical sea duty with the more routine, shoreside classroom lectures in an academic setting.

When the attack on Pearl Harbor took place on 7 December 1941, the federally-sponsored Merchant Marine Cadet Corps had only existed for three years and was even younger in terms of its substantive development. On 15 March 1938, President Franklin Roosevelt signed General Order #23 creating the U.S. Maritime Commission, which was initially chaired by Joseph P. Kennedy. The order directed the Commission, among other things, to establish and assume jurisdiction of a new, federal cadet training effort for the nation's merchant marine. Existing training systems were unable to meet the foreseen requirements. Over the previous four or more decades, the training had been suspect in quality and was projected as inadequate in terms of capacity. The goal of the new effort was a trained and efficient citizen manpower pool which could serve a merchant marine capable of the carriage of a substantial portion of peacetime foreign commerce, as well as one that could serve as a fourth arm of defense in time of military emergency.

Cadet training was a prime source of merchant marine officers up until that time, and included individual state-sponsored schoolships (one of which dated back to the early nineteenth century) as well as cadet billets on board merchant ships which carried U.S. mail. In addition, shipping companies on their own had employed cadets with the expectation that, when trained and qualified, those young mariners would replenish the company's ranks of licensed personnel.

The U.S. Merchant Marine Cadet Corps was considered in that context to be a necessary new effort as America moved forward in the rebuilding of its maritime capabilities in the face of a deteriorating world situation. It is worth noting that the authorizing date for the Cadet Corps was only four days before Nazi Germany's invasion of Austria on 19 March 1938. A chain of events had commenced which assuredly led to World War II. Imperial Japan already had a series of conquests to its credit on the China mainland. Understandably, a song composed for the Academy included the characterization "our strifeborn Alma Mater."

The first national competitive examination for Cadet Corps applicants was held across the country on 17 April 1939. Out of 450 applicants, 166 cadets were chosen. They joined the ranks of the small Cadet Corps that had already been established through absorption of a limited number of existing industry trainees. Also absorbed were a number of young graduates of state-sponsored schools who could not immediately be employed but whom the government realized would be sorely needed as new ship construction entered service. The latter were given Cadet Officer status and a stipend, thus encouraging them with their new licenses to "stay with it." The wisdom of that policy was soon apparent, as the thin oversupply of personnel that existed before Pearl Harbor rapidly changed after the U.S. entered World War II into a huge manpower shortage.

The strength of the embryonic Cadet Corps on 15 June 1939 was 266. The authorized strength was 400. These numbers were considered adequate at that time for the licensed officer needs of the existing merchant fleet and the 150 new ships under construction. The original planning for improved officer training contemplated a gradual build-up, but the international events of the late 1930s and the early 1940s altered those plans. As late as 1941, however, the Corps had no permanent home base ashore. While the visionary Rear Admiral Richard R. McNulty planned an Academy homeport, the four year program was then heavily skewed towards shipboard service with practical assignments and correspondence courses. A total of twelve months of the planned four years (but not all consecutively), were to be spent in classrooms and laboratories rented from existing institutions.

However, rapidly developing world events in 1941 and a significant acceleration in the build-up of the U.S. merchant marine stimulated an intense search for a permanent shore base for the expanding Cadet Corps. The leisurely development, including non-proprietary shore facilities, could not continue. The site selected for the permanent campus of the U.S. Merchant Marine Academy was Kings Point, New York. The president approved acquisition of the multiple private estates involved on 4 March 1942, but the Corps had already begun to move to the site some three months earlier. As Brad Mitchell, author of the history of the early Corps and Academy put it, with the acquisition of that campus, "new curricula, new disciplines and a new tempo of life were being forged. The long planned United States Merchant Marine Academy was at last in being."

In addition to Kings Point, the Corps acquired regional wartime sites on the Gulf and Pacific coasts. Pass Christian, Mississippi and San Mateo, California, along with other sites, filled the expanded wartime need for dispersed induction and preliminary training. The desired sequence was shipboard assignment followed by completion of training at Kings Point, but in the hectic expansion that followed Pearl Harbor, some members of the Cadet Corps actually completed their programs without once setting foot on the Kings Point campus.

Just how rapid that growth (and then contraction) became can be illustrated by the 1 January total on-board strength of the Cadet Corps before, during, and after the war:

1938 - 99	1943 - 4,658
1939 - 187	1944 - 7,148
1940 - 282	1945 - 4,912
1941 - 425	1946 - 3,746
1942 - 461	

During that peak year of 1944, 2,668 cadets were at the Academy; 3,350 were serving on board armed merchant ships, and 1,130 were at regional schools. This 1944 Corps dispersal illustrates the distinction between the program concept at USMMA and that of its fellow service academies. "Cooperative education," or a strongly practical career exposure, was a dominant component of the USMMA experience. Even today, two members of the Corps (now Regiment of Midshipmen) serve on a typical commercial freighter, tanker, or containership, one as a deck major and the other as an engineering major. This integral part of the fifty-year-old program has prevailed during war and peace as well as during the transition from a war-shortened trade school approach to a highly competitive and accredited four-year college.

World War II did, however, shorten the course for a substantial number of the graduates. Global logistical requirements drove the shipbuilding program, and that in turn defined manpower needs. The Cadet Corps had to abandon all pretense of a fully rounded education as the program was reduced in stages. Briefly, with brand new ships urgently in need of licensed officers, the War Shipping Administration and the U.S. Coast Guard, as the licensing agency, collaborated to the extent that by mid-1942 Cadet Corps members found themselves at sea as third mates or third assistant engineers in as little as sixteen months after their date of enrollment. Generally, those sixteen months included ten months at sea. Shipboard assignments were, in concept, learning experiences with a mixture of supervised, hands-on tasks and not less than four hours daily of study on academic projects. In fact, Cadets often became fully engaged, valued crew members on armed merchant ships sailing both in convoy and independently. With the depletion of the licensed complement which sometimes occurred due to casualty, illness, or other factors, cadets not infrequently found themselves holding down shipboard billets nominally requiring a license.

In light of the Cadet Corps' exposure to enemy action during the war, it is not surprising that the Corps sustained casualties. The story of the U.S. Merchant Marine Cadet Corps and conflict at sea, however, even pre-dates Pearl Harbor. In October 1939, two Cadet officers assigned to the American merchant ship *City of Flint* were taken prisoner along with their ship and shipmates by the German pocket battleship *Deutschland* in spite of the U.S. Neutrality Act. Subsequently released, the ship and crew returned safely to an American port. Those members of the Cadet Corps had experienced a comparatively mild preview, two years before Pearl Harbor, of the forthcoming Battle of the Atlantic.

The American *City of Rayville* provided the next preview of events to come for the Cadet Corps. In November of 1940 this ship, whose complement included two Cadet Corps members, struck a German mine off the coast of Australia. The sole fatality, three months before Pearl Harbor, was the third assistant engineer who drowned while abandoning the sinking ship.

The Cadet Corps' good luck held, in terms of fatalities, throughout the months of the Neutrality Act and even though the January and February following Pearl Harbor. This is surprising in retrospect, since the commander of the German submarine fleet, Admiral Karl Dönitz, triggered off the hammer blows of Operation *Drumbeat* in mid-January of 1942, and the tragic devastation and destruction of American and Allied shipping along the U.S. Atlantic coast soon followed. The Corps was well exposed.

Its luck ran out, however, on 19 March 1942 when the U.S. freighter *Liberator*, operated by Lykes Brothers Steamship Company for the government, met a German submarine off the North Carolina coast. Cadet Howard P. Conway and four shipmates lost their lives when a torpedo struck the ship on her port side and exploded into the engine room. Conway was the Corps' first World War II battle casualty, number one in the tragic count that reached the 142 now commemorated on the Battle Standard.

While the young members of the Cadet Corps knew little about 1942's Operation *Drumbeat* and the enemy's carefully planned commitment to strike America a staggering blow along its own shores, they quickly became aware that their chosen profession entailed a huge risk. Nevertheless, they continued to sail in growing numbers on board unarmed merchant ships during the first few months of 1942 and in the increasing fleet of armed merchantmen. The Corps was a certain participant in the American and Allied disaster at sea that occurred during the first half of 1942.

The U.S. Navy was not prepared to deal effectively with the German submarine offensive in the Atlantic during that period. A contemporary of Admiral Ernest J. King expressed relief that, with the mission of CinCLant in King's hands, another Pearl Harbor would not occur. But as 1942 progressed, another Pearl Harbor did take place. The destruction of merchant shipping along the brightly illuminated Atlantic coastline became a "turkey shoot" for the merchant mariners who sailed those ships. Authorities continued to permit coastal shipping to be silhouetted targets for enemy submarines. Even major navigational lights burned brightly, permitting the enemy to navigate accurately and position themselves for the kill. By late February 1942, "sixty-two ships had been lost in waters closely abutting the U.S. and Canadian shorelines. . . . In March a total of seventy-nine Allied and neutral vessels would be sunk worldwide; of that number seventy-four went down in the Atlantic"[1]

With explosions, fires, and sinkings visible to the public from ashore, the administration and the navy had not only a public morale problem but also were faced with the fact that the enemy was close to interdicting the Atlantic supply line and threatening U.S. ability to support the Allies as well as prosecute the war. For months it appeared that the only U.S. response was to strive to build more merchant ships than the enemy could sink, and this effort was successful. American shipyards rapidly moved into high gear, and sinkings by enemy submarines could not keep pace with launchings. Furthermore, during the second half of 1942, the navy's efforts were more successful as well and the U.S. had a more acceptable response to the enemy than accelerated new launchings.

This was reality in 1942, the world within which the fledgling Cadet Corps members and their fellow merchant mariners existed. There were eighteen American sinkings in January, thirty in February, thirty-five in March, forty-two in April, ninety-four in May, fifty-six in June, and forty-eight in July, but August saw seventeen losses. The high in 1943 was thirty-seven in March. December proved high with sixteen in 1944 and April with fifteen in 1945. All told, over 700 American merchant ships were lost in World War II and over 6,600 merchant mariners lost their lives.[2]

The American World War II shipbuilding effort was magnificent, and it swelled the number of merchant ships flying the Stars and Stripes to over 5,000. Those ships became a formidable, globe-spanning logistical tool; without them total victory could not have been achieved. The U.S. Merchant Marine Cadet Corps also expanded at an equally impressive pace, first to overcome the losses by enemy action but subsequently to meet the demands of the shipbuilding program.

The wartime service of the Cadet Corps is dramatically revealed in two sources: the required combat reports filed by Cadets after they returned from a voyage which included enemy action (often including loss of their ship), and the growing number of fatalities now commemorated by their inclusion in the Battle Standard's "142". Almost one-third of the World War II related Corps fatalities were recorded in 1942 and another 50 percent of the war's final casualty total for Cadets occurred in 1943, when a greatly expanded Corps was exposed to enemy action.

---

[1] Michael Gannon, *Operation Drumbeat: The Dramatic True Story of Germany's First U-Boat Attacks Along the American Coast in World War II* (New York: Harper & Row Publishers, 1990), 266.

[2] See James E. Valle, "United States Merchant Marine Casualties," *supra*, 259 and tables on 263 and 266.

One of those early 1942 fatalities was particularly inspiring and deserving of the posthumus recognition represented by the Corps' second, out of a total of five, Distinguished Service Medals. His fatality also prompted the naming of a major campus building. The Liberty ship *Stephen Hopkins*, armed but sailing alone westbound in the South Atlantic, encountered the German surface raider *Stier* accompanied by its supply ship *Tannenfels*. Author Brad Mitchell effectively describes the engagement:

> Less evenly matched adversaries could hardly be found; yet when *Stier* opened fire she launched what was an anachronism in twentieth-century naval war, an individual ship-to-ship gun duel to the death.
>
> Predictably, *Stephen Hopkins* was smashed and sinking in twenty minutes. But astonishingly, the raider too was mortally wounded.[3]

Mitchell uses the word "astonishingly" because *Hopkins* fought with a single four-inch stern gun, two 37-millimeter bow guns, and four .50-caliber and two .30-caliber machine guns. All but the four-inch gun were primarily designed for anti-aircraft defense. The *Stier* weighed in with a destroyer-like armament of six 5.9-inch guns, two torpedo tubes, and an array of machine guns. The *Tannenfels* was more lightly armed.

The *Hopkins* armament, manned by a combination of Naval Armed Guard and merchant crew ably assisted by the shipmaster's maneuvers, fought the enemy from maximum range down to where both sides utilized their machine guns. With the *Hopkins* afire, mortally wounded and immobilized by multiple engine room direct hits, and sinking by the stern, the shipmaster ordered abandon ship. The eighteen-year-old engine Cadet Edwin J. O'Hara, finding the naval gunners and their commanding officer dead, dying, or having followed the general abandonment order, singlehandedly pumped out the five remaining four-inch shells in the ready box, scoring hits on both of the enemy ships. O'Hara was killed in the close-in return fire, but the *Stier*, with four ships and 29,000 tons of Allied shipping to her credit on its cruise so far, had met her match. She sank after a series of explosions caused by the *Hopkins* fire. The deck Cadet, Arthur R. Chamberlin Jr., also lost his life in the engagement which later resulted in the *Hopkins*'s designation as a "Gallant Ship." After a harrowing month in an open lifeboat, during which four of the original survivors perished, fifteen of the *Hopkins* combined crew of fifty-five

---

[3] C. Bradford Mitchell, *We'll Deliver* (Kings Point, NY: USMMA Alumni Association, 1977), 115.

merchant mariners and naval armed guard made landfall on the Brazilian coast. The other forty were casualties.

While neither of the *Hopkins's* two cadets survived that ship's enemy action, many other cadets lived to file their reports of such encounters. No less than 450 cadets turned in reports of attacks. Those reports covered enemy action involving 250 ships of which 220 were lost.[4] They read today like Hollywood fiction, but they are fact.

Torpedoings, bombings, and shell fire were a constant and often-experienced threat for the members of the Cadet Corps on their anything-but-routine, professional sea training assignments during World War II. The dangers of the frigid run to Murmansk (including the devastated Convoy PQ 17, abandoned by its naval escort) and the struggle to reinforce and save Malta all became part of the Corps' training experiences. Cadets who were still expected to complete their shipboard training and accomplish their lesson plans had, unique to the academic world, legitimate excuses for failure to turn in required assignments on time.

Cadet Raymond P. Holubowicz had one of the most irrefutable excuses to offer as to why he had not completed his assigned studies on time. He was assigned in May of 1942 to the freighter *Syros*, which joined Murmansk-bound convoy PQ 16.[5] On 26 May the ship was torpedoed in the Barents Sea. Holubowicz survived and was taken to Murmansk. He joined the westbound *Hybert* of Convoy QP 13 and arrived in the shambles of eastbound PQ 17 in time to be sunk a second time, this time by mines. Due to poor weather, the Convoy Escort Commander had failed to obtain a good position fix. Rescued and repatriated, Holubowicz headed back to Murmansk on the Liberty ship *J.L.M. Curry* with Convoy PQ 18 in September of 1942. Having made port after heavy opposition and wintering in Murmansk, the *Curry* headed home in March of 1943 and, weakened by further enemy action, foundered in heavy seas off Iceland.[6] Halubowicz gained the dubious distinction of a third ship loss in one round trip. Fortunately he survived once more. The following year Cadet Holubowicz was awarded the medal for Distinction in Action by the Soviet government. In 1977 the U.S. government, over three decades late, presented former Cadet Holubowicz its decorations.

All members of the Corps of Cadet were also midshipmen in the United States Naval Reserve. This latter status translated into a most

---

    [4] Ibid., 111.
    [5] Captain Arthur Moore, *A Careless Word. . . A Needless Sinking* (Farmington, ME: Knowlton and McLeary Company, 1983), 274.
    [6] Mitchell, *We'll Deliver*, 114.

unique situation with respect to some fifty-five members of the Corps. Early in 1942 the navy, desperate for manpower with any significant shipboard skills, discovered within its reserve ranks the midshipmen (inactive) who were members of the U.S. Merchant Marine Cadet Corps. Their shipboard training service aboard merchant ships, particularly on the engineering side, appeared most attractive in a frantic search to bridge the gap between current navy shipboard manning priorities and the output of existing and expanding navy training programs. As one of the fifty-five midshipmen activated in early 1942, Russell H. Holm speculated he was one of the first midshipmen to be regularly assigned to a combat ship since the founding of the Naval Academy in the nineteenth century. When Holm reported aboard the USS *Heywood* (APA5), the commanding and executive officers felt compelled to break out navy regulations to determine where a midshipman fitted into the roster of a twentieth-century combat ship. According to Holm the answer was "with but after Chief Warrant officers."[7]

There were a multitude of heroic actions and distinguished service by American forces during World War II, and the contributions of members of the Army, Navy, Marines, and Coast Guard are well-known. But the contributions and sacrifices of the U.S. Merchant Marine Cadet Corps, like those of their merchant marine shipmates, were rarely recognized as being of equal significance. It was not until 1988 that by congressional action the U.S. government granted participating merchant mariners, including Cadet Corps members, status as veterans of World War II. Many who were directly involved at the time did understand, however, that an awful toll was exacted from those who participated in a unique program. A war memorial at the U.S. Merchant Marine Academy contains the following inscription:

> To Commemorate Cadet Midshipmen and Graduates
> of the U.S. Merchant Marine Academy
> Lost in World War II

Cast in bronze are 210 names.

---

[7] Russell H. Holm, conversation with author, 1991.

18

Port in a Storm: The Port of New York in World War II

Joseph F. Meany, Jr.

While the origins and growth of the Port of New York have been the subjects of a number of studies,[1] historians have neglected its period of apogee from 1942-1945. The preeminence of the Port of New York[2] during that period stemmed from a combination of pre-existing factors. These include the geography of the harbor, the economic, industrial, and educational resources of the port, and the resources of the New York metropolis itself.

First was the remarkable geographic situation of New York harbor. As *Life* magazine reminded its readers in November 1944: "With its seven bays, four river mouths, [and] four estuaries, it is by far the world's best and biggest natural harbor and most of the world's major ports could easily be tucked into it."[3] The harbor comprised more than 430 square miles of water, including the 122 square mile expanse of the Lower Bay,

---

[1] See, for example, Robert Albion, *The Rise of New York Port, 1815-1860*, 3d ed. (New York: Charles Scribner's Sons, 1970); Richard C. McKay, *South Street: A Maritime History of New York* (New York: Haskell House Publishers Ltd., 1971); James Morris, *The Great Port: A Passage through New York* (New York: Harcourt, Brace and World, Inc., 1969); and Writers' Program of the Works Projects Administration for New York City, comp., *A Maritime History of New York* (New York: Haskell House Publishers Ltd., 1973).

[2] U.S. Navy, Third Naval District, *Historical Summary of the Third Naval District*, 5 vols., *Unpublished Histories of U.S. Naval Administration in World War II*, vol.2 (Navy Department Library, Naval Historical Center, Washington Navy Yard, Washington, D.C.), 1-2.

[3] Julien Binford, "War is Fed Through the World's Biggest and Busiest Harbor," *Life*, 20 November 1944, 55.

and above the Narrows, the deep, protected waters of the Upper Bay.[4] From the north, the Hudson River linked the harbor with the continental interior, channeling the produce and products of the upper midwest to New York via the Great Lakes and the New York State Barge Canal. To the east, Long Island Sound provided an avenue from the harbor to coastal New England and the Atlantic beyond.

By 1942, the Army Corps of Engineers had delineated six hundred individual ship anchorages able to accommodate ocean-going vessels.[5] On the peak day in 1943, there were a total of 543 merchant vessels at anchor in New York harbor, a figure very close to maximum capacity.[6]

Throughout the war, entrance and egress were monitored by Harbor Entrance Control Posts (HECPs), joint service activities, located at Fort Wadsworth on the Staten Island shore of the Narrows and Fort Schuyler on the Bronx shore of Long Island Sound. In 1943, advance posts were established at Fort Hancock on Sandy Hook, Fort Tilden on Rockaway Point, and at Fort H.G. Wright on Fisher's Island in Long Island Sound.[7]

Harbor entrance control presented a complex problem. The primary requirement was an immediate, accurate identification of all in-bound vessels. This determination had to be made well to seaward of the Ambrose Channel. It was critical that no hostile vessel be allowed to enter the main ship channel, which at the outer harbor entrance was only two thousand feet wide and forty feet in depth. Sea mines or block ships sunk in this restricted area might result in the closure of the Port of New

---

[4] Numerous descriptions of the harbor and its component parts have been written, ranging from the scientific to the poetic, from Robert Juet's *Journal* of Henry Hudson's second voyage,in 1609 to Jan Morris's retrospective *Manhattan '45* (New York: Oxford University Press, 1987).

[5] U.S. Army, Corps of Engineers, Board of Engineers for Rivers and Harbors, *Port and Terminal Facilities at the Port of New York*, part 3; *Port Facilities Maps* (Washington, D.C.: U.S. Government Printing Office, 1942). See also U.S. Coast and Geodetic Survey Charts, United States - East Coast, No. 286, New York - New Jersey: Raritan Bay; No. 369, New York Harbor: Gravesend Bay; No. 541, New York Harbor: Upper Bay and Narrows; No. 715, New York Harbor: Liberty Anchorage, Upper Bay; No. 746, Hudson River: Days Point to Fort Washington Point; No. 747, Hudson River: Fort Washington Point to Yonkers; No. 748, Hudson River: Yonkers to Piermont.

[6] Jeannette Edwards Rattray, *Perils of the Port of New York: Maritime Disasters from Sandy Hook to Execution Rocks* (New York: Dodd, Mead and Company, 1973), 211.

[7] U.S. Navy, Third Naval District, *Historical Narrative, Harbor Entrance Control Post, New York Harbor* (hereafter *HECP*), *Unpublished Histories of U.S. Naval Administration in World War II* (Navy Department Library, Naval Historical Center, Washington D.C.), 566-567, 570. See also Frederick R. Black, *A History of Fort Wadsworth, New York Harbor: An Historic Resource Study*, Cultural Resource Management Study 7 (Boston, MA: North Atlantic Regional Office of the National Park Service, U.S. Department of the Interior, 1983).

York for months, an event with potentially disastrous consequences.[8] Despite the critical nature of the ID requirement, at the end of the war the navy estimated that the system was effective only 60 to 70 percent of the time.[9] The sheer volume of traffic strained the system. By the end of 1942, the HECPs were expected to monitor over nine hundred merchant ship arrivals per month, not including naval vessels, and an approximately equal number of clearances. These averages rose to 1,100 per month in 1943 and would peak at 1,200 per month in early 1944. The first six months of 1944 saw 7,121 arrivals and 7,238 clearances. During the build-up to D-day, convoys totalling as many as eighty to one hundred vessels departing in a single night were not uncommon.[10] During World War II the Port of New York saw a total of 1,462 convoy departures.[11]

Army six-inch coast defense batteries in Forts Hancock and Tilden were responsible for fire control of the Ambrose Channel. The primary alert battery at Fort Hancock remained on twenty-four-hour alert throughout the war and was, in theory, prepared to fire in fifteen seconds upon suspicious vessels or those violating harbor entrance procedures. They actually did fire "innumerable" "bring-to" shots across the bows of unidentified vessels which were required to halt for boarding and examination.[12] Fishing vessels, patrol craft, and coastwise traffic complicated problems of identification and control. "Bring-to" shots, fired at ranges of two to seven thousand yards, were often tricky when there might be fifty or more vessels in the vicinity of the ship in question. Conditions of reduced visibility further complicated the problems of identification and control, and it is remarkable that no casualties were caused by this type of "friendly fire."[13]

A secondary battery, located at Norton's Point on the tip of Coney Island, maintained a five-minute alert and was well placed to engage ships approaching the Narrows that might have successfully by-passed the outer harbor defenses, a fairly frequent occurrence.[14] In addition,

---

[8] *Historical Narrative, HECP,* 537.

[9] Ibid., 545.

[10] Ibid., 536-537, 588.

[11] Convoy departures from New York by year were as follows: 1941, 2 convoys of 13 ships; 1942, 346 convoys of 3,747 ships; 1943, 488 convoys of 7,039 ships; 1944, 439 convoys of 7,541 ships; 1945, 187 convoys of 3,119 ships for a total of 1,462 convoys of 21,459 ships. See chart of convoys departing New York by destination, year, and number of ships. U.S. Navy, Third Naval District, *Historical Summary,* vol. 5, microfiche 5.

[12] *Historical Narrative, HECP,* 538-539.

[13] Ibid., 554-555.

[14] Ibid., 555.

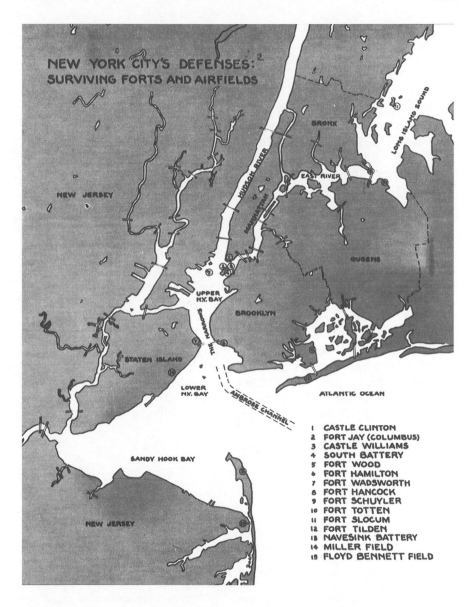

The system of defenses at the Port of New York was a primary reason for its prominence during World War II. From Russell S. Gilmore, *Guarding America's Front Door: Harbor Forts in the Defense of New York City* (Brooklyn, 1983). Courtesy of the Fort Hamilton Historical Society.

ninety millimeter anti-MTB batteries were located at the outer harbor fortifications, at the inner harbor fortifications, at Forts Wadsworth and Hamilton, and at Norton's Point. Theoretically, all maintained a condition of readiness, although after 1942 it proved increasingly more difficult to keep the gun crews on alert.[15]

The Upper Bay was also protected by an antisubmarine net and anti-motor torpedo boat boom across the Narrows. Strong currents of four knots or more swept through the Narrows, making passage of the net and boom a hazardous undertaking in the best of circumstances, complicated by the constant congestion of ship traffic through this natural bottleneck.[16] The numerous accidents, including multi-ship collisions involving considerable loss of life, have been ably compiled by Jeannette Edwards Rattray.[17]

In the event, the Port of New York was closed for only one forty-eight-hour period, 13-14 November 1942, after the discovery of sea mines some two miles southeast of Ambrose Light.[18] Of the ten mines laid by *U 608* on the night of 10-11 November 1942, five were swept and detonated between 13 and 21 November.[19] It was only with the end of the war and the capture of the records of U-boat Command that it was discovered that ten mines were laid. A search for the five remaining mines in May 1945 was unsuccessful. They have never been found.[20]

The need to ensure a smooth and uninterrupted traffic flow at the entrance to the Ambrose Channel was critical. Ships could not be allowed to congregate outside the harbor entrance where they would be easy prey for U-boats.[21] Responsibility for the actual boarding and examination of

---

[15] Ibid., 555.

[16] Ibid., 537-538.

[17] Rattray, *Perils of the Port of New York.*

[18] See Samuel Eliot Morison, *A History of United States Naval Operations in World War II,* vol. 1, *The Battle of the Atlantic, 1939-1943,* (Boston: Little, Brown, 1956), appendix 4, "Mine Fields Laid by U-Boats in Western Atlantic, 1942," 417.

[19] Schuyler M. Meyer Jr., "How We Closed the Port of New York," *Sea History* 44 (Summer 1987): 50-51. The mines were laid directly across the discontinued ship track from Europe. This route had been replaced in 1940 in order to place ships as early as possible over the "deep gorge" as protection from the danger of magnetic mines. Their location was thus an apparent failure of German intelligence. Had they been sewn across the active ship channel they would almost certainly have borne fruit. Letter of Schuyler M. Meyer Jr. to the author, dated 7 April 1992.

[20] Schuyler M. Meyer, Jr., who as a young ensign had swept the original five mines, was unaware in 1992 that a total of ten mines had been laid. Conversation with the author, 31 January 1992.

[21] This was especially important during the U-boat blitz of early 1942, when U-boats were known to loiter around harbor entrances on the east coast of the United States. If evidence of the danger was necessary, witness the massacre of transports outside

vessels was given to the Coast Guard Pilot Command, since pilots would be boarding vessels in any case in order to guide them into port.[22] The task fell to the 123 professional pilots licensed by New York and New Jersey to guide ships into and out of the Port of New York. They were organized into powerful guilds — the New York and New Jersey Sandy Hook Pilots Associations and the Hell Gate Pilots Association — that dated back to the age of sail.

Munitions convoys were often routed through the more protected waters of the East River, Hell Gate, and Long Island Sound, guided by the twenty-three members of the Hell Gate Pilots Association based on City Island in the Bronx.[23] The Coast Guard reserved its highest praise for this tiny band:

> Upon being militarized in the Temporary Reserve in December 1942, the Hell Gate pilots faced the greatest undertaking in their history. . . .
>
> Tugs and tows going up-river could not follow the rule of keeping to the right, for their tows would have ended up in the Brooklyn Navy Yard. Instead, a short distance before reaching Corlears Hook, they started pulling for the Manhattan shore, and on reaching the Hook, headed for the Brooklyn shore to even off. Aside from narrow, confined channels and treacherous currents and mid-stream rocky areas, there were 22 changes of course in the 16-mile run.
>
> Between 1 January 1942 and 31 May 1945, the Hell Gate pilots took 14,539 vessels through these waters without loss of a single ship.[24]

On their busiest day of the war, the Hell Gate pilots guided fifty-eight ships out into Long Island Sound.[25]

Inbound vessels found themselves in the busiest harbor in the world. At the peak of wartime effort, the Port of New York accommodated a daily average of over four hundred ships and averaged a ship clearance every fifteen minutes.[26]

Casablanca harbor following the *Torch* landings of 8 November 1942. Morison, *United States Naval Operations in World War II*, vol. 2, *Operations in North African Waters* 167-174, and appendix 1, "Allied Ships Sunk during Operation *Torch*," 281-282.

[22] Pilots boarded inbound merchant vessels carrying a secret identification signal that was to be immediately checked against a countersignal held by the master of the vessel. *Historical Narrative, HECP*, 560-561.

[23] Records of the Hell Gate Pilots Association are located in the City Island Historical Museum, New York, NY.

[24] "The Coast Guard at War," (Historical Section, Public Information Division, Headquarters, United States Coast Guard, 1 January 1948), 116.

[25] Rattray, *Perils of the Port of New York*, 212.

[26] Karl Drew Hartzell, *Empire State at War: World War II* (Albany, NY: New York State War Council, 1949), 326.

Maritime management of the port was vested in the office of the Port Director, New York, a naval function subordinate to Third Naval District.[27] The office became operational on 15 October 1939, when:

> On that day, Captain Frederick G. Reinicke, USN (Ret) reported for duty to the Commandant of the Third Naval District as Port Director. He established himself in a one room office at the Third Naval District Headquarters with a staff of one officer assistant and a secretary. On 8 May 1945, the day on which hostilities with Germany ceased, four floors of the Whitehall Building at 17 Battery Place were occupied by approximately 1200 Naval personnel who were actively engaged in managing the world's biggest marine traffic job.[28]

Once established, the office of the Port Director, New York experienced explosive growth as more diverse responsibilities were added to the office.

The second factor contributing to the preeminence of the Port of New York was the economically developed condition of the port itself. In reality eleven ports in one, the Port of New York boasted a developed shoreline of 650 miles comprising the waterfronts of Manhattan, Brooklyn, Staten Island, the Bronx, and Queens as well as the New Jersey shore from Perth Amboy to Elizabeth, Bayonne, Newark, Jersey City, Hoboken, and Weehawken.[29] The port included some 1,800 docks, piers, and wharves of every conceivable size, condition, and state of repair. Seven hundred and fifty were classified as "active," and two hundred were able to berth 425 oceangoing vessels simultaneously in addition to the four hundred able to anchor in the harbor. These docks and piers gave access to 1,100 warehouses containing some 41 million square feet of enclosed storage space.[30]

The Port of New York had thirty-nine active shipyards, not including the huge New York Naval Shipyard located on the Brooklyn side of the East River. These facilities included nine big-ship repair yards, thirty-six

---

[27] U.S. Navy, Third Naval District, *Historical Narrative of Port Director - New York . . . 15 October 1939 to 14 August 1945* (hereafter PDNY), District Historical Office Serial 121, *Unpublished Histories of U.S. Naval Administration in World War II* (Navy Department Library, Naval Historical Center, Washington Navy Yard, Washington, D.C.), 295.

[28] *Historical Narrative,* PDNY, 294.

[29] U.S. Army, Corps of Engineers, Board of Engineers for Rivers and Harbors, *Port and Terminal Facilities at the Port of New York,* Part 1, *General Report* (Washington, D.C.: U.S. Government Printing Office, 1942).

[30] U.S. Army, Corps of Engineers, Board of Engineers for Rivers and Harbors, *Port and Terminal Facilities at the Port of New York,* Part 2, *Piers, Wharves and Docks* (Washington, D.C.: U.S. Government Printing Office, 1942).

large dry docks, twenty-five small shipyards, thirty-three locomotive and gantry cranes of fifty-ton lift capacity or greater, five floating derricks, and more than one hundred tractor cranes. Some 575 tugboats worked the port.[31]

Between Pearl Harbor and VJ Day, more than three million troops and their equipment and over sixty-three million tons of additional supplies were shipped overseas through New York. Almost an equal number of men returned by the same route.[32] The army's New York Port of Embarkation (NYPE), first established in 1917, constituted the primary military command in the Port of New York. In actuality a "massive network of rail lines, highways, waterways, piers, and storage houses," between 1941 and 1945 it would grow from a single installation, the Brooklyn Army Terminal, to a total of ten port terminals scattered through Brooklyn, Manhattan, Staten Island, and New Jersey and would employ, at its largest growth, over 55,000 men and women. The Brooklyn Army Terminal was the largest warehouse in the world, with more than 3,800,000 square feet of storage space and room to unload 450 railroad freight cars.[33] The Port Johnson Terminal in Bayonne, New Jersey, with its large motor pool facilities and piers on the Kill Van Kull, was the principal shipment point for combat vehicles. The Claremont Terminal at Craven Point, Jersey City, allowed loading directly from freight cars drawn up on both sides of its giant Pennsylvania Railroad pier. Craven Point was the principal terminal for explosives and ammunition bound for the war fronts of Europe and the Mediterranean. The Howland Hook Terminal, located on the Arthur Kill on the backside of Staten Island, was the principal storage area and shipment point for POL (petroleum, oil, and lubricants) products arriving from the refineries of Bayonne and Elizabeth, New Jersey. The North River Terminal was the principal troop embarkation terminal of the NYPE. Consisting of seven covered piers on the Hudson River, part of the famous prewar "ocean liner row,"[34] the terminal permitted troops to arrive by ferry if necessary and to load directly onto troopships. It was from here that the fast liners, the Cunarders *Queen Elizabeth, Queen Mary, Aquitania,* and *Mauritania,* the French Lines' *Ile de France,* and the Holland-America Lines *Nieuw*

---

[31] Binford, "New York Harbor," 55.

[32] Troops embarked from New York totalled 3,283,678; troops debarked from the port totalled 2,150,065. "Staging Area - BROOKLYN: Record of a Borough at War," *Brooklyn Eagle,* Sunday Supplement, 9 December 1945, 3.

[33] Lt. Col. Herbert S. Crocker, *Army Supply Base, Brooklyn, N.Y.: Completion Report, 1919* (Brooklyn, NY: Construction Division of the Army, 1919).

[34] Francis J. Duffy and William H. Miller, *The New York Harbor Book* (Falmouth, MA: TBW Books, 1986), 37-45.

Amsterdam, departed on their lonely, high-speed crossings of the Atlantic.[35] The Army Postal Terminal in Manhattan handled as many as nine million letters and packages a day at the height of the war. Some three billion pieces of first-class mail were sent and received through the NYPE Postal Terminal during the "duration." Troops bound for overseas were funnelled into the port from the NYPE's three major staging areas: Camp Kilmer, near New Brunswick, New Jersey, Camp Shanks, near Orangeburg, New York,[36] and Fort Hamilton on the Brooklyn shore of the Narrows.

The Naval Shipyard, New York, universally called the Brooklyn Navy Yard, was the navy's premier port facility. The Brooklyn Navy Yard also experienced exponential growth under the pressure of wartime demand. Established in 1801, the Navy Yard comprised at its greatest extent some 290 acres along the Brooklyn shore of the East River around Wallabout Bay. The yard boasted seven dry docks, two building ways, and three hundred buildings, including some of the largest industrial structures in New York City, all connected to the water's edge by thirty miles of standard and narrow gauge railroad track. In 1941, it was already the most congested shipyard in the world. The war brought even greater expansion, including two 1,200-foot concrete graving docks able to handle 60,000-ton ships. The navy added berthing facilities for three more capital ships, enlarged other wharves, and built new waterside facilities, including a giant hammerhead crane with a 350-ton lift for the placement of battleship turrets.

At the peak of its activity, nearly 75,000 men and women were employed at the Brooklyn Navy Yard, making it the largest industrial plant in New York State. The yard generated a monthly payroll of between $15 and $16 million. During World War II, it turned out eighteen warships for the U.S. Navy, including three battleships,[37] five aircraft carriers,[38] two cruisers,[39] and eight LSTs. In addition, the Brooklyn Navy

---

[35] Correlli Barnett, *Engage the Enemy More Closely: The Royal Navy in the Second World War* (New York: W.W. Norton and Company, 1991), 490.

[36] Scott E. Webber, *Camp Shanks and Shanks Village: A Scrapbook* (New City, NY: Historical Society of Rockland County [NY], 1991).

[37] USS *North Carolina* was the first American battleship constructed after the failure of the interwar naval treaties. Her keel was laid in October 1937, and she was launched June of 1940, and commissioned in April 1941. USS *Iowa*, the first of four *Iowa*-class battleships, was commissioned in February 1943, and USS *Missouri*, was commissioned in June 1944.

[38] USS *Bennington*, launched in February 1944; USS *Bonhomme Richard*, launched in April 1944; USS *Kearsage*, launched in May 1945; USS *Oriskany*, launched in October 1945; and the Midway-class USS *Franklin D. Roosevelt*, launched in April 1945.

[39] USS *Helene* and USS *Juneau*, commissioned in March and lost in November 1942.

The USS *Missouri* passes under Brooklyn Bridge during World War II. Photo courtesy of the U.S. Navy.

Yard performed alterations and repairs on countless other vessels.

At the height of the Battle of the Atlantic, as many as sixty-seven ships might be simultaneously under repair. The yard repaired or modified 345 ships in 1942; 869 ships in 1943; 1,539 ships in 1944. In addition, in 1944 the Brooklyn Navy Yard performed routine "voyage repairs" on six cruisers, 262 destroyers, 825 destroyer escorts, and 103 auxiliary ships.

Maritime education, training, and welfare were major activities in the wartime Port of New York and represent the third factor contributing to the port's preeminence. Some institutions that existed before the war experienced exponential growth. In addition, new institutions and facilities were created out of whole cloth in order to meet wartime exigencies. Three programs produced licensed officers for the American merchant service.

Deck and engineering officers for the vastly expanded merchant marine were graduated from the New York State Maritime College, which was founded in 1874 aboard the schoolship *Saint Mary's*. In 1938, however, the Maritime College came ashore, occupying Fort Schuyler, a nineteenth-century coast defense fortress at Throgs Neck in the borough of the Bronx.[40] Plans for a new four-year baccalaureate program that would have graduated its first class in 1943 became a casualty of war as the college was forced to return to its traditional two-year, and later an abbreviated eighteen-month, officer licensing curriculum.

The United States Merchant Marine Academy was founded by the U.S. Maritime Commission in 1940. It was created to meet an anticipated wartime demand for licensed merchant marine officers beyond the capacity of the four state maritime colleges to fulfill.[41] The nation's newest federal academy occupied the former Walter Chrysler estate at Kings Point on Long Island's North Shore, just across the sound from its rival, the New York State Maritime College, on Throg's Neck. In the meantime, radio officers were taught to concentrate on dots and dashes in the isolation of tiny Hoffman and Swinburne Islands, located just below the Narrows in the lower bay.[42]

Perhaps the most ambitious enterprise in maritime education was the Maritime Commission Training Station located on Sheepshead Bay in Brooklyn.[43] Intended to fill the urgent need for merchant seamen to crew the new Liberty and Victory ships, the Sheepshead Bay facility was the largest of three quasi-military training stations established in San Francisco, New Orleans, and New York. Sprawling over seventy-six acres, the Sheepshead Bay facility was constructed during the spring and summer of 1942 and took in its first cycle of trainees on 1 September 1942. The first class of graduates shipped out on 5 December 1942, before the station was even formally dedicated.

Courses varied in length according to curriculum and the urgency of the demand for merchant seamen. During the Atlantic crisis of 1942 and 1943, when shortages in crews were acute, hundreds of recruits were shipped out after only six weeks of training. By 1944, when available ships had full crews, the normal thirteen-week courses for deck and engineering ratings was extended to eighteen weeks.

The full trainee complement was 10,000 men at any given time between December 1942 and August 1945, by which time the facility had

---

[40] Capt. Gerard J. Nolan, *Centennial 1874-1974: State University of New York Maritime College, Fort Schuyler, Bronx, New York*, 6-8.

[41] The four colleges were the New York, Massachusetts, Maine, and California Maritime Colleges.

[42] Francis J. Duffy, "The Dreams, Decline, and Decay of Hoffman, Swinburne Island," *Staten Island Advance*, Sunday, 3 September 1978, L 19.

[43] "Sheepshead Bay Maritime Training Station," in "Staging Area - BROOKLYN: Record of a Borough at War," *Brooklyn Eagle*, Sunday Supplement, 9 December 1945, 20-22. The site of the training station is now occupied by Kings College Community College.

graduated 115,000 trained volunteer merchant seamen. Two men out of three trained for the War Shipping Administration came from the Sheepshead Bay Training Station. More than half of the entire personnel of the American merchant service were Sheepshead Bay graduates. This included some 10,000 sixteen-year-olds who were accepted with their parents' consent.

The expanded wartime Coast Guard, transferred for the duration from the Treasury to the Navy Department, filled its ranks through the Manhattan Beach Coast Guard Training Station, Brooklyn, which after 1 February 1942 was the largest Coast Guard Station in the country. The Coast Guard went from its 1940 total of 12,600 men to a wartime peak of 180,000 men and women. Sixty-five thousand Coast Guard men and women, more than a third of its personnel, were trained at the Manhattan Beach facility. Initial recruits found themselves billeted in 104 vacationer's cottages on the former resort beach. Meals were served in "an overgrown refreshment stand" until barracks and mess halls were completed in October 1942 and the station reached its full complement of 7,000 recruits.[44]

The decision to assign sailors to man guns and communications equipment aboard merchant ships led to the creation of the U.S. Naval Armed Guard. Men assigned to this duty trained at three facilities located on Treasure Island in San Francisco Bay, in New Orleans, and at the huge Naval Militia Armory on the East River at the foot of 52nd Street in Brooklyn. At the peak of wartime activity, the New York center, the largest of the three, was home base for 65,000 armed guardsmen, most of whom were at sea at any given time. The center could accommodate up to 5,000 men at a time.[45]

In addition to its educational and training institutions, the Port of New York was home to the preeminent welfare institution for merchant sailors, the Randall Foundation's Sailors' Snug Harbor. On a grassy, tree shaded campus overlooking the Kill Van Kull on Staten Island, the foundation supported a sailors' retirement home which had grown since the eighteenth century to a handsome collection of neoclassical buildings.[46] Although New Deal legislation had largely diminished the problem of indigent merchant seamen before the war, World War II gave

[44] "Manhattan Beach Coast Guard Training Station," in ibid., 18-19.

[45] U.S. Navy, Third Naval District, *Historical Narrative of the U.S. Naval Armed Guard Center, Third Naval Distract, 20 May 1941 to June 1945*, District Historical Office Serial no. 401, *Unpublished Histories of U.S. Naval Administration in World War II* (Navy Department Library, Naval Historical Center, Washington Navy Yard, Washington, D.C.).

[46] The centerpiece of the facility was a half-scale replica of London's St. Paul's Cathedral.

the home for "disabled, injured or aged seamen," who did not then qualify for servicemen's or veterans' benefits, a new population and a new lease on life.[47]

Thus, geography, economics, education, and welfare were factors that made New York a vitally important port both before and during World War II. Other aspects of the port remain to be studied, such as the relation of the wartime port to the city of New York, the world's most popular liberty port. After all, the port was only the interface between the city and the sea. Moreover, since the nineteenth century New York had been a "world city," and this was never more true than during the Second World War when the streets of New York were crowded with Allied seamen. The British formed the largest foreign contingent — some two hundred British naval officers and other ranks were permanently stationed in New York, and over 150,000 British sailors passed through the Port of New York during the war.[48]

Other areas for study include the economy of vice that flourished around the Brooklyn Navy Yard, or the association of certain drinking and other establishments with specific ships' companies. The question of how the history of the Port of New York relates to the history of the city of New York awaits further study and documentation. What is well documented is the predominant role of the port in the American effort to supply the Allies during the crucial years 1941 to 1943.

---

[47] Barnett Shepherd, *Sailor's Snug Harbor, 1801-1976* (New York: Snug Harbor Cultural Center/Staten Island Institute of Arts and Sciences, 1979).
    [48] Press Release, British Liaison Office, Rockefeller Center, dated 15 August 1945. Provided by Norman Brouwer, South Street Seaport, New York.

19

The Coast Guard
Captains of the Ports

Robert M. Browning, Jr.

On the morning of 6 December 1917, a tremendous explosion ripped through the sleepy town of Halifax, Nova Scotia. The *Mont Blanc*, a French freighter carrying 5,000 tons of TNT, collided with another vessel, caught fire, and exploded. The blast leveled thousands of dwellings and killed about 1,600 people, mostly children. The disaster ranks as one of the worst maritime tragedies of all times. This particular ship sailed from New York on its way to Europe, one of hundreds that loaded explosive cargoes in New York during World War I. It was this disaster that in part stirred American leaders to empower the Coast Guard to ensure that this never happened in the United States.

Logistics is one of the most important aspects of warfare, yet it is frequently the most overlooked. The smooth movement of cargoes in and out of ports in wartime is an important task that often affects tactics and strategy. The Coast Guard, through its Captain of the Port offices, provided logistical supervision, security, law enforcement, and safety measures in all major American ports during World War II. The management of these important logistical functions allowed the United States and its allies to move supplies steadily without delays and disorder and contributed to victory.

The Coast Guard and its predecessor agency, the Revenue Cutter Service, have supervised the movement and anchorage of vessels in U.S. territorial waters since the Revenue Cutter Service assumed this job in 1888 in New York. By 1915, when the Coast Guard was created, the Service was directed by the Rivers and Harbors Act "to define and establish anchorage grounds for vessels in all harbors, rivers, bays, and other navigatable waters of the United States . . . ."[1]

During World War I, the Coast Guard served under the Navy Department and continued to enforce rules and regulations that governed the anchorage and movements of vessel in American harbors. The Espionage Act, passed in June 1917, gave the Coast Guard further power to protect merchant shipping from sabotage. This act included the safeguarding of waterfront property, the supervision of the movement of vessels, the establishment of anchorages and restricted areas, and the right to control and remove persons on board ships. The tremendous increase in munitions shipments, particularly in New York, required an increase in personnel to oversee this activity. The term Captain of the Port was first used in New York during the war for the officer charged with supervising the safe loading of explosives, and a similar post was established in three more U.S. ports.[2]

During World War I Captain Godfrey L. Carden, commander of the Coast Guard's New York Division, was named Captain of the Port in that harbor. The majority of this nation's munitions shipments abroad left through New York. For a period of a year and a half over 1,600 vessels carrying over 345 million tons of explosives sailed from this port. In 1918, Carden's division was the largest single command in the Coast Guard. It was made up of over 1,400 officers and men, four Corps of Engineers tugs and five harbor cutters.[3]

During Carden's tenure the Captain of the Port duties were performed without serious mishap. The most dangerous moment occurred when munitions at a rail yard in Morgan, New Jersey, began exploding and spreading fire into other buildings storing ammunition. Although Captain Carden had no responsibility for this accident, a Coast Guard detachment from Perth Amboy, New Jersey, reached the scene first with other New York units arriving later.

When the Coast Guard arrived the fire was intense. Exploding shells filled the air with shrapnel. They attempted to control the fire and remove the dead and wounded. A party of Coast Guardsmen learned that nine cars of TNT lay in the middle of the facility and were in imminent danger of catching fire. In the inferno the Coast Guardsmen

[1] Act of 4 March 1915, 38 Stat. L 1049, 1053

[2] "Captains of the Port," Statistical Division, U.S. Coast Guard, Coast Guard Historian's Office, 5-6.

[3] Godfrey L. Carden, "Handling of High Explosives in Wartime," *Engineering and Mining Journal* 109 (January 1920), 19; Godfrey L. Carden file, Coast Guard Historian's Office, Washington, D.C.; Robert Erwin Johnson, *Guardians of the Sea: History of the United States Coast Guard, 1915 to the Present* (Annapolis, MD: Naval Institute, 1987), 49.

repaired the tracks and removed the train. During the disaster two Coast Guardsmen died in rescue activities. The explosions of a total of 1,000 tons of TNT at the yard rattled buildings in Manhattan. This served as a reminder to the public of the Halifax calamity and the importance of explosives handling.[4]

After the First World War, these officers continued to regulate peacetime port activities and to be known as Captains of the Ports. In the twenty years following the war, the responsibilities of the Coast Guard grew to include the regulation of anchorages and the movement of vessels in American harbors. In April 1939, with the outbreak of another war in Europe imminent, the Coast Guard was once again called to monitor and enforce new anchorage regulations.[5] Adopted by the War Department, these regulations charged the Captains of the Ports to enforce stricter laws that reflected the growth of the major ports and their increased maritime activity.

In September 1939, President Franklin Roosevelt's neutrality pro-clamation laid the groundwork for Coast Guard activity for the next two years. After the proclamation, the Captains of the Ports were charged with sealing the radios and checking armaments on vessels of belligerent nations. Such actions prevented nations at war from broadcasting the whereabouts of enemy vessels, sailing times, and other intelligence infor-mation while in port. This proved to be a huge task for offices that were usually considerably understaffed; in Philadelphia an eight-man detail sealed over 10,000 radios in the three-year period from 1942 to 1944.[6]

Because the increased traffic in American ports had blurred the authority of the various federal, state, and local agencies responsible for port security and safety, in June 1940 the president proclaimed that the Treasury Department (Coast Guard) would assume functions previously assigned to other government agencies. Then an August 1940 conference attended by federal, state, and local port authorities considered topics that related to anchorages, dangerous cargoes, and vessel movements. The conference clarified several regulations and acts then in effect, giving the Coast Guard more authority and responsibility for the safety and security of navigable waters in the United States.[7]

The Dangerous Cargo Act of October 1940 and the restructuring of

---

[4] Riley Brown, *The Story of the Coast Guard* (Garden City, NY: Blue Ribbon Books, 1943), 74-76.

[5] *The Coast Guard at War; Port Security*, 30 vols. (Historical Section, Public Information Division, Coast Guard Headquarters, 1949), 18: 1-4.

[6] Narrative Histories, 4th Division, Record Group 26, National Archives, Washington, D.C. (hereafter RG 26, NA).

[7] *Coast Guard at War; Port Security*, 5-6.

anchorage regulations the same month clearly laid out and expanded previous regulations and provisions enforced by the Coast Guard. The responsibilities of each Captain of the Port increased, and by November twenty-nine ports had such officers. This set up the machinery for enforcing the laws and regulations which governed the movement of vessels, the loading of dangerous cargoes, and the protection and regulation of anchorages.[8]

In March 1941, the Captain of the Port in Norfolk, Virginia learned that crews of certain Italian vessels were sabotaging their ships in Wilmington, North Carolina and Baltimore, Maryland. After confirming this fact, the Coast Guard determined it would take possession of the vessels under the 1917 Espionage Act. Two officers dispatched to the Italian vessels in Hampton Roads found that a great deal of damage had been done to the machinery and boilers of the ships. The merchant ship control office of the Coast Guard issued orders to investigate. Between 29 March and 5 April 1941, the Coast Guard took into "protective custody" twenty-seven Italian, thirty-five Danish, and later fifteen French vessels.[9] These vessels, with a combined total of over 479,000 gross tons, were later repaired and converted for use by the Maritime Commission.

The duties of the Captains of the Port again increased dramatically and were gradually consolidated after this country went to war. In November 1941, the Coast Guard transferred administratively to the Navy Department. Port security duties also transferred at this time to the Secretary of the Navy. The commander in chief delegated this responsibility to the Commandant of the Coast Guard by letter in June 1942. Regulations for explosives were promulgated in April 1941, and marine inspection and navigation duties under the Bureau of Marine Inspection and Navigation were transferred to the Coast Guard in February 1942.[10]

During the war the Coast Guard's broad responsibilities grew to include:

- Control of the anchorage and movement of all vessels in port.
- Issuance of Coast Guard identification cards, and supervision of ingress and egress to vessels and waterfront facilities.
- Fire prevention measures, including inspections, recommendations, and enforcement.
- Firefighting activities, including use of fireboats, trailer pumps, and other extinguishing agents.

---

[8] Ibid., 8.

[9] Ibid., 9-10; "Captains of the Port," 72.

[10] Memorandum for Assistant Chief Operations Officer from Chief, Port Security Division Merle A. Gulick, 3 August 1945 Port Security Subject Files 1941-45, RG 26, NA.

- Boarding and examination of vessels in port.
- Supervision of the loading and stowage of explosives and military ammunition.
- Sealing of vessels' radios.
- Licensing of vessels for movement in local waters and for departure therefrom.
- Guarding of important facilities.
- Enforcement of all regulations governing vessels and waterfront security.
- Maintenance of water patrols.
- General enforcement of Federal laws on navigable waters, and other miscellaneous duties.[11]

The Coast Guard found it was tasked to do many things with few resources. With so many functions to perform, the service had to rely upon and coordinate the activities of many different groups to ensure that its plethora of tasks could be fulfilled. This relationship did not solidify overnight. It took a great deal of trial and error, experimentation, and coordination from existing organizations to implement a comprehensive port security program.

An early inadequacy in the divisions of authority became evident when *Normandie* burned. In January 1942, the French luxury liner *Normandie* was being converted into a transport in New York City. She caught fire and the lines of authority for fighting the fire proved to be indistinct. Due to delays, confusion, and a few bad decisions, she later capsized to the embarrassment and dismay of all the agencies responsible for her.

This accident, however, helped to bring about a consolidation of the Coast Guard's duties. In February 1942, a Presidential Executive Order directed the Secretary of the Navy to ensure the safeguarding of American and territorial waterfronts and the president advised that the Coast Guard carry out this function. Thus, the responsibility was delegated by letter from the Secretary of the Navy to the Commandant of the Coast Guard, who operated under the Chief of Naval Operations.[12]

Because of the loss of the *Normandie* in 1942, the fire prevention program received early attention. Due to large concentrations of vital war materials, explosives, and other flammable and hazardous cargoes being loaded and unloaded, this role became extremely important. Normally the local municipalities oversaw such functions, but local authorities with their limited equipment could not cope with the increased port traffic

---

[11] "Captains of the Port," 108-109.
[12] Ibid., 108.

brought on by the war. In 1942, the Coast Guard likewise did not have the staff nor the firefighting equipment to lend much aid.

To remedy this situation, the Coast Guard began a program to supplement the number of fireboats in the nation's harbors. It increased its firefighting force immediately by converting 150 small vessels (tugs, luggers, fishing, party vessels) to fireboats. The service likewise built 103 thirty-foot Hanley boats with four gasoline-driven 500-gallon-per-minute fire pumps and several other fireboats, including twenty-nine forty-foot fireboats equipped with seven fire monitors that served on the East Coast. Twenty-two fire barges of fifty-to-sixty-foot lengths were built for the West Coast. These fire barges had eight gasoline-driven fire pumps each with a 500-gallon capacity. By 1944, 253 Coast Guard fireboats served ports around the nation. These boats were generally stationed in strategic areas of the harbors because of their lack of speed. They normally lay at ammunition handling piers, gasoline loading operations, or near other dangerous cargoes.[13]

All firefighting activities involved close cooperation with the municipal fire departments. To supplement the boats afloat, the Coast Guard placed a large number of small fire pumps on board picket and patrol boats. These pumps were capable of extinguishing small fires discovered while on patrol. In conjunction with the water craft, the Coast Guard also maintained trailer units with 500-gallon-per-minute pumps which could be pulled to fires ashore.[14]

As an added precaution, the service placed a great emphasis on fire prevention. Men specifically trained for such work inspected all water-front facilities, checked fire extinguishers and fire alarms, and ensured that private industry and municipal authorities followed safety rules. The Coast Guard liberally distributed fire prevention literature to educate the various groups at the waterfronts and demonstrated its high level of alertness and training during the war. Of all the waterfront fires reported in a one-year period from 1942 to 1943, the Coast Guard discovered over 25 percent and responded to over 91 percent.[15]

The private sector performed similar safety functions. Fires occurring in privately owned property could potentially affect port safety and security. The Captains of the Ports found that they had to "sell" the program to the private facility owners because the Coast Guard had no

---

[13] *Coast Guard at War; Port Security,* 72.

[14] "History of Port Security," United States Coast Guard Seattle, Washingtion District Historical Office, 13th Naval District, United States Coast Guard 1946, Unpublished Manuscript, Coast Guard Historian's Office, 13th Naval District, 102-103.

[15] *Coast Guard at War; Port Security,* 75.

legal authority to force compliance but only to recommend safety measures. As a result of the program, however, many private facilities installed firefighting equipment and took preventive measures to avoid fires. Many also revised their housekeeping by rearranging cargo stowage and by cleaning areas that presented a hazard.[16]

Welding and smoking accidents caused most of the fires on the waterfronts and ship inspection departments received instructions to give special attention to this problem. The Coast Guard began non-smoking campaigns and instituted other fire safety programs. In addition, in the summer of 1943 all Captain of the Port offices requested the pier owners to wet down piers in the hot, dry months to avoid fires.[17]

One of the more visible duties of the Coast Guard was the protection of piers and docks. The service began this job with the understanding that it could not be solely a Coast Guard operation. To perform this tremendous task, the Captains of the Ports had to be the coordinators and their men only a supplement to municipal and private personnel. The protection of waterfront property and facilities was thus a coordinated effort involving military, naval, and Department of Justice intelligence personnel, private organizations and companies, municipal and state police forces, and commercial organizations.[18]

For two years the Captains of the Ports administered protective and security measures for waterfront facilities without any regulations to support this action. The Espionage Act of 1917 did not include land facilities, and thus the Coast Guard had the responsibility to protect waterfronts without legal measures to enforce regulations. An Executive Order of 12 December 1941 authorized the Coast Guard to place guards along all waterfront installations to protect national defense facilities, materials, and utilities. Due to limited personnel, however, the Coast Guard only maintained guards in cases of emergency or in exceptional situations when other guards could not be secured. Even though the Captain of the Port had the responsibility for the security of all the waterfront facilities in the port, the specific burden of security still rested on the owners and operators of the facilities. The Captains of the Ports therefore mainly supervised this duty for the first fifteen months of the war. An act of Congress in July 1943 (effective 1 May 1944) gave the service the proper authority.[19]

---

[16] "History of Port Security," 13th Naval District, 91-97.

[17] Ibid., 97-100.

[18] "Captains of the Port," 109; "History of Port Security," 13th Naval District, 78.

[19] Memorandum for Asst. Chief Operations Officer, 3 August 1945 from Chief, Port Security Division, Merle S. Gulick, Port Security Files, 1941-45, RG 26, NA; "Captains of the Port," 109-110.

A Coast Guardsman stands watch at the Port of New York City. Port Captains were responsible for the security of thousands of ships. Photo courtesy of U.S. Coast Guard.

To protect vessels and important installations within each port facility, the Coast Guard created security zones around the dock areas. Within these areas the Captain of the Port assigned roving guards and enforced the integrity of the zones with Coast Guard personnel and barricaded streets. The men watching the waterfront generally performed their service on foot but used vehicles in isolated spots. The official duties were to locate and report fires, detect saboteurs or unauthorized personnel, check vehicles, check ID cards and watch for cameras, contact watchmen in facilities, and man barricades.[20]

In order to maintain a tighter control over access to sensitive dock areas and to prevent sabotage and subversive acts, the service issued identification cards. Wartime regulations required that everyone working or visiting the waterfront have a card. Likewise, the Coast Guard had the authority to inspect and search vessels and remove persons not authorized to remain on board.[21] The Captain of the Port could issue ID cards to U.S. citizens that made their livelihood on the dock, to those with occasional business, to temporary guards, and to aliens.

Once the duties of the Captain of the Port were fully recognized, it became evident that there was a need for investigative personnel to augment the existing intelligence operations. In March 1942, the Chief of Naval Operations outlined a program for special agents for Captain of the Port work. The main thrust of the program was to uncover sabotage before it occurred. Coast Guard intelligence acted mainly as a clearing house and repository for information. Investigators spent much of their time with security checks and the screening of civilian and Coast Guard personnel. They also interviewed a large number of enemy aliens who held temporary ID cards. Coast Guard intelligence activities usually remained a small program within the Captain of the Port organizations. Such activities did serve to aid Naval Intelligence but were sometimes handled by the Coast Guard District Intelligence Officers.[22]

Harbor patrols were just as important as those from shore and consumed much of the manpower of the Captain of the Port offices. This particular task utilized various patrol craft to watch the multitude of vessels in U.S. harbors. These small harbor craft worked in tandem with offshore patrols and the Beach Patrol to watch the vast shore lines. Harbor patrol craft watched for fires, unauthorized persons, and pleasure

---

[20] "History of Port Security," 13th Naval District, 80; *Coast Guard at War: Port Security*, 14; Port Security Division, Subject files, 1941-45, RG 26, NA; Narrative History, 4th Division, RG 26, NA; *Captain of the Port Manual*, United States Coast Guard, Government Printing Office, 1943, 6-7.

[21] "Captains of the Port," 109-110.

[22] "History of Port Security," 13th Naval District, 189-93.

craft with improper papers. In addition, their crews reported accidents, removed menaces to navigation, rendered assistance, patrolled anchorages and restricted areas, and escorted ammunition and dangerous cargo ships out of the harbor. Most of this duty consisted of identifying and checking personnel on board vessels. The Coast Guard harbor patrols often questioned the occupants of small craft and checked cargoes for proper documentation. Parties of men also inspected ships' equipment for safety, made recommendations for replacing fire fighting equipment, or called fire hazards to the attention of the owners.[23]

Early in the war Auxiliary craft handled some harbor patrol duties, but gradually Coast Guard Reserve craft took over this function. Most reserve craft were small converted pleasure craft given a coat of grey paint. Most carried only small arms — revolvers, rifles and submachine guns. Their equipment might also include fire pumps and hoses. Such boats operated on a full-time basis an average of twenty-one hours a day; They were gradually returned to their owners as the Coast Guard replaced them with eighty-three-footer and thirty-eight-footer picket boats.[24]

Vessel security was also an important part of the responsibilities of the Captains of the Ports. By discretion, the Captains of the Port regulated the guards and the number required according to the size and cargo of the vessel. But the responsibility for providing guards to protect and maintain the security of vessels while in port rested with the owners of the vessels. The vessels' sizes determined the type and number of guards that were required to ensure security. Vessels between 2,000 and 5,000 gross tons were required to have guards at each gangway when moored to a dock or other facility. Vessels over 5,000 tons additionally had to have a roving guard to patrol all parts of the vessel accessible to passengers and crew members. Fire guards stood watch with fire extinguishers and hoses with running water when repairs created special hazards in all vessels over 1,000 gross tons. Special regulations also covered inspections, maintenance of boilers, shipboard electrical power, tending of mooring lines, ventilators, lighting, ships' keys, and much more.[25]

Dangerous cargoes, if not handled properly, could endanger not only a particular ship or warehouse but also the entire port and the movement of all cargoes. This was the greatest single threat to all major ports during the war. A catastrophic accident could cripple logistical activities for months. The safe loading and handling of dangerous cargoes was thus

---

[23] *Coast Guard at War; Port Security*, 79-81.

[24] Ibid.

[25] *U.S. Coast Guard Port Security Regulations*, Title 33, 1944, 13-17.

A security detail man guards the unloading of dangerous cargo. Accidents in munitions handling were rare due to close supervision. Photo courtesy of U.S. Coast Guard.

an integral part of the logistical successes of World War II and an important mission of the Coast Guard.

Early in 1942, those responsible for port safety realized that the peacetime regulations that governed the movement of explosives would have to be amended to handle wartime conditions. On 28 February 1942,

the duties of the Bureau of Marine Inspection and Navigation under the
Department of Commerce were transferred by executive order to the
Coast Guard. These duties included the authority to control the shipment
of explosives on ships. There were, however, some gaps in the oversight
of movement of this type of cargo. For example, in New York, the
Interstate Commerce Commission regulations stopped when the shipment
left the railroad cars and Coast Guard responsibility did not begin until
it was loaded onto the vessels.[26]

After meetings with a joint Army, Navy, and Coast Guard committee,
the Coast Guard promulgated a code for the transportation of military
explosives and ammunition which expedited the movement of important
shipments. Each munitions vessel would be assigned a 24-hour-a-day
detail to supervise the safe transfer of the cargo. A security detail man
watched each cargo hold, one roved the weather decks fore and aft, one
guarded the gangway for illegal entry, and several stayed on the pier.
When loading was complete, the Coast Guard personnel closed and
sealed the hatches and a detail remained until the vessel sailed.[27]

During the war the Captains of the Ports made the appropriate
recommendations for the anchorage of vessels carrying explosives and
dangerous cargoes and designated loading terminals and conditions in
which they could be used. For better control, the Captains of the Ports
issued permits for unloading explosives and also regulated the loading
and unloading of flammable materials. Considerations were given to
dangers to shipping, the degree of isolation from populated areas,
accessibility to shipping and obstacles that might delay the swift
movement of these vessels to and from the terminal. At times the
responsibility of providing the safest possible loading had to be relaxed
to avoid holding up the flow of supplies which might be harmful to the
national war effort.[28]

The Captain of the Port by law had nearly absolute authority to
govern this activity, but his authority could be checked. When explosives
were handled by army and navy facilities, the Captain of the Port could
merely withhold approval if unsafe conditions existed. He could not,
however, take any steps to stop any dangerous activity as long as it lay
wholly under the control of military officials.[29]

The Coast Guard kept accidents in ammunition handling to a
minimum during the war. The most devastating explosion occurred at

---

[26] *Coast Guard at War; Port Security*, 63-64.
[27] Ibid., 65-69.
[28] "Captains of the Port," 111; *U.S. Coast Guard Security Regulations*, 4-5.
[29] "Captains of the Port," 111.

Port Chicago in Suisun Bay, about twenty-five miles from San Francisco. Coast Guard explosive-loading details had been assigned to that port but were removed when safety recommendations were not followed. Eight and a half months later, harking back to the *Mont Blanc*, the steamship *E.A. Bryan*, with 5,000 tons of ammunition on board, exploded, causing extensive damage for miles and killing over 300 people. The only thing that prevented a larger loss of life was that the accident site was isolated from the large population centers of San Francisco and Oakland.[30]

There were some successes too. A good example, which may have had consequences of untold proportions, was the fire on board the Panamanian steamer *El Estero* in New York Harbor. At 5:20 on the afternoon of 24 April 1943, an oil feed pipe burst on board the *El Estero*. The boiler room fire spread rapidly and could not be controlled by the ship's crew. A Coast Guard munitions supervisor who happened to be on board immediately assumed command of the vessel. The ship contained 1,500 tons of high explosives, equal to the amount of explosives that destroyed Halifax, Nova Scotia during World War I. The munitions officer, Lieutenant Commander John T. Stanley, directed his men to fight the fire as best they could. Fire apparatus arrived soon thereafter. The additional equipment did not contain the blaze and the fire began consuming the ship's superstructure.

A real danger now existed. An explosion would be deadly in a metropolitan area where 10 percent of the nation's population was concentrated. The Captain of the Port of New York directed the ship be scuttled, but Stanley's men could not reach the sea cocks due to the fire. Stanley cut the *El Estero* adrift and tugs towed her into the bay while fireboats worked to flood the vessel. The metropolitan area was warned of the possible disaster and local officials took air raid precautions. Two hours of towing and flooding caused the *El Estero* to list suddenly and settle within sight of Staten Island. Lieutenant Commander Stanley received the Legion of Merit for his conduct. What is amazing about this incident is the fact that this was his first day as a munitions officer.[31] This last incident indicated the need for the Coast Guard to control shipping in the harbors and just how valuable this service would prove to be. The Captains of the Ports had the tremendous administrative and supervisory responsibility for the safe and timely movement of vessels within the harbor. The Coast Guard issued licenses for vessels over 100 feet to

---

[30] Ibid., 159; Robert L. Allen, in his book *The Port Chicago Mutiny* (New York: Warner Books, 1989), 69, claims that the Captain of the Port withdrew the detail after observing the "bad conditions."

[31] *Coast Guard at War; Port Security*, 127.

The Panamanian steamer *El Estero* was scuttled by the Coast Guard in April 1943. The ship contained 1,500 tons of high explosives when it caught fire in New York Harbor. Photo courtesy of U.S. Coast Guard.

depart local waters. Seasonally employed vessels such as fishermen and pleasure vessels were also supervised by the Coast Guard. The Captain of the Port defined anchorages and monitored anchorages near bridges, railroad crossings, and cable and pipeline areas to ensure that these valuable logistical and communication conduits would not be affected by a shipping accident.[32]

The work of the Captains of the Ports increased as the war

---

[32] *U.S. Coast Guard Port Security Regulations*, 4-5.

progressed. An increase in activity occurred in all major U.S. ports as America became the major contributor to the war effort. The service, however, never grew as fast as its responsibilities. This created situations in which the Coast Guard had to make daily decisions to balance port security needs with its capabilities.

At the beginning of the war only 250 of the 400 essential piers in New York City were protected by the Coast Guard. In early 1942 only 1,200 active men guarded these piers. When divided into four watches this left only 300 at each watch. There were times when this small number of men was stretched even further. By June 1942, the Coast Guard in the New York area had been augmented to 3,000 present for duty. At this time they guarded only 439 of the 1900 piers. With the increased activity and the port's growth as a logistical center for the war, it was estimated that the Coast Guard would have needed nearly 16,900 officers and men to properly secure the port. At one point in the war 50 million gallons of gasoline sat in drums in the port of New York for several weeks. During this period, guarding the gasoline became a key concern, not checking ID cards or guarding the piers. Shortages of manpower, however, occurred in all the ports. The heavy responsibility of port security duties eventually comprised 22 percent of the Coast Guard's manpower, not including the Reserves.[33]

A lack of manpower proved to be the most serious deficiency that plagued port security operations throughout the war. In June 1942, the Coast Guard Temporary Reserve was established to augment the Coast Guard Regulars. The Temporary Reserve was made up of men and women who were excluded from full-time military service for one reason or another. These reservists could be between the ages of twenty and sixty-five but generally were near middle age. They included businessmen, attorneys, teachers, bankers, librarians and secretaries among their number. The great demand for port security personnel became increasingly critical to meet the demands of the war effort. In May 1942, a Volunteer Port Security Force was created in Philadelphia to utilize the new reserve component. These men and women would eventually augment the regular forces and relieve the Captains of the Port of their single greatest worry — a lack of personnel.[34]

By November the Philadelphia unit had 700 people in training for port security duty. A month later they began their first duty. The experiment in Philadelphia proved so successful that the Coast Guard

---

[33] "Coast Guard at War," 3rd Naval District, 10: 92-95, 100, RG 26, NA; Narrative Histories of World War II, 1941-45, 3rd Naval District, 9: 79, RG 26, NA.

[34] *Coast Guard at War; Port Security*, 127.

created a Port Security Unit and expanded the volunteer forces. Eventually twenty-two major ports had these units employing 20,000 men and women.[35]

The Volunteer Port Security Force performed many of the duties of the regulars and immediately began guarding the waterfront and spearheaded the fire safety program. The volunteers were unpaid, agreed to perform at least twelve hours of work a week, and joined for a variety of reasons. By 1944, 50,000 served in the Temporary Reserves and fulfilled the major portion of pier guard duty and harbor patrols. Women known as the "TR SPARS" participated performing clerical work, serving in the transportation pools, and as messengers and mechanics. These men and women had full military status while on duty and had all rights, privileges, and powers of the Coast Guard Reserves.[36]

The Temporary Reservists demonstrated supreme competence and reliability, serving an important role in the war. This organization freed up over eight thousand regular Coast Guard officers and men to man military vessels. This equalled nearly 20 percent of the Regulars in service. More importantly, it allowed the Coast Guard to carry out the necessary port security tasks.

Allied victory during World War II depended upon the timely movement of supplies and the ability to plan for logistical buildups of supplies and men. By the end of the war, nearly 200 Captain of the Port and Assistant Captain of the Port offices had been established in the United States and overseas. The Captain of the Port's valuable service to ensure the steady movement of supplies was of inestimable value. The logistical centers of the United States remained secure from sabotage, confusion, and mishaps. This function of the Coast Guard is often overlooked, but it was certainly an important duty and a key factor in Allied victory during World War II.

---

[35] Ibid., 39-40; *The Coast Guard at War, Temporary Reserve*, Historical Section, Public Information Division, Coast Guard Headquarters, 1948 20: 39.

[36] *Coast Guard at War; Port Security*, 36-43.

20

The Battle of the Atlantic in Feature Films

Lawrence Suid

The battle for the Atlantic shipping lanes during World War II undoubtedly determined the outcome of the European conflict. Except for the British navy's successful pursuit of the *Bismarck* and the *Graf Spee*, however, the combat consisted almost exclusively of submarine attacks on convoys and destroyer counterattacks. Only on rare occasions did Allied planes come across a German submarine or did German planes bomb Allied shipping. Consequently, at least for American filmmakers, the U.S. participation in the Battle of the Atlantic lacked the visual excitement of air to air, air to surface, or surface to surface combat that made the war in the Pacific so exciting on motion picture screens.

As a result, Hollywood's portrayal of the sea battles between the Allies and the Nazis has taken second place to its recreation of the more cinematically stirring surface and air battles in the Pacific in such films as *They Were Expendable, Task Force, Tora! Tora! Tora!*, and *Midway*. Nevertheless, while these movies contain the most memorable images of World War II at sea, American filmmakers have not ignored the Battle of the Atlantic either during the conflict or since 1945. On their part, British and German filmmakers have also created stories about the struggle to control the Atlantic shipping lanes which conveyed the high drama of the war at sea. To compensate for the lack of visual impact, these movies have inevitably focused on a few individuals in small-scale combat.

During the war, the movies had additional aims beyond simply telling dramatic stories of people trying to survive in a hostile environment. Each tried to inform its audience of how the Allies were fighting an implacable enemy and to demonstrate why that combat must be won. Even during the war, however, filmmakers began to moderate the images of the Germans, anticipating Allied victory and a changed geopolitical world. Following the end of hostilities, the movies about the Battle of the Atlantic, like all the other portrayals of Germany in World War II, have reflected the political realities of the Cold War.

To be sure, governments have used motion pictures to create messages for as long as the commercial film industry has existed. The United States military has a particularly rich tradition of assisting Hollywood to produce movies that present the armed services in a positive light. The navy, for one, began cooperating with filmmakers even before World War I. From the service's perspective, the positive portrayals of its men, equipment, and procedures helped recruitment and informed the public (which, of course, included members of Congress) of where its tax dollars were going. On its part, Hollywood has seen the navy as a stage for action/adventure and romantic stories. The producers of *Top Gun*, for example, denied they had made a navy recruiting advertisement, even though the film clearly served that purpose. Instead, the filmmakers explained that they considered themselves as simply travel agents taking their audiences to new and exotic settings, which were otherwise out of reach.

In hindsight, of course, not all the stories would seem to contain positive images. In *Men Without Women* (the first film in which John Wayne spoke) and *Submarine D-1*, for example, submarines sank and lives were lost. In *Flight Command* and *Dive Bomber*, naval aviators crashed and died while trying to advance flight technology. Unfortunately, audiences did not always recognize the informational purpose of the movies. Reacting to *Dive Bomber*, a viewer wrote to the secretary of the navy on 1 December 1941 to complain:

> "If there ever was a picture shown to discourage anyone from joining the Air Corps it is the picture *Dive Bomber*. [It would lead every] potential draftee to stay clear of aviation [because] every aviator loses his health due to flying. Perhaps this is so, but it seems a queer time to advertise this throughout the country. If this picture was made in Germany and sent here I could see the point. [It] sure won't get any recruits in the air service."[1]

Answering a similar letter, the navy wrote that the film had generally received a favorable response and suggested that if it only showed the positive side of aviation ". . . it would not ring true and would be

---

[1] Arthur Keil to Frank Knox, 1 December 1941, Box 94, Record Group 80, National Archives, Washington, D.C. (hereafter RG 80, NA).

declared propaganda by the public."[2] Ironically, isolationists in the U.S. Senate used precisely that language in accusing Hollywood of making films about Germany and the military in order to draw the United States into World War II.

During Senate hearings in September 1941, filmmakers vehemently disagreed with such attacks. Harry Warner, whose studio had made *Dive Bomber*, argued that his films were ". . . carefully prepared on the basis of factual happenings and they were not twisted to serve any ulterior purpose." Addressing the specific issue of military stories, he said that his company ". . . needed no urging from the government and we would be ashamed if the government would have had to make such requests of us. We have produced these pictures voluntarily and proudly."[3]

After much acrimony, the hearings recessed until 8 December. Pearl Harbor rendered further hearings moot and provided strong evidence that such films as *Dive Bomber* and *Flight Command* did not draw the U.S. into war. The Japanese attack also exposed the lie in these films, since the navy had not been able to protect the nation as the service had represented it was prepared to do. In any event, the U.S. entry into World War II gave Hollywood free rein to portray all aspects of the Allied involvement in the war in positive and, if truth be told, propagandistic terms.

The early portrayals of combat in the Atlantic, such as *The Navy Comes Through* and *Crash Dive*, remained little more than fanciful portrayals of combat designed to inspire patriotism. The latter film, for one, illustrated the training of submariners at New London and then followed the patrol of one of the subs in the North Atlantic. In truth, U.S. submarines saw little if any action in the Atlantic and only rarely did any submarine captain during World War II send a party ashore as happened in *Crash Dive*. Still, the destruction of enemy installations and the triumphant return of the submarine to base were bound to have a positive impact on audiences, particularly in early 1943 when victory was not yet certain.

Action in the North Atlantic, on the other hand, realistically saluted the efforts of the merchant marine to maintain a lifeline to Great Britain during the darkest days of World War II. Fresh from outsmarting the Japanese in *Across the Pacific* and the Germans in *Casablanca*, Humphrey Bogart played his usual hard-bitten persona, this time as a second officer

---

[2] Alan Brown to E.C. Roworth, 26 August 1941, RG 80, NA.

[3] Senate Committee on Interstate Commerce, "Propaganda in Motion Pictures, Hearings Before a Subcommittee of the Senate Committee on Interstate Commerce," 77th Cong., September, 1941, 338-41.

of a tanker setting out from New Jersey to the European theater. After introducing the audience to the typical heterogeneous Hollywood crew, the film goes inside a U-boat as it goes about its business of sinking the ship.

As soon as the surviving crew collects itself aboard a lifeboat, the sub surfaces and proceeds to cut the frail craft in two while a German officer films the scene for posterity. In fact, during the first two years of the war, Hollywood regularly portrayed the Axis committing such atrocities. In *Wake Island* and *Air Force*, for example, Japanese pilots strafed American fliers as they dangled helplessly from their parachutes. Bogart and most of the crew make it to a nearby raft from which they are rescued after drifting for eleven days. Back in port, in a local bar, Bogart meets (and following the strictures of the Production Code Office) marries a singer. Despite her pleas, Bogart rejoins his captain aboard a new Liberty ship for a run to Murmansk, which the film details with great care. The story itself seldom rises above the level of melodrama, although any film in which Bogart appeared gained a significant measure of quality.

More to the point, however, *Action in the North Atlantic* served as a vehicle for explaining the importance of supporting the Soviet Union, the dangers which the German wolfpacks presented to the success of that mission, and the manner in which the merchant marine worked with the navy to counter the submarine threat. In the end, Bogart sails the freighter into Murmansk after his captain is wounded in a running battle with a U-boat.

The film itself does contain a feel of authenticity and accuracy thanks to the assistance which the navy and the Merchant Marine Service provided the production, within the limits of men, resources, and security. Does it become a docudrama? Probably not, since any film conveying the dangers and grimness of convoy duty would probably have had a negative affect on the war effort. As it stands, however, *Action in the North Atlantic* did give the American people some understanding of the nature of the war in the Atlantic.

In contrast, in Alfred Hitchcock's *Lifeboat*, the Battle of the Atlantic served as a springboard for a story about the struggle of a diverse group of people to survive in a small boat on the open sea. To be sure, the occupants of the lifeboat find themselves cast together as the result of the mutual sinking of a freighter and a U-boat. However, except for one element in the plot, the film could just as well have been about survivors of a peacetime shipwreck. In fact, *Lifeboat* becomes a story about the Battle of the Atlantic for one reason: the strongest, most complex, most practical, and most interesting character aboard the boat is the German submarine captain, who has survived the sinking of his ship.

This portrayal of the enemy in such human terms, rather than in the previous, evil stereotypes, reflects the reality that the Allies were winning the war. With victory now only a matter of time, the Office of War Information had informed all the film studios, in late 1943, that the government would no longer tolerate portrayals of enemy atrocities or torture and would not give letters of export to films containing such images. Why a change in policy?[4]

As Allied victory became more certain, American military planners and diplomats were beginning to give thought to the postwar world and to consider the identity of a future threat to the nation. To meet that threat, it had become clear that a friendly Germany and Japan would serve as useful buffers. As a result, government officials realized the need to moderate Hollywood's virile, propagandistic images of the current enemies. So, notifications went to filmmakers to tone down or, as in the case of *Lifeboat*, improve the portrayals.

In any case, the German U-boat commander stood in stark contrast to his squabbling, weak, self-centered companions. Walter Slezak created a shrewd, cunning enemy, one whom the audience could respect, if not like. In response to critics concerned with the implications of Slezak's portrayal, Hitchcock contended that he made the Nazi a strong character in order to remind the Allies not to underestimate their enemy. Ultimately, the other survivors gang up on the U-boat captain and cast him overboard when they realize he had hoarded precious water and navigated the lifeboat to a German supply ship.

In essence, then, *Lifeboat* became a microcosm of the war, containing a cross-section of Allied nationalities and points of view. *The New York Times*, for one, observed that the film stood as a ". . . trenchant and blistering symbolization of the world and its woes today." At the same time, the paper observed that the German was "tricky and sometimes brutal, yes, but he is practical, ingenious, and basically courageous in his lonely resolve. Some of his careful deceptions would be regarded as smart and heroic if they came from an American in the same spot." In this light, the reviewer felt that the filmmakers "failed to grasp just what they had wrought. . . . But we have a sneaking suspicion that the Nazis, with some cutting here and there, could turn *Lifeboat* into a whiplash against the 'decadent democracies.' And it is questionable whether such a picture, with such a theme, is judicious at this time."[5]

Ultimately then, the film undoubtedly had more to say about the

---

[4] John C. Flynn, Society of Independent Motion Picture Producers to Roy Disney, 9 November, 1943.

[5] *The New York Times*, 13 January 1944.

politics of World War II than about the Battle of the Atlantic. Nevertheless, it did remind people of the suffering which the war at sea could inflict on those caught up in it. At the same time, for historians, *Lifeboat* remains a primary document of the war, illustrating how films were used to shape attitudes about current and future enemies.

On the other side of the Atlantic, *In Which We Serve* illustrates the manner in which the British presented the war at sea to its people. Essentially the biography of a destroyer from her launching to her sinking in the Mediterranean, it also portrayed, through a series of flashbacks, the story of the officers and enlisted men who fought the Nazis on the sea. While the destroyer is lost in action off Crete, much of its life afloat is spent in the Atlantic, including support of the Dunkirk evacuation.

Made with the assistance of the Royal Navy and Air Force, the film addressed the audience on several levels. It showed the building of the ship, gave a human face to both the officers and men, provided information on the nature of naval warfare, and, perhaps most important, delivered a strong propaganda message about the evil nature of the enemy.

Interestingly, the visual image that conveyed the message remained the same that had appeared in Hollywood films. As the Japanese had strafed helpless American fliers and German U-boat commanders had cut American lifeboats in two, *In Which We Serve* features Nazi fighters strafing British survivors in the water. Unlike the singular nature of the attacks in the American films, however, the British emphasized the enemy's evilness by having the attacking German planes repeatedly strafe the helpless men as they struggled.

Despite the desperate situation in which the British found themselves in the early days of the war, the filmmakers received considerable assistance in producing *In Which We Serve*. While Hollywood also received cooperation from the military during the war, navy help remained relatively limited until late in the conflict. For example, the primary navy assistance on *Thirty Seconds Over Tokyo* consisted of allowing MGM to film a carrier dockside, the hoisting of B-25 bombers onto the flight deck, and filming some scenes aboard ship.

Once the war ended, of course, the navy was more than happy to assist on all manner of stories, most of which portrayed the fighting in the Pacific, usually in living color. The British, on the other hand, had little to celebrate about their naval actions against the Japanese. However, filmmakers could draw upon the navy's successful fight against the German submarine menace as well as two major victories against the enemy's surface ships in the Atlantic as subjects for inspiring stories.

Probably the best of these films, *The Cruel Sea*, reached the screen in 1953. Adapted from Nicholas Monsarrat's novel of the same name, the movie played down heroism and realistically depicted how the men who fought aboard small escort ships contributed to the successful war effort.

Jack Hawkins portrayed a civilian sailor turned Royal Navy officer who has to mold a group of inexperienced volunteers and inductees into effective crews, first of a corvette and then of a frigate. Uncomfortable as a commander of a combat ship, Hawkins has to face the dilemma of running over British sailors from a torpedoed merchant ship or letting a German U-boat escape. His anguish only increases when the Germans torpedo his ship and he loses most of his crew.

The producers of *The Cruel Sea* peopled the story with believable rather than the stereotypical characters, so many from column A and so many from column B, that usually appeared in war films. As a result, the movie effectively visualized the harshness of the naval war in the Atlantic. In contrast to the films made during the war, however, *The Cruel Sea* portrays the Germans only as prisoners, with no images of evilness to stir up anger and foster the war effort.

Why? The war was now over. The Cold War had reached its height. Germany was becoming an ally. Images of U-boats cutting lifeboats in two served no purpose. Whether the omission of such portrayals made the film more accurate or whitewashed the nature of the war remains another matter. In any case, receiving all necessary assistance from the Admiralty, *The Cruel Sea* enjoyed a feel of authenticity not possible in the wartime movies which had to use miniatures and special effects to recreate combat at sea.

Likewise, the British and American films portraying the Battle of the Atlantic also benefitted from considerable military assistance. Similar in their story line, both *The Pursuit of the Graf Spee* and *Sink the Bismarck* captured with considerable realism the visual excitement of surface warfare. At the same time, both movies raised the issue of dramatic license in cinematic recreations which propose to tell a story of historical events. *The Pursuit of the Graf Spee*, released three years after *The Cruel Sea*, portrays the British pursuit of the German pocket battleship, played by the U.S. Navy's cruiser *Salem*.

Using the same formula, *Sink the Bismarck* detailed the British chase and ultimate sinking of the *Bismarck* before it could reach the open Atlantic and wreak havoc on the Allied convoys heading east. While most of the story closely follows the historical events, the filmmakers replaced the officer who masterminded the pursuit from the basement of the Admiralty with a fictional character. If nothing else, it allowed them to create a love story between the officer and one of his aides, perhaps to help the box office.

Such dramatic license has seldom bothered the U.S. military, unless the portrayal showed its men or actions in a negative light. Unlike the Americans, the British armed services have had little problem providing filmmakers with assistance on stories, even those which might put them in a bad light. The primary criteria has remained whether the portrayal is historically accurate. In the case of *Sink the Bismarck*, however, the film-makers left out one crucial element, the controversy surrounding the British abandonment in the water of hundreds of survivors from the German ship.

Apparently responding to a report that a German submarine was in the area, a British cruiser cut short its rescue effort. By 1960, of course, Germany had become a Western ally and nothing could be gained by dredging up old wounds. On the other hand, a portrayal of the captain's dilemma, if he had had a dilemma, remains the stuff of good drama as visualized in *In Which We Serve*, when the captain decides he must run over British sailors in order to sink a German submarine.

In any event, the political impact of the Cold War on Battle of the Atlantic movies is even better illustrated in the first Hollywood movie on the subject, *The Enemy Below*, released in 1957. Made with full navy cooperation, the movie focused on the desperate battle between an American destroyer and a German U-boat. Humanizing the conflict by creating three-dimensional characters, *The Enemy Below* remains one of the best movies about World War II, if not about naval warfare in general.

To be sure, given the context of the Cold War shift in alliances, Curt Jurgens, as the German submarine captain, receives sympathetic treat-ment in his struggle to outwit Robert Mitchum, the commander of a U.S. destroyer. The duel, which neither man wins, suggests that whatever the system for which they fought, nobility exists between comrades-in-arms. While this is probably true and probably more realistic than showing a submarine run over a lifeboat containing enemy sailors, *The Enemy Below* makes it easy for viewers to forget the true nature of Hitler's Germany. In fact, Jurgens only alludes to the nature of the government for which he wages war, his primary concern being the welfare of his crew.

Nevertheless, the juxtaposition of the honor among warriors and the loss of good men's lives does create an antiwar statement of some power in the film. In contrast, the German film *Das Boot*, released in 1982, attempted to make a not-very-subtle antiwar statement by showing the Battle of the Atlantic only from the German perspective. Moreover, the filmmakers took pains to remove as an issue the nature of the government for whom the sailors were sacrificing their lives. As a result, the audience could easily find itself rooting for the U-boat to succeed in its attacks.

Such manipulation of reality may well have seemed appropriate to the German filmmakers in the political context of the early 1980s. Germany was now allied with the United States against the Soviet Union, which had not yet manifested its underlying weakness. If not completely aware of the evilness of the Nazi regime, the younger generations of Germans recognized the destruction which World War II had brought upon their country and did not want to fight another devastating war. Perhaps most important, however, the very materialism that democracy had brought to the German people worked against any future militarism.

Nevertheless, the manner in which the makers of *Das Boot* manipulated audiences to forget or forgive the true nature of the Nazi government remains insidious for those who remember or know the reality of World War II. In particular, the film opens in the fall of 1942 at a party in which submarine officers openly criticize the German government. While Hitler had suffered some initial setbacks in Russia, his regime would never have tolerated such disloyalty. Nevertheless, throughout the movie, the officers aboard the U-boat make clear their displeasure with the Nazi regime.

Probably even more important, the very environment within the submarine, whatever its authenticity, created sympathy for the crew and ultimately the hope that the men would survive the British attacks. As a result, without necessarily being aware of it, audiences might well hope that the U-boat could sink enemy ships and escape pursuit, instead of realizing which side represented the good guys and which the bad guys.

In fact, many submariners who saw *Das Boot* have attested to the accuracy of the film's portrayal of life aboard a submarine. However, the images in the movie remain at considerable variance to the portrayal of German U-boats in such films as *Action in the North Atlantic, The Enemy Below,* and even documentary footage taken aboard submarines in the same time frame. While filmmakers have undoubtedly sanitized life aboard American submarines, even a causual viewer wonders about the lack of discipline and slovenly nature of the sailors aboard the German submarine in *Das Boot.*

Worse, if all U-boat captains had used the same tactics and enjoyed the same luck as the commander of the film's boat, Germany would have had difficulty achieving as much success with its submarines as it did, at least in the early years of the war. In *Das Boot,* the submarine is easily discovered first by a British destroyer and then by British aircraft, clearly suggesting the captain has not learned the tactics of avoidance. Later, he surfaces in the middle of the night on a blazing sea of oil to observe a stricken tanker he has torpedoed. Although realizing he has mortally wounded the ship, the captain still launches another of his precious torpedoes to hasten the sinking process.

To be sure, U-boats did often attack on the surface. However, they would use their deck guns if necessary to administer a *coup de grace* rather than waste a torpedo. Of course, *Das Boot* had no intention of becoming a documentary about submarine warfare. Instead, when it was released in 1982, the filmmakers intended to make an antiwar statement by showing the futility of combat. In fact, whatever the accuracy of those images, *Das Boot* did make a powerful statement. While a lay person may not question the U-boat commander's exposing his ship on a burning sea, the viewer will certainly understand the horror of war which forced him to leave the British sailors from the tanker struggling in the cruel sea.

Of course, it remained an operational necessity to leave sailors in the water. Submarines had no ability to rescue large numbers of men, enemy or friendly. But *Das Boot* did not concern itself with the reality of its portrayals and so probably had little to say about the true nature of the Battle of the Atlantic. Nevertheless, the film remains one of the few efforts by Germans to portray their side of the Battle of the Atlantic to international audiences and stands as a useful comparison to *The Enemy Below* and other Western movies, including *Sink the Bismarck* and *Pursuit of the Graf Spee.*

Likewise, the issue of operational necessity remains a subject of significant importance and dramatic impact. Gwyn Griffin's *An Operational Necessity*, based on an actual incident, tells the story of a U-boat operating off Africa in the last days of the war. The sub sinks a British freighter loaded with lumber. The submarine captain concludes that search planes will easily spot the debris, rescue the crew, and so be able to track down his U-boat. Consequently, he machine guns the survivors as an operational necessity. Unfortunately for him and his executive officer, one man survives to tell the story. The end of the war finds the German U-boat crew captured. When the ship's log is discovered aboard the sub, the connection is made, and the captain and his executive officer are tried for war crimes and shot.

Such things did happen. After all, as the captain said in *Das Boot*, submarines could not take prisoners. As recounted in *An Operational Necessity*, the German captain's lawyer ultimately argued that the officer must give his primary commitment to his men. The British provided the visual image of this in the 1971 movie *Murphy's War*. While Peter O'Toole's character ultimately becomes an Ahab, pursuing his Moby Dick in the form of a German submarine, the film uses an operational necessity as its springboard to show how war and killing transcend reason.

In this instance, a German submarine sinks O'Toole's ship and machine guns his comrades in the water, without an explanation. O'Toole manages to reach the South American coast, where he awakens from his stupor just in time to see the submarine glide by his resting place and up the river. After his recovery, O'Toole begins his pursuit of the sub. On his part, after intercepting a radio message alerting the allies to his location, the submarine commander, out of "necessity" and because of his "responsibility" to his men, kills the pilot of a British seaplane that had attacked his ship.

Having escaped from the Germans a second time, O'Toole repairs the damaged plane and sets about to destroy the submarine with an obsession which parallels Ahab's pursuit of Moby Dick. When his homemade bomb fails to do the trick, O'Toole ultimately sinks the U-boat with one of its own torpedos. But, like Ahab, O'Toole becomes trapped by the instrument of his attack and dies, like his prey, victims of war.

Murphy's War perhaps stands as the ultimate statement about the Battle of the Atlantic. Men faced each other in mortal combat. Many died. One side won. But *The Cruel Sea, The Enemy Below, Das Boot,* and *Murphy's War* each stated in its own way that man lost for having had to fight. Beyond that, a study of these films illustrates how nations have used the motion picture medium not only to entertain but also to convey messages, each pitched for the particular time in which it appeared.

Glossary

AAF: (U.S.) Army Air Forces.

ABC-1: agreement concluded in March 1941 giving top Allied priority to the European-Atlantic Theater and the defeat of Germany.

Air Gap: area of the North Atlantic where air coverage could not be provided to convoys due to range from air bases.

Armed Guard: a U.S. Navy gun crew stationed aboard a merchant freighter or tanker.

ASDIC: Anti-Submarine Detection Investigation Committee (British). The term is used to describe the instrument which sent out sound waves in pulses that detected U-boats and returned a signal that gave the range and bearing (and after 1944 the depth) of the submarine. *See* sonar.

ASV: airborne microwave (10- and 3-cm) radar.

ASW: antisubmarine warfare.

B-Dienst (Funkbeobachtungsdienst): the German radio-monitoring and cryptographic service.

BdU (Befehlshaber der Unterseeboote): Commander in Chief, U-boats.

Black Pit: part of the air gap (q.v.) southeast of Greenland exploited by German U-boats to sink merchant ships.

Bletchley Park: a mansion in Buckinghamshire, northwest of London, where the Government Code and Cipher School's cryptanalysts analyzed German radio messages. *See* GC&CS.

bombe: word used to describe the electromechanical scanning machine constructed from a series of Enigmas linked together at Bletchley Park.

CinCLant: Commander in Chief Atlantic Fleet.

CinCWA: Commander in Chief Western Approaches.

cipher: a secret system of communication that substitutes letters or other symbols for letters in order to conceal the meaning of a text.

CNO: (U.S.) Chief of Naval Operations.

code: a system of symbols used to represent assigned meanings. *See* cipher.

CominCh: Commander in Chief, United States Fleet.

cryptography: the science or study of code and cipher systems employed for secret communication.

Drumbeat: a translation of *Paukenschlag*. *See Roll of Drums*.

Enigma: another name for the *Schlüssel M* cipher machine. The term was also used to denote the machine's encrypted product.

ESF: Eastern Sea Frontier (U.S. Navy).

GC&CS: British Government Code and Cipher School. *See* Bletchley Park.

guerre de course: French term meaning a war on seaborne trade or commerce.

HF/DF ("Huff-Duff"): high frequency/direction finding.

Hydra: the cipher used by operational U-boats in establishing the daily setting of the Schlüssel M cipher machine.

Kapitänleutnant: Lieutenant Commander.

Kapitän zur See: Captain.

Korvettenkapitän: Commander.

Kriegsmarine: the World War II German Navy, so named from 1935 to 1945.

Kriegstagebuch **(KTB)**: German war diary kept by ships and boats at sea, also by shore-based headquarters staffs.

Kurzsignale: a U-boat's short-signal position report by radio (wireless).

Lend-Lease: U.S. act in early 1941 to support any ally by providing needed war supplies for its defense without a demand for payment. About half of U.S. aid went to Britain and a quarter to Russia.

Luftwaffe: German Air Force.

Mahan, Alfred Thayer: influential American naval strategist who published *The Influence of Sea Power Upon History* (1890), which stressed the necessity for states to build a powerful navy.

Milch-Cows: U-boat tankers used to refuel U-boats.

MOMP: mid-ocean meeting point south of Iceland, where U.S. and British naval escorts exchanged responsibility for guarding Atlantic convoys.

Oerlikon: name given to any of several 20 mm automatic antiaircraft and aircraft canon.

OKM (Oberkommando der Kriegsmarine): German Naval High Command.

ONI: (U.S.) Office of Naval Intelligence.

Paukenschlag: *see Roll of Drums* and *Drumbeat*.

PC: patrol craft, often used as submarine chasers (U.S. Navy).

PG: gunboat (U.S. Navy).

RAF: (British) Royal Air Force.

rake: a patrol line across the pathe of a convoy formed by U-boats.

RCAF: Royal Canadian Air Force.

Reichsmarine: the German Navy in the period 1919-35.

Roll of Drums: translation of *Paukenschlag*, German code name for the U-boat operation in the Atlantic beginning in January 1942, which was devastating to Allied shipping. *See Drumbeat.*

SC: 110-foot submarine chaser, wooden hull (U.S. Navy).

Schlüssel M (Marine-Funkschlüssel-Machine M): Kriegsmarine version of the electromechanical cipher machine used by the German armed forces for telex and wireless (radio) traffic.

Schnorchel (snorkel): a valved air pipe that protruded above the surface and allowed a U-boat to proceed underwater on diesel power.

Seekriegsleitung (Skl): the German Naval Staff.

SLOC: sea lines of communication.

Sonar: an acronym standing for Sound Navigation, Ranging. This was the U.S. Navy's echo-ranging sound apparatus equivalent to the British ASDIC.

Teardrop: Allied hunter-killer operation versus Axis submarines begun in early 1945.

Triton: a U-boat cipher employing four rotors instead of three, introduced on operational boats in February 1942 and not solved by cryptanalysts at Bletchley Park (where it was called "Shark") until December 1942.

U-boat: several U-boat types were employed during the war including Type VIIC boats of 770 tons displacement and a surface speed of 17 knots (7.6 submerged); Type IXB of 1,050 tons; and Type XXI, a large boat of 1,600 tons with a fast submerged speed of 17 knots. Type XXIII was a small boat for use in coastal waters.

Ultra: code name for decrypted German wireless messages when sent out from Bletchley Park to operational commanders.

Wehrmacht: German Army.

Z-plan: Hitler-endorsed 1938 plan for development over ten years of a balanced fleet of capital ships, cruisers and submarines.

Select Bibliography

Abbazia, Patrick, *Mr. Roosevelt's Navy: The Private War of the U.S. Atlantic Fleet, 1939-1942.* Annapolis: Naval Institute Press, 1975.

_____. "When the Good Shepherds Were Blind." U.S. Naval Institute *Proceedings* 101, no. 9 (1975): 49-57.

Bailey, Thomas A., and Paul B. Ryan. *Hitler vs. Roosevelt.* New York: The Free Press, 1979.

Barnett, Correlli. *Engage the Enemy More Closely: The Royal Navy in the Second World War.* New York: Norton, 1991.

Beesley, Patrick, Jürgen Rohwer, Kenneth Knowles, and Harold Deutsch. "Ultra and the Battle of the Atlantic." *Cryptological Spectrum* 8 (Winter 1978): 5-29.

Behrens, C.B.A. *Merchant Shipping and the Demands of War.* London: HMSO, 1955.

Bekker, Cajus. *Defeat At Sea: The Struggle and Eventual Destruction of the German Navy, 1939-1945.* New York: Ballantine Books, 1955.

_____. *Hitler's Naval War.* New York: Zebra Books, 1971, 1977.

Belke, T.J. "Roll of Drums." U.S. Naval Institute *Proceedings* 109, no. 4 (1983): 58-64.

Black, Wallace B. *Battle of the Atlantic.* New York: Crestwood House, 1991.

Blakely, Tom. *Corvette Cobourg: The Role of a Canadian Warship in the Longest Sea Battle in History.* Cobourg: Cobourg Branch of the Royal Canadian Legion,1983.

Bratzel, John F., and Leslie B. Rout, Jr.. *The Shadow War: German Espionage and United States Counterespionage in Latin America During World War II.* Frederick, M.D.: University Press of America, 1986.

Bredemeier, Heinrich. *Schlachtschiff Scharnhorst.* Herford: Koehlers Verlagsgellschaft, 1962.

Buchheim, Lothar Günther. *U-Boat War.* trans. Gudie Lawaetz. New York: Knopf, 1978.

Buckley, John. "Air Power and the Battle of the Atlantic: 1939-1945." *Journal of Contemporary History* 28, no. 1 (January 1993): 143-161.

Carlisle, Robert L. *P-boat Pilot: With a Patrol Squadron in the Battle of the Atlantic.* Santa Barbara: Fithian Press, 1993.

Central Office of Information, Great Britain. *The Battle of the Atlantic: The Official Account of the Fight Against the U-Boats, 1939-1945.* London: H.M. Stationary Office, 1946.

Churchill, Winston S. *Memoirs of the Second World War. An Abridgement of the Six Volumes of The Second World War.* Boston: Houghton Mifflin, 1959.

_____. *Secret Session Speeches.* New York: Simon & Schuster, 1946.

Cremer, Peter E. *U-Boat Commander: A Periscope View of the Battle of the Atlantic.* New York: Berkley Books, 1984, 1986.

Dönitz, Karl. *Memoirs: Ten Years and Twenty Days.* trans. R.H. Stevens in collaboration with David Woodward. Cleveland: World Publishing, 1959.

Farago, Ladislas. *The Tenth Fleet.* New York: Ivan Obolensky, Inc., 1962.

Gallery, Daniel V. *Clear the Decks!* New York: Warner Books, 1951.

Gander, Leonard M. *Atlantic Battle: A Personal Narrative.* London: Hutchinson, 1941.

Gannon, Michael. *Operation Drumbeat: The Dramatic True Story of Germany's First U-Boat Attacks Along the American Coast in World War II.* New York: Harper & Row, 1990.

Gardner, W.J.R. "Prelude to Victory: The Battle of the Atlantic 1942-1943." *Mariner's Mirror* 79, no. 3 (August 1993): 305-317.

Garzke, William H. Jr. and Robert O. Dulin Jr. *Battleships: Axis and Neutral Battleships of World War II.* Annapolis, MD: Naval Institute Press, 1985.

Gröner, Dieter Jung, and Martin Maas. *Die deutschen Kriegsschiffe, vol. 4: Hilfsschiffe I: Werkstattschiffe, Tender und Begleitschiffe, Tanker und Versorger.* Koblenz: Bernard und Graefe Verlag, 1985.

Hancock, W.K., ed. *Statistical Digest of the War.* London: HMSO, 1951.

Harbron, John D. *The Longest Battle: The Royal Canadian Navy in the Atlantic 1939-1945.* St. Catherines: Vanwell Publishing, 1993.

Hayden, Edward L. "The Battle Won by Civilians." *Sea History* 29 (1983): 6-8.

Heinrichs, Waldo. "President Franklin D. Roosevelt's Intervention in the Battle of the Atlantic, 1941." *Diplomatic History* 10, no. 4 (1986): 311-332.

Hessler, Günter. *The U-Boat War in the Atlantic 1939-1945.* London: HMSO, 1989.

Hickman, Homer H. *Torpedo Junction: The U-Boat War off America's East Coast.* Annapolis: Naval Institute Press, 1989.

Hinsley, F.H. et al. British Intelligence in the Second World War: Its Influence on *Strategy and Operations*, 3 vols. New York: Cambridge University Press, 1979-88.

_____."The Enigma of Ultra." *History Today* 43 (September 1993): 15-20.

Hough, Richard. *The Longest Battle: The War At Sea, 1939-1945.* New York: William Morrow, 1986.

Hoyt, Edwin. *U-Boats Offshore: When Hitler Struck America.* New York: Stein and Day, 1978.

Hughes, Terry, and John Costello. *The Battle of the Atlantic.* New York: The Dial Press/James Wade, 1977.

Jones, Reginald V. *The Wizard War: British Scientific Intelligence 1939-1945.* New York: Coward, McCann, & Geoghegan, Inc., 1978.

Kahn, David. *Hitler's Spies: German Intelligence in World War II.* New York: Macmillan Publishing Co., 1978.

_____. *Seizing the Enigma: The Race to Break the German U-Boat Codes, 1939-1943.* Boston: Houghton Mifflin, 1991.

Karig, Walter, et al. *Battle Report: The Atlantic War.* New York: Rinehart & Company, Inc., 1946.

Keegan, John. *The Price of Admiralty: The Evolution of Naval Warfare.* New York: Viking Penguin, 1988.

Kemp, Peter K. *Decision At Sea: The Convoy Escorts.* New York: Elsevier-Dutton, 1978.

_____. *Key to Victory: The Triumph of British Sea Power in World War II.* Boston: Little, Brown, 1957.

Kennedy, Ludovic. *Pursuit: The Chase and Sinking of the Battleship Bismarck*. New York: Viking, 1974.

King, Ernest J. *U.S. Navy At War, 1941-1945: Official Reports to the Secretary of the Navy*. Washington D.C.: The United States Navy Department, 1946.

Knox, Collie. *Atlantic Battle*. London: Methuen, 1941.

Kozaczuk, Wladyslaw. *Enigma: How The German Machine Cipher Was Broken, and How It Was Read By The Allies in World War Two* ed. and trans. Christopher Kaspack. Frederick, MD: University Press of America, 1984.

Lewin, Ronald. *Ultra Goes to War: The First Account of World War II's Greatest Secret Based on Official Documents*. New York: McGraw-Hill, 1978.

Love, Robert W. Jr.. *History of the United States Navy*, 2 vols. Harrisburg, PA: Stackpole Books, 1992.

Lundeberg, Philip K. "The German Critique of the U-Boat Campaign, 1915-1918." *Military Affairs* (1963).

Macintyre, Donald G.F.W. *The Battle of the Atlantic*. London: Severn House, 1961, 1975.

Mahan, Alfred Thayer. *The Influence of Sea Power Upon History, 1660-1783*. Boston: Little, Brown and Company, 1890.

Maier, Klaus A. et al. *Germany's Initial Conquests in Europe*, vol. 2 of *Germany and the Second World War*. trans. Dean S. McMurry and Ewald Osers. Oxford: Oxford University Press, 1991.

Meigs, Montgomery C. *Slide Rules and Submarines*. Washington D.C.: National Defense University Press, 1990.

Middlebrook, Martin. *Convoy*. New York: William Morrow, 1977.

Milner, Marc. "The Battle of the Atlantic." *Journal of Strategic Studies* 13, no. 1 (1990): 45-66.

_____. "Canada's Naval War." *Acadiensis* 12 (1983): 162-171.

_____. "Convoy Escorts: Tactics, Technology, and Innovation in the Royal Canadian Navy." *Military Affairs* 48 (1984): 19-25.

_____. *North Atlantic Run: The Royal Canadian Navy and the Battle for the Convoys*. Annapolis: U.S. Naval Institute Press, 1985.

Morison, Samuel Eliot. *The Atlantic Battle Won: May 1943-May 1945*, vol. 10 of *The History of United States Naval Operations in World War II*. Boston: Little, Brown, 1956.

_____. *The Battle of the Atlantic: September 1939-May 1943*, vol. 1 of *The History of United States Naval Operations in World War II*. Boston: Little, Brown, 1947.

_____. *The Two-Ocean War: A Short History of the United States Navy in the Second World War*. Boston: Little, Brown, 1963.

Mulligan, Timothy P. *Lone Wolf: The Life and Death of U-Boat Ace Werner Henke*. London and Westport, CT: Praeger, 1993.

_____."German U-Boat Crews in World War II: Sociology of an Elite." *Journal of Military History* 56 (April 1992): 261-281.

Munting, Roger. "Soviet Food Supply and Allied Aid in the War." *Soviet Studies* 36 (October 1984): 582-593.

Noli, Jean. *The Admiral's Wolf Pack*. trans. J.F. Bernard. Garden City, NJ: Doubleday, 1974.

Oxford, Edward. "Battle of the Atlantic." *American History Illustrated* 28 (November/December 1993): 33-43, 66-69.

Palmer, Michael A. *Origins of the Maritime Strategy*. Washington D.C.: Naval Historical Center, 1988.

Raeder, Erich. *My Life*. Annapolis,MD: Naval Institute Press, 1960.

Rayner, Denys A. *Escort: The Battle of the Atlantic*. London: W. Kimber, 1955.

Reid, Max. *D.E.M.S. and the Battle of the Atlantic, 1939-1945*. Ottawa: Commoners' Publishing Society, 1990.

Rohwer, Jürgen, *Axis Submarine Successes*. Annapolis: Naval Institute Press, 1983.

Rohwer, Jürgen, and G. Hummelchen. *Chronology of the War at Sea, 1939-1945*, trans. Derek Masters, New York: Arco Publishing Co., 1972.

Rohwer, Jürgen. *The Critical Convoy Battles of March 1943: The Battle for HX.229/SC.122*. trans. Derek Masters. Annapolis: Naval Institute Press, 1977.

Roskill, S.W. *The War at Sea*. 3 vols. London: HMSO, 1954.

Rusbridger, James. "The Sinking of the Automedon, the Capture of the Rankin: New Light on Two Intelligence Disasters in World War II." *Encounter* 64 (May 1985): 8-14.

Russel, Jerry C. "Ultra and the Campaign against the U-Boats in World War II."in *Ultra, Magic, and the Allies*. vol. 1 of *Covert Warfare: Intelligence, Counterintelligence, and Military Deception During the World War II Era*. ed. John Mendelsohn. New York: Garland Publishing, 1989.

Salewski, Michael. *Die deutsche Seekriegsleitung, 1935-1945*. 3 vols. Frankfurt am Main: Bernard und Graife, 1970.

Sand, Ellis. "The Last Cruise of YP-438." *American Heritage* 38, no. 4 (1985): 92-103.

Schoenfeld. Max. "Winston Churchill as War Manager: The Battle of the Atlantic Committee, 1941." *Military Affairs* 52 (July 1988): 122-127.

Seagrave, Sterling. "War At Sea Seared Americans Before Pearl Harbor Attack." *Smithsonian* 12, no. 8 (1981): 100-109.

Seek and Sink: A Symposium on the Battle of the Atlantic, 21 October 1991. Bracknell: Royal Air Force Historical Society, 1992.

Seth, Ronald. *The Fiercest Battle: The Story of North Atlantic Convoy ONS.5, 22nd April-7th May 1943*. New York: Norton, 1961, 1962.

Showell, Jak P. Mallmann. *U-Boats Under the Swastika*. Annapolis: Naval Institute Press, 1987.

_____. *The German Navy in World War II*. Annapolis: Naval Institute Press, 1987.

Smith, Bradley F. *The Ultra-Magic Deals and the Most Secret Special Realationship, 1940-1946*. Novato, CA: Presidio Press, 1993.

Smith, S.E. ed. *The United States Navy in World War II*. New York: William Morrow, 1966.

Steury, Donald, P. "Naval Intelligence, the Atlantic Campaign, and the Sinking of the *Bismarck*: A Study in the Integration of Intelligence into the Conduct of Naval Warfare." *Journal of Contemporary History* 22 (April 1987): 209-233.

Syrett, David. "The Battle of the Atlantic: 1943, The Year of Decision." *American Neptune* 45, no. 1 (1985): 46-64.

_____. *The Defeat of the German U-Boats: The Battle of the Atlantic*. Columbia, SC: University of South Carolina Press, 1994.

_____. "German U-Boat Attacks on Convoy SC. 118: 4 February to 14 February 1943." *American Neptune* 44, no. 1 (1984): 48-60.

Suid, Lawrence, ed. *Guts and Glory: Great American War Movies*, Reading, MA: Addison-Wesley, 1978.

Tarrant, V.E. *The U-Boat Offensive, 1914-1945*. Annapolis, MD: Naval Institute Press, 1989.

Terraine, John. *The U-Boat Wars: 1916-1945*. New York: G.P. Putnam's Sons, 1989.

U.S. National Archives. *Records Relating to U-Boat Warfare 1939-1945*. vol. 2 of *Guides to the Microfilmed Records of the German Navy 1850-1945*. Washington D.C.: The National Archives and Records Administration, 1985.

U.S. Navy Department, Naval Security Group Command Headquarters. *Intelligence Reports on the War in the Atlantic from December 1942 to May 1945 as Seen Through and Influenced by Decryption of German Naval Radio Traffic.* Wilmington, DE: Michael Glazier, 1979.

U.S. Navy Department, Naval Security Group Command Headquarters. *U-Boat Operations: Allied Communications Intelligence and the Battle of the Atlantic.* Washington D.C.: The Command, 1977.

U.S. Navy Department. *U-Boat Operations*. Washington D.C.: U.S. Navy Department, 1945.

Vaeth, J. Gordon. *Blimps and U-Boats: U.S. Navy Airships in the Battle of the Atlantic.* Annapolis: Naval Institute Press, 1992.

Van der Vat, Dan. *The Atlantic Campaign: World War II's Great Struggle At Sea.* New York: Harper and Row, 1988.

Watt, Frederick B. *In All Respects Ready: The Merchant Navy and the Battle of the Atlantic, 1940-1945*. Englewood Cliffs, NJ: Prentice-Hall, 1985.

Whitley, M.J. *German Capital Ships of World War II*. London: Arms and Armour Press, 1989.

Willoughby, Malcolm. *The U.S. Coast Guard in World War II*. Annapolis: The U.S. Naval Institute Press, 1957.

Winterbotham, F.W. *The Ultra Secret*. New York: Dell Publishing, 1974.

Winton, John. *Ultra at Sea: How Breaking the Nazi Code Affected Allied Naval Strategy During World War II*. New York: William Morrow, 1988.

Y'Blood, William T. *Hunter-Killer: U.S. Escort Carriers in the Battle of the Atlantic.* Annapolis: Naval Institute Press, 1983.

Zimmerman, David K. "The Royal Canadian Navy and the National Research Council, 1939-1945." *Canadian Historical Review* 69, no. 2 (1988): 203-221.

About the Book and Editors

They were known as "iron coffins"—the German U-boats that terrorized Allied shipping during World War II. In this volume commemorating the fiftieth anniversary of the Battle of the Atlantic, historians from both sides of the ocean offer new insights into the conflict.

The Battle of the Atlantic was the most important campaign of the war, for Allied success in Europe depended on massive movements of ships, men, and matériel across the Atlantic from the Americas. In spite of an unprecedented Allied shipbuilding effort, German U-boats were causing severe damage to this vital supply line; unless the deadly U-boat menace could be eliminated, the Allies would be unable to defeat Nazi Germany.

The cost in lives lost and ships sunk was appalling, but statistics alone do not reflect the human dimension of this most terrible sea fight. It is a story of incredible courage and unspeakable cruelty, one in which calculated risks and life-or-death decisions became commonplace. It is a story of the combined efforts of planners and strategists, spies and codebreakers, naval officers and crews, merchant mariners, and civilians at home in both Allied and Axis nations to achieve an end to the carnage at sea. And it is a story of the triumph of technology, as Allied advances in radar and sonar ultimately led to victory over the German wolfpacks.

The book makes an important contribution to the history of World War II, examining both much-studied and lesser-known aspects of this critical campaign. Its contributors provide a comprehensive account of all who participated in this long and costly effort: those who planned, those who fought, those who waited, and those who died.

Timothy J. Runyan is professor of history at Cleveland State University and editor of *The American Neptune* journal. **Jan M. Copes** is instructor of history at Cleveland State University and assistant editor of *The American Neptune*.

About the Contributors

Dean C. Allard is Director of Naval History at the Naval Historical Center in Washington, D.C. A graduate of Dartmouth College, Georgetown University, and George Washington University, he is the author of a number of books and articles on U.S. naval history and the history of American marine science.

Jeffrey G. Barlow received his Ph.D. at the University of South Carolina. Formerly an analyst for the Heritage Foundation and the National Institute for Public Policy/National Security Research, he is presently a historian at the Naval Historical Center in Washington, D.C. He is author of *The Revolt of the Admirals: The Fight for Naval Aviation, 1945-1950.*

R. A. Bowling joined the United States Navy in 1940, served on U.S.S. *Cole* in the North Atlantic in 1941, graduated from the U.S. Naval Academy in 1945, commanded seven ships and one unit command of 42 ships, and retired in 1974. He holds a Master Mariner, Unlimited, license and went to sea in the merchant marine until 1991. He earned a doctorate in history at the University of Maine.

John F. Bratzel is a Latin American specialist at Michigan State University. His publications include *Latin American History* and (with Leslie B. Rout, Jr.) *The Shadow War: German Espionage and United States Counterespionage in World War II.*

J. David Brown is Head of the Naval Historical Branch of the Ministry of Defence located at Great Scotland Yard in London. He served in the Royal Navy as an aviator. His publications include *The Guinness Book of Air Warfare* and *The Royal Navy in the Falklands War.* He is a Fellow of the Royal Historical Society.

Robert M. Browning, Jr., received his Ph.D. degree from the University of Alabama. He is the Chief Historian for the U.S. Coast Guard and has written articles on Coast Guard history and *From Cape Charles to Cape Fear: The North Atlantic Blockading Squadron During the Civil War.* He is currently at work on a study of merchant vessel casualties during World War II.

James T. Cheatham is a retired Naval Reserve Commander who practices law in Greenville, North Carolina. He authored *The Atlantic Turkey Shoot: U-Boats off the Outer Banks in World War II.*

Jan M. Copes is assistant editor of *The American Neptune*, a quarterly journal of maritime history. The author of several articles, she is a lecturer in history at Cleveland State University.

Harold D. Huycke is an experienced sea captain and marine surveyor. A graduate of the California Maritime Academy, he is author of *To Santa Rosalia: Further and Back.*

Thomas A. King is a retired Rear Admiral, U.S. Merchant Marine. His posts included Atlantic Coast Director of the U.S. Maritime Administration. He graduated with the cadet class of 1942 and later served as superintendent of the U.S. Merchant Marine Academy.

Theresa L. Kraus is a historian at the Federal Aviation Administration in Washington, D.C. She also worked at the U.S. Army Center for Military History and the Naval Historical Center. Her doctorate is from the University of Maryland. She has authored several articles on naval and military history.

Robert W. Love, Jr., is a member of the history department at the U.S. Naval Academy. He received his Ph.D. at the University of California at Davis and is the author of numerous works on naval history, including *The Chiefs of Naval Operations* and a two-volume *History of the U.S. Navy*.

Philip K. Lundeberg is Curator Emeritus of Naval History at the Smithsonian Institution. He received his doctorate from Harvard and joined the Institution after teaching at St. Olaf and the U.S. Naval Academy. He first probed *Teardrop* events in May 1945 interviewing fellow survivors of *Frederick C. Davis*, prior to preparation of numerous condolence letters and its final action report.

Joseph F. Meany, Jr., received his doctorate from Fordham University in New York City. He is Senior Historian at the New York State Museum in Albany, New York. His recent exhibitions include *The Janes Who Made the Planes*, about women aviation workers in World War II. He is presently at work on a book and exhibition about the Port of New York in the Second World War.

Marc Milner is professor of history at the University of New Brunswick, Fredericton, N.B., Canada. Prior to going to UNB he worked for the Department of National Defence, in Ottawa, on the official histories of the RCN and the RCAF in the Battle of the Atlantic. He is the author of *North Atlantic Run* and *The U-boat Hunters* as well as numerous articles on the Atlantic War.

Werner Rahn joined the Federal German Navy in 1960. He holds a Ph.D. in history from Hamburg University and is now head of the Second World War Research Department, Military History Research Office of the German Armed Forces. He is the author and editor of several books and articles on German naval and military history.

Jürgen Rohwer served as an officer on German destroyers and minesweepers from 1942-1945. He received his doctorate at Hamburg University. He was director of the Library of Contemporary History at Stuttgart and editor of *Marine-Rundschau*. He is the author of numerous works, including *The Critical Convoy Battles of 1943* and *Axis Submarine Successes*.

Timothy J. Runyan is professor of history at Cleveland State University. He is editor of *The American Neptune*. His publications include *European Naval and Maritime History, 300-1500* and *Ships, Seafaring and Society* which won the K. Jack Bauer Award of the North American Society for Oceanic History.

Roger Sarty is Senior Historian at the History Division, National Defence Headquarters, Canada. A graduate of Duke University and the University of Toronto, he contributed to the official history of the Royal Canadian Air Force and is co-author of the forthcoming official history of the Royal Canadian Navy. *Tin-Pots and Pirate Ships* (which he wrote with Michael L. Hadley), won NASOH's John Lyman Book Award.

Donald P. Steury is employed by the U.S. Central Intelligence Agency, where he served as a Soviet naval analyst. He holds a Ph.D. from the University of California at Irvine and has authored articles on the German Navy in World War II.

Lawrence Suid holds a Ph.D. from Case Western Reserve University and is the author of *Guts and Glory: Great American War Movies*, a study of the relationship between the film industry and the American military. He has also published *The Film Industry and the Vietnam War*, and, *Film and Propaganda in America: A Documentary History*, and is completing a study of Hollywood and the U.S. Navy.

David Syrett received his doctorate at the University of London and is professor of history at Queens College of the City University of New York. The author of five books and numerous articles, he recently published *The Defeat of the German U-boats: The Battle of the Atlantic*.

James E. Valle holds degrees from San Francisco State University, UCLA, and the University of Delaware. He is the author of *Rocks and Shoals, Social Order and Discipline in the United States Navy, 1800-1861*, and *The Iron Horse at War*. He is professor of history at Delaware State College.

Index